The Masculine Crisis
How to Rewrite Manhood in an Age of Social Struggle?

Copyright Page for The Masculine Crisis- How to Rewrite
Manhood in an Age of Social Struggle?" Author: Josiah Cornell

ISBN: 9798898605674

Content Warning: Please Read Before Continuing

This book explores men's mental health in raw and unfiltered detail. It includes discussions of depression, suicide, addiction, emotional suppression, trauma, grief, abuse, violence, and the long-term psychological effects of unresolved pain.

Some chapters include references to suicidal ideation, self-harm, childhood trauma, emotional neglect, and interpersonal conflict. These topics are approached with honesty and compassion, but they may be distressing or triggering for some readers.

Please take care of your emotional wellbeing as you read. It's okay to pause, skip sections, or return later if something feels too heavy. You are encouraged to reach out to a therapist, support organisation, or trusted person if you feel overwhelmed.

This book is written with deep respect for the complexity of the male experience and for anyone navigating their own healing journey.
You are not alone. You are not broken. You are human.
And you deserve understanding, safety, and support

Foreword
Masculinity in Crisis – A Rewriting of Manhood

What is a Man?

At its most fundamental level, a man is defined as an adult human male. However, this definition merely scratches the surface of the complexities surrounding manhood. In contemporary society, the concept of a "man" transcends mere biological categorisation; it is intricately woven into the fabric of identity, psychology, and sociocultural dynamics. A man's identity is often sculpted by a myriad of external factors, including cultural expectations, family upbringing, peer influences, and the unspoken societal norms that he internalises throughout his life.

Traditionally, men have been conditioned to fulfil roles centred on protection, performance, and provision often viewed as the pillars of masculinity. However, beneath these societal expectations lies a more profound reality: manhood is not monolithic but rather dynamic and multifaceted, encompassing both vulnerability and strength. Consequently, the modern male experience involves navigating a complex landscape of emotional and psychological demands.

Today, a silent revolution is taking root within the hearts and minds of men worldwide, manifesting as a masculinity crisis characterised not by overt aggression or dominance, but rather by emotional turmoil, confusion, and feelings of isolation. The essence of being a man in the 21st century has become increasingly ambiguous. The societal rules that once appeared clear-cut have evolved dramatically; traditional masculine roles have shifted, and the expectations placed on men can feel overwhelmingly contradictory. Many men now grapple with a poignant question: Who am I, truly, beneath the layers of societal expectation?

The increasing visibility and assertiveness of women across various domains, a necessary and overdue response to the historical patriarchal imbalance have coincided with a profound re-evaluation of traditional male roles. Men who were once celebrated for their stoicism, physical strength, and financial provision are now encouraged to embrace a broader spectrum of qualities, including emotional openness, vulnerability, and meaningful connection. Despite this cultural shift, many essential infrastructures that support these emotional transitions, such as mental health services, educational frameworks, and positive cultural narratives are struggling to keep pace with these changes.

As a result, many men find themselves suspended between two conflicting worlds: one defined by their upbringing, steeped in traditional notions of masculinity, and another in which they are striving to navigate a more nuanced and emotionally aware existence. This emotional disconnect often leads to a sense of fragmentation, where men feel torn between societal expectations and their evolving self-identities. The journey toward understanding manhood today requires not only introspection but also a communal effort to redefine masculinity for the betterment of both men and society as a whole.

Masculinity and the Psychological Lens

To comprehensively understand the transformation of masculinity, it is essential to examine it through the integrated lenses of psychoanalysis, counselling psychology, biopsychology, and contemporary mental health theories. This multifaceted approach enables a deeper exploration of how masculinity is shaped and expressed in today's society.

Freud's Legacy: Conflict and Conformity

Sigmund Freud's pioneering theories on masculine identity reveal that it arises from a complex interplay of desire, fear, and

5

the internalisation of authority figures, particularly within the family structure. Central to Freud's theory is the Oedipal conflict, which occurs during the phallic stage of psychosexual development. In this phase, boys navigate their familial relationships by emotionally distancing themselves from their mothers and seeking to identify with their fathers' societal roles. This process is often driven by a deep-seated fear, fear of emasculation or social exclusion, which compels boys to conform to normative masculinity. In Freudian terms, gender emerges not as an innate characteristic but as a socially constructed identity, curated through interactions with societal expectations. For many men, this process manifests in masculinity becoming a performative role, akin to a costume donned for acceptance, heavily influenced by external societal pressures that dictate what it means to be masculine.

Klein's Contribution: Maternal Envy and Disconnection

Melanie Klein expanded upon and critiqued Freud's foundational theories by emphasising the critical role that mothers play in the emotional development of boys. Her concept of "womb envy" posits that some men may subconsciously harbour feelings of resentment toward women, stemming from the acknowledgment of their unique ability to nurture and create life. This unresolved tension can lead to various emotional challenges, including a reluctance to embrace vulnerability and a tendency toward emotional disconnection. Klein's insights illuminate an essential aspect of masculinity: it is frequently constructed around a rejection of dependence and emotional openness, qualities that are vital for mental health and overall well-being. Such emotional disconnection often results in difficulties in forming intimate relationships and managing stress, as these men may feel pressured to adhere to rigid ideals of stoicism and strength, ultimately hindering their mental health.

By integrating various theoretical perspectives, we can gain a nuanced understanding of the complexities of masculinity while acknowledging the intricate cultural, psychological, and

6

emotional factors that significantly shape men's experiences and expressions of their gender identity.

Horrocks and the Unfathered Man

Joseph Horrocks introduced the concept of the "unfathered man," a term that encapsulates individuals who grow up without access to emotionally available male role models. This absence can have profound implications for men as they transition into adulthood. Many such men enter this phase of life lacking the relational tools needed to effectively navigate interpersonal conflicts, articulate their emotions, or embody positive models of masculinity. Within the context of mental health services, there is an increasing recognition that this emotional void can lead to a spectrum of mental health challenges in men, including substance abuse, heightened aggression, and deep-seated depression. These issues are particularly prevalent when individuals cling to traditional gender roles that value stoicism and self-reliance without engaging in critical self-reflection.

Masculinity as Performance: The Crisis of Modern Manhood

R.W. Connell's theory of hegemonic masculinity posits that masculinity is not a fixed characteristic but rather a socially constructed performance that is reinforced and perpetuated across various societal contexts. Traits that are often celebrated within this framework include competitiveness, emotional stoicism, dominance, and an overarching need for control. In stark contrast, qualities such as emotional awareness, vulnerability, and relational intimacy are frequently marginalised and viewed as weaknesses. This societal construct creates a significant emotional chasm; men are socialized to suppress crucial aspects of their emotional spectrum to achieve social acceptance and avoid stigma.

From a biopsychological standpoint, the enduring effects of such emotional suppression can be incredibly detrimental. Men who find themselves entrenched in continuous emotional repression often develop maladaptive coping strategies. These may include

7

alexithymia, characterized by an inability to identify and express emotions; hypervigilance, which manifests as an overactive state of awareness and anxiety; increased irritability; or emotional numbing, where they struggle to connect with their feelings at all. Psychiatric research highlights a troubling paradox: while men are three times more likely to die by suicide compared to women, they are significantly less inclined to seek therapeutic interventions such as talking therapies. This discrepancy does not stem from a lack of need; rather, it reflects the internalised shame associated with vulnerability and emotional expression that many men grapple with.

Counselling psychologists are increasingly recognizing "gender role strain" as a pivotal concern within the emotional struggles of men. Many men experience both internal conflicts and social repercussions when they deviate from conventional masculine norms. In therapy, it is common for men to present symptoms such as burnout, unexplained anger, isolation, or physical manifestations of stress, only to uncover that the root causes often lie in an outdated script dictating their identities and behaviour's. This script prescribes rigid definitions of masculinity, ultimately constraining their emotional and psychological well-being. By addressing these foundational issues, therapists can assist men in redefining their identities in ways that embrace vulnerability and emotional authenticity.

The Emergence of the New Man

Amidst the turmoil of societal upheaval and shifting cultural expectations, a new narrative around masculinity is beginning to take shape, one that advocates for a more nuanced and holistic understanding of manhood. This evolving narrative recognises that true strength is not solely defined by physical prowess or stoic silence; rather, it coexists harmoniously with qualities such as empathy, vulnerability, and compassion. Emotional literacy, an essential skill that involves recognising, understanding, and expressing one's feelings, is increasingly recognised as a vital component of effective leadership.

In this emerging paradigm, men are not only encouraged to express their emotions freely and authentically, but they are also invited to engage in meaningful relationships without the constraints imposed by traditional notions of masculinity. This shift promotes an environment where men can share their struggles, seek support, and forge deeper connections with others, fostering emotional resilience and well-being.

As we navigate a rapidly changing world marked by complex challenges and diverse experiences, this evolution in the understanding of masculinity holds promise. It paves the way for a healthier, more integrated perspective on what it truly means to be a man, one that celebrates both strength and sensitivity, thereby enriching personal identities and societal interactions alike.

Introduction
Who Am I When I'm No Longer Surviving?

Every man encounters a significant crossroads in his life, a pivotal moment when the silence he once wore like armour, solid, dependable, and seemingly protective, begins its insidious transformation. This silence, a former source of strength, morphs into a stifling shroud that suffocates the very essence of who he is. Initially, this shift is subtle; it emerges like a hollow sensation nestled within the quiet, a creeping awareness that something crucial is missing, even as the outer layers of life appear meticulously in order. This silence is not random; it is inherited, intricately woven into the fabric of our upbringing. From childhood, we are shaped by the culture, the families, and the myriad histories that envelop us.

Boys, whether overtly or quietly, receive an education that profoundly influences their emotional landscape, teaching them to view emotions as perilous and vulnerability as a glaring sign of weakness. Any semblance of softness becomes something to be suppressed and hidden. We are handed an unspoken code, protect, provide, endure. Above all, we learn one pivotal lesson: do not feel.

As a direct consequence, we have adapted. We have morphed into emotional escape artists, expertly burying our fears, grief, sadness, and longing under layers of functionality and productivity. We present ourselves as reliable, diligent, and ostensibly successful, attaining positions or accolades that look impressive on the surface. Yet, inside, something vital begins to fray at the edges. We cloak our depression beneath the guise of workaholism, dismiss our anxiety as mere stress caused by modern living, and mask our pain with temporary relief found in alcohol, compulsive behaviour's, anger, late-night scrolling, or distractions that masquerade as productivity. In this haze, we have become fluent in a language steeped in disconnection, unable to articulate our inner turmoil.

For many of us, we never received the essential permission to be fragile or to feel deeply. We shrink from expressing our vulnerabilities or seeking help, often paralysed by the oppressive weight of shame that accompanies these desires. Within this absence of approval, we risk losing touch with our genuine selves, drifting further from the emotional connections that are foundational to our humanity.

This book serves as that long-overdue permission slip. It is not merely a guide to mental health or another series of "how-to" steps for self-fixing; rather, it invites you to reclaim your humanity in its most authentic form. It is a detailed map designed to help you rediscover the parts of yourself that have been forced into hiding for far too long, betrayed by societal expectations and internalised beliefs. This journey resembles a psychological excavation, firmly anchored in trauma theory, the complexities of men's psychology, practical counselling insights, and the neurobiology of survival itself.

The wisdom contained within these pages is drawn from thousands of hours spent listening to men as they voice their silences, their concealed rage, their shame, and their grief. Some have found a sense of freedom within these pages, liberating their trapped emotions. Others continue their fight, grappling with their internal battles, while some faced insurmountable obstacles and did not make it through. Yet, each one of their stories and experiences is woven into the fabric of this text, compelling us to confront the realities of our shared existence and fostering a sense of connection and understanding.
This book serves as a profound sanctuary for men who have honed the skill of moving forward in life while having forgotten the essence of feeling deeply. It speaks to those who carry the oppressive weight of others' expectations, often silently wondering if anyone could bear the weight of their own burdens. This narrative resonates with fathers who, despite being physically present in their children's lives, find themselves

emotionally numb, haunted by the spectres of their own unfulfilled needs and childhood wounds. It reaches out to partners yearning for a deeper emotional connection but grappling with the uncertainty of how to fully trust in that bond without fear of vulnerability. It acknowledges the man who has never heard words of pride, alongside the boy within him who was never afforded the chance to cry with intention and authenticity. If any part of this speaks to your experience, take solace in knowing that you are not alone; you are truly seen.

Within these pages, we will embark on a thorough exploration of the intricate reality of trauma, viewing it not as mere isolated events but as an expansive system of survival tactics that fundamentally reshapes how we think, feel, and engage with the world around us. We will delve into the complexities of emotional suppression and dissect its manifestations within the male body, from the struggles with mental health and the tight grip of addiction, to the profound challenges that arise in relationships. We will confront the heavy burdens of shame and rage, examine father wounds that resonate across generations, and illuminate the feelings of isolation and burnout that often erode one's sense of self camouflaged beneath a polished exterior of competence.

More importantly, we will illuminate what true recovery looks like, a journey that is neither linear nor a fairy tale ending, but rather a radical redefinition of power, peace, and personal identity. We will cast aside superficial mantras and empty platitudes, choosing instead to embrace clinical insights grounded in bio-psychological frameworks, and the raw honesty that emerges from men who courageously live their truths. Within these pages, you will discover reflections of your own experiences within the diverse patterns illustrated, and even more crucially, within the vast possibilities that lie ahead.

As a trauma-informed writer and practitioner, I have spent countless hours in rooms filled with men who, after years of donning their emotional masks, finally felt safe enough to let go and sob for the first time in decades. I've witnessed men rediscover their innate capacity to trust themselves and others. I've observed them collapse inward, not from a sense of defeat, but from the profound relief that accompanies a long-awaited sense of safety and acceptance. I have been a witness to those sacred moments when the relentless survival instinct begins to loosen its vice-like grip, creating space for something far deeper to take root: restoration, wholeness, and a renewed sense of self-respect that transforms their lives.

This journey is not merely about evolving into a "better man" in the traditional sense, following the prescribed rules of masculinity or adhering to societal expectations. Instead, it's about embracing a profound sense of wholeness, stepping boldly into the fullness of what it means to be a man who actively engages with life rather than existing on autopilot. It's about shedding the facade of invulnerability and strength to explore the depths of your own emotions, recognising that these feelings are not signs of weakness but essential elements of a genuine existence.

You deserve far more than mere endurance in the face of life's challenges; you deserve a state of peace that resonates within you, clarity that allows for introspection, intimacy that fosters deep connections with others, and the freedom to express yourself authentically. You have the right to cry freely without the burden of shame, and to love wholeheartedly without the fear of vulnerability. Moreover, you deserve to transcend the limiting roles that have been imposed upon you and fully embrace the essence of who you truly are.

While this book may not have all the answers neatly laid out, it aims to inspire you to ask the right questions that can lead you to a deeper understanding of yourself. Within those questions, you might rediscover the long-lost voice, the one that has been silenced by years of societal conditioning that you once bravely wielded.

Consider this: What if everything you were taught about manhood has insidiously been eroding your spirit, leaving you in a state of disconnection from your true self?

It's time to unravel those deeply ingrained teachings, to challenge the narratives that have shaped you, and to write a new personal story that aligns with your authentic self.

Welcome to your truth, where vulnerability is embraced and authenticity reigns.
Welcome to healing, the pathway to reclaiming your lost self.

"You don't need to be falling apart to realise you've never fully lived. Sometimes, all it takes is for you to pause your relentless survival mode long enough to remember who you were before the world dictated who you should be."

Act One: The Unspoken Inheritance
(Masculinity, Silence and Collapse)

Chapter 1

The Blueprint of a Man — Expectations That Built and Broke Us

"What if the blueprint you were handed wasn't for a man, but for a machine?"

To fully grasp the complexities of modern male identity, we must first peel back the layers of historical expectations that have shaped it over centuries. What does it genuinely mean to be a man today? This inquiry should transcend theoretical frameworks and engage with the vivid realities, personal experiences, societal conditioning, and the rewards and penalties associated with masculinity. At the core of the struggles that men face in contemporary society lies a profound inheritance of silent, unyielding pressure, a legacy handed down through generations like a sacred script dictating roles: provide, protect, dominate, and suppress emotions.

These rigid expectations did not emerge in isolation; they are intricately woven into the intricate tapestry of our ancestors' lives, deeply inscribed in our cultural narratives and myths. From the blood-soaked battlefields of ancient conflicts, where valour was equated with survival, to the mechanised factory floors of industrial Britain, where men were expected to toil tirelessly for their families, the concept of manhood has been forged not through compassion or nuance, but through resilience, relentless labour, and stoic endurance. In these original contexts, roles such as the warrior or the breadwinner served critical functions, acting as survival mechanisms designed to navigate harsh environmental and economic realities.

However, as societal landscapes shift and evolve evidenced by the rise of egalitarian movements, evolving family structures, and broader definitions of gender identity we must critically question what happens to such an outdated script. What emerges in a world that increasingly values emotional intelligence, collaboration, and vulnerability? How do we redefine masculinity in a way that honours both tradition and the emerging ideals of equality and emotional well-being? The answers lie not only in the faults of the past but also in the ongoing dialogue about what it means to be a man in an ever-changing world.

The Ancient Archetype: The Warrior, The Hunter, The King

In the early days of tribal societies, the transition to manhood was heralded by a series of significant rites of passage complex rituals meticulously designed to test a boy's pain threshold, courage, and endurance. These experiences were not merely ceremonial; they were essential markers that defined masculinity within the community. A boy's worth was intricately linked to his capacity to endure gruelling trials, overcome adversaries, or contribute meaningfully to the tribe's survival.

The warrior, for instance, embodied the ideals of honour and sacrifice, often facing physical threats that demanded not only strength but also strategic thinking and unwavering bravery. With each battle fought, he bled for his community, reinforcing his role as a protector. Similarly, the hunter played a pivotal role in providing sustenance, showcasing not just physical prowess but also vital skills like tracking, stealth, and resourcefulness in the wild. His ability to secure food emphasised efficiency and the necessity of survival.

The king, in his position of authority, wielded power and influence, often navigating the delicate balance between justice and fear in his governance. His decisions directly impacted the tribe's wellbeing and stability, and his ability to command respect and allegiance from his followers was paramount. In this context, boys quickly learned that their self-worth hinged on their ability to demonstrate functionality, invoke fear, or earn respect within these defined roles.

These archetypes held substantial symbolic weight within tribal cultures, yet they also contributed to the emergence of an early performance model of masculinity where emotional expression, such as crying or showing vulnerability was deemed a sign of weakness rather than a natural human experience. This cultural narrative created a formidable blueprint that suggested manhood was synonymous with emotional rigidity, functionality, and stoicism, often at the expense of open emotional discourse. Thus, the expectations placed on men were not only about their physical abilities or roles but also about suppressing deeper fears and vulnerabilities, which became ingrained in the fabric of societal norms.

Industrialisation and the Provider Trap

With the advent of the Industrial Revolution in the late 18th and early 19th centuries, the fabric of traditional societal roles underwent a profound transformation. Men, who once played integral roles in the supportive communal structures of tribal and agrarian societies, found themselves extracted from these cooperative environments. They were redefined as mere cogs in the vast and relentless machinery of industrial production. The battlefield, which had once served as a venue for valour and heroism, was supplanted by the factory floor, where the hunt for sustenance was replaced by the incessant quest for a pay check.

During this pivotal time, the archetype of the "family man" emerged, characterised by stoicism, pervasive exhaustion, and an unsettling emotional unavailability. Men became the primary breadwinners, but this role often came at the cost of their emotional lives. Displays of affection and vulnerability were relegated to the feminine sphere, creating a sharp dichotomy between masculinity and emotional expression. While men brought home the financial resources essential for family survival, they seldom articulated their emotional needs or expressed warmth towards their loved ones. Instead, they frequently sacrificed emotional connection in the name of duty, believing that providing materially was their most significant contribution.

In environments where survival hinged on productivity and efficiency, emotional fluency became not only an overlooked aspect of masculinity but a perceived danger to one's standing. The tacit message reinforced through generations was stark: boys raised by fathers who rarely uttered "I love you" inherited this silence as if it were a family heirloom, a legacy of emotional restraint. Strength was equated with silence, kindness was mistaken for weakness, and an outward display of softness was viewed as contrary to the masculine ideal. This entrenched belief system not only shaped individual identities but also contributed to a broader cultural landscape where emotional disconnect became the norm, stifling genuine relationships and leaving a lasting impact on future generations.

War and the Weaponisation of Emotion

The trials of two world wars irrevocably transformed generations of boys into soldiers, conditioning them not only to fight on the battlefield but also to suppress their emotional selves in the process. In this harsh and unforgiving landscape, compassion became a casualty, often sacrificed at the altar of duty and survival. Rather than addressing the psychological trauma that many soldiers faced, such as post-traumatic stress disorder (PTSD) society chose to stigmatise these afflictions, branding them as signs of weakness. Shell shock, a term first used during World War I to describe the psychological impact of the horrors of war, was often misinterpreted as cowardice. Expressions of grief were seen as indications of unmanliness; shedding tears? Completely unacceptable.

The repercussions of this emotional repression reverberated profoundly within the realm of fatherhood. Many men returning from the front lines were not only physically wounded but also emotionally detached, burdened by invisible scars that ran deep yet remained unspoken. Struggling to articulate their pain, they

19

built lives characterised more by relentless productivity than by genuine emotional connection. In this environment, they raised sons who never witnessed their fathers demonstrate vulnerability or express feelings. Instead, these sons absorbed an unyielding creed from an early age: the belief that real men endure suffering without complaint, triumph over adversity in silence, and forge ahead with stoic resolve, often at the expense of their own emotional well-being. This cycle of repression and silence continued, perpetuating a legacy that profoundly affected the ways in which subsequent generations navigated their own emotional landscapes.

1950s to 1980s: The Stoic Provider and Silent Struggles

As the mid-twentieth century unfolded, the nuclear family model emerged as the cornerstone of Western masculinity, shaping societal expectations and norms. This model was constantly reinforced by various institutions, including the media, religious organisations, and advertising, all of which propagated a singular, idealised image of fatherhood. The archetype of the "ideal father" depicted a man who worked long, arduous hours in a job that often required physical and emotional exertion, while his partner primarily occupied the domestic sphere, managing the home and caring for the children. Underpinning this paradigm was the belief internalised by boys that to lead a successful household necessitated a stoic emotional detachment, a formula for manliness that prized strength and resilience over emotional vulnerability.

Yet, beneath this seemingly stable facade, a myriad of deep-seated cracks began to materialise. The external trappings of success often belied a pervasive despair that many men grappled with, frequently hiding behind the mask of alcoholism as a coping mechanism. Emotional disconnection manifested not simply as a personal shortcoming but was cloaked in a guise of control, where the need to appear unflappable overshadowed the importance of genuine emotional engagement. Countless men toiled tirelessly, not just to provide for their families but as a means of escape from the emotional void that loomed over their lives.

Social spaces such as bars and pubs evolved into informal sanctuaries where men sought solace, transforming into places of unspoken communion. Here, they could forge a semblance of connection with one another while avoiding the vulnerability associated with true emotional sharing. In these environments, conversations often circled around mundane topics or lighthearted banter, masking the deeper struggles they faced. Without the language or understanding to navigate their emotions, many men found emotional literacy to be an alien concept, and the idea of seeking therapy remained firmly relegated to the realm of taboo. As a result, generational wounds festered and deepened, remaining unseen yet profoundly felt, perpetuating a cycle of emotional isolation that echoed through families and communities.

Feminism and the Fracturing of the Script

The arrival of second-wave feminism during the 1960s and 1970s catalysed a crucial societal reckoning regarding traditional gender roles that had long been entrenched in Western culture. Women sought far more than just acknowledgment of their capabilities within domestic spheres; they demanded agency, professional careers, and social and economic equality, all warranted by historical injustices. Their revolutionary efforts, such as the push for equal pay, reproductive rights, and access to education, triggered seismic shifts in collective perceptions and societal expectations.

However, as women were equipped with new tools and opportunities to expand their identities and roles, many men found themselves adrift, struggling to adapt without such insights for their own transformation. Society encouraged them to adopt less dominant roles, to express vulnerability, and to engage more meaningfully in domestic life through active participation in parenting and household duties. Yet, this shift often came without a clear roadmap or supportive framework, leaving many men feeling lost in uncharted territory. The process of feminisation of ethics, which called for emotional intelligence and empathy, was not easily integrated into the traditional masculine identity formed through generations.

While feminism liberated one gender, it simultaneously left many men grappling with the remnants of their own constraints, caught in a dilemma of whether to cling to outdated ideals of masculinity or to cast them aside for a more nuanced understanding of gender dynamics. The battleground of identity evolved, pitting emerging progressive values against deeply rooted societal norms.

What is the outcome of these profound societal shifts? A complex cocktail of confusion, shame, and anger began to brew. Some men successfully adapted to the evolving landscape, embracing more cooperative and emotionally expressive roles, while others resisted the temptation to change, clinging fiercely to traditional notions of masculinity. Most, however, found themselves internalising a growing fear regarding their masculinity, often questioning: Am I still man enough? This introspection led to a variety of responses, from increased engagement in gender discourses to, in some cases, backlash against women's rights movements, revealing the intricate and often conflicting emotions that emerged from this transformative period.

The Age of Conflicting Messages

Today, the modern man finds himself navigating a perplexing intersection of conflicting messages and expectations that often feels overwhelming. He is pressured to embody a myriad of contradictory characteristics: he is expected to be strong and resilient yet simultaneously vulnerable and open to emotional insights; he should take initiative and lead decisively while also practicing active listening and valuing the perspectives of others; he is compelled to provide financially for himself and his loved ones while equally prioritising his own mental and physical self-care; he faces the challenge of advocating for his beliefs while being mindful of the voices and experiences of those around him.

The relentless barrage of social media amplifies these societal expectations, creating a confusing landscape where fitness influencers tout the virtues of discipline and physical prowess alongside therapists who advocate for self-acceptance and mental well-being. On the dating front, norms waver dramatically between the promotion of "alpha male" archetypes, characterised by dominance and assertiveness and the increasing necessity for emotional openness and vulnerability. In professional environments, assertiveness and aggressive behaviour are often celebrated and rewarded, while in personal relationships, these same traits can be met with resistance and rejection.

As a result, today's men find themselves in an ongoing struggle, expected to embody the roles of a warrior, a healer, a lover, and a sage, all while maintaining an impossible balancing act that invites both aspiration and anxiety. This relentless expectation can lead to feelings of inadequacy and confusion, as men strive to meet idealised versions of masculinity that may feel unattainable.

In this evolving cultural landscape, the quest to redefine masculinity is ongoing, marked by deep struggles for authenticity and meaningful connection in a world that increasingly seems to reward disconnection. Men are called to reflect on their identities, forge genuine connections, and embrace a more holistic view of masculinity that allows for emotional depth and complexity without the confines of traditional stereotypes.

The Biopsychology of Emotional Suppression

From a neuroscientific perspective, the long-term practice of emotional suppression, especially in men conditioned to inhibit expressions of vulnerability, can lead to profound psychological and physiological consequences. Extensive research highlights the detrimental effects of such emotional repression, revealing links to various bodily responses, including:

- Elevated cortisol and adrenaline levels: Chronic emotional suppression contributes to a persistent state of stress, characterised by elevated levels of cortisol and adrenaline, hormones that prepare the body for fight-or-flight responses. Over time, this chronic stress can result in serious health complications, such as hypertension, metabolic dysfunction, and an increased risk of conditions like diabetes.

- Disrupted prefrontal cortex-amygdala regulation: Emotional suppression can interfere with the delicate balance between the prefrontal cortex, responsible for higher-order thinking and impulse control, and the amygdala, which processes emotions, particularly fear and anxiety. This disruption often manifests as impaired impulse control and an inability to manage emotions effectively, leading to heightened sensitivity and reactivity during stressful situations, ultimately affecting decision-making and social relationships.

- Increased risk of cardiovascular problems: The ongoing strain of heightened stress responses has been linked to an array of cardiovascular issues. Research indicates that chronic emotional suppression can contribute to conditions such as coronary artery disease and heart failure, as the body constantly works under stress, leading to wear and tear on the cardiovascular system.

- Emotional numbing and dissociation: As individuals suppress their emotional responses, they often experience a profound disconnection from their feelings, a phenomenon that can result in emotional numbing or dissociation. This disconnection may lead to a persistent sense of emptiness or numbness, diminishing one's capacity for joy and fulfilment in both personal and professional realms.

The brain, in its effort to cope with the demands of emotional suppression, can begin to atrophy regarding its capacity for emotional processing. This atrophy weakens empathy circuits, elevates anxiety levels, and may result in the body serving as a repository for unprocessed emotions such as grief, rage, and shame. Over time, these unresolved feelings can lead to a cycle of emotional and physical distress, impacting overall well-being and quality of life.

Counselling and Psychiatric Insight

In contemporary counselling psychology, practitioners are increasingly recognising that many male clients do not initially express their emotional struggles in straightforward or explicit terms. Instead, their presentations may manifest as a range of symptoms, including but not limited to persistent anger, emotional numbness, chronic burnout, sexual dysfunction, social isolation, or substance addiction. At the core of these symptoms frequently lies a singular, profound theme: "I don't know who I'm allowed to be anymore." This sense of uncertainty can stem from societal expectations and traditional masculinity norms that discourage vulnerability and emotional openness.

In response to these challenges, psychiatric models, particularly within NHS men's health initiatives are evolving to integrate gender-sensitive trauma frameworks. This innovative approach includes comprehensive psychoeducation that explores the impact of masculinity scripts, which dictate acceptable behaviour's and emotional expressions for men. Practitioners are also incorporating body-based therapies designed to help clients recognise and release stored emotions that may be trapped in the body, promoting physical and emotional healing.

Moreover, group therapy models are being developed to validate and affirm forms of communication that are often associated with masculinity, such as storytelling, humour, and action-oriented healing practices. These sessions create a supportive environment where men can share their experiences, fostering a sense of community and connection. By normalising discussions

25

around emotional struggles and reclaiming the narrative around masculinity, these approaches aim to empower male clients to explore their identities and express their feelings more freely.

Redefining the Blueprint of Masculinity

It is imperative that we begin to dismantle the outdated blueprint of masculinity while preserving the values that continue to hold relevance in modern society. We must acknowledge that masculinity itself is not inherently toxic; rather, the toxicity emerges from rigid societal roles and stereotypes that stifle emotional growth and expression. Strength should be redefined, not by the ability to dominate or overpower others, but by the capacity to make discerning, thoughtful choices in the face of challenges. True leadership is not undermined by emotional expression; on the contrary, it is significantly bolstered by a deep emotional awareness and the ability to connect with others on a human level.

To foster a healthier understanding of masculinity, we must proactively teach boys that:

- Crying is not a flaw but an essential human expression that reflects vulnerability and authenticity. Tears can signify courage, illustrating the importance of processing and sharing emotions.
- Asking for help is not a sign of weakness; it is a courageous acknowledgement of one's limitations, an essential aspect of self-worth that recognises our interdependence and the strength found in community support.
- Exhibiting softness and empathy do not equate to weakness, but instead demonstrate strength of character and a willingness to engage compassionately with others.
- Protectiveness does not necessitate emotional suppression. Rather, true protectiveness involves empathy, understanding, and the ability to communicate one's feelings effectively to those they care about.

- Embracing love and affection for friends, family, and partners does not compromise their identity; instead, it enriches their experience and connection with others, fostering deeper bonds and understanding.

The new masculine blueprint must encompass:

- Emotional literacy, which includes the ability to identify, articulate, and express feelings in a meaningful way, thus enabling better personal and interpersonal relationships.
- Collaborative and effective communication skills that promote dialogue and understanding, essential tools for resolving conflict and building strong relationships.
- The nurturing of relationships through active listening, empathy, and vulnerability, while eliminating shame or stigma associated with these practices.
- The establishment of boundaries that are both firm and compassionate, ensuring that personal integrity is maintained without disregarding the feelings and rights of others.
- An identity rooted in authentic self-expression and introspection, rather than the mere pursuit of external achievements or societal approval.

By reshaping the narrative around masculinity, we can cultivate a generation of emotionally intelligent, compassionate individuals who understand that true strength lies in vulnerability and connection.

A New Definition of Masculinity

What truly defines a man in today's context? It transcends the mere physical weight he can lift or the burdens he can bear. Instead, it is about the emotional truths he has the courage to articulate and stand by, demonstrating vulnerability and authenticity. Strength is not measured by the silence he endures through hardship; rather, it is reflected in the meaningful connections he consciously chooses to cultivate with others, whether through deep conversations, acts of kindness, or simply being present in the lives of those around him.

Moreover, the idea of masculinity should not be about striving for perfection or fitting into narrow stereotypes; instead, it should emphasise the authenticity he embraces in his everyday life. This authenticity is about being true to oneself, acknowledging flaws, and celebrating the full spectrum of human emotion, from joy and love to fear and sadness.

As we shift the paradigm of masculinity, let us focus on wholeness, integration, and emotional courage qualities that reject cruelty and promote understanding instead. Presence should replace posturing, allowing men to show up as their true selves without the constraints of societal expectations. The new narrative of masculinity invites a rich tapestry of experiences and feelings, urging us to recognise that emotional suppression is not a hallmark of strength, but a barrier to genuine connection.

This transformation signifies not merely an end to outdated notions of manhood but heralds an exciting reinvention one where men embrace their complexities and engage fully with the world around them, fostering healthier relationships with themselves and others. It is a call to redefine what it means to be a man in a way that celebrates emotional intelligence and empathy, paving the way for a more compassionate society.

Therapist Insight: Understanding the Masculine Identity Crisis

Psychologists are increasingly reframing the masculine identity crisis not merely as a sign of dysfunction but as a significant opportunity for profound personal transformation. This experience of disorientation represents a psychological threshold, a critical juncture at which individuals can move away from inherited societal scripts and embark on a journey towards crafting a self-authored narrative that embodies their truth and authenticity.

Rather than failing to embody traditional notions of masculinity, men are awakening to their genuine selves, courageously breaking free from the rigid constraints imposed by societal expectations. This moment can be seen as a liberating permission slip, urging individuals to cease performing a pre-scripted role and instead embrace their true identities. It is an invitation to not only recognise who you are beneath the layers of expectation but to boldly pursue personal growth with authenticity and courage. Embracing this process allows for a deeper understanding of oneself and fosters a more fulfilling and sincere expression of masculinity, paving the way for meaningful connections with others and a more integrative experience of life.

Chapter 2

Forged in Silence — How Boys Become Men

There is no single, defining moment in a boy's life when he learns what it truly means to become a man. Unlike many traditional rites of passage, such as bar mitzvahs or high school graduations, that signify transitions in life, there is no universal guidebook or roadmap to follow in this journey towards manhood. Instead, most boys acquire their understanding of masculinity through a gradual process of osmosis, keenly observing their environments and absorbing the cultural cues that surround them.

This understanding is shaped by a multitude of experiences, including everyday interactions with peers, family dynamics, and moments of correction from authority figures, which may range from teachers to coaches. Boys internalise the myriad messages communicated throughout their formative year's messages that often convey specific expectations about strength, stoicism, and relationships. Unfortunately, these lessons about masculinity are rarely neutral or benign; they are heavily influenced by several critical factors.

The emotional climate of the home plays a pivotal role: a supportive, nurturing environment can foster healthy expressions of masculinity, while a volatile or neglectful atmosphere can lead to confusion and aggression. Economic realities in the surrounding community further compound these influences; boys raised in affluent neighbourhoods may have different opportunities and pressures compared to those in disadvantaged areas. Cultural expectations grounded in their heritage also shape perceptions of what it means to be a man, as traditions, family values, and societal norms dictate specific behaviour's and roles.

Moreover, the presence or absence of influential role models, be they fathers, older brothers, mentors, or community leaders can significantly impact a boy's understanding of masculinity. Positive role models can impart lessons of empathy, respect, and responsibility, while the lack of such figures may lead boys to seek validation through less constructive avenues. Thus, the journey toward manhood is complex and multifaceted, reflecting a blend of societal, familial, and personal influences that boys must navigate as they carve out their identities.

The Geography of Masculinity

Masculinity is a complex and multifaceted concept, significantly shaped by geographic location and social dynamics. For instance, consider a boy raised in a tranquil suburban enclave of Kent; he is likely to absorb a set of cultural messages about manhood that emphasize emotional restraint and academic success. In contrast, a boy growing up in an impoverished inner-city estate in Birmingham faces a vastly different reality. In such environments marked by economic struggle and social instability, masculinity often becomes intertwined with notions of survival, where physical strength and toughness are not just valued traits but essential qualities for navigating a perilous world. As a result, emotional expression may be heavily stigmatised, framed as a vulnerability that can lead to ridicule or even violence. This leads to emotional suppression as a learned defence mechanism, ingrained from an early age due to the harsh realities these boys encounter daily.

On the other end of the spectrum, boys nurtured in middle-class households tend to internalise a version of masculinity that prioritises productivity, academic achievement, and a composed exterior that signals control. The messages prevalent in these families often carry an undercurrent of stoicism and subtlety; while overt expressions of weakness are not punished outright, they may be met with an air of silent disapproval. In this context, boys learn to "be strong" by maintaining a facade of composure, excelling in school, and avoiding any emotional or social turmoil that might disrupt the polished image they are encouraged to uphold.

Demographically, the working-class white British communities often exalt a rugged form of masculinity that values grit, hard work, and the ethos of "getting on with it" even amidst adversity. Boys from these backgrounds are frequently raised with the belief that expressing vulnerability is a sign of weakness. In contrast, cultural norms within South Asian, African, or Eastern European households might frame masculinity around principles such as honour, hierarchical respect, familial duty, and emotional restraint. Though the specifics of these masculinities differ widely, a common thread emerges: across a diverse array of cultures and social classes, boys are rarely taught that emotional literacy that is, understanding and expressing one's feelings can be a valuable aspect of being masculine.

Data from the NHS reveals a troubling trend: young men from lower socioeconomic backgrounds are significantly less likely to seek help from mental health services, while those from minority ethnic communities face even greater stigma and systemic barriers that complicate their access to care.

Globally, these patterns of masculinity manifest in various ways. In countries such as Japan and regions in the Middle East, traditional masculine ideals often remain entrenched in values like stoicism, obedience, and honour, perpetuating rigid gender roles. Conversely, Scandinavian countries are increasingly fostering ideals of emotional balance, gender equality, and open, nurturing fatherhood. This progressive approach contributes to more favourable mental health outcomes for their youth, highlighting the importance of evolving societal values. Thus, the geographical context profoundly influences what messages about masculinity are deemed acceptable for boys, shaping their behaviours and emotional development in significant ways.

Father Figures and the Fatherless Gap

The role of a father, or the absence of one, plays a crucial role in shaping a boy's understanding of masculinity and influencing his future relationships. According to the UK's Office for National Statistics, more than 23% of children now grow up in single-parent households, with a significant portion lacking a father's presence. In certain boroughs of London, this figure can surpass 60%, particularly in communities facing economic hardship or social instability.

When fathers are absent whether physically due to separation, death, or emotional unavailability a psychological rupture often occurs within the child. This phenomenon is frequently referred to as the "Father Wound." It signifies a profound void in attachment and identity that can have lasting implications on a boy's development. Without the validation, structure, or guidance that fathers ideally provide, many boys may cultivate a sense of hyper-independence or emotional detachment. This detachment can be accompanied by a chronic need to prove their worth, often manifesting as overachievement or risk-taking behaviour's.

Even in cases where fathers are physically present, their emotional distance can inadvertently stifle their sons' emotional development. An emotionally unavailable, overly critical, or volatile father may send the damaging message that love is conditional, something to be earned through performance and achievement. Research supports that boys exposed to these dynamics may face heightened risks of developing anxiety disorders, engaging in substance misuse, and grappling with various interpersonal difficulties as adults. Boys raised in families characterised by authoritarian parenting styles are also more likely to adopt maladaptive coping mechanisms, such as emotional repression, aggression, or unhealthy conflict resolution strategies.

In Black, Asian, and Minority Ethnic (BAME) households, it is common for fathers to be present physically but emotionally restrained, often due to deeply ingrained cultural or generational norms. In these contexts, boys frequently navigate strict behavioural expectations without the necessary emotional guidance for nurturing their development. Therapeutic settings often reveal that these boys struggle with self-soothing techniques and face difficulties in forming secure attachments in their adult relationships, which can perpetuate cycles of emotional distress.

Joseph Horrocks' concept of the "unfathered man" poignantly encapsulates this struggle. Whether due to physical absence, neglect, or emotional detachment, the result is often a fragmented masculine identity, one fashioned more from survival instincts than from authentic self-expression. This ongoing discourse about the complexities of masculinity underscores the pressing need for supportive environments that prioritise emotional health, resilience, and a more comprehensive understanding of what it means to be a man in the contemporary world. Addressing these issues is essential not only for the individual well-being of boys and men but also for fostering healthier family dynamics and societal structures.

Learned Behaviours and Emotional Development

Children develop their emotional understanding and responses primarily through a process known as mirroring, which is critical for their emotional development. From the very beginning of life, boys begin to align themselves with the emotional rhythms exhibited by their primary caregivers, most notably their mothers and fathers. When nurtured in an environment brimming with warmth, open emotional expression, and supportive interactions, they internalise these nurturing behaviour's. Such a positive foundation becomes instrumental in shaping their future emotional landscapes, promoting resilience, and fostering healthy relationships.

Conversely, if caregivers, particularly fathers, withdraw emotionally or display negative emotional responses, such as sarcasm, emotional stoicism, or overt anger, boys are likely to adopt these maladaptive reactions as their default emotional responses. This response can lead to significant challenges in their emotional development and understanding.

Delving further into the bio-psychological aspects, it becomes evident that an emotionally barren environment can have profound and lasting impacts on key areas of brain development. Chronic emotional suppression affects critical brain structures. The amygdala, which governs emotional responses and threat detection, may become overactive, while the prefrontal cortex, responsible for impulse control and rational decision-making, can underdeveloped. Additionally, the hippocampus, which is essential for memory formation and emotional regulation, may not function optimally. Boys raised in such challenging conditions often exhibit hyper-vigilance, a heightened state of alertness to perceived threats, and systems of empathy that are markedly underdeveloped, leading to difficulties in social interactions.

This skewed emotional landscape can lead to a psychological condition commonly referred to as alexithymia, characterised by a marked difficulty in identifying and expressing one's emotions. It's crucial to understand that boys experiencing this phenomenon do not lack feelings altogether; rather, they frequently lack the vocabulary and cognitive framework necessary to articulate those feelings accurately. In educational settings, the resulting emotional illiteracy can be misinterpreted as behavioural issues, compounding misunderstandings between students and teachers. Over time, anger tends to ascend as the predominant emotional expression among these boys. This does not indicate an intrinsic propensity for anger; instead, it reflects the learning of survival behaviour, as it becomes the sole emotional language they have been exposed to and can thus articulate fluently.

Attachment theory further elucidates this dynamic. Boys raised with inconsistent caregiving, wherein emotional responses fluctuate or are unpredictable, often develop avoidant or disorganised attachment styles. This can result in emotional oscillation, characterized by vacillation between clinginess to caregivers and complete emotional shutdown. As these boys transition into adulthood, they may grapple with deep-seated fears of intimacy and struggle to build trust in affectionate relationships. This behaviour does not stem from a lack of desire for connection; rather, it arises from the intense discomfort and anxiety linked to pursuing emotional connections that may feel unfamiliar or unsafe. The paradox of their desire for closeness contrasted with their learned behaviour's often leads to emotional isolation, complicating their ability to foster fulfilling relationships.

The Social Scripts That Shape Us

Social learning theory provides deep insight into how children absorb and internalise gender roles through mechanisms of observation and reinforcement within their social environments. For instance, a young boy who is met with ridicule from peers or adults for expressing vulnerability, such as crying quickly learns that these traits are not rewarded. In contrast, when he displays aggression or toughness, he often receives accolades, praise, or acceptance. This dichotomy of reactions shapes his understanding of which behaviours are valued in his particular social context. Such formative experiences contribute to the development of cognitive schemas, which are unconscious frameworks that dictate what is deemed acceptable, valuable, or safe in terms of gender expression.

Cognitive behavioural therapy (CBT) further elucidates how these schemas solidify into core beliefs that profoundly influence a man's self-perception and interpersonal interactions throughout his life. For example, many men might internalise beliefs such as: "I must project strength at all costs, or I risk abandonment;" "My value is tied to my achievements rather than my inherent qualities as a person;" or "Seeking help is a sign of weakness and an indicator of personal failure." Over time, these beliefs become entrenched, forming rigid behavioural frameworks that permeate various aspects of life, including professional settings, personal relationships, and parenting styles. This can lead to patterns of overachievement, emotional detachment, and unhealthy perfectionism. If unaddressed, these internal pressures often culminate in mental health challenges such as burnout, anxiety, or emotional breakdowns, compelling individuals to confront the façades they have built around themselves to navigate societal expectations.

Additionally, media representations play a significant role in reinforcing these rigid scripts. From blockbuster action heroes who epitomise invincibility to romantic leads who exhibit emotional stoicism, men are predominantly depicted as resilient, unattached figures who shun emotional vulnerability. This pervasive cultural narrative conveys the damaging message to boys that genuine emotional expression equates to weakness, while true masculinity is characterised by silence in the face of pain and restraint in times of need. When emotions do surface, they are frequently suppressed or concealed, creating a cycle of emotional isolation that can have lasting effects on mental health and interpersonal relationships.

The Grief Beneath the Armour

An often-overlooked but profoundly significant aspect of men's mental health is the concept of identity grief. This term encompasses not just the sorrow associated with the death of loved ones but also the deeper, more insidious loss of one's authentic self. It captures the pain experienced by the sensitive child who is chastised for expressing vulnerability, the compassionate teenager who faces ridicule from peers for being empathetic, and the adult man burdened by impostor syndrome, feeling the dissonance between his genuine self and the persona he believes society demands.

This underlying grief can be pervasive and insidious, creating a persistent sense of emptiness and dissatisfaction, even amidst seemingly fulfilling external circumstances, such as career success or social status. Rather than presenting as classic depression with overt symptoms, it often manifests as a profound disconnection from one's true emotions and identity. This disconnection can strip individuals of the freedom to live authentically, leaving them trapped in a cycle of performance and conformity, which ultimately undermines their sense of self-worth and fulfilment.

The societal pressures to conform to traditional masculine ideals, such as stoicism, strength, and independence can exacerbate these feelings, silencing the quieter, more vulnerable aspects of one's identity. Consequently, this grief can lead to a range of mental health challenges, including anxiety, substance use, and strained relationships, highlighting the urgent need to address the emotional landscape that many men navigate in silence.

Therapist Insight

In therapeutic circles, the concepts of "Father Wound" and "Father Hunger" are used to articulate the deep psychological and emotional scars that arise from the absence, emotional unavailability, or inconsistency of a father figure. This absence can manifest in two primary forms: physical absence, where the father is simply not present in the child's life often due to divorce, abandonment, or death and emotional absence, wherein the father is physically present yet emotionally distant, disconnected, or unable to provide the nurturing support typically expected from a paternal figure.

For many men, the wound created by this absence leads to a persistent and deep-seated ache, a yearning for visibility, validation, and guidance from a masculine presence that was either missing or insufficiently nurturing. Society often socializes boys to suppress their vulnerabilities, promoting the notion that the need for love, especially from their fathers, signifies weakness. This cultural conditioning can create internal conflicts, making many men bury their longing for paternal acknowledgment beneath layers of societal expectations and stoicism, a trend often echoed in male-oriented social structures and norms.

As adults, the repercussions of the father wound can manifest in various detrimental ways, significantly impacting interpersonal relationships, self-perception, and overall mental health. Some common consequences include:

1. Low self-worth or an inability to self-validate: Many men find themselves grappling with persistent feelings of inadequacy, believing they are unworthy of love or respect. They may seek external validation through achievements, relationships, or social status as a way to fill the emotional void left by their father's absence.

2. Anger toward male authority figures or mentors: A deep-seated mistrust or resentment can develop towards men in authoritative or mentorship roles. This can lead to challenges in both professional environments and personal interactions, frequently resulting in a defensive or confrontational approach to male relationships.

3. Emotional distance in relationships: The inability to connect at an emotional level can create barriers in romantic relationships, where expressions of vulnerability are perceived as threatening. This often results in a cycle of emotional detachment, where intimacy feels out of reach.

4. Fear of becoming a father or overcompensating as one: Some men may develop an aversion to fatherhood altogether due to their own negative experiences, fearing that they will replicate their fathers' failures. Conversely, others may overcompensate in their parenting styles, striving to provide what they felt was lacking in their own upbringing, often leading to excessive pressure on both themselves and their children.

5. Chronic people-pleasing, perfectionism, or an unyielding competitive drive: The relentless pursuit of external approval can foster perfectionistic tendencies, where the need to meet societal expectations takes precedence over personal well-being. This can lead to burnout and feelings of emptiness despite outward successes.

The father wound is often characterised as a form of developmental trauma. It can stem not only from overt abuse but also from the subtler, yet pervasive, neglect or emotional absence experienced throughout formative years. The absence of affirming expressions such as "I'm proud of you" or "You can do this," paired with a lack of affection and emotional support, can leave lasting scars that affect one's sense of self-worth and relational dynamics throughout life.

Importantly, recognising the father wound is not about casting blame on the father but rather about embarking on a journey of acknowledgment and acceptance. By confronting the pain associated with the relationship that was never fully realised, individuals can begin a necessary process of mourning the loss of the ideal paternal figure they needed. This step is crucial in reconstructing an internal father figure characterised by compassion, strength, and emotional security.

While it is impossible to alter one's upbringing or undo the past, it is entirely possible to break the cycle of pain and dissatisfaction that often accompanies it. Healing typically involves redefining personal understandings of masculinity, nurturing oneself with the love and guidance that may have been absent in childhood. This journey towards emotional wholeness invites profound transformation and growth, fostering resilience and a richer capacity for connection and self-acceptance.

Reconstructing Manhood

Masculinity isn't broken; it's an ongoing journey of personal development and self-discovery. This exploration does not require you to completely discard all the lessons you've learned throughout your life; rather, it involves discerning which lessons no longer resonate with your true self or align with your greater purpose. Authentic manhood is not defined by narrow traits such as dominance, invulnerability, or the insistent silence often expected of men. Instead, it embodies concepts such as presence, being fully engaged and aware in each moment, protection, where you support and care for those around you, honest expression, allowing your emotions and thoughts to be communicated openly, and a rooted power that emanates from within, grounded in self-awareness and confidence.

Take a moment to reflect deeply on these essential questions:

-   Who did I become to navigate the challenges of life? - Explore the various masks you've worn, these could include the "stoic provider," the "fearless leader," or the "funny guy" you adopted to gain acceptance or ensure your survival in different social environments. What actions and behaviours were necessary for you to succeed in these roles, and at what personal cost?

-   Who am I beneath the layers of expectation and conditioning? - Delve into your core identity, peeling back societal pressures, familial influences, and personal struggles. This might involve recalling formative experiences from childhood, examining how cultural norms shaped your view of masculinity, and identifying the quiet truths about yourself that may have been overshadowed by external demands.

-   What kind of man do I aspire to be, on my own terms? - Envision a version of masculinity that aligns with your own values and ideals. Consider the qualities you admire in others, traits like empathy, strength, creativity, and resilience. Reflect on how you can embody these traits authentically, free from the constraints of external judgment, and create a definition of manhood that feels true and fulfilling.

Healing is not merely a quest to transform into someone entirely new; rather, it is a profound process of rediscovering the person you were before the world pigeonholed you with limiting labels, suggesting you were either too much or not enough, or somehow flawed altogether. This journey toward wholeness encourages you to embrace your complexity, understand your vulnerabilities, and ultimately, reclaim the fullness of your identity.

Reflection Prompts:

- What did the word "man" represent in your household as you were growing up? Reflect on the specific qualities, expectations, and responsibilities that were associated with this term in your family dynamic. How did these definitions shape your understanding of masculinity, and what models (whether positive or negative) influenced your perception of what it means to be a man?

- Were emotions regarded as a source of strength or as a sign of weakness? Consider how this viewpoint was expressed in your family, through words, actions, or cultural norms. Reflect on how this perception affected your ability to express emotions openly and your willingness to show vulnerability. What barriers, if any, did this create in your relationships with others?

- When did you first feel a sense of shame around your sensitivity, and who instilled that belief in you? Pinpoint the specific moments or experiences that contributed to this feeling, whether it was a comment from a parent, a peer's reaction, or a societal expectation. Examine the influences that led to this internal conflict, and how these experiences shaped your self-image over time.

- What kind of father figure would you aim to become for both others and yourself? Envision the qualities you admire in nurturing figures or role models in your life. Think about what nurturing and support truly mean to you, do you aspire to be emotionally available, encouraging, or perhaps a source of wisdom? How can you actively embody these qualities to foster a positive legacy for future generations?

- What aspects of your identity were stifled during your childhood to "fit in" or merely survive? Acknowledge the parts of yourself, interests, beliefs, or characteristics that you felt compelled to hide to gain acceptance or avoid conflict. Consider how these suppressed aspects have affected your self-acceptance and authenticity in adulthood.

This chapter is not about placing blame on others or yourself; rather, it's an exploration of the experiences that have shaped you and the beliefs you hold. As we transition into the next chapter, you will discover your unique blueprint to empowerment crafted with intention, not merely inherited by default. Embrace the potential for growth and transformation, and reclaim your narrative as you carve out a path that is genuinely your own.

"But even once we've become the men they told us to be, the silence we learned doesn't just disappear, it festers. And sometimes, the cost of that silence is our very will to live."

Chapter 3

The Primal Drivers of Modern Masculinity

What Men Are Searching for (But Don't Know How to Name it)

For many men, there exists an unarticulated longing, an awareness that a critical element essential to their fulfilment is missing from their lives. This absence transcends mere deficiencies in financial resources, career achievements, or romantic connections; it expresses as a deeper, existential gap that resonates within their very core, creating a profound sense of yearning.

This void often manifests in a range of unhealthy behaviour's: aimless late-night scrolling through endlessly refreshing social media feeds that offer fleeting distractions rather than genuine connection; the tension of clenched jaws during mundane conversations, as they grapple with unspoken thoughts and feelings; and a pervasive emptiness during social interactions that, instead of fostering a sense of community, leaves them feeling more isolated. Such emotional turbulence frequently finds expression in overworking, a fruitless attempt to find purpose in relentless productivity, overdrinking to numb the underlying discomfort, and persistent overthinking that spirals into anxiety. The silence that envelops them often speaks volumes, revealing the internal struggles they dare not voice, while underlying hostility may erupt in moments of frustration tiny explosions born from suppressed emotions that feel too overwhelming to articulate.

What we might label as a crisis is, in fact, a profound clash between the primal instincts that have historically shaped manhood, survival, connection, and purpose and the modern cultural landscape, which often leaves many men feeling isolated, disconnected, and directionless. These primal desires are universal among all humans; however, they often become misdirected, muted, or even weaponised in the lives of men, leading to a cycle of unhealthy coping mechanisms and emotional disconnection.

This exploration is not merely an exercise in scapegoating men; rather, it serves as a thoughtful invitation to decode their experiences and emotions. By examining the societal pressures, historical expectations, and personal narratives that shape modern masculinity, we can begin to foster a dialogue that encourages vulnerability, authenticity, and ultimately, healing. Let's delve deeper into this complex terrain together.

Survival and Safety

At the heart of every man lies an instinctual drive for survival, encompassing not only the physical realm but also the social and psychological dimensions of existence. This drive is often amplified by the unrelenting pressure to succeed, leading to an internal mantra that echoes in their minds: he must not fail, nor allow himself to appear weak before peers, family, or loved ones.

In response to these societal expectations, many men alter their behaviour significantly. They may choose the path of silence, suppressing their thoughts and emotions to avoid judgment or perceived vulnerability. This often leads to enduring soul-crushing jobs that disregard their mental health and overall well-being. Additionally, they may tolerate disrespect from colleagues or friends in an attempt to maintain an illusion of harmony and stability in their relationships. Unfortunately, this guise of peacekeeping frequently causes them to render themselves invisible, as their true feelings and needs go unexpressed.

Societal conditioning reinforces the notion that men must project an image of strength and unwavering stoicism. This expectation can result in a façade of emotional numbness; men are not genuinely cold but rather engaged in a primal struggle for survival in a world that often feels hostile or dismissive. From a bio-psychological perspective, the amygdala, our brain's core threat detector becomes hyperactive in men who have faced trauma or significant emotional stress. This chronic state of hyper-vigilance rewires their neurological pathways, causing them to prioritise perceived threats over the nurturing of genuine connections and emotional intimacy with others. Consequently, many men find themselves in a vicious cycle, caught between societal expectations and their innate desire for authentic relationships.

Freedom from Fear and Pain

Men, like all humans, experience pain deeply, yet they are often socialised from an early age to conceal their vulnerabilities. Societal norms frequently dictate that displaying emotions, particularly sadness or fear is a sign of weakness. As a result, emotional pain can manifest in various ways; it might emerge as outward expressions of anger, irritation, or even apathy. Some men may turn to destructive habits such as alcohol dependence, gambling, or other forms of escapism to cope with their inner turmoil. Others might choose to withdraw altogether from stressful environments, isolating themselves from friends and family. Many opt to wear a mask of indifference, projecting an image of strength while concealing their true feelings beneath a veneer of stoicism.

This dynamic is part of why therapy often meets with resistance from men. The challenge they encounter stems not from a lack of caring but from a deeply rooted belief that expressing their pain is akin to admitting defeat or vulnerability. Beneath the tough exterior many men present lies a heart that feels profoundly, a heart that aches under the weight of unexpressed emotions and unaddressed trauma.

The brain's fear centre is finely tuned not only to physical threats but also to the potential emotional vulnerability that comes with open expression. For many men, the avoidance of emotions is often misinterpreted as apathy; in reality, it serves as a form of self-defence. This protective layer of armour is instinctively created to guard against the pain of rejection, judgment, or further heartbreak, perpetuating a cycle of emotional suppression. The challenge lies in unravelling this defence mechanism, allowing men to understand that acknowledging their pain does not equate to weakness, but rather to the courage it takes to confront and heal from it.

Power and Control

In a world characterised by unpredictability and constant change, many men find themselves grappling with a profound sense of uncertainty. In a bid to reclaim a semblance of control over their lives, they often resort to various coping mechanisms: some may express their frustrations through silence, adopting a stoic facade that conceals their inner turmoil, while others might channel their feelings into anger, erupting with a ferocity that masks their vulnerability. Additionally, there are those who dive headfirst into a relentless pursuit of achievement, believing that success will insulate them from feelings of inadequacy.

Conversely, some men, overwhelmed by the weight of this tumultuous emotional landscape, choose to withdraw entirely, resigning themselves to a passive existence in an effort to avoid the painful sting of powerlessness and disappointment.

This complex phenomenon extends beyond issues of wounded pride or inflated ego; it is deeply interwoven with an intrinsic longing for agency, the ability to influence one's own life and circumstances. From a young age, boys are often socialised to stifle their emotional experiences, leading to a pervasive fear that vulnerability equates to weakness. In response, they may seek to exert control over everything within their grasp, relationships, careers, and even their own emotions often with little regard for the collateral damage this behaviour may cause.

The repercussions of this struggle for agency can be strikingly profound. Faced with overwhelming feelings of powerlessness, many men either succumb to the pressure, collapsing under the weight of their own expectations, or respond with explosive outbursts that can alienate those around them.

It's essential to recognise that the individual in this scenario is not simply an authoritarian figure imposing his will on others; rather, he is a man ensnared in a cycle of fear, grappling with a deep-seated anxiety about his significance in a world that can be unforgiving. Understanding the concept of agency within the framework of emotional literacy is crucial. True agency is not about the dominance or control over others; it embodies a clear sense of direction and purpose, a navigation of one's own emotional landscape that empowers rather than oppresses.

Without the necessary skills to effectively process and articulate their emotions, many men find themselves trapped in a self-perpetuating cycle where their expressions of power become defensive reactions fuelled by panic, rather than mindful choices rooted in self-awareness and understanding. This underscores the pressing need for fostering emotional intelligence, allowing men to cultivate healthier relationships both with themselves and the world around them.

Love and Connection

Men undoubtedly desire love; however, many struggle to accept it fully due to societal conditioning from a young age. Traditional norms often teach them to equate their self-worth with achievements, leading them to chase validation through success rather than fostering emotional connections. This approach cultivates performances of strength, men are often seen as protectors and providers, responsible for the safety and well-being of those they love. Yet, when opportunities for emotional vulnerability arise, many find themselves paralysed, unable to express their feelings.

Deep down, these men yearn for genuine intimacy and connection, but they often lack the vocabulary or emotional tools to articulate these desires. This disconnect can manifest in various, often harmful, behaviour's. For instance, some men may choose to ghost romantic partners rather than confront their own emotions, believing that avoidance is easier than facing discomfort. Others might seek solace in infidelity, attempting to fill the void of internal loneliness with fleeting encounters, yet these actions often lead to further isolation.

The root of these behaviour's often stems from an inability to express feelings like "I'm feeling isolated and disconnected." He is not merely distant or uninterested; rather, his struggle with closeness is a reflection of not having been taught how to navigate emotional intimacy. Though oxytocin, often referred to as the bonding hormone, is present in men, it frequently remains underutilised. As a result, the experience of emotional proximity can feel threatening, a reflection of unhealthy models established during their formative years that taught them to suppress vulnerability. This lack of emotional awareness and skill creates a cycle of loneliness and disconnection, hindering their relationships and personal happiness.

Status and Significance

Society frequently communicates to men that their self-worth is closely tied to their achievements, pushing them to pursue prestigious titles, handsome salaries, and external accolades. Beneath this relentless chase lies a profound, intrinsic longing for acknowledgment and a deep-seated need to feel valued and respected by their peers, family, and society at large.

When a man's self-esteem becomes intertwined with his social or professional status, every setback or perceived failure can feel devastating and overwhelming, plunging him into a state of despair. The absence of recognition, whether it's a missed promotion or a lack of appreciation for hard work, can trigger profound feelings of anger, disappointment, and resentment often directed both inwardly, at themselves for not measuring up, and outwardly, at the system or individuals they believe have failed to recognise their worth. This emotional upheaval creates a compelling drive for some men to remain stuck in toxic professional roles. They cling to these positions out of fear that without them, their identities would fade into obscurity and they would lose their sense of purpose and belonging.

In this context, he does not navigate through life with pride and confidence; rather, he exists in a state of perpetual anxiety and uncertainty, consumed by the fear of being unseen and unheard. The dopamine response, a neurological mechanism designed to reward the pursuit of goals can create an addictive cycle within achievement-focused environments. While the initial excitement of success can be intoxicating, the relentless pursuit of more can often lead to a deeper sense of emptiness and dissatisfaction, as the emotional anchor needed for true fulfilment is noticeably absent. Without a healthy relationship to his achievements, he may find himself constantly striving, yet perpetually feeling unfulfilled, trapped in a cycle that underscores the fragility of his self-worth.

Novelty and Stimulation

Men often possess an innate drive for risk-taking, curiosity, and the pursuit of challenges. Yet, in the absence of fulfilling experiences, this adventurous spirit can devolve into reckless behaviour. A man doesn't cheat merely out of boredom or desire for novelty; he may engage in infidelity because he feels an overwhelming emptiness within himself, desperately searching for ways to feel a genuine sense of aliveness again. His pursuit of new thrills should not be mistaken for immaturity; it often represents a deeper yearning for more meaningful experiences and emotional connections.

This desire for excitement should be viewed through the lens of an unfulfilled longing for depth and significance in life, rather than a character flaw. He is not inherently unstable; instead, he is unstimulated, seeking to invigorate his existence through various means. The male brain's reward system is intricately designed to thrive on challenges and the prospect of personal growth. When these essential elements are missing from daily life, whether due to routine, dissatisfaction at work, or lack of emotional intimacy, men may subconsciously generate a sense of intensity that can

51

appear chaotic. This behaviour is not a reflection of a fragile psyche; rather, it is often a response to biochemical processes gone awry, leading him to seek out experiences that momentarily fill the void and provide a fleeting sense of fulfilment.

Meaning and Purpose

At his very essence, a man aspires to have significance in the grand tapestry of life, his ambition often extends beyond the pursuit of personal success to encompass a yearning to contribute to a cause greater than himself. However, in today's fast-paced and often fragmented society, many men find themselves navigating their life journeys without a clear and purposeful path to discover this deeper meaning. They are systematically deprived of traditional rites of passage that once marked the transition into manhood, the invaluable guidance of seasoned mentors, and the clear societal maps that could illuminate their way forward.

Men are frequently admonished to seek out their purpose, yet the pervasive lack of resources, support systems, and community connections can leave them bewildered and adrift in life's vast ocean. This emotional turbulence manifests as a sense of aimlessness, leading many to feel increasingly unmoored. Tragically, this disconnection is all too frequently linked to the alarming rates of male suicide. These numbers do not arise from a lack of care but rather from an overwhelming sense that life feels devoid of purpose, direction, and fulfilment.

It is important to recognise that he does not simply find himself lost; rather, he grapples with a profound longing for a coherent narrative that can provide him with guidance and clarity. The human brain thrives on stories, narratives shape our identities and experiences. Without a strong, engaging story to connect with, a man's sense of self can become fragmented and confused. In this context, meaning transforms from being a mere luxury to an essential lifeline it has the power to restore balance, instil hope, and ultimately enrich a man's life. To aid in this quest for meaning, society must cultivate spaces and narratives that celebrate the journey of manhood, offering support, mentorship, and a shared sense of purpose.

Intersectional Insight

The primal drives residing within every man, such as the profound needs for connection, validation, and authentic self-expression are significantly shaped by the intricate interplay of race, class, culture, and personal identity. For instance, the Black man often grapples with the societal stigma that discourages vulnerability. He may find himself conflicted, fearing that to express emotions like sadness or fear is to risk being perceived as aggressive or weak, perpetuating the harmful stereotype that equates masculinity with emotional suppression. This internal struggle is further complicated by historical narratives that frame Black men within a lens of hypermasculinity, often leading to a detrimental cycle of emotional isolation.

Similarly, the gay man carries the heavy burden of societal shame, having learned through personal experiences and cultural messages that love and acceptance can frequently come alongside rejection and discrimination. The fear of societal backlash can lead him to mask his true self, stifling his ability to express his identity openly. This can result in a profound sense of loneliness, as he navigates relationships while balancing the need for authenticity with the desire for social acceptance.

In contrast, the working-class man often feels suffocated by the relentless pressures of stoicism, conditioned from a young age to suppress his emotions and endure hardships without complaint. This expectation can lead to pervasive feelings of inadequacy when he perceives that he is not living up to the traditional ideals of masculinity, often resulting in a reluctance to seek help or support for mental health struggles.

Therefore, masculinity cannot be understood as a universal truth; rather, it emerges as a dynamic construct influenced by these diverse experiences and expressions. A nuanced understanding of masculinity requires a rebirth rooted in empathy, an appreciation for individual differences, and a commitment to redefining what it means to be a man in today's society. Each narrative adds richness to our collective understanding of masculinity, challenging outdated stereotypes and fostering a more inclusive environment where all men can thrive emotionally and socially.

Therapeutic Tools & Coaching Prompts

- Which primal desires, such as the fundamental needs for affirmation, deep connection, or public recognition, do you currently feel are most unmet or overlooked in your life? Consider reflecting on specific instances where you've felt these needs arise but remain unfulfilled.
- In moments of emotional triggering, perhaps during conflicts, rejections, or even moments of vulnerability, which specific desire do you instinctively find yourself trying to protect or shield from being exposed? Think about how this protection manifests in your behaviour and responses.
- Imagine what it would mean for you to meet that desire in a constructive and healthy manner. How could you actively engage with that need through open communication, self-care, or seeking supportive relationships, rather than pushing it aside or disregarding it?
- Reflect on your upbringing: who in your life taught you which expressions of desire were safe to share and which ones were labelled as weaknesses or vulnerabilities? Consider how these teachings may have shaped your current outlook on emotional expression and your willingness to pursue those desires.
- How might your perspective shift if you began to view your struggles as misdirected expressions of unmet needs rather than as personal failures? Envision the freedom that could come from reinterpreting these challenges as opportunities for growth and a deeper understanding of your inner desires.

The Final Reframe: He's Not Broken. He's Misunderstood.

Imagine if every maladaptive behaviour commonly attributed to men, such as ghosting in relationships, explosive outbursts of anger, or emotional numbing in times of distress was, in reality, a distorted expression of fundamental human needs for connection, validation, and understanding. What if the key to addressing their struggles lay not in attempting to "fix" these behaviour's, but rather in deciphering the underlying emotions that drive them?

These unmet desires do not indicate that men are inherently toxic; instead, they highlight the inherent humanity within each individual. The actual crisis we face is not that men experience emotions too subtly or infrequently, but that societal norms often discourage or invalidate their emotional experiences altogether.

These primal drivers rooted in the need for belonging, acceptance, and emotional security are not intrinsic flaws; they represent a powerful and vibrant flame craving expression and understanding. The more pressing question we should be asking ourselves is: "How do I honour these emotions wisely, instead of suppressing or stigmatising them?"

Healing begins when we transition from a punitive approach towards these instincts to a mentorship model that guides them toward deeper understanding and emotional fulfilment. We need to create an environment where feelings of safety, relief, empowerment, love, self-worth, vitality, and purpose can thrive, not only for men but for everyone who loves and supports them.

Our collective well-being is intricately connected to nurturing whole individuals in a society that desperately needs men who can embrace and embody their complete selves, including their vulnerabilities and strengths. By fostering a culture that values emotional literacy and authentic communication, we pave the way for richer, more meaningful relationships, and ultimately, a healthier community for all.

Chapter 4

Lost Boys in a Fatherless World: The Masculinity Crisis & Cultural Collapse

You can discern his presence without ever laying eyes on him. The man who grew up without a father carries an invisible burden, a shadow intricately woven into the very fabric of his being. This absence is not simply the result of an evil father or one who was perpetually violent, nor is it merely the physical absence of a parent. Instead, it is the intangible void left by a paternal figure, marked by the echo of unspoken words and the comforting absence of arms that should have wrapped around him in moments of need. It is the silence that envelops the heart where meaningful lessons on courage, integrity, and love should have been imparted.

This haunting absence may not always leave visible scars; instead, it often crafts a complex emotional blueprint, a legacy that silently shapes his identity. A boy who grows up fatherless navigates a treacherous path forged by that emptiness, unwittingly replicating the emotional void when he eventually steps into fatherhood himself. Some men inherit a family name rich with history and significance, while others find themselves burdened with profound emotional wounds that colour their perspectives and influence their choices, often leading them to grapple endlessly with feelings of inadequacy or longing.

For those men who rise from these painful depths, determined to redefine their narratives and become what they never experienced in their own childhood, their journey transcends the mere act of parenting. It evolves into a poignant tale of redemption, a reclaiming of what fatherhood could and should be a sacred bond built on love, trust, and understanding. Each step taken becomes a conscious choice to embed warmth where there was once coldness, to offer guidance where there was none, transforming their past pain into a foundation for a more nurturing future.

A Quiet Identity Crisis: When Boys Become Lost Men

He sits enveloped in a nearly suffocating silence, his fingers mindlessly scrolling through an endless feed of motivational quotes that ring hollow against the backdrop of his own turmoil. Each carefully curated image showcases the confident postures of men twice his age, radiating an air of certainty and purpose that he grapples to comprehend. In an era, fraught with the tension between hyper-masculine bravado and the sharp critiques of cancel culture, he is ensnared in the complex web of his own identity. This internal conflict, this relentless struggle for self-understanding, perhaps constitutes the very crisis itself, an identity crisis that echoes throughout society.

Masculinity has become a muddled concept, no longer adhering to a clearly defined narrative or expected norms. The traditional roadmaps, those established roles of provider, protector, and patriarch have either been rendered obsolete or become laden with stigma and misunderstanding in contemporary discourse. In searching for emerging narratives, he finds them fragmented and often ridiculed, frequently shrouded in ambiguity. What remains is far from a sense of liberation; instead, it manifests as disorientation and confusion, leading to a profound sense of loss.

This turmoil has given rise to what some scholars and commentators are now calling the Masculinity Crisis. It is not merely a clamorous demand for a return to traditional values or a blanket resistance against progressive movements. Rather, it represents a profound reckoning with the glaring absence of mentorship, the lack of structured guidance, and the considerable void left by absent father figures. We are witnessing a generation of men raised without the steady hands of guidance, young boys and teenagers devoid of crucial rites of passage. Many lack fathers who could impart the wisdom to lead, as they, too, navigated their own complexities without a guiding hand.

This generational gap leaves young men feeling adrift, yearning for a map to navigate their evolving sense of self in a world that often seems to reject them.

The Collapse of Masculine Landmarks

In generations past, masculinity adhered to a straightforward path that many found comfort in: Work diligently at a trade or profession, marry the person of your choice, become a devoted father, protect your family fiercely, and assume a leadership role within your community. While these directives may have been rigid and often unforgiving, they provided a clear roadmap that guided countless lives, instilling both purpose and identity.

Today, however, that clarity has been obscured, leaving many men in a state of confusion. The world of work has transformed dramatically, becoming precarious and unpredictable, characterised by frequent layoffs and the rise of gig economies that prioritise flexibility over job security. Marriage, once seen as a foundational milestone, is frequently postponed or viewed as an outdated institution; many opt instead for cohabitation or choose to remain single, embracing alternative lifestyles that don't fit traditional templates. Fatherhood, which was once an esteemed role, is now considered optional by many, with societal expectations shifting dramatically. In this evolving landscape, the instinct to protect is often misconstrued as control, and the notion of leadership is met with doubt and scepticism, making it difficult for men to navigate their roles.

As a result, the archetypes of masculinity have drifted into uncertainty. The warrior, who once found purpose in battle, now seeks a challenge in a world that often feels devoid of conflict. The king, once a figure of authority and governance, grapples with feelings of inadequacy in a society that questions traditional power dynamics. The provider, long regarded as a pillar of stability, faces an unsettling sense of irrelevance as job markets evolve and economic pressures mount. Meanwhile, the stoic man, taught to embody emotional resilience, is now urged to embrace vulnerability, yet he walks a fine line, aware that expressing emotions too intensely can lead to judgment or ridicule.

Caught in this intricate web of confusion, many men find themselves paralysed by indecision: Should they rise to lead and claim their space in society, or should they take a step back to allow others to take the forefront? Whatever decision they make is subject to intense scrutiny and dissection by societal standards, leaving them feeling trapped and reluctant to voice their struggles. This silence becomes both a refuge and a burden, compounding their internal conflicts and exacerbating their feelings of isolation in an increasingly complex world.

Biopsychology of the Fatherhood Shift

Amidst the challenges of modern fatherhood, a profound glimmer of hope emerges from contemporary neuroscience. As men embrace the role of fatherhood, their brains undergo a remarkable transformation driven by hormonal changes. Specifically, levels of oxytocin, often referred to as the 'bonding hormone' and dopamine, which is associated with feelings of pleasure and reward, experience a significant increase. Concurrently, testosterone levels may slightly decline, paving the way for deeper emotional connections and nurturing relationships with their children.

Neuroscientific studies have shown that fatherhood goes beyond merely fostering emotional growth; it represents a fundamental biological evolution within the male brain. Advanced brain imaging techniques, such as functional magnetic resonance imaging (fMRI), reveal enhanced empathy and improved emotional processing capabilities in new fathers. These findings suggest that the experience of becoming a father significantly rewires the male brain, fostering a greater capacity for connection, understanding, and emotional attunement that may not have been fully realised prior to this life-changing role.

This biological shift marks the dawn of a new chapter in masculinity, where traditional notions of strength can harmoniously coexist with vulnerability. As men learn to navigate the complexities of fatherhood, their evolving emotional awareness can guide them toward becoming the nurturing, compassionate fathers they were always meant to be. This transformation not only benefits their children but also contributes to healthier familial relationships and a more emotionally intelligent society.

The Father Wound: Unconscious Imitation

Men rarely become their fathers by conscious choice; rather, they often follow their fathers' paths by default, imitating learned behaviour's unless they actively choose to disrupt this inherited script. The unacknowledged trauma stemming from an absent, emotionally distant, or even overbearing father profoundly shapes a man's capacity to express love, assume leadership roles, and navigate the complexities of life. This trauma, left unaddressed, serves as a default blueprint for their behaviour, influencing their interactions, emotional responses, and relationships.

Healing begins with the courageous act of acknowledgment. It necessitates a deliberate choice to break the silence surrounding one's emotions, experiences, and the lasting impacts of paternal relationships. This transformative journey calls for a style of fathering rooted in emotional presence and genuine connection, rather than fear, emotional detachment, or a desire to perpetuate old patterns.

"Most men don't become their fathers by choice. They do it by default, unless they disrupt the script." Yet, countless men find themselves ensnared in a cycle of repetition, unwittingly inheriting the behaviour's and attitudes they observed in their fathers. The cycle of abuse is multifaceted; it does not solely manifest as physical violence but can also surface as emotional neglect, abandonment, infidelity, detachment, or apathetic engagement. For example, sons of divorced fathers may enter subsequent relationships with an ingrained expectation of disappointment or failure, shaped by the emotional turbulence of their upbringing. Similarly, sons of unfaithful fathers might subconsciously seek validation through behaviour's that mirror their fathers' actions, perpetuating patterns of betrayal and insecurity. Such cycles of behaviour continue until one individual consciously decides to challenge the status quo and break free from the chain of inheritance.

This generational cycle extends beyond observable actions; it encompasses deeply ingrained beliefs and unconscious scripts that dictate responses to life's challenges. For instance, a boy who witnesses his father shutting down during arguments may internalise the belief that silence equates to strength or stoicism. If he observes infidelity being normalised within the familial context, he might come to confuse betrayal with notions of bonding and loyalty, failing to recognise the destructive consequences of such beliefs. These emotional inheritances aren't merely replicated; they are assimilated into the core of their understanding of relationships and masculinity, shaping how they relate to others throughout their lives.

To effectively break this cycle requires a resolute commitment to rewriting one's internal programming. It involves making a powerful, definitive statement: "It ends with me." By consciously choosing to reflect on and redefine their experiences, men can initiate a transformative process that not only liberates themselves but also paves the way for healthier relationships and a more authentic expression of love and masculinity.

Rise of Digital Father Figures

In the absence of tangible mentorship, many men increasingly turn to digital figures for guidance, seeking solace in the advice of entrepreneurs, influencers, and self-help gurus like Jordan Peterson and Andrew Tate. Peterson advocates for personal structure and self-responsibility, emphasising values such as discipline, accountability, and the importance of confronting chaos in one's life. His teachings often encourage individuals to take ownership of their circumstances and strive for personal growth through incremental changes and goal-setting.

On the other hand, Andrew Tate thrives on themes of dominance, financial success, and provocative rhetoric, frequently espousing a controversial, hyper-masculine perspective that challenges traditional societal norms. His messages often emphasise aggression, competitiveness, and the pursuit of wealth, appealing to those who seek a more assertive and, at times, confrontational approach to masculinity.

These figures resonate with many men for various reasons. They offer a semblance of direction in a world that can often feel overwhelming and ambiguous. Their absolute statements, whether about personal success, masculinity, or relationships provide a false sense of clarity and control amid the complexities and uncertainties of modern life. In the absence of authentic male mentorship, even rigid answers can act as a temporary lifeline, promising security and validation in a society that often feels fragmented.

However, true masculinity encompasses far more than catchy slogans or simplistic frameworks. It requires a deeper understanding shaped by compassion, emotional intelligence, and relational wisdom. Genuine growth and fulfilment come from the ability to navigate one's emotions, foster meaningful connections, and engage in healthy, respectful relationships with others. As men strive to become more rounded individuals, they must seek guidance that transcends mere doctrine and embraces the richer, more nuanced aspects of human experience.

Intersectional Fatherhood: Race, Class, Queerness

Fatherhood is not a monolith; it is a rich and diverse experience shaped by the unique identity and circumstances of each father. For instance, Black fathers often confront the damaging stereotype of the "absent Black dad," working tirelessly to demonstrate their unwavering presence and commitment to their children. They navigate systemic barriers, such as socioeconomic inequities and discriminatory narratives, which can make their efforts even more challenging. By actively engaging in their children's lives, through attending school events, participating in extracurricular activities, and fostering deep emotional connections, they challenge and redefine what fatherhood looks like in their communities.

Queer fathers are also reshaping the concept of fatherhood by creating chosen families that reflect their values and identities. They embrace adoption, surrogacy, or co-parenting arrangements that defy traditional familial structures, prioritising emotional openness and communication over traditional norms. Many queer fathers share their journeys publicly, dispelling myths and fostering acceptance, which adds richness to the larger narrative of parenthood.

On the other hand, working-class fathers face the dual pressure of being the primary breadwinner while grappling with the expectations of traditional masculinity that often discourage emotional expression. They may work multiple jobs, balancing financial responsibilities with the desire to be present for their families. The intersection of economic hardship and societal expectations can lead to a struggle for these fathers as they seek to convey love and support while feeling constrained by an inherited stoicism.

"Fatherhood isn't one thing. For some, it's a biological role defined by genetics and lineage. For others, it's a quiet act of defiance against the legacies of neglect, absence, and emotional unavailability, as they strive to break cycles and create nurturing environments for the next generation."

Performing vs. Embodying Fatherhood

Some men merely perform the expected roles associated with fatherhood. They may provide material gifts, enforce rules and discipline, and show up physically during significant events like birthdays or graduations. However, there is a stark contrast with those who genuinely embody the essence of fatherhood. These fathers go beyond mere presence; they engage deeply with their children, demonstrating vulnerability by sharing their own struggles and emotions. They are attuned to their children's needs, both physical and emotional, offering a steady presence that fosters trust and security.

True legacy in fatherhood isn't constructed through reaching unattainable ideals of perfection or the flawless execution of traditional roles. Instead, it is built through the seemingly mundane yet profoundly impactful and repetitive acts of showing up each day. This means being there for school events, listening attentively to their child's stories, and providing comfort during tough times. It includes both the laughter shared during ordinary moments and the crucial support offered during crises. These consistent and meaningful engagements, even when challenges arise, create a lasting impact that shapes a child's sense of self and resilience. In essence, a father's true legacy is woven through the fabric of everyday life, marked by emotional connection and unwavering support.

Spiritual Dimension: Sacred Yet Imperfect

Raising a child is a deeply sacred endeavour, embodying the potential for growth and transformation within every child, despite their imperfections. It is a journey where the father, having experienced the voids of his own upbringing, steps up to become a spiritual warrior, a guardian of wisdom and emotional resilience. His legacy is not measured by the accumulation of material wealth or titles but is engraved in the everyday nuances of life.

Picture him settling down each night to read bedtime stories, his voice soft and resonant as he transports his child to far-off lands filled with dragons and heroes. Imagine the silent yet profound exchanges during dinner, where a simple glance can communicate love, understanding, and safety, fostering a bond that transcends words. In moments of imperfection when he inadvertently loses his temper or misses a significant event, he doesn't shy away from offering genuine, heartfelt apologies, teaching his child the importance of humility and accountability.

Above all, he stands as a fierce protector, ready to shield his child from life's harsh realities, cultivating a safe haven where vulnerability can flourish. This nurturing path embodies the essence of masculine redemption, a conscious reclamation of love, guidance, and unwavering support that shapes the next generation. Through these small yet profound interactions, he weaves a tapestry of trust and security, demonstrating that true strength lies in tenderness and compassion.

From Cultural Collapse to Personal Legacy

In today's society, many boys are navigating a complex landscape where traditional rites of passage, mentors, and safe spaces to fail are increasingly scarce. These vital experiences, once integral to the male journey into adulthood, have dwindled, leaving boys to seek refuge in social media platforms like TikTok, Facebook, and Instagram, where trends and fleeting moments of validation provide an escape from their struggles. Additionally, they often turn to the instant gratification of pornography, which can distort their understanding of intimacy and relationships, or they sink into the suffocating silence of isolation, where loneliness can amplify their insecurities and fears.

In such a world, the scrutiny of their missteps has become all too common, with critics quick to judge actions without offering constructive support or encouragement. This harsh environment can make growth feel daunting, but amid this chaotic landscape, some men emerge resilient. They take initiative to build the support systems they need, gathering communities of like-minded individuals who share their experiences, thus recreating the mentorship and camaraderie that were once a given.

These men actively craft their own rites of passage, perhaps through adventure, artistic expression, or community service that empower them to move beyond societal expectations. They undergo personal transformations, becoming the fathers that their younger selves desperately needed. Drawing from hard-earned lessons and personal experiences, they guide their families with wisdom, patience, and compassion, fostering a nurturing environment that encourages open dialogue and emotional intelligence. In doing so, they not only heal their own wounds but also pave the way for future generations to thrive with more awareness and understanding.

Gentle Prompts for Reflection

- What kind of father did you need during your formative years? Reflect on specific traits or actions that would have made a significant difference in your development. For example, did you yearn for a father who was more present emotionally, perhaps by actively engaging in your daily life, or did you desire someone who offered guidance and support during challenging times? Think about how qualities such as patience, encouragement, or a strong sense of humour could have shaped your experiences.

- What kind of father are you becoming in your own parenting journey? Consider the evolution of your values, such as the importance of communication, empathy, or resilience and how these principles inform your role as a parent. How do you strive to nurture your children's individuality while also instilling a sense of responsibility? Reflect on specific moments where you consciously choose to embody these evolving values.

- What does the concept of legacy mean to you personally? Ponder the values, beliefs, and traditions you wish to instil in your children and pass on to future generations. This might include cultural practices, ethical standards, or personal stories that illustrate resilience and love. How do you envision your children carrying these legacies forward in their own lives?

- Where in your parenting do you find yourself acting from a place of fear instead of love? Identify specific triggers, such as moments of stress, past disappointments, or societal pressures that lead you to react defensively or restrictively. Explore healthier approaches to these situations, like practicing mindfulness or seeking open dialogue, and consider how these methods could foster a more nurturing environment for your children.

- What do you wish your father had told you at crucial points in your life, such as during moments of self-doubt or pivotal decision-making? Reflect on the wisdom you longed for, whether it was encouragement to pursue your dreams, reassurance during tough times, or affirmations of your worth. How can you offer that same wisdom to yourself now, cultivating a sense of self-compassion and understanding as you navigate your own challenges?

- What emotional scripts or patterns have you inherited from your upbringing, and which of these no longer serve you? Consider the messages you received about success, failure, or vulnerability, and how they may influence your current behaviour's. Identify the narratives that hold you back and envision new stories you want to create for yourself, ones that foster growth, authenticity, and healthier relationships.

Final Reframe: The Cycle Ends with You

If you are a man who grew up without the guidance of a father, facing the absence of his support, wisdom, and presence, and you are now stepping up to take on the crucial role of a father yourself, know that you are not broken, far from it. You embody the strength and determination to break the chains of generational cycles that too often perpetuate silence and disengagement. Your journey is not defined by the void left in your childhood; rather, it is shaped by the commitment you make each day to be present, nurturing, and supportive.

In choosing to embrace fatherhood with intention, you are actively rewriting the narrative of manhood. This transformation extends beyond simple lifestyle adjustments; it fundamentally alters the legacy you create. With every thoughtful action and meaningful interaction, you infuse your parenting with love, hope, and purpose, crafting a foundation for your children that is rich in emotional intelligence and resilience. You are cultivating a future where your children understand the value of connection, empathy, and respect, ensuring that they are prepared to navigate the world with the tools they need.

By fully engaging in this profound responsibility, you are not only changing your own life but also the trajectory of those who follow you. Your legacy will be one that celebrates vulnerability and strength, encouraging future generations to understand that true manhood is rooted in compassion, accountability, and the unwavering commitment to uplift those around them.

Chapter 5

Across the Ages — Men's Mental Health Through the Lifespan

Introduction: Time as a Mirror for the Mind

Men do not experience mental health challenges in a vacuum; rather, they navigate these complexities amid the evolving seasons of their lives. During their teenage years, many encounter the harsh realities of bullying, an issue that permeates schools and social circles. Bullying not only undermines self-esteem but also forces young men to grapple with their identities in a society that often imposes rigid and limiting definitions of masculinity. Consequently, this struggle can lead to a problematic fear of vulnerability, making them hesitant to express emotions or seek support. As a result, forming healthy relationships becomes increasingly difficult, since emotional openness is often perceived as a weakness.

As they transition into their thirties, many men experience a significant turning point marked by the debilitating effects of burnout. This decade frequently presents overwhelming career pressures, financial responsibilities, and the demands of family life. The weight of societal expectations, particularly the belief that they must be the primary providers can exert immense pressure on their mental health. This burden often manifests as heightened anxiety, feelings of inadequacy, and a sense of being trapped in a cycle of obligation. As a result, personal ambitions and well-being take a backseat, leaving many men feeling lost and unfulfilled.

Reaching their fifties, men often grapple with profound grief and loss, whether through the passing of parents, close friends, or the realisation that cherished dreams have slipped away. This stage of life can trigger a deep existential crisis, prompting a critical reassessment of accomplishments and personal values. Many men find themselves questioning their legacy and the meaning of their lives, which can lead to a dwindling sense of purpose. This reflection is crucial, as it pushes them to confront their emotions and ultimately seek healing.

This chapter embarks on an insightful journey through these formative decades, exploring how the male experience evolves over time. It delves into the deep societal influences and pervasive stigma surrounding men's mental health issues, examining how these cultural narratives shape their experiences. Additionally, it highlights the critical role that personal identity plays in a man's ability to cope, communicate, and heal. By unpacking these dimensions, we gain a deeper understanding of the unique challenges men face throughout their lives, emphasising the vital need for fostering open dialogues about mental health. This exploration not only sheds light on individual struggles but also advocates for a collective movement toward support and understanding in a world that often neglects masculine vulnerability.

Teens (13–19): The Silent Years

Key Themes: Suppression of emotion, peer pressure, confusion of masculine identity, early trauma, bullying, body image issues, and the emergence of anxiety and depression.

Adolescence serves as a critical crucible where the foundations of masculine conditioning are not just established but often rigorously enforced. During this transformative stage, boys encounter both overt and subtle societal pressures that compel them to stifle their emotions. Phrases such as "Man up," "Boys don't cry," and "Be tough" echo throughout their formative years, embedding deeply in their minds as societal scripts that inhibit the expression of vulnerability, sadness, and fear. These messages shape not just their behaviour but also have profound, lasting impacts on their mental health.

70

Research from the Mental Health Foundation in the UK highlights a concerning statistic: 1 in 6 children aged 5 to 16 is likely to experience a mental health condition, with boys particularly disadvantaged in their willingness to seek help. The societal expectations surrounding masculinity erect barriers that deter them from reporting emotional distress or reaching out for support. Bullying serves as a particularly cruel exacerbation of these problems, especially when it targets perceived weaknesses, queerness, or sensitivity. Boys who fail to conform to the rigid "alpha" stereotype may find themselves marginalised, leading to feelings of profound isolation and loneliness.

As symptoms of anxiety and depression take root, they are frequently obscured by behaviour's such as anger, aggression, or emotional withdrawal, further complicating their ability to express their true feelings. The emergence of social media has exacerbated these struggles, intensifying body image issues and fostering unhealthy comparisons between their authentic lives and the curated, idealised images presented by their peers and influencers. This environment can amplify feelings of inadequacy and distress, making the journey through adolescence even more challenging for boys.

Reflection Prompts:

- What specific messages did I receive about masculinity during my childhood and adolescence? Were these messages consistent across different environments, such as home, school, and peer groups?
- Can I recall a particular moment when I first felt compelled to conceal my emotions? What specific event or interaction triggered that feeling, and how did I cope at the time?
- Who were the notable individuals in my life, parents, teachers, friends who acknowledged and validated my feelings? Conversely, who tended to dismiss or downplay my emotions? How did their varying

responses shape my emotional development and my understanding of vulnerability?

20s: Building a Self That Performs

Key Themes: Identity crisis, career pressure, fear of failure, isolation, addictive coping, first major heartbreaks, "performing masculinity."

Your twenties are often heralded as an exhilarating decade, filled with opportunities for exploration, personal growth, and newfound independence. Yet, for many young men, this pivotal period can devolve into a solitary performance coloured by the overwhelming weight of societal expectations. The transition into adulthood brings with it a relentless pressure to define and establish a successful career, build meaningful relationships, and demonstrate one's worth, all while battling an underlying fear of failure that can feel insurmountable.

Statistical Insight: According to a survey conducted by NHS Digital (UK), young men aged 18–24 represent the demographic least likely to seek professional help for mental health issues. This group experiences heightened levels of anxiety, depression, and substance use disorders, yet remains largely silent about their struggles, often due to stigma and fear of judgment.

Heartbreaks during this time are frequently navigated in silence, hidden beneath a carefully crafted facade of bravado and humour. Many young men turn to addictive behaviours, ranging from excessive gaming and substance abuse to compulsive consumption of pornography as a misguided means of coping with deep emotional pain. This decade often lays bare the harsh reality of "performing masculinity," where societal pressures to conform to an adult image magnify feelings of confusion, inadequacy, and profound loss.

Reflection Prompts:

- Who am I when I peel away the layers of my job title, social media persona, and the mask I wear in public?
- What specific behaviour's or habits am I engaging in to shield myself from discomfort or vulnerability, and how are they impacting my mental health?
- Have I ever internalised the belief that asking for help signifies weakness, rather than recognising it as a courageous step toward healing and growth?

30s: The Fracture Beneath the Foundation

Key Themes: Burnout, fatherhood, financial burdens, relationship disillusionment, hidden mental health dips, pressure to "have it all together."

As men transition into their thirties, this pivotal decade is often characterised by a heightened desire for stability and a sense of accomplishment. During these years, careers typically demand increased dedication as professional responsibilities grow with aspirations for advancement. Simultaneously, family responsibilities may multiply, especially as many men find themselves navigating the complexities of raising children, supporting partners, and maintaining active roles in their households. Societal expectations climb, creating an implicit belief that by this stage, individuals should have a well-defined life trajectory marked by solid career progress, intimate personal relationships, and clear life goals.

Yet, beneath this polished exterior, the insidious effects of burnout often lurk, manifesting as a persistent sense of fatigue and emotional exhaustion. The compounded responsibilities of providing for a family, nurturing children, managing romantic or familial relationships, and performing consistently in a demanding career can feel suffocating. The weight of these expectations might lead to feelings of inadequacy and a fear of not measuring up.

Statistical Insight: The Office for National Statistics (ONS) reports that men aged 30–39 have the second-highest suicide rates in the UK. This alarming statistic is frequently linked to the intense pressures stemming from career demands, the emotional toll of relationship breakdowns, and, significantly, feelings of isolation that can accompany these burdens. Many men in this age group, despite appearing to thrive, may be battling an undercurrent of despair that goes unnoticed.

In this challenging phase, not only are many men struggling internally, but they often project an image of stability and success to the outside world. This can lead to a dissonance where they grapple with deep-seated emotional distress while outwardly appearing composed. The societal pressure to maintain a facade of competence can obstruct genuine vulnerability, thereby creating barriers even within intimate relationships, preventing authentic connections that might provide relief and support.

Reflection Prompts:

- What emotional sacrifices am I making to maintain the appearance of having it all together? Are there moments where I suppress my true feelings to project strength?
- Who in my life truly knows the real me, beyond the roles I play as a partner, parent, or professional? Are there trusted confidants I can turn to for support?
- When was the last time I paused to reflect on what I genuinely need, emotionally, mentally, or physically? How can I carve out time for self-care amidst my various commitments?

40s: The Emotional Stalemate

Key Themes: Midlife crisis, emotional stagnation, existential fatigue, loneliness, resurfacing trauma, feelings of invisibility or irrelevance.

Entering one's 40s often signifies a pivotal moment of emotional reckoning for many men. As they survey their lives, an unsettling question frequently emerges: Is this really all there is? The relentless ambition that once propelled them forward often gives way to a pervasive sense of stagnation and fatigue, leading to a profound questioning of the very aspirations that once defined their paths. This emotional shift can feel disorienting, as old wounds stemming from past relationships, career setbacks, personal failures, or unresolved conflicts begin to resurface, demanding both attention and healing.

Family dynamics are also in flux during this decade, as children grow increasingly independent. This shift can create a void in what was once a primary source of identity and purpose, leaving many men feeling disconnected or adrift. At the same time, professional life may reach a plateau, catalysing a deep examination of purpose and fulfilment. Many men find themselves asking whether their career is genuinely aligned with their passions or if they have simply drifted into roles that no longer resonate.

Intimacy within romantic relationships can begin to dwindle as partners face the daily noise of responsibilities and unmet emotional needs. The once vibrant connection can fade into a routine existence, challenging men to find ways to reignite the spark or face the reality of growing apart.

This emotionally charged decade often prompts men to grapple with core questions surrounding self-worth and identity. Such introspection can lead to a pivotal fork in the road: one path may result in a breakdown, where unresolved issues and hidden feelings spiral out of control, while the other offers a breakthrough, an opportunity to courageously confront and integrate these past experiences into a more authentic self.

Research Insight: According to the Campaign to End Loneliness, men in their 40s report some of the highest levels of loneliness in their lives. They are statistically less inclined to cultivate close friendships or establish emotional connections, making them less likely to lean on confidants during this challenging phase. This isolation can further exacerbate feelings of invisibility and irrelevance.

Unprocessed trauma has a way of surfacing in troubling ways during this period. Without meaningful outlets for expression, many men may resort to unhealthy coping mechanisms, such as escapism through excessive work, distractions, extramarital affairs, substance misuse, or emotionally shutting down intensifying their sense of isolation and despair.

Reflection Prompts:

- What areas of my life currently feel emotionally stagnant or devoid of vitality?
- What grief or pain from my past have I never fully acknowledged, and how has it shaped my present?
- What steps could I take to feel genuinely alive again, not for anyone else's expectations, but for my own well-being?

50s: Grief, Grace, and Masculine Rebirth

Key Themes: Grief, health anxiety, career transitions, re-evaluation of masculine roles, emerging openness to therapy despite lingering shame.

Entering one's 50s often marks a significant transitional phase, where the fragility of both the body and life itself become increasingly evident. Health scares can manifest unexpectedly, whether it's a troubling diagnosis, chronic pain, or unexpected physical limitations prompting a thorough reassessment of lifestyle, diet, and overall well-being. The weight of grief from losing parents, close friends, and beloved mentors can become particularly heavy during this decade, serving as stark reminders of mortality and leading many to contemplate their own legacy and the impact they wish to leave behind.

Alongside these emotional challenges, many individuals find themselves grappling with career dissatisfaction. Achievements may feel overshadowed by regret over unfulfilled aspirations or paths not taken. The questioning of one's purpose can feel almost relentless, leading to a deep sense of longing for the ambition and dreams that seemed so attainable in earlier decades. Yet, within this backdrop of uncertainty and sorrow, a quieter wisdom can blossom, offering insights into what truly matters in life beyond professional accolades.

For numerous men, this decade emerges as a pivotal point for emotional growth and awakening. There is a nurturing shift towards viewing therapy and counselling as essential tools for navigating the complex emotional landscape of midlife. Although stigma and shame still linger, especially among those who have been raised to uphold a stoic façade, there's a growing acknowledgment of the importance of mental health. Men, in particular, are increasingly reaching out for support following significant life changes such as bereavement, divorce, career transitions, or retirement. This trend reveals a gradual cultural shift towards understanding that vulnerability can coexist with strength.

In tandem with this emotional exploration is a re-evaluation of traditional masculine roles. The definitions of what it means to be strong are evolving; many men are beginning to recognise the value of openness, honesty, and emotional truth over the previously held ideals of control and dominance. As their emotional vocabulary expands, they find themselves capable of forging deeper connections not only with their inner selves but also in their relationships with others, fostering a greater sense of community and authenticity.

Data Insight: According to recent reports from Mind (UK), men in their 50s are now more likely than ever to seek counselling for the first time. This trend is particularly pronounced in response to significant life changes such as bereavement, divorce, or retirement, showcasing a gradual yet crucial acceptance of the need for mental health support.

Reflection Prompts:

-   What specific losses am I grieving that I have not yet allowed myself the space or the courage to confront?

- In what ways has my understanding of masculinity transformed over the years, and how do I define strength today?
- At this juncture in my life, what does healing look like, and what steps can I take to foster that healing?

This refined text invites a deeper engagement with the complexities and opportunities that can arise during these crucial decades, encouraging thoughtful introspection and growth.

60s and Beyond: Return to Self or Collapse into Silence

Key Themes: As individuals enter the latter stages of life, they often face a myriad of significant challenges. For many, this period is marked by the profound loss of identity that often accompanies retirement. The transition away from a lifelong career can lead to an unsettling void, where feelings of loneliness, cognitive decline, and reflections on past regrets may loom large. This phase necessitates a redefinition of self-worth, moving away from tangible career accomplishments toward a more intrinsic understanding of value and purpose. The contrast between reconciling these inevitable changes and succumbing to despair becomes increasingly stark as one reaches these pivotal life junctures.

For numerous men, the phase often referred to as the "golden years" can feel like an overwhelming burden. This experience resembles being ensnared in rusted chains, tethering them to a past identity that has been heavily defined by professional success and relentless productivity. Retirement can feel akin to a form of erasure, stripping away not just the daily structure and routine that work provides but also the meaning often rooted in one's professional roles. Without the external validation gained through employment, a sense of isolation can begin to seep in, making it all too easy to slide into the depths of loneliness and despair.

However, this stage also presents a unique opportunity for rebirth and reinvention. It is a fertile time for deep reflection

78

upon one's life journey, providing the chance to evaluate the legacies we leave behind. Embracing the self beyond the confines of job titles and accolades can lead to profound peace and fulfilment, away from the relentless pressures of societal expectations.

Statistical Insight: In England alone, a staggering 1.4 million older men report experiencing significant feelings of loneliness. Many of these men attribute their emotional struggles to a deep and profound sense of lost purpose that follows their retirement. This unsettling statistic highlights a critical societal issue, emphasising the urgent need to address the emotional and mental health needs of men as they transition into their later years. It stresses the importance of community, connection, and support systems to mitigate these feelings of isolation.

At this crossroads, the choice confronting many men becomes unmistakable: they can either cling to outdated definitions of masculinity, which prioritise relentless productivity and unwavering stoicism, or they can summon the courage to surrender to a softer, freer, and ultimately more authentic version of themselves. This decision to embrace vulnerability can foster not only self-acceptance but also deeper connections with others.

Reflection Prompts:

- Without productivity, who am I? - This question invites a profound exploration into the essence of one's identity, urging individuals to look beyond their careers and examine their personal values, passions, and the relationships that truly define them.

- What regrets still dwell in me, and what acts of forgiveness might liberate my spirit? - This reflection encourages individuals to confront and understand the emotional burdens they carry, offering pathways to healing and self-compassion through the practice of forgiveness, both to oneself and others.

-   What legacy do I aspire to leave behind, emotionally and relationally? - Considering the emotional and relational impact one wishes to impart to future generations can serve to redefine one's sense of purpose, reinforcing connections and offering a greater understanding of the roles we play in each other's lives.

By engaging with these themes and prompts, individuals can navigate the complexities of this season of life with greater clarity and intention, fostering resilience and deeper connections along the way.

Final Thoughts: Age Does Not Heal — Awareness Does

The journey through life has imparted valuable lessons to many individuals, often emphasising the importance of prioritising performance over authentic emotional expression. Societal expectations have moulded men to take on the role of providers rather than allowing them to be recipients of care, leading to a mindset that values problem-solving over seeking support in times of need. However, each decade of life offers a unique opportunity, a chance to unlearn these deeply ingrained habits and beliefs, enabling a fresh start.

Mental health and emotional understanding are not merely the concerns of the young; they are essential components of a fulfilling life journey at any age. The earlier we initiate honest and open conversations about our feelings, vulnerabilities, and personal experiences, the richer and more authentic our lives can become. Engaging in these discussions can lead to deeper connections with ourselves and others, fostering a supportive community where everyone feels valued.

Embrace your journey with this mantra: "You are not behind. You are not broken. You are becoming." Remember that personal growth is a continuous process, and every step you take, no matter how small, contributes to your evolving narrative.

Call-to-Action:

If you are a man engaging with this text, I encourage you to choose a specific decade from your life, be it your childhood, your teenage years, or even your twenties or thirties and write a heartfelt letter to either your past or future self. Take the time to reflect on the needs and emotions you experienced during that period. What were your dreams, fears, and aspirations? What support did you wish you had, and what lessons have you since learned that could offer reassurance to your younger self? By honouring those needs and acknowledging the person you've become, you can foster a deeper connection with your evolving identity.

If you are someone who supports men, whether as a friend, family member, or therapist consider pausing for a moment to reflect on a crucial question: At what decade do the men in your life seem to stop sharing their thoughts and feelings openly? Is it in their late teens, where societal pressures to conform take hold, or perhaps in their thirties when career demands overshadow personal expression? What factors contribute to this silence, cultural expectations, fear of vulnerability, or past experiences of being dismissed?

Together, let's commit to breaking down the barriers of silence and stigma one season at a time. Start listening attentively to the stories that emerge from these pivotal decades, creating a space where men feel valued and empowered to share their truths. In doing so, we pave the way for a more supportive and understanding environment for all men, encouraging open dialogue about their struggles, triumphs, and everything in between.

Chapter 6

The Father Wound: Becoming the Man He Couldn't Be

There is a moment, often unacknowledged yet profoundly impactful, in nearly every man's life when he finds himself grappling with the haunting question, "Was I ever truly seen by my father?" This inquiry, though it may not always be articulated in poetic terms, can manifest as a torrent of raw anger, a deafening silence that speaks volumes, or the weary frustration that accompanies a relentless pursuit of recognition from a spectre of the past. Each of these responses underscores a universal struggle that many men face, echoing deep within their psyches.

At the core of this question lies the essence of the father wound, a term that encompasses not merely the pain stemming from physical absence, through divorce, abandonment, or the finality of death, but also the profound emotional wounds inflicted by neglect. This neglect often materialises as a lack of guidance during formative years, a dearth of affirming words that reinforce a child's value, insufficient mirroring of feelings that allows a boy to understand himself, and a scarcity of affection that fosters deep emotional connections. Consequently, this leaves the boy within the man in a perpetual state of longing, confusion, and an insatiable desire for validation.

It is crucial to understand that this exploration is not aimed at casting blame; rather, it seeks to illuminate and recognise enduring patterns that have often gone unnoticed. These patterns resemble generational scripts, passed down through familial lines, typically shrouded in silence and unspoken expectations. They may include fathers who themselves were never shown affection, or who prioritised societal expectations over emotional availability. Until these intricate, often painful patterns are acknowledged and comprehended, they are likely to repeat across generations, perpetuating a cycle of emotional pain that can impact not just the individuals involved but their families as a whole. Only through understanding and breaking these cycles can healing begin, allowing for a more fulfilling connection to self and others.

The Invisible Hand: Intergenerational Trauma in Male Lineage

Fathers do not always inflict wounds through overt cruelty; more frequently, they do so through their silence. This silence is a legacy handed down through generations, a heritage rooted in societal expectations that condition men to suppress their emotions, endure hardships, and avoid vulnerability at all costs. This behaviour does not stem from a lack of love; rather, it arises from a profound unknowing, a disconnection from the ability to articulate affection and nurture those around them.

Consequently, this silence creates a lineage characterised by emotional illiteracy, where feelings remain unspoken and love unexpressed. Picture grandfathers returning from wars, their harrowing stories locked away behind stoic facades, incapable of communicating their trauma. Imagine fathers who work tirelessly at multiple jobs, burdened by the weight of responsibility yet never voicing their pride or offering words of encouragement, a simple "I'm proud of you" often left unsaid. As a result, sons grow into adulthood with an aching yearning for affirmation and validation, trapped in a cycle of unfulfilled emotional needs.

This dynamic encapsulates the essence of intergenerational trauma, which is not always born from dramatic or catastrophic events. Instead, it finds its roots in the countless small, consistent absences that accumulate over time. Affectionate hugs that were never shared, meaningful conversations that were sidestepped, and emotions that were too often dismissed as signs of weakness create a void that echoes through the family line.

On a psychological level, this absence manifests in various distressing patterns that complicate interpersonal relationships. Individuals may develop insecure or avoidant attachment styles, which hinder their ability to build meaningful connections with others. Chronic self-doubt can become a pervasive shadow, making them constantly question their worth and desirability. There may also be a tendency to engage in people-pleasing behaviour's or hyper-independence as coping mechanisms, often resulting in an inability to ask for help or acknowledge their own needs. Emotional repression can lead to unexpected outbursts, where repressed feelings surge forth, causing chaos and confusion.

Bio-psychologically, the absence of emotional mirroring from a father figure disrupts the developing nervous system of the child at a fundamental level. Without a role model to guide emotional regulation and expression, the child grapples with managing feelings in a healthy manner. High cortisol levels, a physiological response to stress, remain elevated, and the amygdala, the brain's centre for processing emotions becomes overactive, leading to heightened anxiety or fear responses. Meanwhile, the prefrontal cortex, responsible for impulse control and future planning, faces significant challenges due to the lack of emotional guidance. In the absence of safe emotional attunement, the boy's body remains perpetually on high alert, trapped in a sympathetic nervous system response characterised by hyper-vigilance, a state that lingers long after troubling moments have passed, continuously influencing thoughts, behaviour's, and overall wellbeing.

Absence Has Many Faces: Physical vs. Emotional

While the concept of an absent father can often be described through recognisable scenarios such as incarceration, divorce, death, or simple disinterest, the phenomenon of an emotionally absent father tends to be more insidious and challenging to identify. This type of father may physically inhabit the same space providing financial stability, attending family dinners, or even engaging in activities such as coaching youth sports.

84

However, he remains emotionally inaccessible, often neglecting to ask about his child's feelings, turning away during moments of vulnerability, and failing to share vital lessons on resilience, empathy, and emotional intelligence.

This subtle form of absence can inflict deep wounds. It plants a damaging belief: the need for connection is something to be scrutinised, perhaps even denied. Boys raised in such environments frequently adopt self-protective mantras like:

- "I don't need anyone."
- "I just deal with things on my own."
- "I can't even remember him ever hugging me."

These phrases often mask a deeper, haunting thought: "Maybe I wasn't worth the attention." This belief can poison personal relationships, breed isolation, and perpetuate an ongoing cycle of emotional disconnection that affects not only individual lives but also influences future generations.

By exploring these complexities, we can work toward a better understanding of not just the emotional wounds themselves, but also the potential paths toward healing that may be available.

Lessons Learned by Accident

Boys do not solely learn from the explicit teachings of their fathers; they also absorb lessons from their fathers' omissions, reactions, and the emotional climate they create. The topics that fathers choose to avoid discussing, the triggers for their anger, the boundaries they set, and the emotions they flee from all inform a boy's understanding of masculinity, vulnerability, and relational dynamics.

For instance, a father who never offers an apology sends an implicit message that vulnerability equates to weakness, teaching his son to detach from his feelings rather than embracing them. Conversely, if a father often erupts in anger, he instils the idea that displaying emotion can lead to peril, discouraging the expression of genuine feelings. Additionally, when a father chooses not to share his own past or struggles, he conveys the notion that pain should be hidden rather than confronted, stifling emotional growth and understanding.

As these boys mature, they grapple with profound implications of such lessons: they often find themselves yearning for the approval and validation of women, trying to fill the psychological void left by these paternal absences. Their interactions with peers tend to be competitive rather than connective, making it challenging to forge authentic relationships. Many of these boys ultimately become fathers themselves, stepping into parenthood without having taken the time to address and heal the emotional scars from their own upbringing. This cycle of emotional disconnection, if left unaddressed, can perpetuate itself across generations, compounding the issues of isolation and unmet emotional needs.

By engaging in discussions and reflections on these patterns, we open the door to healing not just for individuals, but for families and communities as a whole...

The Biopsychology of the Father Wound

From a bio-psychological perspective, a father's emotional presence or the absence thereof, plays a crucial role in shaping the neurological development of his son, particularly within the right hemisphere of the brain. This area governs emotional processing, relational depth, and social cognition, making it vital for the boy's overall emotional health. When a father fails to emotionally attune to his son, the consequences can be profound and multifaceted:

- Mirror Neuron Activation: The mirror neuron system is essential for empathy and social understanding. Without appropriate emotional guidance from a father, boys may struggle to read and interpret the emotions of those around them. This can lead to social miscommunications, a diminished ability to connect with peers, and feelings of isolation, which may persist throughout their lives.

- Oxytocin Bonding: Emotional connection is critical for the secretion of oxytocin, often referred to as the "bonding hormone." A deficit in this emotional connection can lead to lower levels of oxytocin, inhibiting the development of trust and intimacy. This can ultimately undermine the boy's capability to form deep, trusting relationships in adulthood, impacting his ability to connect meaningfully with romantic partners and friends.

- Vagal Tone: The vagus nerve is crucial for regulating physiological responses to stress and facilitates emotional self-regulation. A lack of emotional safety and stability, often stemming from inadequate paternal bonding, can hinder a boy's capacity to soothe himself after distressing experiences. This can lead to heightened anxiety, chronic stress responses, and difficulties managing emotional challenges as they grow, potentially resulting in long-term issues with mental health.

The emotional dissonance experienced by boys is not simply a question of character or personality traits; rather, it is fundamentally rooted in the chemical and neurological architecture that is shaped by early relational experiences. Fathers who engage emotionally provide a scaffolding for their sons' emotional brains, influencing not just their childhood experiences but laying the groundwork for their future emotional and relational well-being.

Cultural Archetypes of Fatherhood

Culturally, various societies have established distinct blueprints of masculinity, fostering rich rituals and deep relationships between fathers and sons that transcend mere biological connections. These dynamics play a vital role in shaping character and identity throughout different life stages.

In many Indigenous cultures, fathers often take on roles that surpass traditional expectations of merely being providers. They become initiators, guiding their sons through deeply transformative experiences such as sweat lodges, vision quests, and storytelling traditions. These practices facilitate a profound journey into adulthood, equipping young men with essential emotional, spiritual, and communal responsibilities that bind them to their heritage and identity. This mentorship not only strengthens familial ties but also embeds a sense of belonging within the community.

In various African tribal cultures, fathers and elders serve as pivotal moral compasses. Young men are immersed in elaborate initiation ceremonies designed to promote emotional resilience and spiritual clarity, alongside a strong commitment to their communities. These rites of passage are profound educational experiences, instilling in young men a robust sense of identity, purpose, and the importance of service to others, thereby reinforcing communal bonds and cultural continuity.

Japanese Bushido culture exemplifies a masculine ideal grounded in the principles of honour, loyalty, and discipline. Fathers embody these values not through mere instruction but through daily conduct that reflects mastery over themselves and restraint in their actions. This living example serves as a powerful model for sons, teaching them the importance of integrity, respect, and perseverance within both personal and societal contexts.

In Jewish traditions, the bar mitzvah symbolises more than just a coming-of-age ceremony; it is a critical affirmation of moral and ethical accountability. During this sacred rite, fathers play a crucial role, guiding their sons through significant emotional growth and intellectual development. This fosters a deeper understanding of their heritage while emphasising the importance of continuity in values and legacy, thereby linking generations.

Contemporary Scandinavian societies have seen a notable evolution in the concept of fatherhood, creating arguably one of the most emotionally supportive models worldwide. Modern Nordic fathers are actively encouraged to engage with their children from birth, prioritising the establishment of strong parental bonds and emotional intelligence. This shift in cultural expectations often includes generous parental leave policies, allowing fathers to be present and involved in their children's early lives. Such practices challenge outdated gender norms, demonstrating that emotional openness and nurturing are essential qualities in fatherhood.

These diverse cultural narratives highlight the significance of fatherhood as a social construct that is complex and multifaceted. Emphasising the need for continuous re-evaluation and redefining of what it means to be a father ensures that future generations can carry forward enriched, inclusive, and evolving understandings of masculinity and fatherhood.

Mentorship as Masculine Medicine

Mentorship serves as a vital complement to fatherhood, filling the emotional void that can arise from its absence. While therapists play a crucial role in helping men navigate and process their inner struggles, mentors provide the practical frameworks that empower these individuals to implement new behaviour's and perspectives effectively.

Elders share their hard-won wisdom, offering insights drawn from a lifetime of experiences that can help younger men avoid common pitfalls. In contrast, therapists delve into the psychological undercurrents that shape one's emotional responses, facilitating a deeper understanding of personal patterns and traumas. Male friends enhance this support network by offering companionship and fostering bonds through shared experiences and mutual understanding, reinforcing a sense of belonging and camaraderie. Mentors, on the other hand, provide strategic guidance and direction, encouraging individuals to pursue their personal and professional aspirations with clarity and purpose.

What sets mentorship apart is its distinctive nature: it offers guidance devoid of the pressure to perform, presenting accountability without the degradation that can accompany shame. Unlike traditional educational or professional relationships, mentorship allows individuals to be recognised not only for their accomplishments but also for the journey of self-improvement and growth they undertake. This recognition validates the effort put into becoming a better version of oneself, fostering an environment where personal development can thrive without the fear of judgment or failure. Through this supportive dynamic, mentorship cultivates resilience and empowers men to realise their full potential.

Checklist: Is He Modelling the Father I Needed?

When evaluating the profound influence of a mentor, it's essential to reflect on several key questions that reveal the depth of their character and approach:

- Does he honour his word? A genuine mentor embodies integrity by faithfully keeping promises and commitments. This reliability establishes a foundation of trust and respect, creating a safe and open environment where mentees feel secure to share their thoughts and vulnerabilities, promoting authentic growth.

- Does he model emotional regulation? The ability to manage and express emotions in a healthy way is a critical skill in personal development. A mentor who exemplifies emotional regulation demonstrates how to navigate the inevitable stresses and challenges of life with composure and maturity. This modelling provides mentees with practical tools to handle their emotions, fostering resilience and emotional intelligence.

- Does he encourage growth without comparison? Effective mentorship focuses on individual progress, celebrating unique journeys rather than fostering competition. A mentor should cultivate an atmosphere where accomplishments big and small are acknowledged and appreciated. By encouraging mentees to set their own benchmarks for success, a mentor helps them find their own paths to fulfilment without the burden of comparison.

- Does he speak truth without cruelty? Honest and straightforward communication is vital for nurturing growth, but it must be delivered with compassion and sensitivity. A mentor who provides constructive feedback rooted in truth does so in a way that lifts up their mentee rather than tearing them down. This delicate balance ensures that honesty serves as a catalyst for transformation rather than a source of pain or discouragement.

- Does he show up when it's hard, not just when it's convenient? A mentor's presence is especially crucial during trying times. Demonstrating reliability in moments of challenge reinforces the depth of the mentor-mentee bond, illustrating that support is unwavering even in adversity. This steadfast commitment fosters a profound sense of loyalty and connection, reassuring the mentee that they are not alone in their struggles.

Every individual deserves at least one mentor who serves as a reflective mirror, offering not just affirmation and guidance, but also a steady hand during moments of uncertainty. Such mentorship can profoundly shape a person's journey, leaving an indelible mark on their path toward personal growth and fulfilment.

The Wound Behind the Rage

The father wound, when left untreated, often expresses itself not through overt sadness but rather through a range of more aggressive behaviour's. These manifestations can include:

- Hyper-masculinity: This often presents as an exaggerated need to dominate and control others. Typically, this behaviour is rooted in a deep-seated fear of vulnerability and inadequacy. Men exhibiting hyper-masculinity may believe that showing weakness is synonymous with failure, prompting them to adopt a façade of toughness and aggression as a defence mechanism.

- Controlling Behaviour: Many individuals may feel an overwhelming urge to script or control relationships. This tendency often stems from underlying anxiety about intimacy and connection. By attempting to dictate the terms of relationships, they seek to create an environment where spontaneity and vulnerability are minimised, thereby protecting themselves from the possibility of emotional pain.

- Relationship Violence: Unresolved emotional pain can lead to the outward expression of violence towards others. This aggression is often a misdirected response to internal struggles, where individuals, in an effort to cope with their own hurt, inflict harm on those around them. This cycle can create a dangerous dynamic, perpetuating more harm and conflict in relationships.

- Aversion to Male Authority: A significant resistance to mentorship or guidance from male figures can arise from past experiences of betrayal or disappointment. Such individuals may carry a profound distrust of male authority figures, fearing that they will replicate previous traumas. This aversion can hinder personal growth and limit opportunities for learning and development.

It is essential to recognise that these behaviours' do not stem from inherent flaws within men themselves. Instead, they often arise from a lack of guidance and support in processing grief and emotional pain. For many, anger serves as a mask that conceals deeper feelings of loss, sadness, and vulnerability. Understanding this dynamic is crucial for fostering healing and helping individuals reclaim their emotional well-being.

The Archetype Link: King and Warrior

The impact of the father wound profoundly affects a man's ability to embrace his inner King, an archetype that represents the capacity to lead with calmness, wisdom, and a sense of sovereignty. This wound can also disrupt the Warrior archetype, which is essential for protecting not only oneself but also others with a sense of integrity and honour, rather than through aggression or domination. When fathers exhibit traits of tyranny, weakness, or emotional unavailability, their sons face a challenging dilemma: they may either replicate these damaging behaviour's in their own lives or rebel against them fervently. Unfortunately, both pathways are rooted in reactivity, often perpetuating a cycle of dysfunction.

True maturation and personal growth occur when a man actively claims his throne as the King and takes up his sword as the Warrior, fully embracing the responsibilities that accompany these roles. The King leads with a foundation built on self-worth and inner strength, rather than seeking validation through external achievements or societal accolades. He understands that his value comes from within, empowering him to guide others with confidence and clarity.

Similarly, the Warrior archetype plays a crucial role in establishing and maintaining healthy boundaries. This requires a balance protecting oneself and others without resorting to defensiveness or rigidness. A true Warrior acts with purpose and resilience, ensuring that actions align with values and principles.

Until these essential archetypes are acknowledged and reclaimed, a man risks living a life that feels performative and superficial. He may find himself struggling to stand firm in his identity, often feeling disconnected from his true self and experiencing shallow connections with others. It is only through the conscious integration of the King and Warrior within that a man can foster deeper relationships, lead with integrity, and ultimately experience a profound sense of fulfilment in his life.

Reconciliation & Repair

It is essential to recognise that not every father is willing or able to change, and not every father-son relationship can or should be salvaged. However, the potential for healing and transformation remains open through various pathways, each offering opportunities for growth and understanding:

1. Direct Repair:

   - Engage in Honest Conversations: Approach discussions with openness, encouraging both parties to express their feelings. This can help clarify misunderstandings and create a foundation for rebuilding trust.
   - Establish New Boundaries: Define what is acceptable in your relationship going forward. Healthy boundaries can foster respect and create a safe space for both individuals to engage authentically.
   - Acknowledge the Pain without Attributing Blame: Recognising hurtful experiences is crucial, but it's equally important to avoid blaming each other. Focus on understanding the circumstances and emotions that have contributed to the current dynamic.

2. Symbolic Repair:

   - Write Letters that May Never Be Sent: This method allows for the expression of unvoiced emotions, thoughts, and grievances without the pressure of immediate resolution. It serves as a cathartic release, facilitating a deeper reflection on feelings.
   - Participate in Guided Inner Child Work: Engage in therapeutic exercises aimed at addressing past traumas.

This work can help heal old wounds by nurturing your inner child and understanding past experiences.
- Visualise the Ideal Father Figure: Take time to imagine the qualities and characteristics of the father figure you needed but did not have. This visualisation can help in identifying the gaps in your upbringing and guide you in shaping new relationships.

3. Mentorship:

- Seek Fatherly Energy: Look for mentors in the form of coaches, experienced elders, or male therapists who embody the nurturing, wise qualities you aspire to. Their guidance can provide support, encouragement, and alternative perspectives on masculinity and fatherhood.
- Create Supportive Communities: Surround yourself with groups of men who exhibit the traits you seek. Engaging with others who prioritise healthy relationships can offer insights, camaraderie, and mutual growth.

4. Re-parenting:

- Become the Nurturing Father to Yourself: Acknowledge your needs and practice self-care, compassion, and patience. By nurturing yourself, you can create a stable emotional foundation that allows for healing.
- Cultivate King Energy: Embrace characteristics like patience, care, and a clear vision for your life. This metaphorical "King" energy represents a balance of strength and nurturing, allowing you to lead yourself and others with wisdom and integrity.

Each of these pathways reflects the complexity of father-son relationships while emphasising the importance of self-awareness and proactive behaviour's in fostering healing, growth, and better connections.

Coaching Interventions

To explore personal growth more thoroughly, consider implementing the following detailed strategies:

Father Audit:

- Take time to reflect on the lessons your father imparted regarding love and failure. What messages did he convey about these concepts, both directly and indirectly?
- Identify the spoken or unspoken rules he established in your household. How have these guidelines influenced your behaviour and decision-making throughout your life? Document specific examples to gain clearer insights into your patterns and triggers.

Emotional Relearning Plan:

- Compile a list of five emotional needs that were not adequately met during your upbringing. These may include needs for validation, affection, security, understanding, or autonomy.
- Construct a script that represents how you wish your father had reacted to you in key moments of your past. Be as specific as possible, outlining what you needed to hear or experience in those situations.
- To integrate these new perspectives, practice your scripts in real-life interactions. This could involve role-playing with your son or partner or even engaging in self-reflection through journaling or meditation. Aim to embody those supportive responses and observe the changes in your relationships.

Inner Council Rebalancing

- Analyse which archetypes King, Warrior, Magician, Lover, your father exemplified, distorted, or neglected in his approach to fatherhood. Consider how these representations of masculinity impacted your identity and self-worth.

- Create a daily regimen of micro-practices designed to cultivate the archetypes that were absent in your upbringing. This might include activities like setting boundaries (Warrior), engaging in creative endeavours (Magician), fostering deep emotional connections (Lover), or taking charge in your life (King). Strive for balance by integrating these practices into your routine to nurture a more holistic self.

Gentle Prompts for Reflection

Engage in deep personal introspection with these reflective prompts:

- When did I first sense an emotional distance from my father? Consider the specific moment or experiences that marked the beginning of this separation. Reflect on how that realisation impacted your relationship with him and with yourself.

- What were the words of affirmation or acknowledgment I always longed to hear from him that he never expressed? Think about the specific phrases or gestures that you wished for. Explore how the absence of those sounds resonated in your life and shaped your expectations in future relationships.

- What aspects of my true self did I suppress or hide in order to maintain a sense of closeness to him? Delve into the traits, interests, or feelings that you felt compelled to push aside. Examine how these repressions influenced your self-esteem and identity over the years.

- In what ways do I still act out or perform in hopes of gaining validation from a paternal figure who is no longer present? Analyse the behaviour's or patterns you've adopted that seek approval or recognition from a

97

father figure. Reflect on how these tendencies may affect your current relationships and sense of self-worth.

- How can I nurture and protect my inner child, providing him with the comfort and reassurance that he never received? Consider practical and emotional steps you can take to heal these wounds. Reflect on the ways you can offer yourself compassion, support, and the love you missed, fostering a deeper connection with your inner self.

Use these prompts to create a safe space for exploration and healing, allowing you to uncover layers of your emotional landscape and facilitate personal growth.

Final Reframe

You do not need to wait for your father to transform in order to begin your healing journey. You are not obligated to seek his permission to outgrow the limitations that have been placed upon you. Remember, your silence is not a debt you owe simply because he gave you his name; it is a burden you can release.

Your true mission is not to fix your father but to liberate yourself from the shadows of his shortcomings. This journey requires you to mourn the love and support he was unable to provide, allowing yourself to feel the grief of what was absent in your life. Embrace the process of granting yourself the compassion and encouragement that he could not offer, and in doing so, break the cycle of pain that may have persisted for generations. It is essential to ensure that your own son, whether he is your biological child or a metaphorical representation of your inner child does not carry the same burdens that weighed you down.

Ultimately, the real father figure is not necessarily the man you were given, but rather the one you choose to become through your own growth and healing. The man who confronts and seeks to heal the wounds left by his father does not merely find wholeness for himself; he evolves into a different kind of ancestor, one who cultivates strength, resilience, and wisdom for future generations. In this way, he transforms not only his legacy but also creates a foundation for his descendants to thrive, breaking free from the cycles of pain that have long held sway.

Chapter 7

When a Man Goes Silent, The Hidden Language of Emotional Numbness

It doesn't begin with silence; rather, it culminates there, representing a profound and often painful journey. Long before a man ceases to speak or forgets how to let tears flow unbidden, he has already internalised a deep-seated lesson: expressing feelings is not safe. This harsh realisation is not birthed from a singular traumatic event; instead, it accumulates through a relentless series of subtle betrayals disinterested rolling eyes, biting remarks, and gut-wrenching emotional dismissals. Each moment contributes to the construction of an impenetrable wall of armour around his heart, teaching him that vulnerability is an invitation for hurt and rejection.

Throughout his life, he absorbs a relentless stream of phrases that echo through his mind, each reinforcing the need to suppress his emotions:

- "Be strong."
- "Don't be soft."
- "Man up."
- "Get over it."

Over time, these words penetrate deep into his psyche, reshaping his very identity. He learns to carry his burdens in silence, burying the questions and doubts that once held significance for him, transforming himself into a version moulded by societal expectations, one that may be tolerated and accepted by others but feels strangely foreign and dissonant to him. This metamorphosis is not a sign of weakness; instead, it emerges as a clinical survival mechanism. He cloaks his silence with a facade of strength, convinced that this stoicism serves as a shield, all the while unaware that it is gradually eroding his connection to his true self.

As the silence intensifies, the man becomes increasingly invisible, not to the bustling world around him, with its vibrant tapestry of life and emotion, but to himself. He stands as a ghost in his own life, walking through days devoid of authenticity and genuine connection, his once vivid inner landscape muted to drab shades of grey. In this state of disconnection, he grapples with an insatiable yet unarticulated longing, craving understanding, acceptance, and the solace that comes from a willingness to be seen and heard. But the fear of what that could entail holds him captive, leaving him trapped in the confines of the silence he has come to know all too well.

Numbness Isn't Emptiness

The suppression of his emotions results not only in coldness but also in a profound numbness that pervades his existence, creating a creeping detachment from his own identity. He moves through the rhythms of daily life, attending meetings, raising children, managing household chores, and adhering to relentless deadlines while inside, he embodies a shadow of the vibrant man he once was. In this sombre state, joy feels like a distant whisper, sadness reverberates faintly from a place obscured by fog, and love resembles an old film, its colours faded, just out of reach.

This emotional experience often goes unrecognised. Most men may not even perceive their condition as numbness; instead, they articulate their struggles through familiar phrases that reveal their inner turmoil:

- "I don't know what I feel anymore."
- "I'm tired. All the time."
- "Nothing gets through to me."
- "I'm here, but not really present."

These expressions are not mere indications of laziness or apathy; they are manifestations of a nervous system entrenched in

101

defence mechanisms, cultivated through years of societal expectations and internal conflicts. In a world that often equates strength with emotional stoicism, numbness becomes a protective shield, a muted baseline that continually whispers: keep pushing forward, stifle your feelings, don't let anyone see your vulnerability.

If this state remains unexamined, emotional numbness can transform into a pervasive blueprint for masculinity, one that is handed down through generations, from father to son, peer to peer. This blueprint impacts not only how men navigate their personal lives but also profoundly influences the ways they love, work, grieve, and pursue their dreams. The result is a cycle of emotional detachment that complicates relationships and stifles authentic connections, leaving them in a perpetual state of isolation amidst a crowded world. To break free from this cycle requires courage, courage to confront one's emotions, to embrace vulnerability, and to redefine what it means to be truly present in one's own life.

The Science Behind Going Blank

Within the framework of trauma-informed psychology, the psychological and physiological detachment experienced by individuals can be understood as a state of hypoarousal. This phenomenon is not merely a benign absence of reaction; rather, it serves as an essential component of the autonomic nervous system's defence mechanisms. When individuals face prolonged threats or stressors without resolution, the body is unable to maintain the heightened alertness associated with a fight-or-flight response indefinitely. Consequently, it shifts into a freeze state, which is marked by emotional shutdown, a physical sense of disconnection, and a proclivity to withdraw from the surrounding environment.

From a biological perspective, this transition is significant. The prefrontal cortex, the brain region crucial for higher-order functions such as logical reasoning, emotional regulation, and social interaction essentially goes offline during hypoarousal. As a result, blood flow is redirected away from this area to more primitive and survival-oriented structures, such as the amygdala and brainstem. In this state, the subtlety of emotional responses diminishes, and the ability to think rationally becomes a formidable challenge. The world may appear to dull into a muted haze, stripped of its vibrancy and clarity, making it difficult for individuals to engage meaningfully with their surroundings.

While this state of hypoarousal may seem dysfunctional from an outside perspective, it is important to recognise that it is a tragic adaptation forged from necessity. For a young boy facing emotional invalidation, this detachment once represented a crucial survival mechanism, allowing him to endure emotional hardships. However, as he transitions into adulthood, what was once a protective strategy can evolve into a prison of sorts, constraining his ability to access and express his own inner world fully.

Moreover, prolonged exposure to hypoarousal can have profound implications for hormonal balance within the body. Cortisol, the primary stress hormone, may remain elevated or fluctuate erratically, leading to detrimental effects on various aspects of life, including sleep quality, digestion, libido, and cognitive functions such as memory. Over time, the brain begins to rewire itself to perceive numbness as a form of safety or self-preservation. This misapplication of neuroplasticity highlights the complex interplay between survival instincts and the costs of self-discipline, illustrating how adaptive mechanisms can paradoxically hinder emotional growth and well-being in the long run.

Losing Himself Quietly

A man trapped in a state of emotional freeze can maintain this facade for astonishingly long periods, months, or even decades. To the outside world, he appears not only functional but also engaged; he's often employed in a steady job, meticulously groomed, and exudes an aura of reliability that invites trust. On the surface, he may hit all the traditional markers of success: a stable career, a comfortable home, perhaps even accolades in his field. Yet, beneath this meticulously crafted exterior lies a profound disconnection from the core of his humanity.

His once vibrant passions, which used to invigorate his spirit and spark creativity, have dwindled into shadows of their former selves, relegated to distant memories. Laughter, which once flowed freely and naturally, has become a mere performance, an obligatory mask donned to navigate the complexities of social interactions where vulnerability is avoided at all costs. Romantic relationships, too, devolve into obligatory exchanges marked by an uncomfortable distance and a persistent misunderstanding, leaving his partner feeling not just isolated, but profoundly unheard. Conversations hover at the surface, devoid of depth and authenticity, as he consistently sidesteps true emotional engagement. The tragedy of this existence is that he cannot be fully known by others, largely because he himself is estranged from his own feelings and thoughts.

This is not a man devoid of concern or empathy; instead, he is one who has lost touch with the capacity to genuinely care for himself and, by extension, for others. His past experiences have etched on him a painful truth: vulnerability often leads to hurt, disappointment, or rejection. His partner might lament in frustration, "You're here, but I can't reach you," while his children might describe him as emotionally cold or perpetually absent. The stark reality is that he is ensnared in a cycle of self-disconnection, desperately wanting to bridge the gap that separates his internal world from the external relationships he inhabits but feeling utterly incapable of doing so.

The repercussions of this disconnection are far-reaching and deeply damaging. Research has established clear links between emotional suppression and hypoarousal to a myriad of serious health issues, ranging from cardiovascular ailments and chronic fatigue to autoimmune disorders, among others. The silent but relentless toll of emotional neglect is reflected in the body; it quietly keeps score, chronicling the impact of every repressed feeling and unprocessed trauma. Often, these consequences manifest in silence, showcasing the dire need for reconnection with one's own emotions as a pathway toward healing and fulfilment.

The Clinical Reality: Masked Depression

For many men, the silent suffering associated with masked depression often goes unnoticed by traditional medical frameworks, leading clinicians to label it a complex and insidious form of depression. Concealed beneath a veneer of functionality, this type of depression lacks the overt expressions typically associated with mental health struggles. Rather than displaying explicit sadness or weeping, these men frequently express their distress through a variety of concerning behaviour's that reveal the depth of their emotional turmoil.

One prominent manifestation is persistent irritability, often accompanied by uncontainable anger that can erupt unexpectedly. This anger is typically fuelled by unresolved trauma and buried emotional pain, resulting in outbursts that appear disproportionate to the triggering events. Such reactions can alienate friends and family, causing them to misinterpret these men's struggles as simple moodiness rather than the deeper issues at play.

Additionally, many turn to a range of substance and behavioural addictions as coping mechanisms. Common examples include excessive alcohol consumption, gambling, compulsive use of pornography, and even obsessive exercise routines. These behaviours' may provide temporary relief or distraction from deeper emotional issues but often lead to an exacerbation of feelings of guilt and shame. The cycle of addiction thus becomes a double-edged sword, providing a fleeting escape while simultaneously deepening the emotional abyss.

The drive for achievement can also serve as a means of avoidance, with overworking and perfectionism acting as refuges from confronting painful feelings. In this scenario, success becomes a shield, allowing these men to bury their emotional pain under a façade of productivity. However, this constant striving for external validation can lead to chronic exhaustion, emotional detachment, and a feeling of emptiness, as the accomplishments fail to fill the void within.

In their personal relationships, these men may experience a significant disconnect from sexual intimacy, or alternatively, engage in compulsive sexual behaviour where encounters become purely transactional. This trend reflects their struggle for emotional connection, resulting in relationships that feel hollow and unsatisfying. The lack of genuine intimacy leaves both partners feeling isolated, compounding their existing emotional challenges.

Physically, many of these men endure persistent sleep disturbances, chronic fatigue, and somatic pain with no identifiable medical cause. These symptoms often serve as physical manifestations of their emotional turmoil, leaving them feeling trapped in a body that seems to betray them. The toll of this internal battle can render daily life exhausting and overwhelming.

Moreover, an overarching inability to experience joy or emotional resonance in life contributes to a monotonous existence. In this state, moments of delight and fulfilment seem elusive, further entrenching feelings of isolation and despair. The vibrant colours of life gradually fade, leaving everything tinged in shades of grey.

Because these symptoms diverge significantly from the more commonly recognised image of depression which is typically characterised by profound sadness and withdrawal, many men face significant challenges in obtaining accurate diagnoses. Instead of being understood as individuals grappling with their trauma and emotional needs, they are often labelled as "moody," "distant," or "workaholic." This misinterpretation becomes more complicated by an internal dialogue laden with shame,

106

prompting self-critical questions such as, "What do I have to be sad about?" or "Real men don't get depressed." These thoughts intensify the silence and stigma surrounding their struggles, ultimately leaving them feeling as though they are silently drowning in despair, unable to seek the help they desperately need.

The Origins: Childhood and Cultural Conditioning

The roots of emotional silence often extend deep into childhood, where a young person's nervous system is exceptionally adaptable, absorbing critical messages about safety and social acceptance. For instance, when a boy cries and is met with ridicule or harsh criticism, he swiftly learns that expressing emotions can invite danger and social rejection. Similarly, if he is dismissed or reprimanded for exhibiting signs of fear or vulnerability, he quickly adapts his behaviour to conform to these adverse expectations. This adjustment can lead to a process known as neurodevelopmental pruning, whereby the neural pathways crucial for emotional expression, empathy, and openness are systematically weakened or even eliminated.

Such developmental dynamics set the stage for conditions like alexithymia, a psychological state where individuals struggle to identify and articulate their feelings. Many men find themselves at a loss when asked questions like, "How do you feel?" This inability is not rooted in a lack of desire to express oneself but rather in the fact that their neural circuitry has not been nurtured to facilitate such introspection and emotional dialogue.

Layering this developmental context with the pressures of toxic masculinity creates a particularly fraught environment. The societal narrative often conflates strength with stoicism, power with control, and masculinity with dominance, ultimately resulting in men who function more like emotionless machines than sentient beings with complex emotional lives. Across various cultures, boys frequently receive accolades for showing resilience and enduring hardships, while any indication of softness or emotional vulnerability is met with disapproval or punishment.

By the time these boys become men, many have internalised a rigid emotional hierarchy. Anger, for example, becomes the only socially acceptable emotion, while grief is dismissed as a sign of weakness, fear is veiled in shame, and love is often viewed with conditions and limits. This internalized emotional landscape hampers authentic connection and vulnerability, leaving many to grapple with the emotional detachment that serves as a barrier to personal fulfilment and meaningful relationships.

Intersectionality: When Silence Runs Deeper

It is crucial to recognise that silence affects men in vastly different ways, shaped by an interplay of factors including social location, race, class, sexuality, and religion. These aspects can complicate and intensify the emotional suppression they face. For instance, a Black man might grapple with the internalised fear that expressing anger could lead to perceptions of him as "aggressive," which often stems from societal stereotypes linking Black masculinity to violence. This fear can create a paralysing cycle, where suppressing genuine emotional responses becomes a means of self-protection against potential backlash.

In a similar vein, a gay man often navigates a landscape where his true feelings and desires must be hidden, conditioned from a young age to mask his authenticity to avoid rejection or discrimination. This stifling of emotional truth can lead to long-lasting issues, preventing him from fully understanding or articulating his pain, and creating barriers to building meaningful connections with others.

For those from working-class backgrounds, the pressure to conform to the notion that their worth is solely tied to their productivity can be overwhelming. This belief may compel them to prioritise relentless work over self-care, neglecting emotional needs and reinforcing a belief that vulnerability equates to weakness. Such ideologies often stem from the necessity to survive economically, leading to a cycle where emotional health is sacrificed on the altar of financial stability.

Moreover, neurodivergent individuals often face misconceptions about their emotional expressions. They might be readily labelled as "cold" or "rude" due to their unique communication styles, which can make it difficult for them to articulate feelings that others might express more easily. This misunderstanding only amplifies their struggle, leading to isolation and further emotional suppression.

Geographic, generational, and religious factors also play critical roles in shaping these experiences. Men raised in rural or traditional environments may encounter deeply entrenched beliefs about masculinity that discourage emotional expression, perpetuating a culture of silence. In such communities, patriarchal norms can create a framework where showing vulnerability is equated with failure, leading men to inherit a legacy of emotional deprivation.

Thus, the silence that many men maintain transcends mere coping mechanisms; it becomes a cultural inheritance, a profound and unspoken legacy passed down through generations. This legacy not only binds them to feelings of isolation but also creates barriers to emotional connection, leaving many to navigate their inner turmoil in solitude, often unaware of the collective struggle they share.

Rebuilding from the Inside

The journey back from emotional numbness is a subtle yet profoundly impactful process, often marked by quiet moments rather than dramatic breakthroughs. This path is characterised not by grand gestures or heroic acts, but by its awkwardness, its small but significant steps, and a deep-seated vulnerability that permeates each experience. Reconnecting with our emotions begins with a collection of micro-moments that lay the groundwork for comprehensive emotional revival:

- Awareness of Numbness: The initial step involves cultivating an acute awareness of when you have slipped into emotional numbness. This requires a reflective practice of checking in with yourself and recognising the signs of disconnection, such as feeling emotionally flat, detached, or indifferent. Being cognisant of these states allows you to address them before they become entrenched.

- Naming Your Emotions: The act of acknowledging and articulating your feelings is essential, even if the words feel elusive. This practice involves not just identifying emotions like sadness or anger, but also recognising subtler feelings like disappointment or anxiety. By putting a name to your emotions, you bring clarity to your inner landscape, fostering a deeper understanding of your needs and experiences.

- Breath as a Tool: In moments of heightened anxiety or overwhelming emotion, remember the importance of your breath. Allowing yourself to take deeper, more intentional breaths can serve as a grounding technique, anchoring you in the present moment. This simple yet powerful practice can help regulate your body's responses, reducing feelings of panic and providing a clearer pathway to emotional clarity.

- Vocalising Your Truth: The power of articulating your truth cannot be overstated. Saying, "I'm not okay," out loud can be a significant turning point. This honest declaration offers a release and embodies vulnerability, inviting others into your experience and fostering deeper connections based on mutual understanding and support.

- Embracing Vulnerability: Allowing a tear to fall without the impulse to wipe it away symbolises a profound acceptance of your emotional state. This willingness to be vulnerable can open the door to healing and connection, creating a safe space for yourself to process your feelings without judgment.

Neuroplasticity, the brain's incredible capacity to rewire itself, offers hope that emotional fluency is not a fixed attribute but rather a skill that can be cultivated over time. With the right support, tools, and patience, individuals, particularly men who may struggle with expressing emotions, can reclaim a more profound connection to their bodies, hearts, and authentic inner experiences. Engaging in trauma-informed practices such as EMDR (Eye Movement Desensitisation and Reprocessing), somatic therapy, breath work, and narrative therapy provides constructive and effective pathways to facilitate this transformative return.

Healing thrives within safe and supportive relationships. These unique spaces allow men to feel seen and valued without the pressure to perform or conform to societal expectations of masculinity. Here, they can begin to unlearn the conditioned fear of feeling, establishing a new relationship with their emotions that fosters growth and understanding.

Ultimately, reconnection is not a singular destination but an ongoing journey, made moment by moment. It requires continual commitment and a willingness to explore the complex landscape of our emotions, opening ourselves to the possibility of deeper joy, connection, and authenticity.

Gentle Prompts for Reconnection:

Emotional Awareness: Reflecting on Early Experiences with Emotions

- When did I first learn that expressing certain emotions, such as sadness, anger, or vulnerability, was deemed "unacceptable" in my environment? Was it a specific incident or a gradual realisation?
- What feelings have I consciously trained myself to hide or ignore, even from my own awareness? How has this

111

suppression affected my overall well-being and relationships?

- If I were to vividly describe my emotional landscape today, what imagery would it evoke? Would it be a stormy sea, a barren desert, or perhaps a vibrant garden full of contrasting colours?

Body as Messenger: Attuning to Physical Sensations

- Where in my body do I routinely notice tension, tightness, or numbness? Is it my shoulders, jaw, chest, or perhaps my gut? Can I identify any patterns related to specific emotions tied to these sensations?
- How does my body respond when I attempt to discuss my emotions? Do I experience physical discomfort, a racing heart, or even avoidance responses like fidgeting or withdrawing?
- Which physical sensations do I find myself most susceptible to experiencing, such as a racing heart in stressful situations, overwhelming fatigue when faced with emotional demands, a foggy mind during anxious moments, or stomach knots when confronted with discomforting feelings?

Emotional Safety: Identifying Safe Spaces

- Who are the individuals in my life that have historically offered me a profound sense of safety, allowing me to express my emotions fully without fear of judgment or reprisal? What actions or words from them contribute to that safety?
- In which situations, or around which people, do I frequently find myself shutting down emotionally? What triggers this pattern, and how does it impact my ability to communicate and connect?
- If I could articulate my truth openly, without fear of negative consequences, what emotions or thoughts

would I want to express? What fears might hold me back from expressing these feelings?

Emotional Memory: Reconnecting with Past Feelings

- When was the last moment I truly experienced a strong emotion, whether it was an exhilarating joy, profound grief, intense rage, or awe-inspiring wonder? What circumstances surrounded that moment, and how did it affect me?
- Are there specific emotions that now feel inaccessible or distant to me? If so, what internal or external blockages might be preventing me from accessing these feelings? Are they tied to past experiences or current situations?
- Reflecting on my childhood emotional environment, were emotions encouraged and welcomed, or were they discouraged and shut down? How has this formative experience shaped my relationship with my emotions today?

Reconnection: Exploring Authentic Feelings

- If I were liberated from the expectations to be strong for others, what emotions would I allow myself to fully experience? How would embracing those emotions change my interactions and self-perception?
- What daily signs indicate that I've retreated into numbness or emotional detachment once more? Is it a lack of enthusiasm, difficulty connecting with others, or an overwhelming sense of emptiness?
- What is one small, concrete action I can commit to this week that honours my emotional life? How can I integrate this action into my routine, ensuring I take steps toward a healthier emotional connection?

Bonus Coaching Insight:

If numbness functions as a form of self-preservation, what insight does that provide into the hurdles I have faced throughout my life? It's important to recognise that authenticity doesn't necessitate dramatic expressions of emotion; your existence is just as valid in those quieter, introspective moments. You don't need to reach a breaking point to deserve the rest and care you require. Healing is a journey, and it's entirely feasible to reconnect with your true self, nurturing one emotion at a time. This process of rediscovery reminds us that even the smallest steps toward feeling can lead to significant transformation. Embrace each feeling as it comes, honouring the lessons and growth that emerge from both the silence and the chaos.

Chapter 8

When Numbness Becomes Normal: The Silent Collapse of Men's Emotional Lives

The Slow Fade to Silence

The journey into silence seldom begins with a dramatic outcry; rather, it unfolds quietly in the subtle, often overlooked corners of childhood. Imagine a young boy, brimming with curiosity and wonder, who cries out in frustration or fear. Instead of receiving comfort and reassurance, he finds himself met with harsh admonitions to stem his tears. When he tentatively confides his worries or fears, he is greeted not with empathy but with laughter, leaving him feeling small and misunderstood. Any display of tenderness is quickly dismissed as weakness, further reinforcing the message that vulnerability is to be avoided at all costs.

These crucial moments do not need to be explicitly articulated; the reactions of the world around him impart powerful lessons. Emotions become intertwined with peril, teaching him that to feel deeply is a liability. The message is clear: openness is fraught with risk, and so he learns to shield his heart behind a facade, where emotions are seen as dangerous and vulnerability becomes synonymous with shame.

As these formative experiences accumulate, layer upon layer, they shape a belief system that permeates every aspect of his life. He begins to tread carefully, curbing any impulse to reveal what lies beneath the surface. Tears that once flowed freely are stifled, pain is rephrased in socially acceptable terms, and emotional masks are donned to help him navigate a world that appears to celebrate stoicism while punishing softness and sensitivity. This transformation is not a sudden collapse; it is more akin to erosion, slow, imperceptible, and ultimately devastating.

Joy gradually dissipates, replaced by a quiet resignation. Sadness morphs into a hollow echo, filling the spaces where genuine emotion once thrived, while hope retreats silently, often until it is barely a whisper. One day, he finds himself staring into the mirror, grappling with a disconnection from the man reflected back, an unfamiliar visage that feels foreign and estranged.

Yet, even as he constructs these walls, he does not entirely extinguish the flame of feeling. Instead, he learns to cloak his emotions, relegating them to clenched jaws, tightened fists, sleepless nights, and compulsive habits that play out like a tragic dance of denial. Over time, he develops a profound schism within himself, a carefully curated version intended for public consumption, and a hidden self-buried deep beneath the surface, away from prying eyes. The emotional amputation becomes so deeply ingrained that he begins to consider this disassociation as normal. In doing so, he loses touch with the vibrant essence of being fully alive, trapped in a world that has painted authenticity as an unnecessary risk.

The Biology of Going Blank

What many perceive as emotional laziness or detachment is often a profound and complex response from the nervous system, known as hypoarousal, also referred to as the freeze state. This biological reaction serves as the body's instinctive mechanism for preserving energy and protecting itself from further harm after experiencing chronic emotional overwhelm. Unlike the more overt responses such as panic or rage, hypoarousal manifests as an internal state characterised by stillness, coldness, and a disconcerting sense of numbness.

During hypoarousal, the prefrontal cortex, the region of the brain responsible for higher-order emotional regulation, decision-making, and social behaviour essentially shifts into a low-power mode, much like an engine idling without engaging.

116

Meanwhile, the limbic system, particularly the amygdala, remains highly reactive, continuously signalling a sense of danger, but without prompting an appropriate or effective response. This can lead to an agonising feedback loop of internal tension and distress. Neurotransmitters that are crucial for mood regulation, such as serotonin and dopamine, are significantly depleted in this state, resulting in a pervasive sense of emotional flatness and lack of motivation.

Men experiencing hypoarousal may articulate their struggles through phrases like:
- "I'm just tired all the time."
- "I feel nothing."
- "I'm here but not really present."

These expressions should not be mistaken for a lack of interest or motivation; rather, they are symptoms of neurological burnout stemming from prolonged exposure to stress and emotional fatigue. It is a survival mechanism, where individuals are desperately attempting to conserve their dwindling energy reserves to endure just one more day in a seemingly unending cycle of internal chaos. Externally, he may present as dependable, fulfilling responsibilities and even achieving success, but internally, he is often running on empty, trapped in the grips of an invisible crisis that underscores the disconnect between outward appearances and inner reality.

Masked Depression: Functioning in Disguise

Depression in men often emerges in ways that starkly contrast with the traditional image of sadness. This phenomenon, often referred to as masked depression, conceals deep emotional turmoil beneath a façade of normalcy. Men, conditioned by societal expectations to suppress their feelings, frequently exhibit the following manifestations:

- Chronic Anger and Irritability: Rather than displaying sadness, men may express their internal struggles through persistent frustration and irritability. This anger

117

can easily surface in their daily interactions, alienating friends and family and leading to strained relationships.

- Relentless Drive to Overwork: Many men respond to their emotional pain by immersing themselves in work. This relentless pursuit of productivity can lead to a cycle of overwork and eventual burnout, leaving them feeling exhausted and unfulfilled.

- Hyper-sexuality or Sexual Numbness: While some men may seek solace in exaggerated sexual activity, using it as a distraction from their emotional pain, others may experience a stark contrast, falling into a state of sexual numbness that deprives them of intimacy and connection.

- Excessive Reliance on Substances: Coping mechanisms often include a heavy dependence on alcohol, drugs, pornography, or gaming. These substances provide a temporary escape from emotional distress but often lead to further isolation and exacerbation of underlying issues.

- Sarcastic or Cynical Humour: Many use humour, especially in a sarcastic or cynical form as a shield to deflect attention from their emotional state. While it may entertain others, it often masks a deeper sorrow and serves to further isolate them from genuine emotional connection.

- Emotional Withdrawal: A pervasive tendency to avoid forming close relationships can develop, as men may withdraw emotionally to protect themselves from vulnerability. This withdrawal can result in a profound sense of loneliness, even among those they are closest to.

- Persistent Physical Ailments: The psychological toll of masked depression often manifests physically, with men experiencing ongoing health issues such as gastrointestinal problems, chronic pain, or persistent headaches, conditions that can be exacerbated by stress and emotional turmoil.

Despite these evident struggles, men may find it difficult to articulate their feelings. The phrase "I'm fine" becomes a common refrain, concealing their inner turmoil. Their eyes, often devoid of the vibrancy that reflects joy, reveal a deeper, unacknowledged sorrow. Recognising these signs is crucial in providing the necessary support and understanding, fostering an environment where men can feel safe to express their emotions without fear of judgment.

When Survival Becomes a Personality

Over time, survival mode can become an all-consuming aspect of a person's identity, gradually suffocating their true self beneath layers of armour. This individual often finds themselves disconnected from the rich tapestry of emotional nuances, struggling to access feelings such as curiosity, tenderness, and vulnerability that once coloured their experiences. Instead of embracing life's complexities, they navigate existence through a rigid lens focused solely on logic, productivity, and unrelenting action. Despite their outward achievements, they grapple with a profound sense of detachment, making it difficult to be genuinely present for themselves or within their relationships. This emotional disconnection diminishes the depth and richness of their interactions with others, leaving a vacuum where authentic connection should thrive.

As a result, relationships may falter, not out of indifference or lack of care, but due to an overwhelming inability to communicate genuine feelings. Love transforms into a rehearsed performance, where gestures are meticulously scripted, and intimacy feels like a series of tasks to be managed rather than a spontaneous sharing of selves. Laughter, once an effortless expression of joy, now emerges as something strained and hollow, stripped of its warmth and sincerity.

119

Deep within, he yearns for a connection to his emotions, silently pleading for the courage to embrace the vulnerability that comes with it. Yet, he remains paralysed by an ever-looming fear. That fear, a persistent whisper in his mind, warns him: "If I open this door, it won't merely let in a trickle of emotion it will unleash a torrent that I may not know how to handle." This internal struggle creates a chasm between who he is and who he longs to be, perpetuating a cycle of isolation that leaves him feeling lost and yearning for genuine connection.

Emotional Repression Starts in Boyhood

From the earliest stages of life, boys are often conditioned to suppress their emotions, a societal expectation that shapes their understanding of masculinity. When a young boy stumbles and falls, he is frequently admonished to pick himself up, wipe away his tears, and exhibit strength rather than vulnerability. This pressure to conform to rigid gender norms filters emotional expression, leading to a distorted view of acceptable feelings: exuberant joy is encouraged but must be loud and boisterous, sadness is relegated to shame and should be hidden, and fear is often displaced into aggression or bravado.

This cultural conditioning begins in toddlerhood and extends well into adolescence, creating deep-rooted patterns of behaviour. In many Western countries such as the UK, the US, and Australia, boys are frequently discouraged from showing vulnerability; they learn from an early age that doing so is a sign of weakness. Conversely, in numerous cultures throughout Asia and Africa, stoicism and emotional restraint are exalted as virtues, further complicating the dialogue around masculinity and emotional expression. Regardless of geographical or cultural context, however, the underlying message remains consistent: boys must exchange emotional safety for social acceptance.

The sources of these messages are diverse and pervasive, including influential figures such as fathers, teachers, coaches, and even the media. Boys encounter these sentiments across countless situations, often reinforced through common phrases like:

- "Stop crying."
- "You're acting like a girl."
- "Grow up."
- "Don't be weak."

These phrases, rather than being innocuous, have profound implications: they shape the neurodevelopmental landscape of a boy's brain in significant ways. The emotional responses that are validated are the ones that become reinforced neural pathways, while those deemed unacceptable are systematically pruned away. This leads to a troubling outcome: as these boys grow into men, they often find themselves disconnected from their full emotional range. They may struggle to articulate their feelings or connect meaningfully with others, resulting in relationships that lack depth and emotional richness. The lifelong impact of this early conditioning can hinder personal growth, mental health, and overall well-being, underscoring the urgent need to challenge and redefine societal expectations surrounding masculinity and emotional expression.

When Nothing Feels Like Anything

When a man experiences a profound emotional shutdown, he may feel as though he has become a mere spectre in his own life. Days seamlessly blend into one another, each indistinguishable from the last, while conversations pass by without leaving any mark on his psyche. Events that once held significance drift past him like distant memories, devoid of resonance or connection. The world takes on a de-saturated, monotone palette; foods that once delighted his senses lose their flavour, music that once stirred his soul no longer elicits any emotional response, and moments of intimacy morph into mere mechanical routines or, worse, vanish entirely.

In a desperate attempt to reclaim some sense of feeling, he may turn to heightened experiences. He might engage in dangerous affairs or make reckless business decisions, driven by an insatiable need to pierce through the fog of apathy. He may find himself speeding down roads, feeling the rush of adrenaline as a brief remedy to his emotional numbness, or getting caught up in physical confrontations, seeking the visceral sensation of a fight. Excessive workouts may become his release, though these pursuits are not merely about thrill-seeking; they are frantic attempts to rekindle the ember of emotion that has dimmed within him.

Yet, when these desperate attempts yield no relief or escape, isolation often becomes his only sanctuary. Silence wraps around him like a comforting shroud, and he may find solace in substance use or an obsession with work, both of which offer a fleeting distraction but a deepening sense of disconnection from himself and those around him. As frustration and despair bubble to the surface, he may fixate on external chaos, pouring his energy into news cycles or political discourse, searching for any semblance of distraction or a false sense of control.

Beneath this chaotic façade, however, resides a haunting whisper that echoes in the depths of his mind: "I don't know who I am anymore." This unsettling self-questioning reveals a profound identity crisis, one that derives from feeling lost in a world once rich with meaning and connection. It is a struggle that stretches beyond the surface, silently begging for acknowledgment and understanding.

Gentle Prompts for Emotional Reconnection

Emotional Numbness as Protection

- What feelings have become so unfamiliar to me that I struggle to name them? Reflecting on past experiences, which specific events or relationships may have contributed to this disconnection from my emotions?
- At what point in my life did I start to believe that it was safer to simply avoid my emotions altogether? Was it a

gradual realisation, or was there a specific moment that marked this shift?

- How have I mistakenly equated numbness with strength and control, convincing myself that being "fine" and emotionally guarded is preferable to feeling vulnerable? What does this say about my understanding of resilience?

The Mask I Wear

- What facades do I habitually present to the world that effectively conceal my true feelings? Are there particular situations or people that prompt me to adopt these masks?
- When someone asks how I am, do I respond with authenticity, or do I merely go through the motions, providing a rehearsed answer that keeps my true feelings at bay?
- If I were to find the courage to momentarily drop my guard, what deeper truths would emerge? What long-ignored emotions would I need to acknowledge, and what fears might be at the root of this guardedness?

Dissociation & Survival Mode

- Do I frequently feel as though I am disconnected from my surroundings, often zoning out or operating on autopilot, as if I'm merely a spectator in my own life?
- What is my go-to escape mechanism when emotions begin to overwhelm me? Do I find myself mindlessly scrolling through social media, reaching for substances, or using humour as a protective shield to deflect deeper feelings?
- Is there a particular time of day or week when I find myself feeling especially emotionally distant or disconnected from those around me? What patterns can I identify that contribute to this dissociation?

Early Lessons About Feeling

- What messages about emotional expression did I receive during my upbringing? Were emotions welcomed and validated, or was I taught to suppress and hide them?
- When I experienced sadness or pain, was I comforted and supported, or did I receive cues to hide those feelings and put on a brave face?
- What aspects of my emotional self, did I learn to suppress in order to fit in, receive validation, or feel a sense of security? How have these lessons shaped my current emotional landscape?

The Desire to Reconnect

- What emotions do I yearn to experience deeply again, whether it be joy, love, excitement, or hope? Why do these particular feelings resonate with me now?
- Are there small, fleeting moments in my daily life that unexpectedly spark even a brief flicker of emotion? What are they, and how can I cultivate more of these experiences?
- If I truly knew it was safe to feel again, which part of my emotional self would I be most eager to reconnect with first? What steps can I take to begin this journey towards rediscovering my emotions?

Bonus Coaching Reflection

"If emotional shutdown served as a protective mechanism during moments of distress, could embracing emotional presence now be the key to my healing journey?" This chapter extends an invitation to transcend the confines of mere survival and engage in a deeper exploration of wholeness. Healing is not necessarily an all-or-nothing endeavour; rather, it unfolds gradually through the simple act of saying 'yes' to our emotions allowing ourselves to fully experience each feeling as it arises. This process is not about rushing toward resolution but involves nurturing ourselves in a gentle manner, taking it one breath, one truth, and one moment at a time. Through this approach, we can cultivate a richer understanding of our emotional landscape, facilitating true growth and transformation.

If feeling nothing kept you safe, imagine how much safer you'll be when feeling everything no longer feels like a threat.

Chapter 9

The Soundless Exit: Male Suicide and the Weight of Unspoken Pain

The Man Who Doesn't Speak

It is often the man who projects a veneer of calm and composure that warrants our deepest concern, for beneath this façade lies a tumult of unspoken struggles and silent battles. While those who openly express their need for help receive the attention and compassion they desperately seek, it is the man who seems to fade gradually into the background, his ever-present smile becoming a mask for his internal turmoil who may be precariously teetering on the edge of despair. He bears a heavy burden, one that is most profoundly felt in moments of stillness, where silence reigns and the weight of his thoughts can be crushing.

This man is the kind of person who routinely checks in on others, always appearing as a steadfast beacon of reliability and support. Friends and family turn to him in times of need, often unaware of the chaos he conceals. His laughter, once a source of joy, has become a tool to mask his loneliness; charming anecdotes and witty banter serve to deflect attention from the sadness simmering beneath the surface. Each day, as he engages with those around him, his own spiralling thoughts remain hidden, obscured by the very guise of dependability he has so carefully cultivated. When the inevitable question arises "How are you?", he responds with a rehearsed, "I'm fine," his smile practiced yet strained, a façade that belies the turmoil raging within.

In his world, silence is not a sign of tranquillity; rather, it often acts as the last bastion of defence, a form of emotional armour designed to shield him from the probing gaze of those who might see through his disguise. Yet, with every passing moment, the weight of his unexpressed struggles grows heavier, threatening to overwhelm him. For this man, the quiet spaces in life, filled not with words but with the heaviness of his unacknowledged fears and sorrows, carry a significance that speaks volumes, a silent cry for understanding and connection.

A Global Epidemic Hidden in Plain Sight

The crisis of male suicide transcends mere statistics on mental health reports; it represents a profound and urgent public health emergency that calls for immediate attention and action. Globally, suicide has emerged as one of the top causes of death for men under the age of fifty, illuminating a critical issue that often goes unnoticed. In the United Kingdom, disturbingly, three out of every four suicide deaths are men, reflecting deep underlying cultural and societal factors. In the United States, the situation is similarly dire, with over 30,000 men taking their own lives each year, an average that reveals the silent suffering experienced by countless individuals. In Australia, the crisis is alarming, with a man dying by suicide every four hours.

Particularly concerning is the situation in Canada, where Indigenous communities grapple with significantly elevated suicide rates. In some areas, the rate for men may be as high as six times the national average, pointing to the complex interplay of historical trauma, social disenfranchisement, and limited access to mental health resources. The plight of these individuals is compounded by broader systemic issues that remain largely under-discussed.

In Eastern Europe, the soaring suicide rates among men can often be linked to economic instability and prolonged unemployment, exacerbating feelings of hopelessness and despair. The absence of adequate psychological support services further intensifies this crisis, leaving many to navigate their struggles alone. In contrast, in countries like Japan and South Korea, deeply ingrained cultural norms surrounding honour, shame, and an unyielding work ethic contribute to what has been termed "silent suicides." These tragic outcomes often follow years of accumulated stress and societal pressure, where individuals feel trapped in their despair, unable to seek help without facing stigma.

Moreover, veterans returning from active duty represent a particularly vulnerable group, facing elevated risks of suicide due to the trauma of combat, the burden of PTSD, moral injury, and the feeling of betrayal by the very systems designed to support them. These brave individuals often find themselves isolated, grappling with the ghosts of their experiences while lacking adequate resources for mental health care.

Each of these statistics translates into human lives, fathers, brothers, sons, colleagues, and friends. Behind each number lies a poignant story of someone who likely wore a smile to conceal their pain, who faced societal demands to 'man up' far too many times, and who battled the heavy weight of silence, unsure of how or where to voice their struggles. By acknowledging this crisis and fostering open conversations about mental health, we can move toward breaking the cycle of stigma and finding constructive paths for support and healing.

The Invisible Man

There exists a disconcerting contradiction in society's approach to male vulnerability that warrants deeper investigation. Men are often expected to embody unwavering strength and resilience, standing as pillars of support and protection for their families and communities. Yet, in the same breath, they are frequently left to navigate their emotional turmoil in isolation, shunned from seeking the very support that could aid them in their struggles. Society celebrates men for their sacrifices, whether in the workplace, in relationships, or through acts of bravery, while simultaneously discouraging any display of emotions that could be perceived as fear, weakness, or softness. This cultural dichotomy creates a challenging landscape for men, many of whom find themselves existing as emotional exiles; they may be physically present among their friends and family yet remain profoundly emotionally invisible.

The tragic reality is that the man who eventually succumbs to the depths of despair may not fit the traditional image of depression that society has constructed. He could very well be the life of the party, radiating charm and humour, a steadfast colleague who never misses a deadline, or a loving father who attends every soccer game. This outward persona often masks an internal chaos that is seldom recognised or acknowledged by those around him. Loved ones might recall, with confusion and heartache, that in the days leading up to his tragic decision, he appeared to be lighter, almost liberated from the weight of his struggles. What they fail to grasp is that this newfound lightness can signify a painful turning point; it often reflects a final resolution or acceptance of his overwhelming despair, a quiet farewell to the turmoil that he had concealed for so long. This tragic misunderstanding underscores the urgent need to foster an environment where men feel safe to express their emotions without fear of judgment and to seek support in their darkest moments.

A Childhood Without Tears

From an early age, many boys receive a message that discourages the open expression of emotions such as sadness, grief, or fear. Instead of being encouraged to share their feelings, they are handed a rigid emotional script that rewards suppression and shames vulnerability. Phrases like "Don't cry," "Be a man," and "Stop being soft" become ingrained in their psyche, serving not merely as casual remarks but as powerful social mandates that dictate what is deemed acceptable behaviour within their communities. This conditioning reinforces the idea that emotional expression, particularly of negative emotions, is a sign of weakness.

Emotional literacy, an essential skill for mental health and well-being is seldom cultivated in boys during their formative years. Fathers, often unaware of the implications of their actions, may unintentionally pass down a legacy of silence, viewing emotional stoicism as a badge of honour in coping with life's adversities. Teachers, tasked with maintaining discipline, frequently prioritise academic performance over emotional wellbeing, often overlooking the emotional needs of their students and dismissing cries for help. Meanwhile, mothers, who may instinctively recoil from their son's displays of vulnerability, often lack the tools to nurture such openness, having been raised in similar environments that prioritise toughness over tenderness.

As boys progress through adolescence, peer groups become increasingly influential, reinforcing these damaging narratives. The pressure to conform to societal expectations of masculinity often leads to a deep-seated belief that expressing feelings of sadness or fear is a profound weakness. This internalised lesson, learned in childhood and adolescence, resonates painfully into adulthood, creating a cycle where emotional suppression becomes the norm. Men may find themselves grappling with unresolved feelings, struggling to communicate needs and desires, and ultimately suffering from the consequences of their learned detachment, which can manifest in relationships, mental health struggles, and overall life satisfaction.

A Practitioner's Truth

In my role on the frontline, where I provide support to men navigating their most challenging moments, I've come to recognise the importance of one pivotal question. This question isn't simply a habit or formality; it is the culmination of my experiences and the invaluable lessons gleaned from countless heartfelt conversations. When a man voices thoughts of wanting to end his life, I gently but firmly ask, "Do you want to die, or do you want your current situation to die?"

Time and again, the answer unveils a profound truth that is often overlooked:

"I want my situation to die."

This statement encapsulates the essence of their struggle. Most men do not possess an inherent desire for death; rather, they find themselves ensnared in a relentless web of despair, feeling as though they are trapped with no possible way out. They grapple not only with their immediate circumstances but also with the heavy burdens of silence, shame, and an overwhelming struggle for survival. The pain they experience does not stem from a death wish; it arises from the unbearable weight of a life that feels unliveable.

What they truly seek is not an escape from life itself but rather a pathway to connection and understanding. They yearn for support, safety, and a compassionate witness who truly sees them beyond the masks they feel compelled to wear. In these moments, I realise that recognising their pain and validating their feelings is essential. It is through compassion and honest dialogue that we can begin to dismantle the barriers of isolation and despair, gently guiding them toward hope and healing. Such moments are powerful reminders that even in the darkest times, connection can ignite a spark of resilience and a renewed sense of purpose.

The Mask of Functioning

Within society, a notable number of men become skilled at donning a mask of competence and reliability, expertly navigating their professional lives while fulfilling family responsibilities. They often rise to positions of leadership and command respect from their peers. However, behind this meticulously crafted facade, many are silently struggling, weighted down by unseen burdens that threaten to overwhelm them.

These men might:

- Overwork themselves relentlessly, using their jobs as an escape to avoid confronting a pervasive sense of emptiness that quietly gnaws at their core. The long hours and relentless deadlines serve as distractions, allowing them to suppress feelings of inadequacy or despair that they fear might surface if they slow down.

- Employ humour as a defensive mechanism, skilfully dodging deeper, uncomfortable conversations about their emotional well-being. By making others laugh, they create an illusion of emotional wellbeing, diverting attention from their struggles and maintaining a social mask that prevents vulnerability.

- Turn to substances, alcohol, or compulsive behaviour's as a means of self-medication, believing that these temporary escapes will numb their emotional pain. In their minds, the quick fixes offer an invaluable respite, albeit fleeting, from the overwhelming feelings they are not ready to face.

- Gradually withdraw from meaningful relationships while cloaking themselves in excuses of busyness or fatigue. This retreat not only exacerbates their isolation but also deepens the chasm between their outward persona and their inner turmoil, leading to strained ties with loved ones who may be unaware of their silent suffering.

- Become fixated on tasks and rigid routines, seeing these as a way to regain a sense of control over the chaos that feels insurmountable in their lives. This need for order can mask their anxiety, providing a false sense of security in the face of emotional and existential uncertainty.

To the outside observer, these men may not seem to be suffering; they are often perceived as high-functioning individuals, successfully managing their responsibilities. Yet, their internal struggles can be profound and destabilising. The more invisible their pain becomes, the closer they edge toward a potential crisis point, where the weight of their unaddressed emotions could lead to devastating consequences, both for themselves and those around them.

Understanding Suicidal Thinking

Suicidal ideation often emerges subtly, rarely announcing itself with overt or dramatic signs. For many men, it starts as a hushed murmur of despair, expressed through thoughts that might echo quietly in their minds, such as:

- "I wish I wouldn't wake up."
- "I just want everything to stop."
- "Everyone would be better off without me."

These expressions of despair are typically passive; they reflect a deep yearning for escape from emotional turmoil rather than indicating immediate plans or intentions to harm oneself. This longing arises from an overwhelming desire for relief from the suffocating pain that can feel insurmountable. Unfortunately, such thoughts frequently go unnoticed, not only by those around them but often by the individuals themselves who are wrestling with these feelings.

When passive suicidal ideation is ignored or dismissed, there's a risk that it can escalate into active ideation, where the desire for escape transforms into concrete plans. This transition can happen with alarming speed, particularly among men who may not feel empowered to express their vulnerabilities. Cultural expectations often discourage open discussions about mental health struggles, leading many to suffer in silence. As a result, there are seldom visible warning signs or gradual build-ups of distress; instead, there is a profound silence that can unexpectedly culminate in tragic outcomes, leaving loved ones reeling from the sudden absence of someone they cared for.

Recognising and addressing these whispers of despair is vital. Open, honest conversations about mental health can create an environment where individuals feel safe to share their struggles, potentially averting a progression from passive thoughts to active plans.

The Intersectional Realities of Suicide

It is essential to recognise that the challenges faced by men are not uniform; rather, they are shaped by a complex interplay of identity and societal factors. Understanding these nuances is vital for fostering meaningful discussions about their experiences, particularly in the context of mental health and well-being.

- Black and Brown Men: These individuals often confront systemic racism that manifests in various aspects of life, including employment, education, and the criminal justice system. Cultural marginalisation can leave them feeling that their experiences are invalidated, leading to a profound sense of isolation. Additionally, biases within healthcare systems frequently mean that their pain and suffering are overlooked or misdiagnosed, further exacerbating mental health challenges.

- Gay and Bisexual Men: Navigating life as a gay or bisexual man can mean facing a landscape riddled with rejection and homophobia. This can start from a young age and perpetuate feelings of shame and internal conflict. Unfortunately, these feelings can be magnified within their own communities, where adherence to traditional masculinity can lead to additional marginalisation. Many experience a lifelong struggle to find acceptance and love, which can deeply impact their mental well-being.

- Trans Men: The journey for trans men is fraught with violence, discrimination, and social erasure. High rates of hate crimes and workplace discrimination create an atmosphere of fear and anxiety, complicating their pursuit of mental health. The lack of visibility and understanding in society often means their struggles are rendered invisible, leading to increased risks of depression and suicide.

- Working-Class Men: Globalisation and economic restructuring have profoundly affected working-class

135

men, often leading to job instability and financial insecurity. As traditional forms of masculinity are tied to economic provision, this upheaval can trigger a crisis of identity, eroding self-esteem and leading to feelings of helplessness. The societal implications of these economic changes can foster a sense of disenfranchisement that is difficult to overcome.

- Disabled Men, Immigrants, Refugees, and Veterans: These groups often navigate the intersectionality of various social challenges. Disabled men may face both physical limitations and societal stigma, while immigrants and refugees often encounter xenophobia and cultural alienation. Veterans grapple with the traumas of combat and the challenges of reintegration into civilian life. These overlapping pressures can lead to feelings of neglect and abandonment by the systems meant to support them, resulting in compounded mental health issues.

In any discussion of male suicide, it is crucial to consider these intersecting pressures and the rich tapestry of experiences that contribute to an individual's mental health journey. The pain that many men carry is not solely emotional; it is deeply rooted in the fabric of social, economic, political, and historical realities that shape their lives. Acknowledging these complexities is essential for creating effective support systems and interventions that truly address their needs.

Gentle Prompts for Self-Reflection

Understanding One's Internal Landscape: A Path to Healing

Gaining insight into one's internal emotional landscape is crucial for the journey toward healing and self-discovery. Below are thoughtfully crafted prompts designed to encourage deep self-reflection and facilitate a more profound understanding of our personal experiences.

Silent Struggle

- Connection and Authenticity: When was the last time someone truly checked in on me, pausing to listen for an authentic response rather than offering a quick "How are you?" What feelings arose from that interaction?
- Embodied Pain: What physical sensations or reactions do I experience in my body when I try to articulate my deepest pain? Do I feel tension in my chest, a lump in my throat, or heaviness in my limbs?
- The Weight of Silence: What kind of silence have I been carrying within me? Is it a silence that protects me, one that reflects my exhaustion, or perhaps a silence shrouded in feelings of shame and isolation?

Suicidal Thinking (Handled Gently)

- Identifying Passive Thoughts: Have I faced moments of passive thoughts emerging, such as "I wish I could disappear" or "I don't feel like waking up"? What specific life circumstances or emotional events triggered these feelings during those times?
- Emotions in Preceding Moments: What emotional states often precede these troubling thoughts? Do I typically feel overwhelmed by grief, engulfed in shame, haunted by a sense of failure, or trapped in loneliness?
- Fear of Judgment: If I could express my struggles without any fear of judgment or repercussions, what specific thoughts and feelings would I want to share with the world?

Masked Emotions

- Social Facades: How do I hide my pain in social situations? Do I turn to humour, throw myself into intense work, exhibit anger, withdraw from interaction, or simply pretend to be okay when I'm struggling inside?

- Subtle Signals: What silent signals or signs do I emit when I am in distress, even if these cues go unnoticed by those around me? Are there subtle changes in my demeanour or body language that indicate my internal struggle?
- Surviving with a Smile: Can I recall instances when I forced a smile just to make it through another day, masking my true emotions for the sake of others or to fulfil certain expectations?

Identity & Isolation

- Invisible Aspects of Self: What aspects of my identity feel neglected or invisible to those around me, including my closest companions? Are there parts of me that I've hidden away, fearing they won't be accepted?
- Expectations of Strength: Who in my life expects me to always be the "strong one"? What specific pressures come with that expectation, and how does it affect my sense of self-worth and vulnerability?
- Contradictory Roles: In what ways have I been pushed into roles that clash with my authentic feelings? How do these expectations contribute to my internal conflict and sense of disconnection?

Worth & Connection

- Asking for Help: If I genuinely believed that I was not a burden to others, how would my approach to seeking help change? Would I feel more empowered to express my needs freely?
- Supportive Presence: What types of presence or affirmations have helped me during my most challenging moments in the past? Who offered genuine compassion and a listening ear when I needed it most?
- Reaching Out: If I were certain that someone would listen without rushing to "fix" my problems, who would

be the person I'd choose to reach out to in times of distress?

Survival to Staying

- Moments of Despair: In those desperate moments when I contemplated giving up, what specific reasons or goals compelled me to choose life? Were there particular thoughts, memories, or aspirations that sparked hope within me?
- Fleeting Moments of Relief: What has provided me, even if just for brief moments with peace, a sense of connection, or relief from my struggles? Are there activities, people, or places that evoke a sense of calm?
- Making Staying Attainable: If I consider that choosing to stay is still an option, what changes or adjustments in my life would make that choice feel more viable? Are there actionable steps I can take or support systems I can lean on to make this path more attainable?

Exploring these prompts can lead to increased self-awareness, deeper understanding, and ultimately, a broader perspective on one's journey toward healing.

Bonus Coaching Reframe:

"Perhaps I don't want to die. Perhaps I just don't know how to live in a world that never taught me how."

This shift in perspective has the potential to be life-saving. It highlights the truth that men do not inherently need fixing; rather, they need to be seen, heard, and supported. It's crucial to remind them that their silence is not a sign of weakness, but rather a reflection of their resilience in a world that often overlooks their struggles. They are not alone in their battles, and it is vital for them to understand that they can share their experiences without fear of judgment. Building connections and fostering open dialogue can empower them to navigate their journeys together, finding strength in vulnerability and solidarity.

"Your story isn't over just because you can't see the next chapter yet. Sometimes, survival is the bravest thing a man can do and tomorrow might be the day everything begins to shift."

Chapter 10

The Language of Silence - Why So Many Men Can't Name What They Feel

For many men, the act of expressing emotions can feel akin to attempting to communicate in a foreign language that they were never taught. Their emotional landscapes are often rich, nuanced, and complex, yet they frequently find themselves grappling with the inability to articulate these deep-seated feelings due to a limited emotional vocabulary. This predicament is not simply a matter of personal struggle; it is a consequence of the societal norms that have, from an early age, guided them away from introspection and emotional exploration. Instead, these norms often direct their focus toward functionality, practicality, and stoicism, reinforcing an unhealthy relationship with their emotions.

Messages such as "toughen up" and "man up" replace opportunities for tender exploration of sadness and vulnerability. These directives discourage men from articulating their fears and doubts, prompting them to suppress their feelings in silence. Consequently, we observe a generation of men who have been conditioned to transmute their emotions into actions: sadness morphs into silence, shame manifests as irritation or anger, longing drives them to over perform in various aspects of life, and vulnerability is often transformed into avoidance or numbing behaviour's.

This emotional repression is neither a personal failing nor a sign of weakness; it is a systemic issue deeply embedded within cultural narratives that elevate strength while dismissing the importance of emotional expression and sensitivity. The conditioning often begins in boyhood, with lessons imparted through a myriad of channels, parents, teachers, peers, and even well-meaning role models who may unintentionally reinforce these harmful beliefs. The communication of these lessons can be subtle yet pervasively influential, as boys learn that their feelings are liabilities and that silence is equated with masculinity.

In this chapter, we will embark on a thorough exploration of the intricate layers of emotional illiteracy, examining its origins in cultural history and its manifestations in adult life. We will delve into how societal pressures create barriers to emotional expression and understanding, and we will highlight the neuroscience behind emotional shutdown, a survival mechanism that, while adaptive in certain contexts, ultimately hinders emotional growth.

Throughout our journey, we will share poignant stories from men who have navigated this difficult path, offering insights and reflections that shed light on their experiences. In addition, we will provide practical tools and strategies designed to cultivate emotional fluency, enabling individuals to break free from damaging patterns. By unlearning the restrictive beliefs surrounding masculinity and embracing a broader emotional vocabulary, we hope to foster a healthier and more compassionate understanding of what it means to truly connect with one's emotions. Together, we will piece by piece construct a framework that encourages emotional expression and nurtures genuine connections with ourselves and others.

Emotional Illiteracy: The Epidemic No One Talks About

Being emotionally illiterate does not necessarily mean one lacks the capacity to feel; rather, it highlights a deficiency in safe and constructive methods for understanding and expressing those feelings. This issue is particularly pronounced among men, who often find themselves constrained by a complex web of unspoken societal rules and expectations regarding emotional expression:

- Don't cry — it's perceived as a sign of weakness and vulnerability.

142

- Don't talk too much – it suggests neediness and dependency.
- Don't admit fear – it's regarded as unmanly and a departure from traditional masculinity.

When young boys internalise the belief that showing emotions, whether through tears or open conversation, will expose them to ridicule or punishment, they learn to suppress these feelings as a means of self-preservation. This learned behaviour acts as a survival mechanism, but over time, it results in a profound disconnection from their emotional selves.

For example, instead of being able to articulate feelings such as shame, a boy might choose to retreat into silence, believing that any expression of vulnerability could lead to mockery. In circumstances where anxiety arises, he may resort to overcompensation, seeking excessive control in various aspects of his life. Importantly, the original emotions do not simply dissipate; they become buried under layers of unresolved feelings, mislabelled, or transformed into reactions that are often unrecognizable.

This cycle contributes to a hidden epidemic: many men navigate through life shouldering the burdens of their emotional histories, yet they lack the vocabulary and frameworks to articulate their experiences and struggles effectively. They often feel isolated, grappling with emotions that remain unprocessed and unshared. This emotional disconnect not only affects their mental health but also influences their relationships with others, compromising their ability to connect on a deeper level. Ultimately, fostering emotional literacy is crucial for breaking this cycle and enabling men to engage with their feelings in a healthy, constructive manner.

The Brain's Role in Emotional Shutdown

Scientific research has increasingly supported the intuition that many men have long sensed emotional suppression is not solely a psychological issue; it is deeply rooted in neurological processes. When individuals experience trauma or frequent emotional invalidation, the amygdala, which acts as the brain's alarm system, becomes hyperactive. This heightened state often results in a heightened sensitivity to perceived threats. In contrast, the prefrontal cortex, responsible for higher-order functions such as logic, language, and emotional regulation becomes less active or even temporarily incapacitated.

This neural disconnect elucidates why many men in states of emotional distress may express confusion with statements like, "I don't know what I'm feeling." Such statements should not be misconstrued as avoidance or lack of awareness; rather, they reflect a brain entrenched in survival mode, overwhelmed by emotional demands it struggles to process.

Moreover, this cycle of chronic emotional invalidation conditions the nervous system to perceive emotional expression as a potential threat, reinforcing a behavioural pattern where even the mere thought of expressing vulnerability triggers an automatic shutdown response. As these reactions become ingrained, neural pathways are formed that link feelings of safety to silence, essentially creating an emotional cage.

However, there is a silver lining: the human brain possesses a remarkable capacity for neuroplasticity, meaning it can rewire itself. By consistently engaging in practices that promote emotional awareness and expression, such as therapy, journaling, mindfulness, and embodied work these rigid patterns can be softened and redesigned. This journey allows for the fostering of an environment that encourages safety, articulate expression, and authentic connections.

By embarking on a path toward emotional fluency, men can begin to reclaim their personal narratives. They can find profound strength in vulnerability, ultimately nurturing deeper and more meaningful connections with themselves and others. This transformative process not only enhances individual well-being but also enriches interpersonal relationships, creating a ripple effect that extends to families, communities, and beyond.

How Emotional Illiteracy Impacts Daily Life

The inability to identify or articulate emotions extends far beyond an individual's internal state; it significantly impacts various facets of life, including relationships, parenting, friendships, workplace dynamics, and overall health. When individuals lack emotional literacy, the capacity to recognise, understand, and express feelings they often face considerable challenges in effectively navigating their environments. These challenges can manifest in several notable ways:

- Explosive Anger: Intense anger frequently serves as a superficial emotional response that masks deeper feelings of grief, fear, or even disappointment. This explosive reaction not only alienates loved ones but can also escalate conflicts to a point where resolution becomes increasingly difficult. Often, those who lash out may not even fully understand the root causes of their anger, leading to cycles of misunderstanding and hurt.

- Emotional Withdrawal: When confronted with conflict, many individuals may choose to disengage emotionally, retreating from discussions or ignoring pressing issues that require resolution. This withdrawal creates a communication void, which can give rise to significant misunderstandings and exacerbate conflicts, preventing the development of healthy, constructive dialogue.

- Struggles to Articulate Needs: Numerous people find it challenging to articulate their needs, aspirations, or boundaries clearly and confidently. This ineffectiveness in communication can breed feelings of frustration and resentment in both personal and professional relationships, as unexpressed needs often lead to unmet expectations and growing dissatisfaction.

- Connecting with Children: For parents, a lack of emotional literacy can hinder their ability to connect with their children on an essential emotional level. This disconnection can lead to feelings of alienation for both the parent and child, impairing the development of a secure attachment that is crucial for a child's emotional well-being and future relationships.

- Shutdown Responses: In situations that require intimacy or confrontation, some individuals may resort to emotional shutdowns as a coping mechanism. This avoidance creates significant barriers to forming authentic relationships, as genuine connection necessitates vulnerability and openness, which they may fear or misunderstand.

- Shame and Sensitivity: The societal stigma surrounding emotions often characterised by phrases like "feeling too much" or "being too sensitive" can induce a sense of shame in individuals. As a result, they may suppress their emotional experiences rather than acknowledge and understand them. This suppression not only deprives them of personal insight but also stunts their emotional growth and well-being.

Ultimately, relationships often deteriorate not due to a lack of love or affection, but because of an insufficient emotional vocabulary. Take, for example, many men who long for emotional closeness yet struggle to initiate or maintain such connections. They may feel lost in their attempts to express themselves, leading to frustration and a sense of isolation. By fostering emotional literacy, individuals can create healthier connections and navigate their personal and professional relationships with greater empathy and understanding.

Relearning the Emotional Alphabet

The encouraging aspect of emotional literacy is that it is indeed a skill that can be developed over time, regardless of one's past experiences with emotions. No matter how long someone has lived disconnected from their feelings, the possibility for reconnection is available at any moment. This transformative process generally consists of several key steps:

Step One: Permission

The journey begins with self-acceptance, which is crucial for fostering emotional literacy. Grant yourself the permission to feel and express emotions without the weight of judgment. It's perfectly valid to acknowledge feelings of uncertainty; for instance, saying, "I feel something, but I'm not sure what it is," represents a significant and courageous first step toward cultivating emotional awareness. This acknowledgment allows individuals to create a safe space for exploration, free from self-criticism.

Step Two: Awareness

Developing awareness involves tuning in to the physical sensations that often accompany emotional experiences. Emotions frequently manifest in the body long before they are articulated in words. Being mindful of bodily signals, such as tightness in the chest, gastrointestinal discomfort, tension in the shoulders, or a lump in the throat can serve as valuable indicators of what you may be feeling. Engaging in practices like mindfulness meditation or body scanning can enhance this awareness, helping you recognise how emotions are expressed physically.

Step Three: Vocabulary Building

A key aspect of emotional literacy is expanding your emotional vocabulary. Utilising tools such as a "feeling wheel" or an emotion chart can help refine your ability to articulate your feelings with greater precision. Rather than broadly categorising emotions as "stressed," take the time to explore more specific terms, like "overwhelmed," "irritated," "frustrated," or "guilty." This nuanced understanding not only enhances self-awareness but also improves communication with others, allowing you to express your emotions more clearly and effectively.

Step Four: Expression Practice

Engaging in intentional practices that promote emotional expression is vital in building emotional literacy. This can take many forms, such as having open and honest conversations with trusted friends or family members, journaling your thoughts and feelings, or using voice memos to articulate what you're experiencing. Speaking your emotions aloud, whether in conversation or in solitude serves as valuable practice that solidifies your emotional fluency. Creating art, music, or other forms of creative expression can also facilitate the release and understanding of your emotions.

Step Five: Support and Re-parenting

Reflecting on the words and affirmations you needed to hear as a child is a crucial step in nurturing emotional growth. Begin practicing these affirmations aloud to yourself, fostering a sense of self-compassion and acceptance. Creating an emotionally safe environment involves nurturing that inner child and becoming the supportive figure you may have lacked in your formative years. This process not only strengthens your emotional resilience but also builds a foundation for healthier emotional connections with yourself and others.

By diligently working through these steps, individuals can develop a deeper understanding and connection to their emotional landscape, ultimately leading to a more fulfilling and authentic life.

Sidebar: The Neuroscience of Healing

Scientific research highlights the transformative role of labelling and discussing emotions, a process that significantly strengthens the neural connections between the brain's emotional and language centres. By explicitly identifying and articulating our feelings, we enhance our ability to regulate mood, engage in effective communication, and nurture more profound connections with others.

For instance, advanced MRI studies reveal that when individuals label their emotions, there is a notable decrease in activity within the amygdala, the brain region primarily responsible for processing fear and distressing emotional responses. This reduction in amygdala activation is particularly important, as it allows individuals to respond to emotional stimuli in a more measured way. Concurrently, the prefrontal cortex, which is crucial for rational thought and decision-making, shows heightened activity in these moments. This activation creates a dual impact: not only does it help to mitigate fear and anxiety, but it also promotes a clearer, more rational perspective on emotional experiences.

The implications of this enhanced emotional literacy extend beyond individual well-being; it plays a critical role in improving interpersonal relationships. As we become more adept at identifying and articulating our emotions, we cultivate empathy and understanding in our interactions with others. This process fosters deeper emotional connections and creates healthier communication patterns. Ultimately, the ability to label emotions contributes significantly to overall mental well-being and cognitive resilience, equipping individuals with the tools necessary to navigate life's challenges with greater ease and clarity.

Gentle Prompts to Explore Emotional Fluency

1. Naming Emotions

- What am I feeling in this moment? Take a deliberate pause and allow yourself to connect with your current emotional state. Engage in a self-inquiry process: Is your heart feeling light with joy, heavy with sadness, or perhaps weighed down by anxiety? Try to dissect the emotion further, do you sense a flutter of excitement mingled with apprehension, or a lingering melancholy that won't quite dissipate?

- Have I felt this emotion before? Reflect on the tapestry of your past experiences to identify moments that may have triggered similar feelings. Think about specific events, relationships, or situations that resonated with this emotional response was it a personal loss, a significant life change, or a moment of triumph? How did you handle those feelings then?

- If my feeling had a colour or texture, what would it be? Visualise your emotions as vibrant images or tangible sensations. Picture the brightness of a sunflower for joy or the coolness of a foggy morning for sadness. Is your feeling represented by warm, inviting tones, or do darker, subdued shades come to mind? Consider the textures as well, does your emotion feel smooth and flowing, or jagged and burdensome?

2. Body Awareness

- Where do I feel tension right now? Gently conduct a body scan, moving your attention from your head to your toes. Are you holding tension in your shoulders, perhaps clenched tightly in your jaw, or is your back protesting with discomfort? Pay close attention to how these physical sensations correlate with your emotional state.

- What changes in my body when I suppress emotions? Observe the physical reactions that accompany emotional suppression. Do you notice a tightening of your chest, an acceleration of your heartbeat, or changes in your breathing patterns? Recognising these signals can help you understand the impact of emotional suppression on your overall wellbeing.

- When did I last feel physically at ease? Take a moment to recall a time when you felt completely relaxed and at peace, perhaps it was a leisurely afternoon spent in nature or a cosy evening at home. Reflect on the circumstances that allowed you to unwind and think about actionable ways you can recreate that calming environment in your current life.

3. Connection and Expression

- Who do I feel safe being vulnerable with? Identify the individuals you trust wholeheartedly to share your inner thoughts and emotions, without fear of judgment or backlash. Consider what attributes, such as empathy, understanding, and non-judgment make these relationships feel supportive and nurturing.

- What do I fear will happen if I speak my truth? Acknowledge any anxieties or concerns that arise when you consider being vulnerable and honest. Contemplate your fears: Are you apprehensive about risking rejection, facing conflict, or losing someone's approval? Understanding these fears can empower you to address them more effectively.

- How would I support a friend feeling the way I do? Imagine approaching a friend who is experiencing emotions similar to yours. How would you comfort and encourage them? Allow that compassion to flow towards yourself, recognising that you deserve the same kindness and understanding in your moments of struggle.

4. Vocabulary Building

- What words do I use repeatedly for emotions? Reflect on the vocabulary you typically use to describe your feelings. Are there particular words, such as "happy," "angry," or "sad," that come up often? Consider how these words resonate with you and the emotional nuances they capture.

- What words feel unfamiliar or inaccessible? Challenge yourself to expand your emotional lexicon by exploring words that may feel out of reach or hard to articulate. Think about emotions like "discontent," "nostalgia," or "ennui." Delve into these unfamiliar terms and allow yourself the opportunity to articulate nuanced feelings.

151

- What might I be feeling beneath anger? Recognise that anger often serves as a protective shield for deeper emotions, such as hurt, fear, or disappointment. Take the time to explore what lies beneath your anger, what underlying issues might you be facing? Unpacking these feelings can lead to greater emotional clarity and healing.

5. Re-parenting Practice

- What words did I need to hear when I was younger? Connect with your inner child by recalling the affirming phrases and supportive expressions you longed for during formative years. Reflect on how these words might have shaped your emotional landscape if you had received them. What missing affirmations can you offer yourself now?

- What can I say to myself today to offer comfort? Consider nurturing language that you can actively use in times of distress. Craft personal affirmations or comforting statements that resonate with you, how can you build emotional resilience through intentional self-talk?

- What does "emotional safety" look like to me now? Visualise and articulate what it means to feel emotionally safe in your present life. Delve into the relationships and environments that foster this sense of security. What qualities do they embody, and how can you cultivate more of that emotional safety in your current circumstances?

Final Reframe

"Emotional fluency isn't about achieving perfection; it's about embracing honesty and authenticity in our feelings and expressions. Recognise that the journey toward emotional understanding is a deeply personal one, unique to each individual. You don't need to possess all the right words or perfectly formulated answers to begin the process. The most crucial step is to take that first leap toward self-expression, even if it feels awkward or unrefined at times.

Each small step you take in articulating your truth, no matter how messy or imperfect, is a meaningful return to your authentic self. It's important to understand that every emotion you experience, whether joy, sadness, frustration, or vulnerability, holds significance and warrants acknowledgment. Allow this insight to act as your permission slip: Your feelings are not only valid, but they also deserve to be recognised and shared.

As we embark on this journey together, let's commit to exploring the depths of our emotions, creating an open space where we can speak freely and listen actively. Remember, the process of understanding our emotions is an evolving one, and each moment of vulnerability contributes to our growth. Let's begin this journey afresh with openness, courage, and the knowledge that every step forward matters."

Call to Action:

Pause for a moment and take a deep breath. Now, think of one specific feeling you've been holding back, just one. It might be a feeling of sadness, frustration, joy, or even anxiety. Allow yourself to name it out loud, giving voice to this emotion that has perhaps been tucked away for too long. Listen to the sound of your own voice as you articulate this feeling. By doing this, you not only acknowledge its presence, but you also begin to witness it without judgment. This simple yet powerful act of honesty can serve as a gateway to deeper emotional exploration and understanding, helping you connect with your inner self and fostering a greater awareness of your emotional landscape. Embrace this moment; it may lead to transformative insights about your feelings and experiences.

"The ability to name our emotions is the beginning of healing. Language doesn't just describe our feelings; it gives them permission to exist."

Chapter 11

Smart Enough to Stay Numb

There's a particular trap that many men unwittingly fall into, one that often masquerades as intelligence and rationality. This deceptive allure presents itself as a sign of strength and logical prowess, creating an illusion of safety and control. However, this trap is more commonly known as overthinking, a term that only scratches the surface. Beneath it lies a more insidious mechanism referred to as the Cognitive Exploit.

The Cognitive Exploit functions as a self-hijacking mechanism of the mind. It initiates a loop of logical reasoning so meticulously constructed that it transforms into a psychological prison. This fortress, rather than offering protection, cultivates deep isolation. Men often find themselves not fully engaging with their pain; instead, they navigate around it, lingering in the periphery, avoiding the confrontation of their emotions. While this cognitive strategy might seem practical for a time, shielding them from immediate discomfort, it ultimately leads to complications, as those genuine emotions cannot be evaded indefinitely.

Consider the archetype of "The Man Who Solved Everything (Except Himself)." He emerges as an individual equipped with strategies for every conceivable scenario in life. A master at reading people and predicting outcomes, he plans several steps ahead, making him a desirable ally in high-pressure situations. Friends admire his composed demeanour during crises, and partners often express admiration, saying, "You never open up." Yet, beneath this calm exterior lies an unrelenting battle, a turmoil that frequently goes unseen.

His meticulous preparation often masks a profound fear of life's unpredictability. The Cognitive Exploit adeptly converts this fear into a façade of logical reasoning, transforming emotional pain into compulsive productivity and heartbreak into a dispassionate analytical exercise. The underlying trauma does not simply dissipate; instead, it adopts a new guise, draping itself in the fabric of control and an illusion of mastery over life.

This psychological mechanism is known as cognitive avoidance, a defence strategy whereby individuals utilise reasoning and intellectual analysis to evade genuine emotional experiences. In therapeutic settings, it is common to encounter individuals who articulate insightful understandings of their emotional states without any observable shift in their feelings. A man may confidently assert, "I understand why I respond this way," "I recognise my trauma response," or "I've read extensively about this topic." However, this awareness is not synonymous with genuine emotional engagement.

This understanding is the crux of the Cognitive Exploit: the brain tragically substitutes superficial awareness for profound healing. In counselling practices, we often explore how this emotional bypassing originates from early childhood experiences. Boys frequently receive praise for exhibiting rationality and logic, while their sensitivity is usually dismissed or punished. This leads to the development of men who grapple with their fear through logical constructs rather than emotional expression. While this approach may appear productive at first glance, it manifests as a patterned avoidance, akin to meticulously cleaning one's house to dodge a daunting conversation. On the surface, everything seems orderly, but underneath simmers a chaotic emotional landscape, yearning for authentic expression and healing. The conflict between intellect and emotion continues, highlighting the pressing need for men to confront their inner turmoil rather than circumvent it. Only then can they embark on the path toward true healing and emotional liberation.

Biopsychology: The Logic Shield

The prefrontal cortex, a critical brain region responsible for higher-order functions such as logic, planning, and decision-making, becomes hyperactive among individuals who engage in cognitive exploitation. This hyperactivity is typically triggered by stressors that threaten one's emotional safety, causing the brain to operate in an overdrive state. Concurrently, the limbic system specifically the amygdala, which is pivotal in processing emotions like fear and anxiety remains in a heightened state of vigilance. This interaction forms a damaging feedback loop that can significantly impair emotional well-being.

The process begins when either an external trigger, such as an interpersonal conflict, or an internal cue, such as a negative thought pattern, prompts an individual to perceive a threat to their emotional safety. In response, the brain rapidly transitions into analytical mode as a defence mechanism, striving to pre-emptively navigate overwhelming feelings. Unfortunately, this response circumvents genuine emotional processing, preventing the individual from truly addressing and understanding their emotional state.

This misalignment results in a paradox: although the person may appear composed, articulate, and outwardly functional, beneath the surface lies a potential for emotional upheaval and cognitive disarray. From a bio-psychological viewpoint, research illustrates that cortisol levels remain consistently elevated in men who operate within this high-alert intellectual framework. This chronic state of stress does not manifest as overt panic; instead, it surfaces as a spectrum of physical symptoms, including persistent migraines, insomnia, gastrointestinal issues, and, in severe cases, an emotional or physical breakdown.

While the body may exhibit multiple signs of distress, such as fatigue or chronic pain, the mind often remains ensconced in denial, avoiding an acknowledgement of its own struggles. This discrepancy not only exacerbates the individual's condition but can also lead to a cycle of unresolved emotional turmoil, underscoring the critical need for effective strategies to reconnect

157

with one's emotional experiences and navigate through them healthily.

Emotional Intelligence vs. Emotional Surveillance

Individuals who may present themselves as possessing high emotional intelligence often reveal a different reality through their behaviours. Rather than genuinely engaging with and processing their own emotions, they operate on a framework of emotional surveillance. Their primary focus is on scanning their environment for potential threats, meticulously cataloguing the actions and reactions of those around them. To them, interpersonal interactions resemble a strategic chess game, where each move is calculated and every nuance is analysed with a keen, almost clinical attention to detail.

Yet, when asked a seemingly straightforward question like, "How do you feel right now?", many find themselves at a standstill, struggling to articulate their feelings. This difficulty arises from the intrinsic complexity and unpredictability of emotions, which defy neat categorisation into data points.

Often, these individuals are caught in a loop of emotional monitoring, concentrating more on assessing risk than nurturing genuine connections. They may obsess over their partner's tone of voice, minute changes in body language, or the subtle shifts in mood, all to gauge potential threats rather than fostering intimacy. This behaviour is frequently a manifestation of a trauma response, masquerading as logical and rational assessment. Beneath this facade lies a profound disconnect between themselves and their emotions, intertwined with an underlying sense of anxiety that colours their interactions and hampers their ability to connect authentically with others.

Coaching Insight: Cognitive Traps

From a coaching perspective, men who find themselves trapped in this cognitive loop often voice sentiments like, "I just want to make sense of it," "I don't do feelings," or "What's the solution here?" This pattern indicates a strong inclination towards logic and problem-solving, leading them to gravitate towards strategies that offer clarity and decisive answers, rather than seeking the emotional support that could aid their healing.

However, the journey of healing is seldom linear or straightforward; it's more like a mighty flood, sweeping through one's consciousness with a force that can feel overwhelming and chaotic. Despite one's intellectual capabilities or analytical skills, it is unrealistic to think that these complex emotions can be contained or suppressed indefinitely. They demand to be acknowledged and processed.

Authentic healing involves more than just intellectual engagement; it requires the bravery to confront and embrace the messiness of emotions, joy, pain, anger, and confusion. It calls for a willingness to sit with discomfort and uncertainty instead of rushing toward solutions. This process can lead to deeper self-understanding and resilience, ultimately fostering a more profound sense of connection with oneself and others. Embracing this emotional journey, though challenging, is pivotal in transforming not just the self but also relationships and life experiences.

Cultural Conditioning: Emotion as Error Code

In many upbringing environments, particularly for men, emotions are frequently viewed as a malfunction or a weakness that needs to be corrected. Common phrases like "Toughen up" in response to sadness, "Control yourself" when anger arises, and "Let it go" after feeling hurt serve to frame emotions as obstacles that must be overcome. This societal conditioning encourages individuals to perceive their feelings not as natural human experiences, but as problems that require fixing or eradicating.

As a result, many develop the mindset of highly effective problem-solvers, adept at manoeuvring through challenges while maintaining an exterior of calm and composure. They become skilled at rationalising situations and finding practical solutions, yet this very skill set often erects a barrier to authentic emotional connectivity. This emotional inaccessibility can leave partners and friends feeling distant and misunderstood, as these individuals struggle to express or acknowledge their own feelings, let alone engage with the emotions of others.

One client encapsulated this experience with a poignant revelation: "I thought feelings were what you erased to get to the solution. Turns out, they were the solution." This profound realisation highlights the critical, yet frequently ignored, role emotions play in nurturing genuine connections and facilitating actual resolution. Embracing rather than suppressing emotions can lead to deeper understanding, empathy, and stronger relationships. Acknowledging and expressing feelings, instead of viewing them as hurdles, is essential for personal growth and compelling connections with others.

NHS Pathway Gaps: Masked Emotional Distress

Within the NHS mental health services, a concerning number of men who embody traditional emotional conditioning often go unnoticed, slipping through the cracks of the system. These individuals, conditioned to suppress their feelings from a young age, tend to mask their emotional distress behind a façade of functionality. They manage to hold down stable jobs, pay their bills punctually, and occasionally offer emotional support to colleagues and friends, all while silently spiralling into a state of burnout.

Rather than expressing their struggles through visible chaos or dysfunction, their distress manifests itself in an outwardly competent persona. They might say, "I'm just tired," a statement that belies the profound internal battle they are facing one filled with feelings of existential dread, anxiety, and despair. This careful articulation of their struggles in logical, often composed terms becomes a double-edged sword. Many NHS assessments, which are designed to identify clear indicators of mental illness, overlook these individuals entirely because they do not exhibit traditional signs of being "ill" or dishevelled.

Instead, they present as articulate, capable, and in control, leading clinicians to mistakenly perceive them as emotionally stable. Yet, beneath the surface, they may be eroding under the burden of unprocessed emotions, wrestling with thoughts of inadequacy, disappointment, and loneliness. The dissonance between their outward composure and inner turmoil highlights a critical gap in mental health care, where the nuanced needs of men conditioned to prioritise functionality may be inadequately addressed or simply ignored. This silent suffering underscores the necessity for a more comprehensive understanding of mental health that acknowledges and validates the diverse expressions of distress.

The Male Empath Dilemma

Interestingly, some individuals who exploit cognitive dynamics display a remarkable degree of empathy, allowing them to intuitively grasp the emotions of those around them. However, rather than using this empathy to cultivate authentic relationships, they often implement it as a strategic tool to expertly navigate their social environments. This leads to a preference for observation over genuine engagement, interpretation over personal revelation, and a focus on adaptation rather than the courage to vocalise their own needs and feelings.

This behaviour resonates with a concept in neuro-linguistic programming (NLP) known as hyper-calibration. In this adaptive strategy, individuals adeptly adjust their responses and behaviour based on the emotional cues of others, all while suppressing or disregarding their own feelings. Externally, their body language may project warmth and approachability, characterised by gestures such as nodding, maintaining eye contact, and assuming a relaxed posture. However, beneath this facade, their internal emotional state often remains stagnant and unexpressed, resulting in a stark dissonance between their outward demeanour and their inner emotional reality. This disconnect not only affects their well-being but can also complicate their interactions, leaving them feeling isolated despite their apparent sociability.

Therapeutic Techniques for Breaking the Loop

- Somatic Interrupts: When you notice yourself spiralling into an overactive thought process, take a moment to pause. Identify and name three physical sensations you are experiencing in your body. This technique serves to interrupt the relentless logic loop and reconnect you with your embodied experience.

- Emotion Mapping: After a recent event, write a paragraph detailing the circumstances. Highlight objective facts in blue and underline your emotional responses in red. If the majority of your writing appears blue, take a moment to question why you might be avoiding the emotional aspects of the experience.

- Vulnerability Vocabulary: Create a personal catalogue of emotional words that resonate with you. Use this vocabulary to articulate your current emotional state, express how you truly feel with specific terms, like "I feel disrespected," rather than generalizations such as "I feel off."

- Core Belief Inquiry: Ask yourself, "What would happen if I didn't understand this perfectly?" This question encourages exploration into the underlying fears that drive the need for rigid logic and control.

- Compassionate Exposure: Make it a daily practice to reveal one emotional truth about yourself. Start with small admissions, like "I'm disappointed" or "I felt hurt," and gradually build the courage to express deeper emotions.

- Somatic Anchoring: Take note of how your body reacts in moments of safety, whether your breathing slows or your shoulders relax. Create a physical anchor, such as squeezing your fist, touching your heart, or placing a hand on your stomach, to reinforce this feeling of safety as an embodied experience, rather than just an abstract concept.

- Mirror Statements: Practice vocalizing emotional truths in front of a mirror. For example, say, "I am afraid of being left." Repeat this statement until it resonates as part of your identity, helping to integrate your feelings into your self-perception.

Gentle Prompts – The Cognitive Exploit

- What intellectual understandings have I grasped but still haven't processed on an emotional level?
- What would it mean to sit with discomfort without the compulsion to resolve it immediately?
- How did I learn that prioritizing logic is safer than embracing vulnerability?
- Who do I become when I allow myself to simply exist without the need to rationalize everything?
- What emotional truths am I evading while cloaked in the guise of clarity?
- What messages have I internalized regarding the implications of being 'smart'?
- Who benefits when I choose silence over self-expression?

Final Reframe

You are not flawed for thinking deeply or questioning your emotions. Your search for understanding does not make you wrong or inadequate. However, it's essential to recognise that the intellect has its limits; true healing often arrives through a process of surrender, not to weakness, but to a sense of wholeness.

You are not merely an intricate system to optimise; you are a multifaceted soul deserving of compassion and understanding. Allow yourself to experience the flood of emotions, let the confusion breathe and give voice to the pain you feel. Real strength lies not in relentlessly solving every problem but in allowing yourself to be truly seen, especially by yourself. There's no need to make sense of every feeling; sometimes, the most profound step is simply to feel.

Chapter 12

Clocked in, Checked Out — Men's Mental Health at Work

He clocks in to the familiar hum of machinery and the clatter of tools, shaking off the exhaustion that clings to him like a second skin. As he pulls on his work boots, he also dons a mask more convincing than any safety gear found on the site. He's known as the reliable one, the quiet workhorse who goes about his day with unwavering determination. He never complains, never sheds a tear, and is often regarded as someone who can withstand immense pressure without faltering.

Yet, beneath this hardened exterior lies a fragile mind, battling silent storms that no one sees. The unwavering façade he presents to the world is a product of years spent navigating a culture that equates vulnerability with weakness.

This is the untold truth of men's mental health in the workplace: behind the stoic veneer, many are wrestling with deep-seated struggles that threaten their very wellbeing. The systems in place, which demand exceptional strength and resilience, simultaneously punish any hint of emotional fragility. In boardrooms filled with ambition and on construction sites echoing with labour, the prevailing narrative is clear: be strong, be silent, and above all, be perpetually productive. But such expectations come with a heavy price, extracting a toll on their mental health and diminishing their humanity.

As he moves through his day, performing mundane tasks and meeting deadlines, the invisible weight of expectations presses down on him. Each unspoken worry, each suppressed emotion adds to the burden, creating a chasm between who he is and who he feels he must be. In the pursuit of relentless productivity, are these men losing touch with themselves? And at what cost to their emotional and psychological wellbeing?

Capitalism's Silent Trade-Off: Productivity Over Personhood

Modern work culture, driven by the relentless demands of capitalism, centres on output, efficiency, and an unwavering expectation of consistency. For men, this societal narrative is deeply ingrained, suggesting that their worth is not based on who they are as individuals, but rather on what they can produce. From an early age, this ideology becomes a form of psychological conditioning, where boys are frequently taught to evaluate their self-worth through external metrics, grades, trophies, salaries, and social status. As they transition into adulthood, their self-esteem often morphs from an internal compass reflecting their values and passions into a transactional measure directly linked to their productivity and success in the workplace.

Consequently, when employment becomes precarious or comes to an abrupt halt, it can trigger a profound crisis in their sense of identity and purpose. For many men, the stakes feel insurmountable, as their job titles and professional achievements have come to define them. This disconnect can lead to a cascade of emotional struggles; the male nervous system, traditionally conditioned to suppress emotions, turns into a vessel for chronic stress and anxiety. Feelings of anxiety may surface as an unrelenting sense of urgency, while symptoms of depression are often mischaracterized as mere fatigue. Panic attacks can be dismissed as simple heartburn, rather than recognised as a serious emotional response.

From a bio-psychological perspective, the sympathetic nervous system, which orchestrates the body's fight-or-flight response, becomes chronically overstimulated. In contrast, the parasympathetic functions responsible for promoting rest, digestion, and emotional balance become severely compromised. As a result, many men find themselves trapped in a perpetual state of overdrive where their minds are constantly racing. Society, however, often labels this relentless drive as "ambition," failing to recognise the detrimental toll it takes on mental health.

The consequences can be dire. This unchecked chase for productivity and status often culminates in severe physical and psychological conditions, including illness, burnout, or complete emotional exhaustion. This cycle perpetuates a damaging stereotype that equates masculinity with stoicism and relentless work, leaving many men feeling isolated in their struggles and in desperate need of an alternative narrative that values holistic well-being over mere output.

When Masculinity Isn't the Only Mask

It is essential to understand that not all men face the same challenges within their work environments. The experience of masculinity is multifaceted, often intersecting with factors such as race, class, neurodivergence, disability, and sexuality. These intersections can amplify the pressures to perform at work, conform to societal expectations, and navigate the complex dynamics of simply surviving in a demanding atmosphere.

Take, for example, Black men in predominantly white workplaces. They frequently confront the expectation to over-compensate and over-perform, driven by both the desire to prove their worth and the weight of societal stereotypes. The stereotype of the "angry Black man" often forces them to suppress their emotions, striving for an unattainable standard of perfectionism in their behaviours. This overwhelming pressure means that even a minor misstep can put their job security at risk and threaten their dignity or sense of justice in the workplace.

Similarly, working-class men often grow up embracing the cultural mantra of "just get on with it," which instils a deep-seated stoicism that shapes their primary coping mechanism. In labour-intensive and trades-related jobs, emotional literacy is seldom cultivated or valued, leading to a silent struggle with burnout. These men may feel trapped, unable to articulate their emotional needs, resulting in mental and physical exhaustion that goes unnoticed and unaddressed.

Autistic men, too, face unique challenges in the workplace. Many engage in masking behaviour's, adapting their natural expressions and reactions to conform to neurotypical social norms. This constant performance not only drains their cognitive and emotional resources but can also be deeply harmful over time. The necessity of self-monitoring and continual adjustments can lead to emotional burnout, increased vulnerability to meltdowns, and shutdowns, which can be misinterpreted by colleagues and supervisors as mere disengagement or lack of competence.

Furthermore, gay and queer men navigating heteronormative workspaces often find themselves engaging in code-switching, downplaying their identities or striving for exceptional performance to create a sense of safety. The persistent fear of facing homophobia, exclusion, or microaggressions complicates their professional journey, making it difficult for them to pursue a sense of psychological safety and acceptance in their environments.

Male caregivers, whether responsible for children, ageing parents, or disabled partners, bear an often invisible burden of emotional labour in addition to their full-time careers. This dual responsibility frequently goes unrecognised in the workplace, leaving them without the support or acknowledgment they rightfully need and deserve.

Ultimately, burnout transcends the mere tally of hours worked; it encompasses the emotional masks that men feel pressured to wear in order to be recognised as "enough." These silent struggles are not just personal experiences; they underscore a critical need for systemic change in workplace culture and mental health support. Addressing these issues could pave the way for healthier, more inclusive, and ultimately more productive work environments for all.

The Strong Colleague Myth

Expressions such as "He's got it together," "He never lets anything get to him," and "He just keeps going" may initially appear to be compliments, yet they often serve as a eulogy in disguise. This reflects a concerning cultural myth surrounding the idea of the strong male colleague, where emotional detachment is glorified and emotional suppression is erroneously valorised. This mindset rewards men who internalise stress through means like working excessively long hours, taking on excessive workloads, and masking their vulnerability, all while they quietly endure the crippling weight of their struggles.

Men who subscribe to this damaging narrative frequently avoid taking mental health days, prioritising the false ideal of relentless productivity over their own well-being. In doing so, they are often faced with severe health crises, including heart attacks and other stress-related conditions. Instead of seeking the therapeutic support they desperately need to cope with their mental and emotional challenges, many men find themselves attending the funerals of colleagues who have succumbed to this hidden suffering. This tragic trend becomes particularly urgent when we consider that men are statistically more likely to die by suicide while in full-time employment, their pain concealed beneath the societal pressure to perform and maintain an image of invulnerability.

Consequently, many men suppress their emotions and isolate themselves from others, maintaining a facade of strength even when dealing with debilitating burnout and mental exhaustion. This pervasive silence around mental health issues not only impacts individual lives but creates a toxic work culture where vulnerability is misconstrued as weakness.

It is crucial to redefine resilience in this context; it should not be seen as the absence of pain or challenge, but rather as the active presence of recovery and the courage to face one's struggles openly. Acknowledging this critical distinction is essential for fostering healthier workplace environments where vulnerability is embraced as an integral part of the human experience, encouraging individuals to seek help, share their burdens, and ultimately thrive both personally and professionally. By shifting this narrative, we have the potential to create a support system that prioritises well-being and acknowledges the complexities of emotional health, benefiting both individuals and organisations as a whole.

Executive Burnout & the Fall from Identity

In high-performance roles, the threat of what is termed high-performance collapse is a daunting reality. Executives, entrepreneurs, and leaders often find themselves particularly vulnerable, as their professional titles become entwined with their sense of self. This deep integration means that when they face significant life changes, such as redundancy, job loss, or the transition into retirement the repercussions extend far beyond financial instability; they confront a profound existential crisis that shakes the foundations of their identity.

Biopsychology sheds light on this phenomenon through the lens of role-based ego fusion, a concept that highlights how deeply individuals can become connected to their occupational identities. The prefrontal cortex, a critical area of the brain responsible for planning, decision-making, and self-perception, can become heavily burdened by this identification. Consequently, when these high-performing individuals experience an abrupt loss of their roles, they are often thrust into a state of disorientation and emotional turmoil. This can manifest as depression or, in more severe cases, suicidal ideation.

In the absence of structured emotional outlets, many of these individuals resort to unhealthy coping strategies. Overwork becomes a way to fill the void left by the loss of identity, while alcohol consumption serves as a temporary escape from overwhelming feelings. Social isolation further compounds the issue, creating a cycle of loneliness and despair. Therapy, which could provide essential support, is often stigmatised and perceived as a sign of weakness, leading many to believe that seeking help might jeopardise their careers or how they are perceived by peers.

The costs of this cycle are extensive and tragic. Families may become fractured as the individual withdraws into themselves, and their physical health can deteriorate due to stress and neglect. Ultimately, a pervasive sense of lost purpose takes hold, leaving these high achievers feeling empty and disconnected from their former selves.

True strength, it turns out, is not merely defined by the accolades one accumulates or the ventures one builds, but by the capacity to endure and navigate through loss. It is within the moments of vulnerability, the courage to confront uncomfortable realities, that genuine resilience is forged. Embracing these challenges can lead not only to personal growth but also to a richer understanding of oneself beyond professional titles and achievements.

The Tradesman's Trauma: Silent Stress in Blue-Collar Men

Mental health challenges do not discriminate based on occupation; they permeate every sector, including blue-collar industries. Within this sphere, tradesmen, builders, delivery drivers, and mechanics often stand out as some of the most emotionally isolated individuals in society. They contend with long hours and demanding physical labour, coupled with work environments that seldom facilitate open discussions about mental health. This can create a breeding ground for unmanaged stress and emotional turmoil that frequently remains unaddressed.

Many tradespeople operate under contractual agreements that provide minimal or no support regarding sick pay, mental health leave, or access to Employee Assistance Programs (EAPs). Even when these resources are available, deeply ingrained societal stigma around mental health can inhibit individuals, particularly men from seeking help or utilising support services. This combination of inadequate support and cultural barriers creates a formidable challenge for those in these professions.

The psychological toll of these conditions can manifest in various distressing ways, including:

-   Chronic Pain: Many tradespeople experience physical discomfort that is often linked to the repression of emotions, suggesting that their emotional struggles are somatically expressed.
-   Increased Substance Use: As a means of coping, some individuals may turn to alcohol or drugs, leading to a cycle of dependency that exacerbates both their mental and physical health issues.
-   Strained Relationships: Heightened domestic tensions, emotional withdrawal from loved ones, or avoidance behaviours can disrupt personal relationships, leaving family members feeling confused and helpless.
-   Emotional Dysregulation: Sudden outbursts of anger or emotional numbness can alienate friends, family, and colleagues, contributing to feelings of isolation and despair.

While these men are often praised for their resilience exemplified by the saying "crack on" in tough times many are grappling with profound inner struggles that go unnoticed. Alarmingly, the suicide rate among construction workers is more than three times the national average, revealing a tragic reality often overshadowed in broader discussions. Notably, wellness programs frequently neglect this demographic, failing to address their unique needs and the silent crises many face daily.

Understanding and addressing the mental health challenges facing blue-collar workers is not just a moral imperative; it is crucial for fostering healthier workplaces and communities. By prioritising mental well-being and creating supportive environments where these individuals can speak openly about their struggles, we can help dismantle the stigma surrounding

172

mental health and pave the way for a more understanding and compassionate society.

EAPs: A Lifeline Men Don't Use

Employee Assistance Programs (EAPs) are valuable resources designed to provide crucial support for employees grappling with mental health challenges, yet they remain significantly underutilised by men. This underutilisation can largely be attributed to a pervasive sense of psychological insecurity associated with seeking help. Despite EAPs promising confidentiality, many men are hindered by an apprehension of being judged or facing potential backlash within their workplace environments. This underlying fear creates substantial barriers that deter them from reaching out for assistance when they need it most.

Furthermore, a significant number of men may not even be aware of the existence of these programs, which compounds the issue. For those who do know about EAPs, the thought of discussing personal feelings, vulnerabilities, and struggles with a stranger can feel overwhelming and alienating, intensifying their reluctance to utilise these services.

A revealing 2023 survey conducted by Mind UK sheds light on this pressing issue. The survey found that while a concerning 60% of men reported experiencing symptoms of burnout, ranging from emotional exhaustion to decreased productivity only a mere 17% accessed the mental health resources provided by their workplaces. This stark disparity highlights a significant gap between the recognition of mental health challenges and the willingness to seek help. It underscores the urgent need for a cultural shift within organisations that fosters an environment in which discussing mental health is normalized, stigma is reduced, and employees feel safe and supported in seeking help when necessary. Only through such efforts can we hope to increase the utilisation of EAPs and promote a healthier workplace culture for all employees.

Solution Loops:

To effectively tackle the mental health crisis affecting men in the workplace, organisations must implement comprehensive and empathetic strategies that resonate on both personal and professional levels. Here are several key initiatives:

Make Mental Health Breaks Visible: Senior leaders should lead by example by openly taking mental health days themselves. By sharing their experiences, they create an environment where it is acceptable to prioritise well-being without stigma. This visibility is crucial in normalising discussions around mental health issues, allowing employees to feel empowered to take time off when needed. Regular communications, such as newsletters or company meetings should emphasise the importance of mental health breaks, reinforcing that employee well-being is as vital as productivity.

Trauma-Informed Onboarding: From day one, new hires should be immersed in a workplace culture that prioritizes psychological safety. This can be achieved by implementing trauma-informed training programs for all staff, emphasising the recognition of trauma's impact on individuals. New employees should be introduced to resources that encourage open communication about mental health, including access to support systems, counselling services, and clear channels for discussing any mental health challenges they might face. By fostering an atmosphere that values transparency and support, organisations can help employees feel secure in expressing their needs and concerns from the outset.

Peer-Led Men's Circles: Establishing peer-led support groups specifically for men within the workplace can create invaluable spaces for connection and discussion. These circles should be designed to promote a sense of community, allowing participants to share their experiences and challenges in a non-judgmental environment. Facilitated by trained leaders, the circles can provide guidance on mental health topics and personal development, thereby encouraging men to share insights and strategies for managing their mental well-being. This initiative not only helps break down barriers around mental health but also fosters a support network that can significantly enhance resilience.

Furthermore, it's essential to recognise that a workforce that has faced trauma cannot be effectively managed through metrics and productivity goals alone. Acknowledging the complexities of mental health is crucial in developing a more holistic approach to employee management. Many men, in particular, may feel hesitant to engage with mental health resources that appear unwelcoming or stigmatised. The foundation for fostering a safe and supportive workplace culture begins with a commitment to understanding and valuing the mental health of all employees. By implementing these initiatives, organizations can cultivate an environment where men feel empowered to seek help and prioritize their mental health without fear of judgment.

Workplace Myths That Kill

The modern workplace is frequently influenced by a set of damaging beliefs that can profoundly impact men's mental health and overall well-being:

- Rest is laziness: This widespread misconception equates the act of resting with a lack of ambition or productivity. In reality, rest is not merely a luxury; it is a critical component of both mental and physical recovery. Regular periods of rest allow individuals to recharge, maintain focus, and enhance creativity. Ignoring the necessity for rest can lead to severe burnout, resulting in diminished performance, a lack of motivation, and potentially harmful consequences for both individuals and organisations. A culture that prioritizes constant work over well-deserved breaks is ultimately detrimental to sustained success and productivity.

- Men who talk are weak: Society often perpetuates the harmful narrative that emotional expression is

175

synonymous with weakness. This belief discourages men from sharing their feelings and seeking support, creating a culture of emotional suppression that can lead to isolation and heightened stress levels. As a result, many men suffer in silence, which not only exacerbates mental health issues but also hinders personal and professional growth. In contrast, embracing vulnerability and open communication fosters resilience and builds stronger connections among colleagues, ultimately enhancing a supportive workplace environment.

- If you're not productive, you're replaceable: This dehumanising belief positions workers as mere cogs in a vast machine, stripping away their individuality and worth. Such a mindset fosters a toxic atmosphere where employees feel immense pressure to perform at all costs. Recognising that burnout is not just a malfunction but a symptom of overwhelming pressure is crucial. It signals a need for support, understanding, and intervention. Cultivating an environment that values the unique contributions of each team member can promote loyalty, engagement, and a healthier work-life balance.

These myths create a volatile workplace atmosphere that can lead to significant mental distress. If left unaddressed, they act like a ticking time bomb, threatening not only individual mental health but the overall efficacy and morale of the organisation. Addressing these damaging beliefs requires a concerted effort to foster a culture of empathy, support, and understanding, which is essential for long-term success and well-being in any workplace.

Coaching Interventions

To further support men in the workplace, implementing targeted coaching interventions can provide impactful strategies aimed at fostering personal growth and enhancing emotional resilience. Below are two comprehensive approaches:

1. Workplace Identity Audit: Encouraging employees to undertake a reflective journey regarding their perceptions of self in relation to their professional roles can yield profound insights. This can be facilitated through guided questions designed to provoke thought and self-examination, such as:

- What role does work play in shaping my self-image? This question invites men to consider how their careers influence their self-perception and the traits they associate with their identities.
- If my job were to vanish tomorrow, what would remain of my sense of self? This reflection helps individuals distinguish their professional identities from their personal worth, fostering a healthier separation between work and self-esteem.
- Have I mistakenly linked my value and self-worth to my performance metrics? Encouraging critical thinking about the impact of performance evaluations can empower men to reassess their definitions of success and worthiness, promoting a more balanced self-view.

2. Emotional Regulation Toolkit for Men at Work: Providing practical techniques and resources for emotional management can empower men to navigate high-pressure scenarios with greater confidence and composure. This toolkit could encompass a variety of strategies, such as:

- Grounding Techniques: Simple exercises that can be performed before or after stressful meetings, such as focused deep breathing or mindful awareness, can help individuals maintain emotional stability and clarity.
- Breath Work Exercises: Incorporating specific breath control practices aimed at alleviating the adrenaline rush that often follows conflict can promote a sense of calm. Techniques such as the 4-7-8 breathing method encourage relaxation and can help participants regain composure in heated moments.

- Boundary Scripting: Providing men with phrasing that allows for thoughtful and measured responses during challenging interactions can create essential space for emotional processing. For instance, a phrase like, "I'll need to revisit this topic once I've had time to reflect," can enable men to pause and collect their thoughts rather than reacting impulsively.

By investing in these strategies and addressing the cultural issues that contribute to workplace stressors, organisations can effectively dismantle barriers and promote a healthier, more supportive environment for all employees. This approach is particularly beneficial for men, equipping them with the tools and skills necessary to thrive both personally and professionally.

Burnout Recovery Map

Recognise the Signs:

Burnout often manifests through a variety of distinct and subtle signs that can be easily overlooked. It's crucial to pay attention to persistent fatigue that lingers even after adequate rest; this isn't just tiredness but a deep exhaustion that feels all-encompassing. Additionally, a growing sense of cynicism towards work and life can emerge, leading you to question your purpose and diminish your enthusiasm for tasks that once brought joy. Emotional depletion is another hallmark symptom, which manifests as feeling drained or detached from both your work and personal relationships. Acknowledging these symptoms is the essential first step toward recovery, as it allows you to confront the issue rather than ignore it.

Reflect:
Take dedicated time to introspect and identify your unmet emotional needs, as understanding these can be a transformative step in your healing journey. Ask yourself critical questions about your current mental and emotional state: What aspects of your wellbeing have been neglected? Are you yearning for validation, connection, or perhaps a deeper sense of belonging that has

been absent in your life? Reflect on what fulfils you and what drains you; this self-awareness will provide clarity on the changes needed to foster a healthier mindset and emotional resilience.

Reset:
Formulate a personalized plan for micro-restoration, incorporating small, actionable steps that can seamlessly integrate into your daily routine. These might include taking short, invigorating walks in nature, which have been shown to enhance mood and reduce stress, practicing mindfulness or meditation to ground yourself amid chaos, or engaging in therapy for more targeted support tailored to your individual needs. It can also be beneficial to reach out to peers to forge connections and share experiences, decreasing feelings of isolation. Schedule intentional time off to truly recharge without guilt; even brief moments of escape can significantly enhance your energy and overall well-being when used wisely.

Managerial Reframe (for Workplaces):
To cultivate a supportive and thriving work environment, organizations should adopt several key strategies:

- Train Leaders in Trauma-Informed Communication: Equip leaders with the skills necessary to understand and respond compassionately to the emotional needs of their teams. Training should focus on building a culture of empathy and support, helping leaders recognize signs of distress and approach conversations with sensitivity and understanding.

- Normalize Flexible Hours for Mental Health: Create policies that prioritise mental health with the same importance as other personal responsibilities, such as childcare needs. This could include allowing employees flexible work hours or the option to work from home, facilitating their ability to manage stress and care for their well-being effectively.

- Provide Anonymous Check-In Portals: Establish platforms that empower staff to express their concerns or feelings without fear of judgment or retribution. These anonymous channels encourage openness and foster a culture where self-care is actively promoted, making it clear that mental health is a priority for the organization. This approach contributes to a workplace environment where employees feel safe to share their struggles and seek support.

By implementing these strategies, workplaces can not only support their employees but also cultivate a healthier, more engaged workforce.

Gentle Prompts for Self-Discovery:

- Who am I outside of my work? Take a moment to reflect deeply on your identity beyond job titles and professional responsibilities. Consider what activities ignite your passion and bring you joy, whether it's a hobby, a cause you care about, or simply time spent with loved ones. What interests define you as a person? Rediscover these elements and explore how they shape your sense of self.

- What belief do I carry about rest, and who taught it to me? Delve into the narratives surrounding rest that have influenced your mindset. Think about your upbringing, cultural contexts, and social circles, what messages about rest did you absorb? Who instilled these beliefs in you, and how have they shaped your approach to relaxation and self-care? Challenge the stigmas associated with rest as unproductive or indulgent; recognize its importance for well-being and effectiveness.

- Where do I still believe that asking for help is a sign of failure? Examine the misconceptions that equate vulnerability with weakness. Reflect on your past experiences, family dynamics, educational background, or workplace culture that may have reinforced this belief. Consider the moments when seeking support has actually led to growth or success. Embrace the strength found in acknowledging your limitations and reaching out for help as a proactive and courageous act.

- What would it mean to show up as a human, not a machine? Contemplate the importance of embracing your humanity in the professional sphere. Think about the ways in which we often dehumanize ourselves through relentless productivity and constant self-discipline. Recognise the value of expressing emotions, joy, frustration, gratitude and how this authenticity can foster stronger relationships with colleagues, enhance collaboration, and create a more compassionate work environment.

- When did I last feel seen, not just used? Reflect on the moments in your career when you felt truly valued for your essence, rather than simply your output. Consider experiences where your opinions, ideas, and personality were acknowledged and appreciated. How did those instances impact your motivation and engagement? Understand the significance of feeling recognized as a whole person and how it contributes to a nourishing work culture.

The 5 Rs: Recovery Plan for Working Men

1   Recognise the Cost of Over performance: It's essential to acknowledge that an unyielding pursuit of success can take a significant toll on your energy reserves and overall mental well-being. This relentless drive often leads to burnout, anxiety, and feelings of inadequacy. By understanding the detrimental effects of over performance, you can begin to set healthier boundaries and prioritise self-care, allowing for a more sustainable approach to achieving your goals.

181

2   Reframe Help-Seeking as Masculine: It's time to redefine the narrative around masculinity to embrace the concepts of vulnerability and strength in seeking help. Traditionally, many cultures have viewed asking for assistance as a sign of weakness; however, it takes immense courage to acknowledge when we need support. By fostering an environment that values emotional openness, we can encourage men to express their struggles and seek help when necessary, promoting mental health and resilience.

3   Reset Your Nervous System Daily: To combat daily stress and anxiety, integrate practices into your routine that help calm and rejuvenate your nervous system. Mindfulness techniques, such as deep breathing exercises, meditation, or gentle yoga, can significantly decrease stress levels. Additionally, engaging in regular physical exercise not only boosts your mood but also strengthens your body, creating a more balanced emotional state. Establishing this daily reset allows you to approach challenges with clarity and composure.

4   Rebuild Your Identity Beyond Your Job: In our fast-paced world, it's easy to become defined solely by our professional roles. Taking the time to explore and cultivate interests, hobbies, and relationships outside of work can be transformative. Whether it's engaging in creative activities, volunteering, or nurturing friendships, developing a multifaceted identity enriches your life. This exploration fosters a deeper sense of self-worth and fulfilment that goes beyond career accomplishments.

5   Reconnect with Real Human Needs: To foster true well-being, it's crucial to prioritise the foundational elements of life that contribute to a healthy, balanced existence. Ensure you are getting adequate rest, as sleep is vital for both physical and mental health. Cultivating a sense of purpose and establishing connections with your community can also enhance your life satisfaction. By

focusing on these essential human needs, you create a holistic approach to well-being that nurtures your mind, body, and spirit.

Final Reframe

You are not defined by your payslip, nor is your value determined by the promotions you receive or the relentless hours you log at work. Your worth transcends any job title or paycheck, and it's essential to recognise that.

Your body is not just a machine designed to produce results, nor is your mind merely a cog in the wheel of productivity. Moreover, your masculinity should not be measured by the burdens you carry or the pressures you withstand. Our society often champions the notion that strength lies in endurance, but true power lies in self-awareness and the wisdom to recognise when you need to pause and reflect.

Resilience is not merely about toughing it out until you crumble; it requires the courage to reach out for support even before you feel pushed to your limits. It's about understanding that asking for help is a sign of strength, not weakness.

So, what does authentic masculinity entail? It's not the glorification of working until you are physically and mentally exhausted; instead, it involves the ability to take deep breaths, step back from the chaos, and reconnect with your inner self. This is especially vital in a world that often celebrates the relentless pursuit of hustle and achievement.

The strongest individuals are not those who never face hardships or setbacks. True strength comes from those who learn from their struggles, who rise again with grace and humility, embracing their vulnerabilities along the way.

This is your invitation to take a moment to reflect, to step back from the demands of life, and to reclaim your path, one that aligns with your values and priorities on your own terms.

Consider this a call to honour your mental and emotional well-being, challenging the traditional narratives of masculinity and paving the way for a healthier and more balanced life.

Chapter 13

The Provider Trap: When Being "Enough" Breaks You

The Weight of Provision

He provides. Not always from a place of desire, and often not because he possesses the capacity to do so. He offers because, from his earliest memories, he was conditioned to fulfil this role. Fathers who spoke sparingly yet laboured diligently into the night demonstrated to him the profound value of silent sacrifice, teaching him that actions often spoke louder than words. Mothers who celebrated compliance over emotional expression instilled within him a deep-seated sense of quiet responsibility that frequently eclipsed his personal feelings and needs.

Teachers rewarded conformity, hammering home the lesson that being useful equated to being worthy of love and respect. Cultural narratives that lauded him only during acts of generosity often turned a blind eye to his moments of faltering or struggle, tightening the unrelenting grip of pressure to consistently perform without falter. From the moment he took his first tentative steps, he was imbued with the belief that his value rested squarely on his ability to produce, repair, and safeguard those around him.

A reasonable person helps without being asked, often anticipating the needs of others rather than focusing on their own. A good man builds not only for himself but for everyone he loves, erecting structures, both physical and emotional, that serve as shields against the harshness of the world. The unspoken rule was clear: to rest is to reveal a hint of weakness; to fail is nothing short of unacceptable.

185

Even the simple act of acknowledging fatigue felt like a perilous admission, a small crack that could threaten to bring down the entire carefully constructed edifice of expectations, responsibilities, and survival roles he had painstakingly erected over the years. Thus, he stands resolute, compelled to push through adversity and to endure discomfort, believing that perseverance is the hallmark of strength. He outruns the pervasive ache that gnaws at his resolve, dismissing moments of vulnerability as luxury he can ill afford. However, this relentless march forward, this stubborn insistence on endurance ultimately transforms into the very force that dismantles him from within. Each time he sacrifices his own needs for the sake of obligation, he further distances himself from his true essence, sowing the seeds of internal conflict that threaten to uproot his very identity.

The Collapse You Don't See Coming

Burnout doesn't arrive abruptly; it seeps into his life like a slow, unnoticed leak in a dam, gradually eroding the foundation he once took for granted. At first, it manifests in subtle ways that seem almost trivial: a fleeting irritability that colours his interactions, lapses in memory that leave him grappling to recall simple details, and an emotional detachment that begins to cloud the warmth of his relationships. Once-thrilling milestones, like the joyous celebrations of birthdays or shared moments of laughter, start to blur into the monotonous backdrop of his existence. Passions that once ignited sparks of joy and creativity now morph into burdensome chores that add weight to his already heavy heart. Each day blends into the next, passing in a haze where he feels like a mere automaton, going through the motions without any real engagement or purpose.

His body begins to send distress signals that he can no longer ignore: aching shoulders that throb ceaselessly, a jaw clenched so tightly it feels as if it might shatter, and persistent headaches that look like dark clouds, casting shadows over his thoughts. Yet, he dismisses these tell-tale signs as mere fatigue, attributing them to the relentless demands of his chaotic workplace. "I'm just tired," he reassures himself, brushing aside the worries like dust on a shelf. "Things have been hectic. I'll bounce back soon."

What he fails to realise, however, is that this is not simply a phase of exhaustion; it's cognitive fatigue, an insidious state where his nervous system operates as if it's perpetually under siege. His sympathetic nervous system, the one tasked with triggering the fight-or-flight response, is stuck in overdrive, flooding his bloodstream with cortisol. This relentless onslaught ignites a cascade of inflammation, wreaking havoc on his sleep patterns and leaving him in a state of restless unrest. As his physical fatigue deepens, his libido wanes, and he becomes emotionally unavailable, not out of indifference, but because he has become too worn down to feel anything at all.

Despite the toll this takes on him, he insists on pushing forward. What once earned him admiration, his relentless work ethic and commitment now siphons away his sense of identity, unraveling the threads of who he is at his core. The cracks beneath the surface deepen into painful fractures; relationships that once thrived with intimacy and connection begin to fray, and the joy that once illuminated his world retreats into darkness. He dons a smile like a suit of armour, a protective shield against the growing sense of emptiness within, until one fateful day, that carefully constructed façade finally shatters, revealing the depth of his despair.

Burnout as a Trauma Response

For many men, burnout transcends mere time management issues; it's often a profound trauma response rooted in deep-seated childhood experiences. In environments where love and acceptance were conditional upon achievement, usefulness transformed into a crucial means of survival. In such households, expressing emotions openly often invited disdain, while vulnerability was perceived as a weakness to be shunned. Consequently, boys internalised a damaging message: "If I'm not useful, I'm disposable."

This internalised belief solidifies into a comprehensive blueprint for adulthood, where the relentless pursuit of validation manifests through productivity and achievement. These individuals become prone to denying themselves the essential need for rest, viewing every moment of downtime as a threat to their self-worth. They silence their emotions, prioritising functionality over feelings, which leads to a disconnection from their true selves.

The cyclical nature of this mindset creates not only a body that never truly relaxes but also a mind that becomes a battleground for unprocessed emotions. Their nervous systems oscillate dramatically between the extremes of fight or complete shutdown, leading to a heightened state of alertness that proves to be physically and mentally exhausting. In a society where their struggles often go unnoticed, it becomes all too easy for them to resort to numbing behaviours. They might turn to excessive drinking, overindulgence in food, compulsive gambling, or simply withdraw from their own lives, seeking temporary relief from the relentless pressure they place on themselves.

This ongoing cycle of striving, achieving, and ultimately crashing can leave men feeling isolated and overwhelmed, reinforcing the very beliefs that led them to this state of burnout in the first place. Recognising and addressing these patterns is crucial for breaking free from this exhausting cycle, allowing for the possibility of healing, emotional expression, and a more balanced way of living.

Somatic Symptoms of Burnout

Burnout in men often eludes verbal expression, manifesting instead through somatic symptoms that convey distress in a language many men have yet to learn how to interpret. This silent struggle can take various forms: chest pain without an identifiable cardiac issue serves as an insistent signal that something is amiss. At the same time, the burden of relentless tension often reveals itself as persistent headaches that resist relief.

188

Men may find themselves wrestling with tightness in their shoulders or a clenched jaw, physical reminders of the emotional weight they carry. Digestive issues may emerge, such as bloating or irritable bowel symptoms, signalling a profound internal struggle that often goes unnoticed. Chronic fatigue creeps in, wearing down their resilience, making even the simplest tasks feel monumental.

Muscle tightness, particularly in the back and neck, serves as a constant reminder of ongoing stress and unresolved tension. These physical symptoms are frequently dismissed, overlooked, or temporarily masked through quick fixes like pain relievers or caffeine. However, they embody the body's urgent call for rest, recovery, and a reconsideration of lifestyle choices, urging men to acknowledge their limits and prioritise self-care before the toll of burnout becomes overwhelming. Recognising and addressing these signs is crucial not only for physical health but also for mental and emotional well-being.

The Guilt of Slowing Down

Ideally, rest should be a sanctuary for solace and healing, a necessary pause in the relentless march of life. Yet, for individuals conditioned by the unyielding imperative to provide, the act of pausing becomes a treacherous landscape filled with an overwhelming tide of guilt. This guilt is often not their own but rather inherited, a haunting echo of the silent struggles faced by their fathers who persevered through deep-seated grief. These parents epitomised stoicism, teaching their children that emotional expression is a sign of weakness, and instilling in them a profound reluctance to embrace vulnerability.

Such guilt is intricately woven into the fabric of a culture that reveres tireless effort and views rest as a luxury rather than a necessity. Within this mindset, when physical exhaustion sets in, relationships begin to fray, and the once-vibrant spark of joy diminishes; the instinctual response is rarely to step back and reassess. Instead, they grip tighter onto their responsibilities, doubling down on their efforts to fix what seems to be unravelling. They work more earnestly, sacrificing their own well-being in a desperate attempt to regain control over their chaotic lives.

This cycle culminates in a painful irony: the provider, who was once seen as the pillar of strength, ultimately becomes the one in dire need of support. Caught in this exhausting and heartbreaking loop, they may struggle to recognise their own depletion. It is only by confronting and acknowledging this painful truth that the path to genuine healing can begin. By embracing vulnerability, they can break free from the expectations that bind them and reclaim their joy, leading to a more balanced and fulfilling existence.

When Identity Becomes a Cage

In our modern society, the concept of work has transcended traditional employment; it has become deeply intertwined with a man's identity and sense of self-worth. This transformation carries significant implications, particularly when an individual finds himself at risk of losing this defining aspect of his life. The question arises: without the role of provider, who is he really? When faced with challenges such as injury, unemployment, or emotional exhaustion, he may confront a haunting void that threatens to unravel his very sense of purpose.

This sensation extends far beyond mere sadness; it manifests as an existential crisis, a profound and often unsettling confrontation with one's core essence and life's intended purpose. As this internal struggle intensifies, feelings of shame can take root, usually triggering a downward spiral into depression. The individual may find himself wrestling with feelings of inadequacy, struggling to reconcile his self-image with his current circumstances.

In the shadows of this crisis, compulsive behaviours may emerge, not simply as acts of defiance or indulgence, but as desperate attempts to regain a sense of well-being and fulfilment.

Infidelities, for example, may transpire not out of passionate desire, but as a profound plea for connection in a world that suddenly feels isolating. Similarly, gambling can shift from a casual pastime to an obsessive pursuit for significance, where each bet is a frantic attempt to reclaim a sense of control over an increasingly unpredictable life.

Self-numbing behaviours, such as excessive drinking or substance use, can emerge not from indifference, but as painful indicators of an overwhelming sense of dislocation. These actions serve as coping mechanisms, revealing the depth of the internal chaos and the yearning for solace in a landscape where purpose feels lost. Ultimately, the journey through this turmoil reveals not just the fragility of identity through the lens of work, but also the profound need for connection, meaning, and recognition in the face of life's adversities.

Intersectional Burnout — When the Weight Doubles

It's crucial to recognise that not all men experience the burdens of identity and mental health in the same way; factors such as race, sexual orientation, immigration status, and socioeconomic background significantly influence their experiences.

For instance, Black men often grapple with an unyielding societal pressure to excel and prove themselves, feeling the need to be "twice as good" to be considered merely acceptable in environments fraught with bias and discrimination. This constant striving for validation frequently leads to silent suffering, as they mask their vulnerabilities to avoid being perceived as weak or threatening. The weight of these expectations can create a profound internal conflict, leaving many to navigate their emotions in isolation.

Similarly, gay, bisexual, and transgender men face a unique set of challenges that compound their mental health struggles. These individuals are often caught between societal expectations of masculinity, pressured to fulfil roles as providers, and the urgent need to affirm and validate their diverse identities in a world that constantly questions their legitimacy. This dual burden can intensify feelings of inadequacy, loneliness, and alienation, making it difficult for them to find safe spaces where they can express their true selves.

Immigrant men carry a profound sense of responsibility as they bear the aspirations and dreams of their families and previous generations. Their perceived failures, whether in securing employment, adapting to a new culture, or achieving professional success, can feel like a betrayal of familial legacies, weighing heavily on their shoulders. This intense pressure often leads to a relentless pursuit of success, compounded by the fear of letting down loved one's back home.

Working-class men encounter a different but equally challenging set of pressures, where their self-worth is often tied to their financial success. This intertwining of moral value with economic achievement fosters a relentless hustle, motivated not by ambition or desire for advancement, but by a primal instinct for survival. The pressures of making ends meet can strip away the sense of fulfilment and leave them feeling trapped in a cycle of stress and anxiety.

Indigenous and culturally marginalised men face formidable obstacles that stem from historical injustices, including colonial trauma and ongoing cultural silencing. The burdens they carry often extend beyond personal experiences, manifesting as a collective weight of systemic, generational, and historical fatigue. This deeply rooted cultural trauma can hinder their ability to seek help, as the unresolved grief of their ancestors intertwines with their own struggles, creating layers of complexity that magnify their challenges.

Through understanding these nuanced experiences, we can better appreciate the diverse realities faced by men from various backgrounds and the intricate factors shaping their mental health journeys.

Clinical Insight: Burnout vs. Depression in Men

While burnout and depression often coexist in individuals, it is crucial to recognise that they are distinct conditions with unique characteristics. Understanding the differences can lead to more effective strategies for prevention and treatment.

Burnout is characterised by:

- Task-related exhaustion: This form of exhaustion arises from prolonged and relentless demands at work or in personal commitments. It reflects a depletion of physical and emotional energy, often leading to a sense of being overwhelmed by responsibilities.

- Irritability and detachment: Individuals experiencing burnout may find themselves increasingly irritable and detached, not only from their work but also from personal relationships. This emotional distance can create feelings of isolation, making it challenging to connect with colleagues, friends, or family.

- Fleeting moments of satisfaction: Despite the overall sense of exhaustion, a person experiencing burnout can still derive occasional joy from small successes or accomplishments, indicating that there remains a glimmer of hope for recovery.

- External performance metrics: Those suffering from burnout often feel a compulsion to meet external performance expectations, which can exacerbate their stress. Their self-worth may hinge on achieving goals set by others, driving a relentless pursuit of validation through work.

In contrast, depression encompasses:

- Pervasive emotional numbness: This numbness deeply affects all facets of life, leaving individuals struggling to find joy or motivation in activities that once brought them happiness. It is not merely sadness but a profound disconnect from the emotional experiences that define human life.

- Loss of interest: Depression leads to an overwhelming sense of apathy, making previously enjoyable activities feel meaningless. Hobbies, social interactions, and even basic self-care may fall by the wayside, contributing to a cycle of isolation and despair.

- Identity collapse: This condition can lead individuals to feel as if they have lost their sense of self. Feelings of shame and worthlessness can envelop them, leading to withdrawal from social engagements and responsibilities. It transcends the boundaries of specific roles, impacting how individuals perceive their value and place in the world.

The distinction between burnout and depression is crucial not only for diagnosis but also for treatment. Burnout may whisper, "I'm failing," indicating a struggle against external pressures and expectations. In contrast, depression can roar, "I am a failure," representing a more profound internal battle that erodes self-esteem and shapes one's self-identity.

Recognising and differentiating between these two states is imperative. Mislabelling one for the other can lead to misdiagnosis or mistreatment. In severe cases, it may result in overlooking critical emotional support that could facilitate healing and recovery. For men navigating the intricate landscape of identity and mental health in a demanding world, understanding the nuances of burnout and depression is not merely academic; it is a vital step toward regaining control and fostering resilience.

Rest as Repair — A Biological Necessity

Rest transcends the notion of a simple mental break; it acts as a vital neurological recalibration crucial for both our bodies and minds. When we intentionally pause our hectic activities and embrace the concept of rest, we facilitate a profound transformation within our nervous system. This shift moves us from a state dominated by the sympathetic nervous system, commonly referred to as the fight-or-flight response, into the realm of parasympathetic dominance, a state often characterised as the rest-and-digest mode. This transition is paramount as it initiates the healing process our bodies desperately need.

During this critical period, a series of significant physiological changes occurs. The vagus nerve, which is a central component of the parasympathetic nervous system, becomes activated. This activation sparks a cascade of restorative effects throughout our body. For instance, heart rate begins to slow down, breathing becomes deeper and more rhythmic, and the muscles, often constricted and tense from stress, gradually release their accumulated tension. As a result, stress hormones such as cortisol start to decrease, allowing sleep to evolve into a genuinely restorative experience rather than a mere interruption of consciousness.

Additionally, as blood flow redirects to the prefrontal cortex, the brain region responsible for higher-order thinking, logic, and emotional regulation, our cognitive functions are sharpened. Clarity of thought is enhanced, fostering a feeling of safety and enabling us to forge deeper, more meaningful connections with those around us. It's crucial to recognise that without sufficient rest, our ability to function at our best becomes significantly impaired; thus, rest should not be viewed as an optional luxury, but rather as a fundamental necessity vital for our overall well-being and repair.

Gentle Prompts for Reclaiming Yourself

Provider Identity

- Reflect on the moment when you first began linking your self-worth to your capacity to give and provide for others. Was this correlation a lesson instilled by your family dynamics, cultural expectations, or societal norms at large? Consider whether early experiences shaped your understanding of value and self-identity in ways that prioritised others' needs over your own.

- Delve into the various roles you find yourself taking on, often out of a sense of obligation rather than genuine desire. How have these roles, not just been defined by the duties they entail, but by the emotional weight they carry, contributed to your sense of identity? Are there specific roles that resonate more deeply within you, defining a part of you that struggles to be authentic?

- Contemplate what it might mean to perceive your value independently of your productivity. How might recognising that your worth is inherent, rather than earned through achievements, influence your perspective on self-worth? Consider the potential liberation that could come from esteeming yourself for simply being, rather than for constantly doing.

Burnout Check-In

- Take a moment to envision how burnout manifests in your life across various domains, emotionally, physically, and relationally. What does that look like for you? Do you often feel drained, disconnected, or overwhelmed by your responsibilities?

- Have you started to notice specific signs of burnout that you previously brushed aside, perhaps feelings of irritability, fatigue, or a sense of detachment, because you felt compelled to maintain a facade of strength? Reflect on times you ignored these indicators in the name of resilience.

- What messages does your body convey to you when you finally allow yourself the quietude of rest? When you create space for reflection and relaxation, what sensations emerge in your body? Consider whether you encounter physical signals of stress or relief, and how these responses inform your understanding of well-being.

196

Rest and Guilt

- Explore your relationship with rest in greater detail. What emotions come to the surface when you contemplate allowing yourself time to recharge? Do thoughts of unworthiness or unproductiveness compel you to push through exhaustion?
- Do you experience feelings of guilt or anxiety when you take a break or slow down, and what contributing factors, whether societal, familial, or personal, might be influencing these feelings? Are they echoes of a performance-driven culture that equates busyness with value?
- Reflect on who instilled in you the belief that rest equates to weakness. What messages did you receive deliberately or inadvertently that have shaped your present attitudes toward self-care and the right to rest? How have these teachings created barriers to embracing your need for downtime?

Intersectional Realities

- Examine how your personal background, cultural, socio-economic, or otherwise, shapes the way you navigate and present yourself in the world. How do these intersections affect your interactions with others, and how do they define your experiences of privilege or marginalisation?
- What unseen burdens do you carry that others might overlook, and how do these burdens impact your daily life and interactions? Consider the emotional toll of these invisible struggles and how they influence your mental and physical health.
- Reflect on where in your life silence has been equated with safety. What historical or personal experiences taught you to prioritise quietude over vocalising your thoughts and needs? How have these experiences

shaped your ability to assert yourself in various environments?

Redefining Strength

- Consider the possibility that true strength may be soft, slow, and steady, rather than aggressive or hurried. What does it look like to cultivate resilience that honours your emotional needs rather than dismisses them?
- Imagine what self-worth might look like if it were not tethered to societal markers of success such as career achievements or financial stability. What internal values like kindness, empathy, or authenticity might take on greater importance in this redefined framework?
- If you had the chance to redefine manhood for yourself, what beliefs and definitions would you alter? How might this transformation support a healthier relationship with the concept of rest, allowing for more self-acceptance and less pressure to conform to traditional ideals of strength?

Coach's Corner: Rebuild Your Identity

1   Rewriting Your Provider Script:

Take an intentional moment to reflect on and articulate your deeply ingrained beliefs about masculinity and your sense of self-worth. Write down statements such as "Real men don't cry" or "You must always earn your worth." Once you have your list, engage with each belief critically. Ask yourself: Where do these ideas come from? How do they serve me, and how might they limit me? Next to each outdated belief, write a new truth that embodies compassion and understanding. For example, replace "Real men don't cry" with "Expressing emotions is a sign of strength" or change "You must always earn your worth" to "My worth is inherent and unconditional." These new truths should acknowledge the importance of taking breaks, our shared humanity, and the fundamental right to exist and thrive without the relentless burden of continuous productivity.

2   Permission Slip to Rest:

Craft a tangible permission slip that symbolises your commitment to self-care. Write: "I, [your name], grant myself full permission to rest without guilt, shame, or the need for justification." Emphasise that your value does not depend on your output or productivity levels. To solidify this commitment, choose a place where you will frequently see the slip, such as on your desk, in your wallet, or on your bathroom mirror. Read it aloud daily, allowing the words to sink in and resonate deeply within you. You might also consider adding a personal affirmation or a short mantra that reinforces this sentiment, such as "I am enough as I am." By doing this, you cultivate a mindset that prioritises your well-being and acknowledges the importance of rest in your life's journey.

Bonus Coaching Reframe:

Remember that you were never created to operate solely as a machine. Your worth is not contingent on your productivity, and you do not need to justify your need for rest. Recognising that you are inherently deserving of rest is essential for your well-being. Embracing rest is not a sign of giving up; rather, it is a vital part of the healing process, allowing you to recharge both physically and mentally. Taking time to rest enables you to resist the pressures of a fast-paced world, helping you reclaim your sense of identity and humanity. By prioritising rest, you acknowledge your value and reinforce the idea that a meaningful life requires balance and self-care.

"Burnout is not a badge of honour. It's your body whispering what your soul has been screaming that it's time to come home to yourself."

Act Two: The Inner Reconstruction
(Shame, Ego, Desire, Healing)

Chapter 14

The Man Who Forgot Himself

He forgot who he was, but this transformation didn't happen all at once; it unfolded gradually, like the slow erosion of a once-mighty cliff face, each piece weathered away by time and tide. Each moment he held his tongue, suppressing the urge to speak up when his heart raced with unexpressed ideas, each forced laugh at jokes that landed with a dull thud, and every dismissal of his own raw emotions with a weary "I'm fine", chipped away at the very foundation of his identity. These seemingly innocuous daily compromises wove together a complicated tapestry of silence, each thread representing a quiet surrender to the expectations imposed by others.

This subtle cruelty, the gradual erasure of a person's essence, was not marked by overt violence or chaotic upheaval, but rather by the numbing weight of compliant existence. With each passing day, he felt more like a spectre of himself, drifting through memories of a different time, a time when laughter spilled from him like sunlight, warm and infectious; a time when he felt empowered to stand fiercely for his beliefs, his voice steady and resonant; a time when his dreams unfurled boundlessly, soaring above the constraints of reality, chasing horizons unfettered by fear.

But that was before. Now, he has perfected the art of careful calculation, weighing his words as if they held the power to tip a scale precariously balanced. He plays the roles society expects of him with a mechanical precision that feels both foreign and familiar, each performance a reflection of what he believes is necessary for survival in a world that often feels hostile to authenticity. Yet in this adaptation, he has lost something vital, the ability to thrive amidst the cacophony of life.

Burdened by the relentless demands of existence, he has become a man rewritten, not due to any inherent weakness, but because he has adapted in ways that he thought were crucial for navigating the tumultuous waters of social expectation. And as he stands before the mirror, he finds himself searching for the flicker of the person he once was, a glimmering ghost of his former self, lingering just beneath the surface, patiently waiting for the day he might remember how to truly live again.

The Story You Didn't Mean to Lose

Every man carries within him an intensely personal narrative, one that begins to take shape in the formative years of childhood. This internal story is often infused with dreams and aspirations, filled with an innocent hope for strength, kindness, brilliance, and a yearning for freedom. Yet, as life unfolds and presents its complexities, a subtle yet profound editing process starts to emerge. The introduction of elements such as shame, heartbreak, and unexpected challenges those gut-wrenching moments that leave an individual gasping for breath begins to reshape that initial script. In this often lonely struggle, silence descends, suffocating in its persistence, accompanied by the burdens of obligatory responsibilities and debts that weigh heavily, both financial and emotional.

As these pressures accumulate, he unwittingly begins to rewrite his original narrative. The vibrant expression of his passion for art, which once served as a vital outlet for joy and identity, is gradually pushed aside and relegated to the background. Long hours spent in the office become the new norm, with late-night scribbles and weekend paint sessions sacrificed at the altar of relentless productivity. In his quest for validation, he finds himself seeking affirmation in work performance rather than in creative expression. In this transformation, he builds walls around his heart, crafting a façade that aligns itself with a rigid, often toxic definition of masculinity, one that prioritises strength and stoicism while dismissing vulnerability and empathy as weaknesses.

The most disheartening realisation during this metamorphosis is that it often attracts unsolicited praise. Friends, family, and colleagues offer labels such as dependable, rugged, and reliable qualities celebrated within a society that usually overlooks the anguish beneath the surface. No one pauses to inquire about the dreams he has shelved or the laughter that has faded from his world; few consider where the spirited essence of his former self has gone.

And therein lies the tragedy: men do not simply vanish with grand gestures or dramatic exits; instead, they fade quietly into the background, subordinated by their compliance with societal expectations. The once vibrant individual who embraced joy, passion, and purpose becomes a mere shadow of his potential, enveloped in silence, haunted by the life he might have lived. As the world continues to move around him, he exists in a perpetual state of longing for the man he once was, left to grapple with the questions of what could have been and what still might be, if only he dared to reclaim his narrative.

The Narrative Neutraliser

This isn't merely the stuff of science fiction; it is a stark reality woven into the fabric of survival in today's world. At some pivotal moment in his life, the vibrant and ambitious story he was destined to live becomes overshadowed by the heavy burden of societal expectations. The relentless pressures of culture, the deep scars of past trauma, the weight of embedded shame, and the unyielding demands from those around him conspire to rewrite his narrative. Instead of embracing his true self, he finds himself adopting behaviours that are deemed socially acceptable, sacrificing authenticity on the altar of the illusion of stability.

The so-called Narrative Neutraliser is not a fantastical gadget from a futuristic tale; it takes on more insidious forms, manifesting as a parent's disappointed gaze, a teacher's cutting sarcasm, or a partner's stinging rejection. Each instance is a thread in the collective fabric of a world that sends the message: "We will love you more if you conform to our comfort."

Gradually, he complies with this unspoken agreement, modifying his thoughts, feelings, and actions to seek approval and acceptance. In doing so, he slowly erases the vibrant essence of who he truly is, drifting further away from the identity he once cherished as he forfeits his dreams for the sake of fitting into a mould crafted by others.

The Neuroscience of Erasure

Here's the unsettling reality about trauma: it possesses the alarming ability to shrink your hippocampus, the vital region of your brain responsible for forming and recalling memories. This diminishment can severely impact your capacity to reflect on your past and envision your future. At the same time, trauma takes hold of your amygdala, exacerbating your fears and heightening your responses to perceived threats. The prefrontal cortex, which governs reasoning and emotional regulation, often falls offline, leaving you adrift without the ability to derive meaning or understanding from your experiences.

In its fervent effort to shield and protect, the brain does not accurately record instances of pain; instead, it edits these memories, safeguarding them and selectively erasing the most excruciating parts. This results in a distorted narrative, where the essence of suffering is transformed into an unrecognisable haze.

Consequently, he finds himself struggling to recall the last time he experienced genuine joy or held onto the beliefs that once fuelled his sense of purpose. Instead of clarity, all that remains are mere fragments of a daily existence ruled by survival instincts. He does not lack warmth or potential; instead, he is ensnared in a complete system shutdown, an emotional paralysis that renders him unable to engage fully with the world around him. The relentless narrative looping in his mind is hauntingly familiar yet deeply damaging: "You're too much." "You're not enough." "Stay small. Stay silent. Stay useful." Caught in this exhausting cycle, he desperately searches for a pathway to reclaim the lost chapters of his life, yearning for a bridge that might reconnect him with the joy and purpose that seem to elude him.

The Survival Lies Men Live By

Men frequently carry profound, unspoken burdens that intricately shape their identities and how they interact with the world. Within their minds, thoughts and beliefs often echo, such as:

- "My needs don't matter."
- "If I break, they'll leave."
- "Real men keep going, no matter the cost."
- "If I'm not useful, I'm replaceable."
- "Vulnerability is a trap."

These mantras aren't merely fleeting thoughts; they represent a deep-seated code ingrained in their very beings through years of social conditioning that insists on the mantra of "man up." This conditioning emphasises stoicism, self-sufficiency, and the denial of weakness, pushing many to suppress their emotions rather than expressing them. Most men do not consciously adopt these beliefs; instead, they find themselves succumbing to societal expectations that dictate that strength and resilience are paramount.

As a result, countless men silently grapple with their internal struggles, feeling compelled to maintain an exterior of toughness. They accept the weight of these narratives as usual, often at the expense of their mental and emotional well-being. This ongoing internal conflict can lead to feelings of isolation, as they fear opening up about their vulnerabilities lest they be viewed as less than "real men." In a world that often celebrates stoicism over authenticity, these men unknowingly carry the heavy burden of unexpressed fears and desires, yearning for understanding yet feeling trapped by their own beliefs.

Sidebar: What Men Tell Themselves (But Never Say Out Loud)

In the hidden corners of their minds, they wrestle with emotions that remain unspoken:

- "I don't know who I am without this job that consumes my life; it's as if my identity is woven into my professional role, leaving no space for the person I used to be."
- "Once, I was filled with dreams and aspirations, but now it feels like those hopes have been buried under the weight of daily responsibilities and endless commitments. I struggle to remember what ignited my passion."
- "I feel invisible, even when I'm surrounded by colleagues or friends. It's as if I'm merely an outsider in my own life, watching as others connect while I remain disconnected."
- "I'm so tired of pretending everything is fine. I put on a brave face for the world, yet inside, I'm crumbling, overwhelmed by an emptiness that I can't explain."

The Therapist's Perspective:

In therapy sessions, men often shy away from expressing feelings of numbness directly. Instead, they might label themselves as tired, burnt out, or simply fed up with the relentless grind. However, beneath these surface-level descriptions lies a deeper, more poignant reality:
"I've forgotten how to feel alive in a world that demands so much from me, where I'm left to navigate my existence without the joy and vitality I once knew."

The Cultural Rewriter

Society consistently rewrites the narrative for men, layering heavy expectations onto their identities that can feel suffocating and contradictory. We hear phrases like:
- "Be strong, but never soft."
- "Be reliable, but don't show emotions."
- "Achieve success, but do so without ever struggling."

This societal blueprint often portrays masculinity as a relentless one-man show, where the script is rigid and offers no chance for intermissions, rewrites, or a second act. Men find themselves weighed down by the pressure to perform this predetermined role perfectly, to the point where they forget that these script lines were never intended to define their true selves.

Reflecting on his past, there was a time when he engaged in creativity with unbridled enthusiasm, when the world was a canvas for his unfiltered imagination. He would sketch fantastical dragons soaring through realms only he could see, and he poured his heart into poetry that resonated with genuine emotion, echoing the deepest parts of his soul. In those moments, he believed he was destined for something extraordinary, as if each creative act was a stepping stone toward self-discovery and fulfilment.

Yet, the vibrant landscapes of his imagination have gradually been replaced by the sterile confines of spreadsheets, deadlines, and the monotonous routine of adult responsibilities. Each day blurs into the next, punctuated only by the mechanical phrase, "Let me check my calendar," as laughter fades from his life, replaced by a quiet resignation. This shift isn't merely a sign of growth or maturity; it is a slow, insidious form of disappearance. The essence of who he is, the imaginative dreamer, the passionate poet, has been overshadowed by the relentless demands of a life that feels more like an obligation than a choice. In the pursuit of success and reliability, he stands at a crossroads, yearning to rediscover the lost parts of himself and reclaim the joy that once defined him.

The NHS Perspective: When Men Are Misunderstood

When a man enters a room radiating palpable anger, society often hastily labels him as aggressive, quick to judge without understanding the roots of his emotions. If he appears perpetually consumed by work, he might be seen as merely a high-functioning individual, admired for his productivity yet overlooked for his struggle. When he shuts down emotionally, he is frequently categorised as emotionally unavailable, a label that masks the complexity of his inner world. However, beneath these superficial labels lies a profound and often tragic truth: he may simply be lost in a society that demands relentless performance while offering little compassion or understanding.

For many men, expressing vulnerability has become an infrequent and even perilous territory. Instead of openly sharing their feelings, they often wrap themselves in the cloak of busyness, convinced that by maintaining this façade, they can navigate safely through a world that usually misinterprets emotional honesty as a sign of weakness. This perpetual state of self-protection can lead to a detachment from their true selves, leaving them struggling to identify what they genuinely desire or need. In a culture that glorifies stoicism and dismisses sensitivity, many individuals find themselves grappling with a profound sense of loss, not only of their emotional connections but also of their own sense of identity. The weight of unexpressed feelings and unacknowledged struggles can become a heavy burden, obscuring the significance of their existence and their innate worth.

Intersectional Considerations

Navigating the complexities of masculinity, men from diverse backgrounds face unique challenges that shape their identities and self-perceptions. Consider the Black man who, often burdened by societal expectations and stereotypes, feels compelled to suppress his anger to avoid confrontation or the stigma that comes with being labelled as "aggressive." This internal struggle can lead to a profound sense of isolation, as his genuine emotions remain hidden beneath a veneer of stoicism.

Similarly, the gay man often grapples with the necessity of masking his tenderness and vulnerability to conform to heteronormative standards. In doing so, he may feel that he has to sacrifice authenticity for acceptance, creating a tension between his true self and the persona he presents to the world.

This disconnect can result in significant emotional turmoil, as he navigates the challenges of belonging and self-expression.

The working-class man faces a different yet equally pressing dilemma. He internalises the belief that taking a moment to rest equates to laziness, driving him to constantly push himself to meet harsh economic demands. This relentless pursuit of productivity can lead to burnout and a sense of worthlessness, as he feels that his value is tied solely to his labour.

Meanwhile, the autistic man often finds himself misjudged, perceived as distant or indifferent, when in reality, he might be overwhelmed by sensory stimuli that others barely notice. This misunderstanding can exacerbate feelings of alienation, as he longs for genuine connection but struggles to communicate in ways that are readily understood by those around him.

Together, these narratives highlight how societal pressures and expectations can lead to disparate experiences rooted in a shared theme: the erasure of individual identity. Each man's journey reveals the complexities of their emotional landscapes and underscores the importance of empathy and understanding in recognising the rich tapestry of human experience.

The Coaching Reframe

Life coaching isn't a one-size-fits-all solution; rather, it serves as a powerful tool for empowering individuals to reclaim their personal narratives. It invites you to take control of your life's story, to pick up the metaphorical pen and begin crafting the tale you genuinely wish to tell. Take a moment to reflect: What narratives have been handed to you by family, society, or past experiences that feel misaligned with your authentic self? In which chapter of your life did you pause your self-expression, burying your genuine emotions and desires under expectations?

Consider the roles you've been compelled to adopt to gain acceptance and conformity. Were you the peacemaker, the overachiever, or perhaps the silent observer? How have these roles shaped your identity, and are they reflective of who you truly are?

Most importantly, consider the ending that resonates with your true self, not just a survival story that gets you through, but one that vibrantly captures your authenticity and aspirations. You don't have to erase or forget your past; instead, embrace and reclaim the parts of yourself that have remained unwritten, the thoughts, dreams, and expressions that wait patiently for you to acknowledge them. This journey of self-discovery and renewal can lead you toward a life that reflects your deepest values and aspirations, allowing you to write a narrative that is entirely your own.

Narrative Therapy: Healing Through Self-Authorship

To embark on a journey of true healing and personal growth, it is essential to take a step back and examine the narrative of your life, the story you have crafted over the years. Begin by identifying the edits and revisions that have been made, sometimes unconsciously, as a means of self-protection. Acknowledge those protective lies that once served a purpose, providing comfort or safety in difficult times, yet may now be holding you back from embracing your authentic self.

Reflect on the survival strategies you've employed throughout your life. These coping mechanisms, whether they were avoidance, overachievement, or perfectionism, have shaped who you are today. It's essential to acknowledge and appreciate how these strategies have helped you navigate challenges, while also recognising when they have outlived their usefulness.

Now, turn your gaze to your origin story. This is the narrative that truly encapsulates who you are at your core, one that is not clouded by societal expectations or the opinions of others. Embrace this story wholeheartedly, as it holds the key to your true identity and aspirations.

As you acknowledge your past, reclaim the power within your own hands. Begin to write the next chapter of your life with intention and authenticity. Remember, you are not defined by past failures or setbacks. Instead, view yourself as the sole author of your narrative, navigating the pages of your life with the authority to reshape your story. Give yourself permission to pen your own tale, one that reflects your dreams, desires, and the person you strive to become.

Five Stages of Story Recovery

1 **Awareness:** Begin by acknowledging how your personal narrative may have been altered or influenced by external factors. Recognise that specific experiences and inputs may have shaped your perspective without your consent, resulting in a disconnection from your authentic self.

2 **Grief:** Allow yourself the space to mourn not only the events that have passed but also the dreams, ambitions, and facets of your identity that have been suppressed or overlooked. Recognise the emotional weight of these losses, and give yourself permission to feel the sadness, frustration, or anger that may surface as you reflect on what has been lost.

3 **Reconnection:** Take the necessary steps to revisit and rediscover the passions, interests, and joys that once defined you. Engage in activities that reignite your spirit and remind you of your true self. This may involve trying new hobbies, reconnecting with old friends, or simply taking time to reflect and uncover what truly excites and fulfils you.

4 **Reframing:** Make a conscious effort to challenge the limiting beliefs that have kept you feeling small, insignificant, or unworthy. Critically examine these thoughts and their origins, and then actively work to rewrite your internal narrative. Replace negative self-talk

with affirmations that celebrate your strengths, capabilities, and inherent value.

5   **Reclaiming:** Ultimately, embark on the empowering journey of finding your voice. Share your truth with confidence and vulnerability, allowing your story to resonate with others. Live authentically, aligning your actions and choices with your true self, and embrace the freedom that comes from fully expressing who you are in all aspects of your life.

Gentle Prompts – Reflecting on the Silence Beneath the Surface

- What was my authentic self like before the weight of expectations labelled me as "the strong one"? Did I have dreams and aspirations that were vibrant and full of life, or was I already conditioned to suppress them in favour of resilience?
- What passions and interests did I hold close to my heart before I fell into the routine of merely surviving day by day? Were there activities that brought me joy and fulfilment that I have since neglected or forgotten?
- Which aspects of my identity am I eager to reconnect with, perhaps those parts that once defined me and provided a sense of belonging? Are there traits or characteristics that I have silenced to fit into a mould created by others?
- Whose approval have I sought in my journey of self-redefinition, and when I reflect on this, is it truly justified? Have I compromised my ideals and values to gain acceptance, and at what cost?
- What would it feel like to stand in my truth and express my thoughts, feelings, and desires openly and honestly? How liberating would it be to shed the masks I've worn and embrace my true self without fear of judgment?

By deeply engaging with these reflective questions, you can begin to unravel the complex layers of societal expectations that have shaped your life, allowing you to rediscover and embrace your true essence with clarity and confidence.

You're Not Erased. You're Buried.

You are not merely the silence that envelops you; you are the voice within, longing to break free from beneath its weight. You are not just the provider who fulfils others' needs; you are the individual who once dreamed fervently of a future prosperous with passion and endless potential, eager to delve into the uncharted depths of who you truly could become.

You are not the man moulded by the expectations and pressures of society; you are that spirited boy who once burned brightly with audacious dreams and vibrant ambitions. Deep inside, that spark still resides, waiting patiently for you to ignite it once more.

Recognise that your story has not reached its conclusion; it hasn't been erased from existence. Instead, it has simply been placed on pause, awaiting your courage to continue writing the next chapter of your life.

So, I encourage you to pick up the pen again. Write with the fervour of your heart, infusing each word with the intensity of your emotions and experiences. Speak your truth boldly, regardless of how it may be received by those around you. Remember who you are at your core, the essence that defines you beyond the roles you've assumed.

The world may often favour the version of you that appears self-sufficient and untroubled, but true healing begins when you confront the raw emotions simmering beneath the surface. Acknowledge the reality of your feelings: "I miss who I used to be. I want him back."

You possess the power to reclaim that lost part of yourself, one deliberate step at a time. One honest word at a time. One deep, grounding breath at a time. One poignant line at a time. Even now, in this very moment, you hold the power to begin anew to reshape your narrative and rediscover the vibrant dreams that once filled your spirit with light. Embrace the journey of rediscovery, and allow yourself the grace to evolve into the person you were always meant to be.

Chapter 15

The Villain Construct – Why Men Become the Bad Guy in Everyone's Story (Even Their Own)

He often comes across as cold, distant, and controlling, and to some, he might even appear abusive. Yet, it's crucial to recognise that these labels may not reflect the whole reality of who he is. Despite his potential for depth, he frequently finds himself cast as the antagonist in the stories of those around him. In moments of conflict, instead of responding with anger or defensiveness, he retreats deep within himself, sealing off his emotions behind a formidable wall of silence. This withdrawal isn't an act of defiance; it's a survival mechanism, a way to cope with an overwhelming internal storm of feelings that he struggles to articulate.

To his partner, this silence can feel like abandonment, igniting fears and assumptions that lead to grim conclusions: that he must be hiding something, that he does not care, or worse, that he embodies the traits of a narcissist, a gaslighter, or a manipulator. These interpretations, however, overlook the possibility that his silence is not meant to inflict pain or create distance. Instead, it can be seen as an instinctive act of self-preservation. When faced with emotional turmoil, he may feel that expressing his feelings would only exacerbate the situation or expose him to vulnerabilities he isn't ready to confront.

This leads to a poignant consideration: what if his retreat is indicative not of a lack of emotion, but of an overwhelming tide of feelings he simply cannot express? This struggle to communicate places him squarely within what I call the Villain Construct, a label he never chose for himself but one that is thrust upon him by the misinterpretation of his actions. With time, he begins to absorb this perception, shaping not only how others view him but how he sees himself. The tragedy lies in the realisation that the distance he thought would protect him ultimately leads to a profound sense of isolation, and a search for connection that seems ever elusive. Misinterpretation of his actions. More painfully, it is how he begins to see himself through that lens.

The Social Mask of the Villain

Men often find themselves navigating a perilous social landscape that offers them minimal encouragement to embrace their emotional complexity. Within this landscape, society presents a limited framework of acceptable identities that often confines them to two extremes: the stoic hero and the fallen man. These archetypes leave little room for nuance, usually invalidating the rich spectrum of emotions and experiences that men may encounter.

The cultural narrative glorifies the archetype of the strong, silent type, suggesting that true masculinity lies in emotional restraint and stoicism. However, this praise is paradoxically accompanied by profound criticism of men who display emotional unavailability. For instance, when a man chooses to detach himself to avoid confrontation, he may be labelled as controlling or manipulative. Conversely, if he attempts to assert healthy boundaries, he risks being marked as toxic. The dichotomy extends to communication; silence can be interpreted as manipulation, while speaking plainly or expressing vulnerability may be deemed aggressive or overly emotional.

This barrage of conflicting expectations creates an exhausting performance of masculinity that can feel like a trap. Men find themselves in a position where they are damned if they do and damned if they don't. When subtlety and complexity are stripped away, the Villain Construct emerges, reducing multifaceted individuals to mere caricatures within someone else's narrative. As a result, men often internalise this reductive perception, gradually shaping their self-concept to align with the distorted lens through which they are viewed. This self-image can lead to profound feelings of isolation and inadequacy, as they struggle to navigate a world that seems increasingly unforgiving of their authentic selves.

Contrast and Double Standards

There exists a striking double standard in how emotional withdrawal is interpreted across gender lines, leading to significant misinterpretations that can impact individuals and their relationships. When a woman withdraws emotionally, society often responds with empathy and understanding. Cultural narratives frame her need for space as a vital aspect of self-care and personal growth. A woman's detachment is typically viewed through the lens of emotional overload or the necessity for introspection, allowing her to prioritise her mental well-being without stigma.

In stark contrast, when a man chooses to retreat emotionally, the narrative shifts dramatically, often with negative consequences. He is frequently labelled as distant, dangerous, or cold, terms that carry a weight of judgment and misunderstanding. His solitude is not seen as a necessary form of self-care but rather as a punitive action against those around him, suggesting a lack of emotional engagement or inability to connect. This disparity in interpretation reflects deep-rooted gender biases that influence our perceptions of emotional expression.

This cultural dissonance contributes to the perpetuation of the Villain Construct, where negative assumptions about men arise not necessarily from their actions but from how those actions are perceived. The bias often leads to a mischaracterisation of his intentions; what may be an earnest attempt to cope with overwhelming emotions can be misconstrued as a sign of malevolence or emotional unavailability. In this context, men find themselves ensnared within a web of false identities, burdened by societal expectations that do not align with their true selves. Such misunderstandings not only complicate individual emotional experiences but also strain interpersonal relationships, highlighting the urgent need for more nuanced discussions around gender, emotional health, and the complexities of human behaviour.

Psychological Framing: The Protector and the Exile

In the realm of trauma therapy, particularly through the lens of Internal Family Systems (IFS), a profound and intricate pattern emerges that sheds light on the complex interplay within a man's psyche. Often, expressions of anger, silence, or withdrawal are not simply emotional responses; they represent the voice of a Protector, a crucial part of his internal system that develops early in life to safeguard a more vulnerable aspect known as the Exile.

The Exile embodies deep-seated wounds from formative experiences. These wounds can manifest as feelings of emotional neglect, betrayal, humiliation, and rejection. The Exile is not just a distant memory; he is the child who was ridiculed for showing sadness, which instilled the belief that vulnerability would only lead to disdain. He also embodies the adolescent who, in his attempt to express his authentic self, faced harsh judgment from peers and authority figures. As a young adult, he may have taken a courageous step toward openness, only to be labelled as weak or inadequate, further deepening the fissures in his self-worth.

In response to these early traumas, the Protector emerges, adopting various masks and strategies to maintain emotional safety. One common manifestation is anger, which can serve as a formidable barrier against perceived threats. However, anger is merely a singular expression within the Protector's wide range of responses. More frequently, the Protector's influence is felt as numbness, apathy, or relentless over-functioning behaviours that superficially resemble success, control, and rationality. Beneath this carefully constructed facade lies a psyche in profound turmoil. One part strives tirelessly to suppress the painful feelings associated with the Exile, while another instinctively seeks to avoid others' scrutiny, fearing judgment and rejection.

Unfortunately, societal norms often deprive men of the opportunity to explore these intricate internal dynamics.

Culturally prescribed notions of masculinity frequently valorise stoicism, self-reliance, and emotional suppression, leaving little room for vulnerability or introspection. As a result, many men begin to conflate their protective personas with their true identities. They lose sight of the fact that within their silence often lies a flickering ember of safety, a once-reliable refuge. They may forget that what outwardly manifests as aggression can frequently be a profound expression of grief and loss, revealing not just personal struggle but also a broader commentary on the emotional landscape that men navigate in a society reluctant to embrace their vulnerability.

Biopsychology and the Survival Blueprint

Exploring the intricate biological foundations of male behaviour reveals how significantly the male nervous system is influenced by early exposure to testosterone as well as prevailing cultural scripts surrounding masculinity. This conditioning fosters a predisposition for action-oriented responses over introspective contemplation. When confronted with stressors, the amygdala, the brain's powerhouse for fear and survival, becomes activated, often overpowering the rational decision-making capabilities of the prefrontal cortex. This activation can elicit three foundational responses: fight, flight, or freeze.

For many men, the "freeze" response may present itself as emotional withdrawal during conflicts. This might involve shutting down communication, refusing to engage in discussions, or suppressing feelings altogether. Such behaviour can create significant distress in relationships, often leaving partners feeling ignored or unvalued. The "flight" response typically manifests as avoidance or disengagement, wherein an individual distance themselves physically or emotionally from loved ones to escape the discomfort of conflict. This can lead to escalating feelings of isolation and disconnection. In contrast, the "fight" response often bubbles to the surface as reactive anger, a defence mechanism that is rooted in deep-seated feelings of vulnerability and frustration. This kind of explosive reaction can result in verbal or physical confrontations, further damaging interpersonal relationships.

It is essential to understand that these responses are not the result of conscious thought or calculated choices; instead, they are instinctual, biological reactions deeply embedded in our evolutionary survival mechanisms. These responses echo back to our earliest ancestors, who navigated a dangerous world where swift decisions between safety and peril were paramount.

Layered on top of these biological mechanisms are complex biochemical factors that further complicate emotional regulation. Chronic elevation of cortisol, a hormone released during periods of stress can lead to emotional numbness, making it challenging to connect with feelings or display emotional responses. Conversely, it can also provoke bouts of explosive rage. Additionally, a decrease in oxytocin levels, especially following traumatic or distressing experiences, can significantly impair an individual's ability to form and maintain emotional bonds with others, leading to profound feelings of isolation and loneliness. Furthermore, dysregulation of dopamine pathways may drive individuals toward compulsive behaviours, such as excessive consumption of pornography, overworking, or substance abuse, as maladaptive strategies for self-soothing and coping with emotional pain.

While grasping these biological and psychological processes does not excuse maladaptive behaviours, it provides essential context for understanding them. Such insights bridge the often vast gulf between judgment and compassion, fostering not only a richer understanding of the challenges many men face in their emotional lives but also encouraging a more empathetic approach to their struggles. This deeper comprehension can facilitate healthier communication, emotional expression, and interpersonal connections in the quest for emotional well-being.

Clinical Sidebar: Attachment Styles and the Mislabelling of Men

Grasping the concept of attachment styles is essential for illuminating how societal norms and expectations often mislabel and stigmatise men. These attachment styles, which stem from early relationships with caregivers, profoundly influence emotional regulation and interpersonal dynamics in adulthood. By exploring the intricate connections between formative attachment experiences and adult behaviours, we can develop a more nuanced understanding of emotional responses that many men exhibit throughout their lives.

For instance, men who exhibit avoidant attachment may be perceived as emotionally distant or unapproachable, when in reality, their behaviour may be a learned response to early experiences of neglect or emotional unavailability. This misinterpretation can lead to stigma, reinforcing damaging stereotypes about masculinity and emotional expression.

Furthermore, acknowledging these patterns underscores the importance of empathy and support in therapeutic settings. Mental health professionals can better assist their clients by considering how societal expectations shape their emotional experiences and behaviours. By fostering an environment of understanding, we can challenge prevailing norms and promote healthier models of masculinity that embrace vulnerability, emotional expression, and genuine connection. Such an approach not only aids individual healing but also fosters a broader cultural shift towards acceptance and compassion.

Attachment Theory and Adult Intimacy Patterns

Attachment theory provides crucial insights into how our formative relationships shape our capacity to forge intimate connections in adulthood. This concept is particularly relevant when examining men, whose attachment styles are often misunderstood or oversimplified in societal narratives.

Avoidant Attachment: Men with avoidant attachment styles are frequently labelled as cold or emotionally unavailable. This characterisation fails to capture the complexity of their experiences. Many of these individuals harbour a profound fear of engulfment, which can stem from past experiences where emotional closeness felt overwhelming or invasive. As a protective mechanism, they may withdraw from emotional engagement, prioritising their independence and autonomy over vulnerability. This can lead partners to misinterpret their need for space as aloofness or disinterest, rather than recognising it as a shield against perceived threats to their individuality.

Anxious Attachment: In contrast, men exhibiting anxious attachment styles are often viewed as needy or controlling. However, this perception neglects the underlying psychological drivers of their behaviour. These men typically experience a heightened fear of abandonment, which can manifest as a constant need for reassurance and validation from their partners. This anxiety can lead them to engage in behaviours that may seem overwhelming or suffocating to their partners. Unfortunately, rather than fostering a sense of intimacy, this dynamic can push loved ones away, creating a cycle of distress and misunderstanding. Recognising that this clinginess emerges from a place of vulnerability rather than a desire for control can cultivate greater empathy and patience in relationships.

Disorganised Attachment: The disorganised attachment style presents a particularly intricate challenge, often manifesting as a confusing array of clinginess and avoidance. Men with this attachment style may have histories marked by complex trauma, characterised by inconsistent or abusive caregiving in their formative years. As a result, their erratic behaviours oscillating between desperation for connection and a withdrawal from intimacy can be mistaken for manipulation or emotional gamesmanship. In reality, these patterns reflect an internal struggle marked by unresolved fear, anxiety, and a desperate yearning for safety and security. Understanding this dynamic paves, the way for compassion rather than judgment, allowing partners to provide the support these individuals desperately need.

By gaining a deeper understanding of these attachment styles, we can challenge and reframe harmful stereotypes that skew our perceptions of male emotional experiences. This awareness fosters a more compassionate and empathetic approach to relationships, paving the way for healthier interactions and connections built on mutual understanding. By acknowledging the complexities of these attachment dynamics, we create opportunities for healing and fostering secure attachments in our own relationships.

Psychiatric Misdiagnosis and Masculine Shame

Research undertaken by the NHS and various psychiatric case reviews reveals a concerning trend: men are disproportionately misdiagnosed with antisocial personality traits, particularly when they present with symptoms related to trauma. This misdiagnosis often occurs because emotional detachment, an adaptive response to trauma, is frequently misconstrued as coldness or lack of empathy. Simultaneously, expressions of anger and frustration, which may actually stem from deep-seated pain and distress, are too readily interpreted as aggressive threats rather than as cries for help.

Moreover, conditions like Post-Traumatic Stress Disorder (PTSD) often go unrecognised, especially when a man's experience does not align with the stereotypical narrative of a "broken veteran." This oversight is particularly troubling because it overlooks the diverse backgrounds of trauma survivors and the manifestations of their suffering, which can vary widely.

A significant barrier in effective clinical practice is that many men remain unaware of the trauma they carry; they may perceive themselves not as survivors but merely as "broken" individuals. This critical misperception can entrench the most dangerous internal conflict: the damaging belief that "Maybe I am the problem." Such thoughts can lead to a toxic shame that seeps into their self-identity, fostering the conviction that there is something irreparably flawed within them, rather than recognising that the issues lie within their coping mechanisms and the circumstances they've faced.

Understanding these dynamics is crucial for mental health professionals. By reframing how we interpret male emotional responses and acknowledging the nuanced presentations of trauma, we can create a more inclusive and practical approach to diagnosis and treatment.

Sexuality, Shame, and the Villain Construct

In the realm of sex therapy, a powerful insight often emerges surrounding the Villain Construct, particularly concerning men and their experiences with intimacy. Many men, rather than pursuing authentic emotional connections, find themselves measuring their self-worth through their sexual encounters. This approach stems from a pervasive fear of impotence, which breeds feelings of inadequacy and defectiveness. On the flip side, incidents of successful sexual performance can lead to heightened anxiety about being reduced to mere objects of desire or utility. Such dynamics can transform intimacy into a transactional exchange, where a partner's plea for emotional openness is perceived not as an invitation for connection but as a stipulation for acceptance: "If you don't perform, you're not enough."

Moreover, when men experience sexual shutdown, their withdrawal is frequently misinterpreted as a form of rejection. Yet, this behaviour often arises from deeper issues such as anxiety, past trauma, or profound shame. When a man pulls away, it is not an act of emotional punishment toward his partner; rather, it serves as a protective strategy to shield parts of himself he fears are unlovable or inadequate. This withdrawal can exacerbate feelings of disconnection, leading the partner to perceive their emotional distance as harmful. In turn, this perceived harm can tighten the grip of the Villain mask, a facade that many men feel obligated to don to navigate their relational experiences. Thus, the cycle of disconnection deepens, entrenching both partners in a struggle that hinders genuine intimacy and understanding.

Relationship Breakdown and the Shame Spiral

When men are viewed through the lens of villainy, it creates an internal narrative that can be damaging and self-defeating. They may grapple with thoughts like, "I ruin everything," "I'm the reason she's unhappy," or "I'm a failure as a man." This relentless cycle of negative self-talk breeds a pervasive sense of shame that stifles growth and personal development, often steering them toward emotional collapse rather than progress.

As this shame festers, the consequences can be profound. Men may find themselves retreating into isolation, numbing their feelings with distractions such as excessive work or unhealthy habits. This response is a misguided attempt to mask their pain but ultimately leads to deeper struggles. For instance, when a partner expresses feelings of exclusion or disconnect, the man might instinctively think, "If you truly saw what's inside me, you would leave." Such thoughts not only exacerbate feelings of inadequacy but also create a wall of misunderstanding that separates both partners.

As a result, both individuals in the relationship may feel isolated and misunderstood, trapped in a cycle where only one partner is often branded as the problem. This dynamic can lead to a tragic stalemate, where emotional walls grow thicker, communication breaks down, and the potential for intimacy and connection becomes increasingly elusive. Recognising and dismantling this narrative is crucial for healing and fostering healthier relationships, where both partners can feel valued and understood.

A Life Coaching Reframe: The Misunderstood Man

By reframing the narrative surrounding the experiences and behaviours of men, we open the door to a more profound understanding of their struggles and complexities. This paradigm shift invites a sense of compassion and empathy, fostering a more constructive dialogue about emotional health and intimacy. Recognising the nuances of men's emotional landscapes is essential in providing the support they need on their journeys toward healing and meaningful connection.

Life coaching serves as a powerful tool that challenges the traditional narrative, which often casts individuals, particularly men, in a villainous light within their own stories. Instead of perpetuating stereotypes, coaching delves beneath the surface, peeling back the layers of societal expectations to reveal not a villain, but a shape-shifter. This is someone who has skilfully learned to navigate a world laden with outdated expectations and pressures that were never genuinely their own.

The transformative journey of life coaching begins with thought-provoking questions designed to disrupt ingrained beliefs and foster self-awareness. These questions challenge the status quo and invite introspection, such as:
- "Who told you that silence was safer than speech?"
- "What part of you are you trying to protect?"
- "Who benefits from you believing you're the villain?"

The essence of this coaching work lies in the concept of re-parenting the self. It involves crafting a new narrative for one's life, an empowering script that acknowledges the importance of voice and expression. This process is vital in teaching the nervous system that proper safety does not require the suppression of thoughts and emotions. By engaging in this inner dialogue, men can begin to rewrite their life stories, embracing vulnerability and authenticity as strengths rather than weaknesses. This journey not only paves the way for personal growth but also facilitates deeper, more genuine connections with others, fostering a community built on understanding and shared experiences.

Healing Through Relationship

It is crucial to recognise that healing is rarely a solitary journey, particularly for men. Authentic healing unfolds through safe and supportive connections that allow individuals to feel seen and heard, rather than being subjected to judgment or criticism. This relational approach fosters an environment where vulnerability is not only accepted but celebrated, encouraging emotional expression and honest dialogue.

For partners engaged in these relationships, adopting mindful communication strategies can significantly enhance the quality of interactions. Instead of using phrases like, "You always...," consider rephrasing your observations with "I feel..." This subtle shift focuses on your feelings, minimizing the chance of blame and promoting a more empathetic exchange. Additionally, asking the question, "What are you protecting when you shut down?" can invite deeper insights into emotional barriers, fostering a greater understanding between partners. Emphasising the intention behind your words with "I want to understand, not attack," helps to create a safe haven for open dialogue, reducing defensiveness and building trust.

For men, the journey towards emotional growth often begins with embracing what are termed "micro-truths." These are small, yet significant acknowledgements of one's feelings, such as, "I don't know what I feel, but I'm trying." Such honesty opens the door to genuine self-exploration and reflection. A meaningful practice to start this journey is journaling about your earliest memory of emotionally shutting down; this exercise can illuminate patterns and coping mechanisms that may have developed over time. Strive to name your emotions before slipping into defensiveness, as this practice not only cultivates emotional literacy but also empowers you to respond to emotions in a healthier, more constructive way. By taking these steps, individuals can foster a deeper understanding of themselves and their connections with others, paving the way for more enriching and authentic relationships.

Clinical Data Insights

Research highlights significant patterns in men's emotional experiences, revealing that a striking 44% of men tend to suppress their feelings to avoid the stigma associated with appearing weak, as reported by the UK Men's Health Forum in 2021. This suppression can lead to detrimental consequences for mental health, as emotional expression is crucial for processing feelings and reducing stress.

Moreover, the impact of childhood experiences on adult behaviour cannot be overlooked; men who have faced four or more Adverse Childhood Experiences (ACEs) are four times more likely to be perceived as aggressive. This correlation suggests that unaddressed trauma from childhood can manifest in behaviours that reinforce societal stereotypes about masculinity.

Compounding these issues is the alarming rate of misdiagnosis of trauma-related disorders among men, particularly in UK psychiatric settings, where over 60% of cases are inaccurately assessed. This misdiagnosis not only perpetuates misunderstandings about male mental health but also underscores an urgent need for a comprehensive understanding of how trauma manifests in men. Addressing these issues is essential for improving mental health support and fostering an environment where men can express their emotions without fear of judgment.

Gentle Prompts for Reflection

To facilitate deep and meaningful personal growth, consider taking time to reflect on the following prompts:

- When did I first decide that I was the problem? Recall the moment this belief took root in your mind. Was it a specific event, a relationship, or perhaps a recurring pattern that led you to internalise this narrative?

Understanding the origin can help you unravel its impact on your current self-perception.

- What part of me is trying to shield myself from feelings of shame? Explore the facets of your personality that may be guarding you against vulnerability. Is it a fear of judgment, rejection, or the pain of past experiences? Identifying these protective mechanisms can aid in understanding how they influence your behaviour and interactions with others.

- What do I need from others to feel safe, even when I might be misunderstood? Consider what you seek in relationships: empathy, validation, patience, or perhaps open communication. Acknowledging these needs is crucial for building connections that foster your sense of safety and security, especially during challenging times of confusion or emotional upheaval.

- Who would I be without the constant need to defend myself? Reflect on how your life would change if you let go of the instinct to justify your actions or feelings. Envision the potential freedom that comes from embracing vulnerability. What passions, joys, or relationships could flourish in an environment of self-acceptance?

In this journey of self-discovery, remember: You are not the villain of your story. You are the boy who was never truly shielded from life's challenges, now inhabiting a man's body as you search for a way back to your authentic self. Understand that you do not need to earn redemption; your worthiness is inherent. You deserve to be seen, understood, and embraced just as you are, whether you find yourself in moments of silence, grappling with confusion, or feeling vulnerable. Even in your most challenging times, you are enough. Cultivating self-compassion and nurturing your sense of belonging is vital for your growth and healing.

Chapter 16

The Mirror and the Mask: Unpacking the Male Ego

He steps into the bustling café, the myriad voices and clinking of cups fading into a background hum as he carries himself with a confidence that seems almost palpable. The tailored suit, a blend of fine fabric and meticulous craftsmanship, brushes softly against his skin, a tactile reminder of the armour he dons daily. When he speaks, his voice cuts through the ambient noise, steady and resonant, each word delivered with precision, as if he's navigating a carefully choreographed dance. His handshake is firm, the grip a deliberate expression of self-assuredness, with every movement crafted to convey an image of unwavering strength. And yet, beneath this polished exterior lies a complex reality: an intricate architecture known as the male ego, a delicate yet resilient construct built brick by brick throughout his life, designed to protect, assert, and thrive in a society that often demands a facade of fortitude.

This reliance on ego is not merely a manifestation of vanity; it is a sophisticated form of armour, forged in the crucible of childhood expectations, societal norms, and personal experiences. The ego acts as a shield, erecting barriers that separate him from the world around him. It consumes his shame like bitter medicine, burying fears deep within the recesses of his mind and silencing the gentler emotions that linger in his heart. The vulnerable boy who once roamed freely and curiously is now obscured behind a facade of stoicism that he feels compelled to uphold. This ego endeavours to embody certainty in every aspect of his life, even when, beneath its fortified walls, self-doubt pulses relentlessly, an ever-present rhythm like a second heartbeat.

Over time, the pressure of maintaining such a facade inevitably reveals its toll. The cracks do not erupt dramatically but instead emerge as micro-fractures, subtle yet revealing, often unnoticed by those around him. In moments when tensions rise, he finds himself interrupting conversations, a subconscious attempt to reclaim control; his voice, betraying him, slightly lifts in pitch, an instinctive response to perceived threats. When emotions draw too close for comfort, he instinctively retreats, hiding behind layers of indifference and bravado, presenting a tough exterior while internally wrestling with vulnerability. Constructive feedback, designed to foster growth, becomes a prick to the delicate fabric of his ego, sending him into a defensive posture, where he bristles or, at times, lashes out in anger when he feels his worth is questioned. Silence often blankets him, not as a pursuit of peace, but as a calculated strategy to protect the carefully crafted mask he wears.

Yet, amidst the stillness that follows these reactions, when the clamour of external expectations diminishes and the world quiets, something stirs deep within the recesses of his being. A deeper longing begins to surface, a subtle whisper beneath the layers of ego that yearns to be acknowledged. This voice craves not accolades or fleeting admiration but a raw, authentic connection that transcends the superficiality of daily performances. It seeks understanding, acceptance, and the profound realisation that vulnerability and strength are not mutually exclusive. This inner dialogue echoes a powerful desire to reconcile the man he has become with the boy he once was, to embody a fullness of self where both tenderness and resilience can coexist harmoniously.

The Cultural Mirror: How Class, Race, and Identity Shape Ego

Not all egos are shaped from the same mould; they are influenced by a tapestry of experiences, cultures, and societal expectations. For the working-class man, ego is often intricately tied to the dignity of craftsmanship. It embodies the calloused hands that tell the story of a lifetime dedicated to hard work, and the immense pride that comes from showing up day in and day

232

out, despite enduring pain, hardship, and the struggles of economic uncertainty. This steadfast commitment to one's trade becomes a core aspect of one's identity, a source of pride that fuels one's self-worth.

For the Black man, ego transforms into a vital form of armour, essential for navigating a world rife with systemic racism and social inequities. This ego acts as a shield against relentless forces that seek to diminish, dehumanise, and discredit him at every turn. It is a complex survival mechanism, honed through generations of resilience. The struggles he faces are not merely personal; they resonate with a collective history, making his ego both a personal fortress and a testament to the strength of heritage.

Similarly, for the queer man, ego often serves as both a protective shield and an elaborate performance. It is meticulously forged through years of concealing his true self, battling societal expectations, and confronting the internalised fears that arise in a world that frequently questions his masculinity and worth. His ego becomes a space where defiance and authenticity collide. As he navigates this intricate landscape, he learns that to embrace his identity entirely is both a radical act of self-acceptance and a challenge against the stereotypes imposed upon him.

Yet, ego is not merely a personal trait; it is deeply influenced by historical context, cultural narratives, and the weight of trauma. For many men, it is not an inflated sense of self that leads to conflict and dysfunction, but rather a distorted version of the ego they have inherited. This warped perception reinforces the damaging notion that "You are only as valuable as your ability to dominate, produce, or remain unshaken in the face of adversity." Such beliefs can create a cycle of validation based on societal standards that often overlook the complexities of individual identity.

True evolution of the ego requires an initial acknowledgement of its layers and origins. Recognition must unfold in stages: first, as a protector earning its place in the psyche, and then as a prisoner, confining him to outdated beliefs and behaviours that no longer serve him. As the silent performer confronts this intricate dance with his ego, he embarks on a transformative journey towards genuine self-acceptance and liberation. This process involves untangling the threads of identity shaped by external expectations, ultimately leading to a more authentic and fulfilling existence.

The Silent Performer

The ego acts not merely as a protective shield, but also as a complex filter, functioning as a suit of armour against the vulnerabilities that lie just beneath the surface, threatening to be exposed. This carefully constructed façade obscures deep-seated feelings of shame, inadequacy, and self-doubt, effectively locking away the broken boy who is yearning for acceptance and love behind the guise of a confident adult. This intricate construct serves to replace the chaotic landscape of uncertainty with a comforting cloak of certainty, providing a semblance of stability and control that can be upheld, albeit only temporarily, until a crack inevitably emerges in the façade.

These fractures, however, rarely present themselves through loud tantrums or overt breakdowns; instead, they manifest in subtler, more insidious behaviours that often go unnoticed. Perhaps it's the habit of interrupting others during conversations, a desperate need to assert control and be heard at all costs, or an inclination to retreat from emotional intimacy, preferring to build walls that keep others at arm's length. It can also be seen in the unpredictable eruptions of anger that arise without clear triggers, leaving both the individual and those around them bewildered and hurt. After perceived slights or moments of disrespect, a chilling silence often envelops the individual, a deep withdrawal into isolation that reflects their inner turmoil and hurt.

Underneath it all lies a pervasive and gnawing terror of being fully seen beyond the carefully crafted mask, the dread of revealing the vulnerabilities that the ego has desperately fought to conceal.

Yet, in those rare, quiet, unguarded moments, an inner longing begins to stir, urging the individual to acknowledge and embrace the depths of their true self. This yearning highlights a more profound need for authenticity and heartfelt connection, a desire to step beyond the confines of the ego's defences and experience genuine intimacy with others, free from the fear of judgment and rejection. It is in that space of vulnerability that true healing and connection can begin to unfold.

The Cultural Mirror: How Class, Race, and Identity Shape Ego

Not all egos are shaped from the same mould; they are profoundly influenced by the cultural and social contexts surrounding individuals. For the working-class man, ego is intricately tied to the dignity of hard labour. His calloused hands and weathered features serve as a testament to a lifetime devoted to toil. This man draws immense pride from his unwavering resilience, showing up day after day, often at the expense of his own comfort and aspirations, all for the sake of providing for his family. His ego reflects a narrative woven into the fabric of his identity, one that celebrates perseverance, sacrifice, and the often-unseen struggles of daily life.

In contrast, for the Black man, ego becomes a vital form of armour, essential for protecting himself against the relentless systems of oppression that aim to diminish, dehumanise, and discredit him at every turn. Living in a society that frequently reduces him to harmful stereotypes, this man navigates an existence laden with the burden of proving his worth beyond the unjust narratives inflicted upon him. His ego, therefore, is not merely a reflection of self-esteem but a necessary shield that enables him to confront and challenge the societal forces that seek to undermine his identity and humanity.

Similarly, for the queer man, the ego often takes on a dual role of both shield and performance, painstakingly forged through years of concealing his authentic self and battling prevailing societal expectations. Striving to assert his identity, he faces the continual challenge of demonstrating his worth in a world that often questions his masculinity and humanity. The conflict between the desire for acceptance and the quest for authenticity creates a tumultuous landscape for his ego, compelling him to navigate the complexities of societal judgment while seeking to embrace his true self.

Thus, the ego transcends the realm of personal traits; it is a construct shaped by historical narratives, cultural influences, and individual traumas. For many men, it is not an inflated sense of self that leads to harm and dysfunction; rather, it is a distorted version of ego inherited from generations past, a narrative that conveys a damaging message: "You are only as valuable as your ability to dominate, produce, or remain unshaken in the face of adversity."

However, the true evolution of the ego cannot occur without first acknowledging its existence. Recognition must unfold in stages: initially, as a protector that has earned its place in one's psyche, and later, as a constraining prisoner, confining the individual to outdated beliefs and behaviours that no longer serve him. Only when the silent performer confronts this intricate dance with his ego can he embark on a transformative journey toward genuine self-acceptance and liberation. In doing so, he frees himself from the chains of societal expectations, redefining his worth beyond the narrow confines of traditional masculinity and embracing a more multifaceted sense of self. Ultimately, this process fosters a richer understanding of identity, allowing for a more authentic expression of ego that honours both individuality and shared humanity.

The Nervous System: When Ego Feels Like Survival

The ego is not merely a construct of our thoughts; it is deeply intertwined with our physical selves and manifested through our physiological responses. When a man's social status or self-worth comes under scrutiny, his nervous system reacts as though it is

236

facing a genuine threat. This reaction triggers a complex cascade of physiological responses: cortisol levels spike, heart rates quicken, and breathing becomes shallow and rapid. This phenomenon aligns with polyvagal theory, which suggests that our bodies are in a perpetual state of vigilance, continuously scanning our environment for signals that indicate safety or danger. These signals can range from subtle cues of respect to stark experiences of rejection or direct challenges to one's power and authority.

Research indicates that in the male brain, threats to status engage the same pain centres that respond to physical injuries. Consequently, when a man experiences feelings of dismissal, criticism, or humiliation, his body reacts as if it is enduring an actual attack. This visceral response helps explain why interpersonal disagreements can evoke feelings as intense and damaging as those experienced during outright warfare. Silence during conflicts can breed a profound sense of shame, amplifying the emotional turmoil. Moreover, the act of expressing vulnerability may feel akin to stepping into a perilous situation, as it can leave a person feeling exposed and at risk.

By cultivating an awareness of and learning to interpret these somatic cues, individuals can begin to disentangle their egos from automatic survival mechanisms. What might initially appear as defensive posturing could, in fact, be a manifestation of emotional dysregulation, a signal that there are deeper, unresolved feelings at play. Understanding this connection between mind and body is crucial for fostering healthier relationships and promoting emotional resilience.

Trauma-Linked Ego Patterns: Narcissistic Shields and Shame Collapse

Some individuals create grandiose, boastful personas not out of genuine self-belief, but rather from a profound fear of being perceived as inferior. This phenomenon is often rooted in childhood experiences characterised by neglect, excessive criticism, or conditional affection. As a result, the ego becomes a

237

defensive fortress, a barrier against the anticipated threats of judgment and rejection from others. This grandiosity functions as a shield, masking insecurities and providing a semblance of control in social situations.

Conversely, there exists a contrasting response known as shame collapse. Individuals who experience this may find themselves unable to meet both internal expectations and external societal standards. This struggle can lead to a debilitating cycle of self-loathing, diminishing the ego instead of inflating it. Those in this state often withdraw from social interactions, over-apologise for their perceived shortcomings, and develop a pervasive sense of invisibility, feeling as though they are fading into the background of their own lives. This withdrawal serves as a protective mechanism against further judgment, illustrating an internal battle with self-worth and identity.

Both of these responses can be understood as adaptations to trauma, revealing the complex ways in which the ego manifests in response to psychological distress. While one response may lead to an inflated sense of self, the other results in a retreat from self-assertion. This dichotomy showcases the varying degrees of ego, either towering above as a defence or shrinking away in defeat.

As Dr. Gabor Maté aptly states, "The false self is always trying to prove something. The real self is just trying to live." This poignant observation highlights the disconnection often present between the projected ego and the authentic self. When individuals become entangled in the pursuit of an idealised persona, they risk losing touch with their true identities and the ability to engage with the world on a genuine level. The journey toward self-acceptance involves recognising these defences, understanding their origins, and ultimately reconnecting with the authentic self, which seeks to live authentically and in harmony with one's own values and desires.

Ego in the Mirror of Others

The true nature of the ego becomes increasingly apparent within the realm of interpersonal relationships, shedding light on the often unconscious motives that drive our interactions. Take, for instance, a disagreement with a partner. In such moments, one may find themselves entrenched in the mindset of "I need to be right," leading to defensiveness and further escalation rather than constructive resolution. This fixation on being correct can cloud judgment and stifle open communication, ultimately creating a chasm instead of bridging one.

In the context of friendships, the ego can manifest as a reluctance to reveal vulnerability, fostering connections that remain superficial and devoid of genuine intimacy. The fear of being perceived as weak can hinder authentic exchanges and prevent deep emotional bonds from forming. Friendships built on a facade rather than transparency often lack the support and trust necessary for genuine companionship.

When examining fatherhood, the ego can impose a cumbersome burden. A prevailing belief that one must "never fail" can create immense pressure to perform flawlessly in all aspects of parenting. This expectation can lead to burnout and a sense of inadequacy, as the reality of parenting is filled with imperfection and unpredictability. However, children are not in search of a perfect father; they yearn for a father who is emotionally available, nurturing, and genuinely engaged in their lives. This emotional intelligence is far more impactful than any ideal of perfection.

Similarly, partners do not seek a heroic saviour; instead, they desire a soulful companion who can navigate life's peaks and valleys with them. They cherish the moments of vulnerability and honesty that create a safe space for shared experiences. In the sphere of brotherhood, the yearning is not for bravado or competition, but for authentic camaraderie and understanding qualities that foster trust and loyalty.

Ultimately, cultivating a deeper understanding of ego dynamics, especially regarding their impact on relationships, can pave the way for healthier interactions. By recognising the limitations that the ego imposes, individuals are better equipped to express their true selves. Embracing authenticity not only enriches our connections but also supports personal growth, leading to more fulfilling and meaningful relationships.

When Ego Is Good: The Gift of Healthy Pride

Ego is not always the enemy. In its most constructive form, it acts as a driving force, providing individuals, especially men with critical attributes like motivation, purpose, clarity, and a sense of structure. A healthy ego empowers men to assert solid personal boundaries, value their achievements, and walk confidently within a world that frequently attempts to undermine their self-worth.

A constructive ego communicates several essential truths that are vital for emotional and personal development:
- "I matter, and my feelings are valid." This affirmation helps cultivate self-respect and emotional awareness.
- "I have a right to be seen and heard." This encourages individuals to express themselves authentically, fostering interpersonal connections.
- "The work I contribute has intrinsic value." Recognising the worth of one's contributions strengthens self-esteem and encourages continued effort and diligence.
- "I can lead and inspire others without exerting control." This perspective promotes collaborative leadership, emphasising influence over authority.

Such a form of ego allows men to enter rooms with genuine confidence, marked by an absence of arrogance. It enables them to take pride in their achievements without feeling superior to others. A healthy ego gives the strength to hold firm in one's beliefs, fostering resilience while simultaneously respecting differing opinions and perspectives.

The ultimate goal, therefore, is not to eradicate the ego entirely, but rather to achieve a process known as ego integration. This involves striking a balance in which the ego supports and enriches one's identity, rather than detracting from it or becoming a source of conflict.

As bell hooks wisely stated, "To know love, we have to tell the truth. We have to be able to be honest." This honesty is integral to understanding the complex layers of our own identities and relationships.

The Ego Audit: From Armour to Awareness

Engaging in meaningful self-reflection can illuminate various aspects of your ego that require attention and understanding. To facilitate this process, consider the following introspective questions:

- Where in my life do I seek validation instead of pursuing my own truth? Identify the areas where external approval might overshadow a more profound understanding of your intrinsic self-worth.
- When do I find myself defending my position rather than striving to understand others? Acknowledging this tendency can help foster compassion, open-mindedness, and empathy in your interactions.
- What part of me feels most fragile, and how do I instinctively protect it? Understanding your vulnerabilities can help develop healthier coping strategies and responses to perceived threats or criticism.
- Who am I performing for? Reflect on whether you are adapting your persona to meet the expectations of others instead of expressing your authentic self, and consider the impact this has on your relationships.
- What am I afraid they'll see if I cease performing? Confronting these fears and insecurities can lead to profound personal growth and greater authenticity.

Ultimately, allow your ego to express its truths, and then extend to it the grace to soften, making space for personal growth, genuine connection, and heartfelt understanding.

Bookmark This Truth

The ego is not inherently evil; instead, it often bears the burden of weariness. Throughout your life, it has tirelessly fought for your worth, dignity, and voice in a world that can sometimes feel dismissive. Like a protective shield, your ego has worked diligently to help you navigate through the challenges and adversities you've faced, assisting you in your quest to survive. However, it's essential to recognise that mere survival does not equate to truly living life to its fullest potential.

You are no longer limited to the role of a man who feels an incessant need to prove his strength and dominance. Instead, you are evolving into a man whose power is rooted in genuine self-assurance and grace. This transformation allows you to embrace authenticity, fostering deeper connections with others and within yourself. As you continue this journey, you'll find that true empowerment comes from a place of inner peace and confidence, rather than the constant need for validation or superiority. This is the essence of living fully and abundantly.

Final Reframe: The Most Powerful Man Is the One Who No Longer Needs to Be

True power is not about exerting control over others; it resides in alignment with your authentic self. This authentic power is not characterised by a need for dominance or manipulation, but rather by a profound depth of character, empathy, and understanding of both yourself and those around you. Real strength is not found in the facade or mask that individuals often wear to navigate social situations; it lies in the essence of the person beneath that mask, in their vulnerability and sincerity.

You don't need to hide behind your ego, which often serves as a shield against perceived threats or insecurities. Instead, the goal is to return to that authentic self that your ego was trying to safeguard. When you achieve this connection with your true self and enter any space not with a desire for validation or admiration, but to be fully present in your own truth, you transform into an unstoppable force.

This form of strength does not come from instilling fear or exerting authority over others; instead, it emerges from the ability to cultivate genuine connections with those around you. When you engage with others from a place of authenticity, they can feel your truth resonate, and this creates strong, meaningful relationships based on trust and mutual respect. Authenticity fosters an environment where people are drawn to you not out of obligation, but out of genuine admiration for the real you.

Chapter 17

The Voice in Your Head Is Lying — Rewiring the Inner Critic, the Trauma Brain, and the Imposter Within

- "You're not good enough."
- "They're going to find out."
- "You've just been lucky."
- "Everyone else has it figured out but you."

These statements are not just passing thoughts; they are insidious invaders that stealthily infiltrate our minds, often disguising themselves as absolute truths. For countless men, these negative affirmations have a profound resonance, echoing in their own internal voice and casting long, suffocating shadows over their sense of self-worth.

Imagine this: what if I told you that the voice narrating your inner dialogue is not actually your friend? Your brain, shaped by past traumas, feelings of shame, and a lifetime of ingrained beliefs, has become the architect of a narrative so convincing that you have unwittingly performed according to its script for most of your life.

You are not broken, despite what that inner critic might insist. Instead, you have simply been misled, trapped in a cycle of self-doubt where the true deceiver resides within the labyrinth of your own mind.

This internal struggle can lead to the perception that you are alone, navigating a world where it seems everyone else has mastered their lives while you're stuck in turmoil. But it's time to confront this misleading voice. By recognising that these thoughts are not reflective of reality but rather distortions crafted by past experiences, you can begin to rewrite your narrative. Empower yourself to challenge these harmful beliefs, reclaim your worth, and forge a path toward genuine self-acceptance and resilience.

When the Brain Becomes the Enemy

Biopsychology reveals a fascinating and pivotal insight: our brains are fundamentally hardwired for survival rather than the pursuit of happiness. This evolutionary design means that during moments of stress or crisis, our brains naturally prioritise the detection of threats over the quest for truth. As a result, we often become adept at recognising patterns in our environment while neglecting to explore new possibilities that could foster growth and peace.

When faced with emotional vulnerability, criticism, or uncertainty, our brain's immediate response is to trigger a primal fear reaction. This is primarily managed by the amygdala, a small, almond-shaped structure deep within the brain that plays a crucial role in processing fear and emotion. Under the influence of this fear, the amygdala releases stress hormones such as cortisol and adrenaline into our bodies. These chemicals prepare us for a fight-or-flight response but simultaneously inhibit the function of the prefrontal cortex, the part of the brain associated with logical reasoning, decision-making, and self-reflection.

In this state of heightened emotional arousal, we often find ourselves at the mercy of a relentless inner critic, an anxiety-driven narrator whose primary goal is to protect us from perceived dangers. This inner voice, rather than supporting us, tends to undermine our self-worth and amplify our insecurities. It whispers insidious fears that can undermine our confidence and clarity, such as:
- "You're going to fail."
- "They're just being polite."
- "You're not truly qualified."
- "You're just winging it and they're bound to notice."

These messages, commonly associated with Imposter Syndrome, do not accurately represent our abilities or true selves. Instead, they emerge from a brain grappling with the dissonance between our accomplishments and a pervasive belief in our unworthiness. This internal conflict can be debilitating, leading us to doubt our successes and fear future endeavours. Understanding this dynamic is crucial, as it allows us to recognise that these thoughts stem from a protective mechanism rather than a reflection of our reality. Embracing this awareness can be the first step toward dismantling the illusions created by our inner critic and fostering a more authentic sense of self-worth.

The Mask of High Functioning Self-Doubt

Men grappling with Imposter Syndrome often present a polished façade of success to the world around them. Many excel in their professional lives, climbing the corporate ladder or attaining high-achieving roles that command respect and admiration. They become reliable providers and pillars of their communities. However, beneath this seemingly confident exterior lies a profound and relentless internal struggle, a deep-seated fear of exposure, an anxious worry that their true selves will be discovered, revealing the inadequacies they work so hard to conceal.

While they may smile and graciously accept accolades from colleagues and loved ones, internally, they often feel an overwhelming urge to deflect compliments, convinced that they are unworthy of such praise. Despite achieving significant milestones, landing promotions, earning prestigious awards, or completing ambitious projects, these men can feel a pervasive sense of numbness, as though the joy and satisfaction that should accompany their accomplishments are perpetually just out of reach. This conflicting dynamic engenders a complex fear of success as much as it does of failure; both outcomes threaten the fragile identity they have constructed, potentially unmasking their feelings of inadequacy.

From a counselling perspective, this internal struggle frequently has roots in early life experiences and conditioning. Take, for example, the boy who was consistently praised only for his achievements, never receiving affirmations simply for being himself or for the qualities that make him unique. This lack of unconditional acceptance can carry into adolescence, where the young man may learn to equate his self-worth with his performance and external validation. Such experiences create a cycle of over-functioning, where the relentless pursuit of success becomes not just a goal, but a necessity for feeling adequate. Ultimately, this path can lead to burnout and emotional depletion, leaving them exhausted and disconnected from both their accomplishments and their core selves.

As they navigate through life, the need for external validation can manifest in various ways, such as a fear of taking risks, an aversion to failure, or an inability to celebrate personal victories. Only through recognising these patterns and addressing the underlying beliefs can they begin to dismantle the walls they've built, ultimately fostering a healthier relationship with themselves and their achievements.

Why the Brain Lies: A Bio Psychological Breakdown

Let's delve deeper into the complex neurological mechanics involved in our emotional responses. The limbic system, a critical component of our brain, is primarily responsible for regulating our reactions to fear, pleasure, and emotions. In contrast, the prefrontal cortex plays an essential role in higher-order functions such as reasoning, decision-making, and language. When an individual experiences trauma, the intricate connection between these two structures can become disrupted, leading to a significant imbalance. This disconnect often manifests as emotional chaos, where individuals may feel intense feelings of anxiety or sadness but lack the coherent language to articulate those emotions effectively.

For many men who have never been equipped with the tools necessary for effective emotional regulation, this can lead to default behaviours that prioritise silence, stoicism, or even self-sabotage. These behaviours are often protective mechanisms developed over time, as expressing vulnerability can feel threatening. The absence of supportive emotional frameworks means that, without conscious intervention, the inner critic can dominate one's thoughts, shaping a distorted perception of reality and leading to further emotional distress.

It's crucial to understand that this struggle is not a mark of weakness; rather, it is a reflection of neural wiring shaped by past experiences and societal expectations. However, the good news is that these patterns can be altered through conscious effort and therapeutic intervention, allowing individuals to cultivate healthier emotional responses and a more constructive dialogue with themselves. Rewiring the brain to foster emotional resilience is not just possible; it is a path to greater self-awareness and emotional well-being.

Life Coach Reframe: Separate the Voice from the Self

One of the crucial steps toward liberating yourself from the lingering grip of the inner critic is to recognise a fundamental truth:
"That critical voice does not define who you are. It is a complex compilation of past experiences, the perceptions imparted by others, and defensive mechanisms rooted in fear."

When you find yourself engulfed by a wave of self-doubt, it's essential to take a moment to pause and engage in thoughtful reflection. Consider the following questions:

- Is this critical voice emanating from my own beliefs, or is it merely the echo of someone else's opinion, a parent, teacher, bully, or abuser? Reflecting on the origins of this voice can help identify its true nature.
- What age does this voice seem to reflect? Is it immature in its reasoning or overly harsh, reminiscent of a particular life stage? Recognising its age can help you understand the developmental context behind those thoughts.
- Would I ever speak to a child or even a friend in the harsh manner that I'm currently talking to myself? This

question encourages empathy towards yourself, fostering a more compassionate inner dialogue.

This reflective practice, often referred to as cognitive diffusion, invites you to unhook your sense of identity from your thoughts. You are not your thoughts; instead, you are the observer of these thoughts, endowed with the ability to step back, gain perspective, and choose how to respond. By acknowledging that these critical narratives are not absolute truths but rather subjective interpretations, you empower yourself to cultivate a more nurturing and supportive inner environment.

Imposter Syndrome in Adult Men

Counselling sessions have shed light on how Imposter Syndrome manifests in men, revealing a complex interplay of thought patterns, emotional responses, and behavioural tendencies. Here's a more detailed exploration:

Many men grapple with an internal turmoil that is often rooted in deep-seated emotional wounds. Thoughts such as "I don't belong here" frequently originate from profound feelings of shame or insecurity. These feelings can lead men to either overcompensate by working excessively in a bid to validate their worth or, conversely, to withdraw entirely to evade the risks of perceived failure. The belief that "If I fail, it proves I was never good" is often fueled by a crippling fear of exposure, a fear that can precipitate a vicious cycle of perfectionism or total avoidance. This relentless pursuit of unattainable standards can create immense pressure, resulting in chronic and debilitating stress.

When a man finds himself thinking, "I got lucky, that's all," it highlights a pervasive sense of low self-worth. This internal dialogue often leads him to downplay his own accomplishments, ignoring the hard work and skill that contributed to his success. Such dismissals not only undermine his confidence but also hinder his ability to truly appreciate and embrace his achievements.

249

Furthermore, the comparison trap can take a profound toll. The thought "I'll never be as good as him" typically stems from a sense of inadequacy, fuelled by relentless and toxic comparisons with peers. This sense of inferiority often manifests in either an unhealthy drive for competitiveness, as he feels the need to outshine others, or in complete emotional burnout, where the pressure becomes overwhelming and paralysing.

These thoughts and feelings are not random; they represent a predictable pattern of reactions rooted in deeper emotional narratives and societal expectations that men face. Recognising these connections is crucial in the journey to break free from the cycle of self-doubt.

By fostering an understanding of these experiences, men can empower themselves to reclaim their self-worth and redefine their identities. It becomes essential to shift the narrative from merely what they accomplish to who they are as individuals, recognising that their inherent value does not solely depend on their achievements but also on their unique qualities and contributions. Embracing this perspective can be transformative, leading to healthier self-esteem and a more fulfilling outlook on life.

Understanding the Inner Critic

At its core, the inner critic is not an inherently malevolent force; instead, it emerges from a place of deep-rooted fear and vulnerability. This internal voice often acts as a representation of a younger version of ourselves, a part that has internalised the belief that love and acceptance are conditional. It equates success with survival and sees vulnerability as a potential pathway to pain or rejection.

When we find ourselves confronting thoughts such as:
- "You'll mess it up."
- "You're too much."
- "You're not enough."

250

What our inner critic is truly articulating is a profound plea for safety and reassurance:
- "Please don't let me get hurt again."
- "Please don't abandon me in this vulnerable state."
- "Please protect me from the world's judgments and expectations."

These thoughts are not merely derogatory statements; they reflect the protective instincts of a part of us that has been wounded in the past. In essence, what we often label as weakness is frequently just the manifestation of past injuries seeking acknowledgement and healing. By recognising this, we can start to reframe our inner dialogue, fostering a sense of compassion for ourselves instead of criticism. Acknowledging these feelings can pave the way for healing, allowing us to confront our vulnerabilities and transform them into sources of strength.

Rewiring the Inner Narrative

Thanks to the incredible concept of neuroplasticity, we possess the innate ability to reshape our internal narratives, turning harsh, trauma-induced scripts into ones grounded in truth, compassion, and self-acceptance. This transformative process involves a series of reflective and proactive steps that can significantly enhance our mental well-being. Here's a practical framework to guide you through this journey:

1. Catch the Thought

When the inner critic steps into the spotlight, it's essential to take a moment to pause and observe. Take out a journal or a piece of paper, and meticulously write down the thoughts exactly as they emerge. This practice not only externalises the critic, allowing you to gain a clearer perspective on its pervasive influence, but it also helps to reduce its power over you. By documenting these thoughts, you create a tangible reference point, enabling you to examine and challenge them later.

2. Trace the Origin

Once you've articulated the critical voices in your mind, engage in a reflective exploration of their sources. Ask yourself questions like, "When did I first encounter this voice? Whose beliefs or opinions am I internalising, and how did they shape my perception of myself?" This step is crucial, as it can help unravel the origins of these negative narratives, illuminating the societal, familial, or personal influences that have contributed to your inner dialogue. Understanding the context of these voices can often weaken their hold over your self-esteem.

3. Speak the Counter-Truth

With a better understanding of where your critical thoughts come from, it's time to stand firmly in your truth. Actively challenge the negative narrative by gathering evidence that contradicts the critic's claims. Reflect on your experiences, achievements, and strengths. What would your closest friends or loved ones affirm about your character and abilities? This crucial step helps create a more balanced perspective, fostering a mindset that acknowledges your worth and accomplishments, rather than succumbing to self-doubt.

4. Create a Compassionate Reframe

Now, it's time to transform those harsh judgments into a more compassionate and nurturing narrative. Instead of allowing thoughts such as "I'm a fraud" to dominate, reframe this into something more empowering, like "I'm on a journey of learning and growth, and I deserve to occupy this space." This reframing process encourages you to focus not on limitations or perceived failures, but on recognising and celebrating your journey, resilience, and the progress you've made. By consistently practising this compassionate reframe, you reinforce a more supportive and loving internal dialogue that fosters self-acceptance and personal growth.

Through these steps, you not only challenge and reshape your inner critic but also cultivate a healthier, more affirming relationship with yourself, empowering you to live authentically and confidently.

Gentle Tools for Healing from the Voice Within

Here are several gentle yet powerful tools designed to help you heal and nurture a kinder internal dialogue, providing greater depth and clarity on each method:

1 Mirror Dialogue

Stand confidently in front of a mirror, allowing yourself to make eye contact with your reflection. Vocalise a series of positive affirmations that challenge any negative beliefs you hold. For example, affirmations such as "I belong here," "I am capable of growth and learning," and "My worth is inherent and unconditional" can serve to reinforce your self-acceptance. Take a moment to feel the weight of each word as you say it; this practice can foster a deeper connection with yourself and gradually shift your internal narrative toward positivity.

2 Timeline Reprocessing

Create a visual timeline of your significant achievements, mapping out key milestones and moments of success in your life. For each accomplishment, take the time to reflect on the inner critic that surfaced during that period, noting how it attempted to undermine your success. Consider the specific thoughts, feelings, and actions you experienced during those challenging times. Reflect on how you overcame these obstacles, celebrating your resilience. This exercise allows you to recognise patterns of self-doubt and reminds you of your capacity to push through adversity.

3 Embodied Grounding

Practice the technique of grounding yourself by placing one hand gently on your heart and the other on your abdomen. While doing this, recite the affirmations, "I am here. I am enough. I am safe." As you say each phrase, take slow, deep breaths, allowing the physical connection to your body to anchor these beliefs viscerally. Visualisation can enhance this practice; imagine roots growing from your feet deep into the earth, providing stability and security. This method not only reinforces the positive messages but also helps cultivate a sense of calm and presence within your body.

4   Future Self-Journaling

Engage in a reflective writing exercise by composing a letter from your future self, who has successfully conquered feelings of imposter syndrome and embraces their true worth. In this letter, explore the lessons and insights your future self has gained along the way. What wisdom have they discovered that could guide you now? What encouraging words and affirmations would they share to uplift you in your current journey? Allow your future self's voice to fill you with hope and possibility, infusing your present with guidance and motivation to continue moving forward.

These techniques not only promote self-acceptance but also invite you to reframe your experiences in a way that nurtures growth and resilience.

Final Reflection

It's crucial to recognise that some of the most dangerous lies we tell ourselves are those we accept without question. Often, these insidious narratives are filled with self-doubt and can arise from our inner critic, the scars left by past traumas, or the pervasive storyline of imposter syndrome. Yet, it's vital to understand that these narratives are not definitive truths; they are merely survival stories rooted in our experiences. You have the strength and resilience to transcend them.

Reflect for a moment: you are not present in this world by mere accident. Your accomplishments are not just products of luck or random chance; they are the fruits of your hard work, determination, and the unique qualities that make you who you are. You are not deceiving anyone by navigating life as you do. Instead, you are on a profound journey of learning and personal growth, actively crafting a new narrative that reflects your true self.

In this new narrative, your worth is unquestionable and intrinsic. Embrace the realisation that your voice is a powerful tool, one that can become the safest refuge in your life, a source of comfort and clarity amidst the noise of doubt. Let's embark on this transformative journey of rebuilding, rediscovering, and amplifying that voice together. As we do, we will weave a story that not only honours your past but boldly charts a course toward a brighter, more authentic future.

Chapter 18

Neural Rewiring – Changing the Path You Walk Every Day

For countless years, you've navigated the same mental pathways, not because they lead to enriching or rewarding destinations, but because they have become familiar and somewhat comfortable. These routes may have initially provided a sense of safety or certainty in a chaotic world. When shame creeps in, it feels like a well-worn shortcut you habitually take, allowing you to bypass the dense undergrowth of uncomfortable emotions that lie beneath the surface. This familiar route offers a fleeting sense of control, even as it leads you further away from genuine healing.

Similarly, numbness acts as a bypass when faced with feelings that unsettle you. It creates a protective barrier, dulling the impact of emotional turbulence, but it often comes with a hidden cost: the disconnection from joy and fulfilment. Anger, in contrast, frequently seems like the only substantial thoroughfare available, especially when more profound, more vulnerable emotions, such as sadness and fear, are deemed too overwhelming to face head-on or are buried under years of denial. These emotions can feel like a construction zone, complex and messy, yet necessary for actual emotional progress.

The routes you've followed throughout your life weren't consciously chosen; they were etched into your psyche through a complex tapestry of experiences, often marked by trauma, repetitive patterns, and an ingrained survival instinct. Each choice to travel these familiar paths may have offered temporary relief or distraction, but they can also reinforce a cycle of avoidance and emotional stagnation.

However, just because your brain has carved these pathways does not mean you are condemned to traverse them indefinitely. Awareness of these entrenched patterns is the first step toward forging new paths that can lead to true self-discovery, healing, and emotional resilience. By consciously recognising these connections and choosing to explore new emotional landscapes, you can begin to reshape your journey toward a more fulfilling life.

The Neuroplasticity Revolution

Let's be clear: Your brain is not a fixed entity; it is a dynamic organ capable of remarkable transformation and adaptability. With every thought you entertain, every emotion you experience, and every action you undertake, specific neural pathways are activated and reinforced. This process, known as Hebbian learning, illustrates the principle that "neurons that fire together, wire together," emphasising how our experiences shape the very structure of our brains.

This means that each time you:

-   Censure yourself for not achieving enough, framing your self-worth solely through the lens of productivity, you activate a neural circuit that associates your value with your output, perpetuating feelings of inadequacy.
-   Choose to numb your feelings with distractions, whether through mindless scrolling on social media, binge-watching television, or succumbing to unhealthy habits instead of confronting and processing the underlying pain. You strengthen habits that inhibit emotional healing and self-awareness.
-   Opt for silence in moments when reaching out could foster connection and healing; you reinforce isolation, making it more challenging to seek support and communicate your needs in the future.

In each of these scenarios, you are not merely reacting to your environment; you are actively reinforcing established neural pathways, creating habitual grooves in your brain that signal, "This is how we navigate and survive in this environment." Over time, these grooves become entrenched, making negative self-perceptions and avoidance behaviours feel like inevitable responses.

However, here's where the transformative potential of your brain shines through: Your brain possesses an extraordinary ability to unlearn these entrenched patterns and forge new pathways. This incredible capacity is known as neuroplasticity. It signifies that regardless of how deeply rooted your trauma may be, how entrenched your habits have become, or how long you've felt trapped in negative thought cycles, change is always within your reach.

This transformational process encompasses not merely emotional shifts but also profound changes at the neurological level. When you engage in practices like mindfulness, self-compassion, or healthy communication, you can actively nurture new pathways that encourage resilience, self-acceptance, and healthier coping mechanisms. Thus, the journey of change is not just a possibility; it is a powerful reality that invites you to reshape your mind and life in fundamentally positive ways.

Trauma Wires the Brain for Threat

Growing up in environments marked by chaos, neglect, or relentless pressure to excel can hardwire the brain for survival. This adaptation often comes at the expense of forming genuine, fulfilling connections with others. In these turbulent settings, the amygdala, commonly referred to as the brain's smoke alarm, becomes hyperactive, causing it to trigger a fight-or-flight response even in situations that pose no real threat. As a result, moments that should be peaceful or enjoyable may be perceived as perilous. This overactivation can lead to chronic anxiety and a heightened sense of paranoia regarding safety and stability.

Simultaneously, the prefrontal cortex, which is responsible for logic, calm reasoning, and executive planning, becomes overshadowed by overwhelming emotional reactions. The consequence is a tendency to react impulsively rather than to engage in thoughtful deliberation in response to various stimuli. You may find yourself withdrawing from social situations that could foster connection or growth, believing it's easier to avoid potential discomfort. While you navigate life in a state of survival, this approach leaves you feeling perpetually on edge, grappling with a sense of instability that can be hard to shake.

Within this persistent state of heightened alertness, even basic feelings of safety and comfort can become elusive or tainted with suspicion. For instance:

- Love may evoke an instinctive bracing for loss, with an internal narrative that perpetually anticipates abandonment. The very notion of attachment becomes intertwined with fear, leading to self-sabotage in relationships or avoidance of closeness altogether.

- Rest triggers an internal conflict, often perceived as laziness or unworthiness. The belief that productivity is the sole measure of one's value can compel you to sacrifice necessary downtime, pushing against your mental and physical limits, which ultimately hinders your well-being.

- Compliments are frequently dismissed as insincerity, making it nearly impossible to accept positive affirmations as valid reflections of your worth or capabilities. This leads to a pervasive sense of inadequacy that clouds your self-esteem and distorts your self-image.

This conditioned response does not accurately reflect your true personality or potential; instead, it emerges from a protracted process of conditioning that has reshaped your reality. It moulds your responses to fit a survival mode, rather than allowing the space for a thriving, flourishing existence where you are free to engage, connect, and grow. Understanding this dynamic is a crucial step toward recognising your inherent worth and reclaiming your ability to engage with the world in a more balanced, wholesome manner.

The Loop of Familiar Pain

Have you ever found yourself ensnared in the same patterns, unable to break free despite your best intentions? You might notice recurring arguments with loved ones, a constant sense of fatigue, or a frustrating tendency toward self-sabotage. These experiences are not mere coincidences; instead, they stem from a neurological loop shaped by your brain's innate preference for familiarity over the unpredictability that change brings.

Our brains are wired to establish patterns, and even pain can feel familiar and safe compared to the uncertainty that accompanies transformation. This preference can lead us to cling to behaviours and situations that are ultimately unfulfilling or damaging. For instance, think of the man who longs for inner peace yet often finds himself drawn into tumultuous circumstances that disrupt his serenity. Or consider the individual who craves meaningful connections but inadvertently pushes away those who seek to get close.

Even with a clear understanding of healthier choices, whether through personal reflection or advice from others, many struggle to make those choices a reality. This internal conflict often persists until one embarks on the crucial journey of rewiring their brain. This process involves stepping outside of ingrained habits, challenging long-standing beliefs, and embracing the discomfort of change. Only through this dedicated effort can one begin to break the cycle, fostering new, healthier patterns that align more closely with their desires and aspirations for a fulfilling life.

The Science of Rewiring

So, how does meaningful change actually occur?

Awareness: The journey to transformation begins with a deep, honest acknowledgement of the persistent thought and behaviour patterns that govern your life. This involves not only recognising your actions but also delving into the underlying motivations that influence those actions. Reflecting on why you respond a certain way can shed light on long-held beliefs and fears, which are often the proper drivers behind your behaviour.

This self-awareness is not merely an observation; it's a profound realisation that sets the stage for genuine transformation.

Interruption: Once you have gained clarity about these automatic responses, the next step is to consciously disrupt them. This can be as simple as taking a moment to pause when you feel an emotional trigger. Techniques such as taking a deep breath, stepping away for a moment, or even changing your physical environment can serve as effective interruptions. This brief moment of conscious reflection allows you to step outside the habitual loop, allowing you to respond thoughtfully rather than react impulsively, laying the groundwork for significant change.

Repetition: After interrupting your typical responses, the key is to consistently choose a new, healthier way of reacting over time. This involves making a deliberate effort to respond differently, whether through mindfulness, patience, or self-reflection. Each time you opt for this new response, you are not only reinforcing different neural pathways in your brain but also allowing them to gradually overshadow the old, ingrained patterns. Change takes time, but with persistent effort, the new responses become more natural and instinctive.

Practically speaking, this process can manifest in several ways:

- When feelings of anger start to surface, pause for a moment. Ask yourself reflective questions like, "What deeper emotions or situations are truly influencing this reaction?" This inquiry can help uncover hidden triggers that might not have been apparent before.

- Instead of responding to failures with harsh self-criticism, embrace an attitude of curiosity. Frame these moments as opportunities for growth and learning, helping you to cultivate introspection that leads to personal development and resilience.

- Practice self-compassion actively. Communicate with yourself using kind and understanding language, just as

261

you would with a friend going through a tough time. Acknowledge your feelings, affirm your worth, and allow yourself the compassion needed to navigate challenges without judgment.

By understanding and actively engaging in these steps, you can facilitate meaningful change in your life.

Coaching Insight: The "Micro-Rewire" Rule

Change doesn't have to be perceived as an intimidating or drastic transformation. In fact, a wealth of research underscores the idea that minor, consistent adjustments are often more effective in fostering long-term change than infrequent, sweeping reforms. By dedicating yourself to selecting one slightly improved thought, a more compassionate reaction, or a healthier behaviour each day, you actively engage in the process of cultivating new neural pathways within your brain.

These incremental shifts, though seemingly minor at first, have the power to accumulate over time. As you consistently choose these better responses, the newly established pathways in your brain will become more frequently travelled routes. This gradual repetition not only strengthens these neural connections but also reshapes the way you respond to life's various challenges. Ultimately, this process can lead to a profound transformation in your mindset and behaviours, resulting in a more resilient and positive approach to life's ups and downs.

Healing Is Unlearning

Consider this: you don't need to completely transform into a different person to find your true self. Instead, your journey is about unlearning the traits and beliefs that have been instilled in you over the years through a myriad of experiences, some uplifting, others deeply challenging.

That tightness you feel in your chest, that constant sense of urgency and pressure? It's not a reflection of who you genuinely

262

are. Instead, it serves as a reminder of past traumas and emotional wounds that linger, shaping your present interactions and feelings. These experiences can create a façade that distracts you from your authentic self.

Take a moment to reflect on that nagging inner critic filled with doubt and criticism. This voice doesn't stem from your true identity; rather, it is a narrative crafted from the external expectations imposed on you by society, family, and peers. It often echoes the sentiments and judgments of others, rather than allowing you to embrace your unique worth and potential.

Moreover, think about the compulsion to project an image of unwavering strength and the need to remain silent about your struggles. This instinct, rooted in a desire for acceptance and fear of vulnerability, has been reinforced over time. It often becomes a protective armour against judgment, but it doesn't define who you are at your core.

Remember, you were not born predisposed to self-sabotage or to harbour negative beliefs about yourself. These patterns have been learned through various life encounters, and just like they were adopted, they can also be unlearned. It's a powerful realisation: with patience, self-compassion, and support, you can strip away the layers that no longer serve you and reconnect with the authentic self that has always been there, waiting to be embraced.

Gentle Prompts:

Pattern Recognition

- What are three recurring reactions or behaviours in my life that no longer contribute to my overall well-being? Reflect on instances where you find yourself reacting in ways that leave you feeling drained, anxious, or unfulfilled. Consider how these patterns manifest in your daily interactions, decision-making, or emotional responses, and recognise that acknowledging them is the first step towards change.

- What is the earliest memory I have of this pattern forming, and how did it impact my personal growth and development? Try to trace back to childhood or significant moments in your life when you first adopted these behaviours. Consider the environment, influences, and experiences that may have shaped this pattern. Reflect on how these formative moments may have hindered or propelled your growth, leading you to where you are today.
- When I feel triggered, what is the first thought or impulse that typically arises, and how can I effectively challenge or reframe it? Identify the automatic thoughts or reactions that surge when you're faced with challenging situations. Acknowledge these impulses without judgment and explore techniques or counterarguments that can help you reframe them into more positive or constructive perspectives.

Micro-Rewiring

- What is one belief about myself that I can gently challenge this week, and how could this shift in perspective influence my self-view and actions? Choose a limiting belief that you hold, such as "I am not capable," and examine its origins. Consider how actively challenging this belief, perhaps by acknowledging your strengths and past achievements, could alter the way you approach challenges and opportunities.
- What new thought, mantra, or daily action would I like to cultivate in my life to promote positivity and growth? Think about what resonates with you, whether it's an uplifting mantra like "I am enough" or a simple daily ritual, such as gratitude journaling or mindful breathing. Contemplate how incorporating this small change could enhance your mental well-being and invite greater joy into your daily routine.

- How would I communicate with a child experiencing similar feelings to those I am grappling with right now? Picture yourself as a nurturing guide. Consider the empathy, reassurance, and understanding you would offer. Reflect on how this compassionate internal dialogue can help soothe your own struggles and foster self-compassion in challenging times.

Building New Roads

- What emotion have I hesitated to fully embrace, and what underlying fear has contributed to this reluctance? Identify the emotions that evoke discomfort, such as sadness, anger, or anxiety. Dig deeper to uncover the concerns at their core, whether it's the fear of vulnerability, rejection, or loss and recognise that allowing yourself to feel these emotions can pave the way for healing.
- What choices or behaviours would the version of myself that I aspire to become demonstrate in similar situations? Visualise your ideal self, someone who embodies resilience, confidence, and authenticity. Reflect on how this aspirational version would handle obstacles or conflicts differently and integrate this perspective into your current decision-making process.
- How might I reframe this journey of rewiring my thoughts and behaviours as a process of healing and rediscovery? Embrace the notion that growth is not a linear path but rather a winding journey. Rather than viewing challenges as setbacks, consider them as opportunities for profound self-exploration and the chance to rediscover your authentic self, ultimately leading to a richer and more fulfilling life experience.

You're not broken. Your brain just did what it had to do to keep you alive. Now it's time to teach it something new: how to live.

Chapter 19

The Desire Decoder – What Men Really Long for (Even When They Don't Say It)

Men are frequently perceived as beings primarily driven by instinct, chasing desires such as sex, success, and power. This perspective, however, oversimplifies the intricate emotional landscape many men navigate. Beneath the surface-level desires lies a rich architecture of emotional needs, a complicated web of feelings and yearnings that most men are neither trained to recognise nor articulate with precision. While society often equates male pursuits with tangible, material success, many of these external ambitions may echo deeper, unfulfilled emotional needs or a profound longing for love, connection, and acceptance.

This gap in understanding should not be viewed as a deficiency in masculinity; instead, it highlights a crucial shortfall in emotional education. From an early age, many men receive the message that emotional expression is secondary to performance and achievement. Consequently, they may struggle to find the appropriate language to convey their inner experiences. In contrast, female emotional expression tends to be more openly validated and recognised, creating a stark dichotomy in emotional visibility between genders. Male desire is frequently subjected to scepticism, often painted as merely sexual, egocentric, or even threatening.

In reality, male desire encompasses a much broader spectrum of needs and emotions. Beyond the pursuit of physical or material gain, many men long for deeper connections; they yearn for recognition as their authentic selves, a sense of emotional security, and the respect of their peers. They seek to be known and understood, to experience safety in their relationships, and ultimately, to feel whole and fulfilled. Understanding these nuances not only enriches the dialogue around masculinity but also fosters a more compassionate and supportive framework for men to express their feelings and navigate their emotional worlds.

The Mask of Misunderstood Desire

Desire, in its myriad manifestations, often cloaks itself in various disguises, making it essential to peel back the layers to uncover its true essence. For instance, a surface-level longing for sexual intimacy may actually mask a more profound craving for genuine emotional closeness and connection. Similarly, what initially appears to be an insatiable drive for ambition may, upon closer examination, reveal an underlying yearning for acknowledgement and validation from others.

When a man distances himself from those around him, this behaviour is frequently misinterpreted as an outright rejection. In reality, it may be a self-protective mechanism to shield himself from the vulnerability that comes with emotional exposure. Conversely, the urge to impose control over situations or relationships often arises not from a thirst for power, but rather from deep-rooted fears and insecurities associated with feeling powerless.

From a psychological standpoint, desire extends far beyond mere sexual appetite or primal instincts; it functions as an internal compass that navigates men toward unmet emotional needs. Many men seek out romantic relationships, career advancements, or exhilarating escapades not from a place of pure intention, but as compensatory strategies to fill the voids of absence or deprivation in their lives. For instance, the compulsion to assert dominance may have its roots in early life experiences characterised by a sense of helplessness or inadequacy. The desire for affection often stems from instances of parental neglect or emotional unavailability, leading to an adult life marked by difficulties in forming intimate connections. Likewise, the relentless pursuit of achievement and the necessity to prove oneself can often be traced back to childhood experiences where one felt overlooked or undervalued.

A psychiatrist might explore these intricate patterns through the lens of unresolved attachment trauma, highlighting how formative relationships shape an individual's adult behaviour. A therapist may refer to this phenomenon as "legacy burdening," which signifies the way past emotional experiences mould current behaviours and attitudes. Likewise, a life coach might characterise this disconnect as "misalignment," emphasising the disparity between one's current actions and the true self that is evolving beneath the surface. Understanding these dynamics is pivotal in crafting pathways toward emotional healing and fulfilling relationships.

The Neuroscience of Wanting

In the intricate landscape of biopsychology, the dopaminergic reward system emerges as a pivotal mechanism driving human behaviour and guiding the pursuit of desires. This system plays a crucial role in reinforcing behaviours that lead to pleasurable experiences by releasing feel-good neurotransmitters like dopamine. However, a significant limitation of this system is its inability to distinguish between genuine fulfilment and superficial rewards. It indiscriminately reinforces any activity that triggers dopamine release, which can lead individuals into a cycle of seeking temporary pleasures that ultimately leave them feeling unfulfilled.

This dynamic reveals why many men find themselves in a relentless pursuit of societal markers of success, be it career achievements, sexual encounters, or thrilling experiences, only to confront an underlying sense of emptiness and dissatisfaction. The neurochemical loops activated in their brains reward the act of chasing these goals. Yet, they fall short of providing the deeper meaning or fulfilment that individuals truly seek on a psychological and emotional level. Compounded by societal pressures that often stigmatise vulnerability, the desire for achievement becomes increasingly detached from authenticity, leading to an internal conflict that many struggle to navigate.

Testosterone, commonly associated with male libido and aggression, also significantly influences aspects of male drive, competitiveness, and motivation. When testosterone levels become dysregulated, particularly under conditions of chronic stress, men may experience a variety of issues, including increased irritability, impulsivity, and emotional detachment.

These hormonal fluctuations can stifle one's ability to form meaningful connections, driving a wedge between personal aspirations and social interactions.

Conversely, oxytocin, the hormone closely tied to bonding and emotional connection, can promote feelings of trust and intimacy in men. The release of oxytocin typically occurs through experiences of emotional closeness, physical touch, and social bonding. However, in a culture where many men feel deprived of physical affection or emotional intimacy, the oxytocin system may remain underutilised. This deprivation can make genuine connections feel precarious and intimidating, further complicating men's emotional landscapes.

While dopamine may fuel the fervent pursuit of goals and instant gratification, it often proves inadequate in addressing the profound longing for authentic relationships and deeper connections. Consequently, many men find themselves ensnared in a cycle of addiction to performance, pornography, or an unending quest for achievement. They are driven by dysregulation in their dopamine systems, which rewards the chase itself rather than the meaningful outcomes. As a result, the fulfilment they seek remains elusive, leading to a stark realisation that the very pursuits designed to bring satisfaction may instead lead to hollow and unsatisfying experiences.

Sidebar: Porn & The Dopamine Loop
The regular consumption of pornography can significantly alter an individual's dopamine sensitivity, which is crucial for regulating pleasure and reward pathways in the brain. As a result of this shift, men often begin to perceive arousal primarily through the lens of superficial, visual stimuli rather than through authentic intimacy. This alteration in arousal patterns can lead to a disconnection between sexual desire and meaningful emotional connections, making it increasingly difficult to experience genuine closeness with partners.

Over time, these altered perceptions can contribute to a psychological phenomenon known as "intimacy avoidance." In

271

this state, men may find themselves struggling to form deep, emotional bonds with their partners. The decline in oxytocin production, often referred to as the "love hormone," which plays a vital role in fostering emotional closeness and attachment, further exacerbates this detachment. As the brain becomes wired to respond to instant gratification through pornography, the ability to connect intimately with a partner diminishes.

This pattern not only complicates personal relationships, making communication and emotional sharing more challenging, but it also deepens the emotional void that many men experience within themselves. They may feel isolated or disconnected, grappling with feelings of inadequacy or frustration in their attempts to create meaningful relationships. Understanding this dynamic is essential for addressing the underlying issues that contribute to intimacy challenges and fostering healthier interpersonal connections.

Attachment Theory & Desire

Attachment styles play a crucial role in shaping how men experience and express their desires within romantic relationships, often leading to complex and sometimes conflicting patterns of behaviour.

Men with avoidant attachment styles typically harbour a deep-seated fear of engulfment. This anxiety regarding emotional closeness causes their expressions of desire to appear aloof, distant, or even controlling. They may intentionally withhold affection and intimacy as a means of self-preservation, striving to maintain their sense of autonomy. This self-protective strategy, while seemingly beneficial for safeguarding their independence, can lead to significant emotional distance. As a result, their partners may find it difficult to forge a meaningful connection, often feeling rejected or sidelined. The avoidant man's internal conflict between the desire for closeness and the instinct to retreat can create a frustrating dynamic in relationships, causing partners to feel unappreciated or emotionally neglected.

Conversely, men with anxious attachment styles exhibit a relentless craving for closeness and emotional intimacy, yet they often grapple with intense feelings of insecurity. Their longing for connection can manifest in a heightened pursuit of sex or external validation, as they mistakenly believe that such encounters will alleviate their deep-seated fears of abandonment and rejection. However, this quest for approval frequently provides only temporary relief and can ultimately leave them feeling more isolated and unsettled. The emotional turbulence caused by this cycle of pursuing connection and subsequently feeling rejected can exacerbate their anxiety, leading to heightened emotional volatility and potential difficulties in maintaining stable relationships.

Men with disorganised attachment styles, often stemming from histories of trauma or inconsistent caregiving during childhood, face a particularly complicated interplay of desire and fear. They may experience an intense longing for closeness, coupled with an overwhelming dread of being hurt or abandoned. This internal conflict often manifests in erratic behaviours, resulting in complicated push-pull dynamics within their romantic relationships. One moment, they may fervently pursue intimacy, seeking to bridge the emotional gap, while in the next, they retreat in fear, overwhelmed by the vulnerability that closeness entails. This unpredictable oscillation can create significant challenges for both partners, as the disorganised man navigates his conflicting needs, leaving both parties feeling confused and emotionally drained.

Ultimately, understanding these attachment styles and the underlying motives behind men's expressions of desire can facilitate more profound empathy and communication within relationships, allowing partners to address their individual needs more effectively.

Internal Family Systems (IFS)

The Internal Family Systems (IFS) model provides a profound framework for understanding the complexities of human dynamics, particularly in navigating emotional experiences. In this model, each individual is viewed as a system composed of various "parts," each with distinct needs, fears, and behaviours. For many men, specific patterns frequently emerge within this system:

- The Protector part often manifests as a drive for success, social status, or even superficial relationships, such as sexual conquests. This part is motivated by a desire to shield the individual from deeper emotional wounds, such as fear, shame, or grief. It constructs a façade of strength and invulnerability, which can make it difficult for men to connect with their authentic feelings. While the Protector may achieve outward accomplishments, these successes may ultimately serve as temporary distractions from unresolved emotional pain.
- The Exile part serves as a repository for the emotional scars stemming from painful experiences like rejection, abandonment, or neglect. These deeply ingrained wounds are frequently suppressed to enable survival amidst emotional trauma. Consequently, men may find themselves grappling with an inability to embrace their vulnerabilities, often feeling isolated in their struggles. The Exile longs for acknowledgement and healing but remains hidden due to the fear of overwhelming pain resurfacing.
- The Manager part diligently works to impose order and structure in daily life, often prioritising responsibilities over emotional expression. This part's primary aim is to prevent chaos and discomfort, creating a protective barrier against feelings that might disrupt a semblance of stability. However, this relentless pursuit of control can lead to the suppression of genuine emotional needs and desires, resulting in a disconnect from one's true self and an inability to form deep, authentic connections.

To facilitate deeper self-reflection and exploration within this framework, a thought-provoking IFS prompt is: "What part of you is craving this desire, and what part is protecting you from experiencing deeper pain?" This question encourages individuals to delve into the intricate motivations behind their desires and the interplay between their various parts, fostering greater understanding of their emotional landscape and the complex ways they seek safety.

The Diversity of Desire

It's essential to recognise that not all men experience desire in the same way; a multitude of factors contribute to how desire is both expressed and suppressed. Elements such as cultural background, race, socioeconomic status, neurodivergence, and individual trauma history significantly shape a man's experience of desire, creating a complex landscape of emotions and behaviours.

For example, many Black men carry the weight of historical trauma and societal pressures that influence how desire is expressed. This legacy often involves a cultivated façade of strength, which can complicate their ability to show vulnerability or articulate their desires without fearing judgment or misunderstanding. The societal stigma surrounding emotional expression may inhibit them from revealing their true feelings, leading to a conflict between their internal experiences and outward behaviours.

Similarly, men on the autism spectrum may face unique challenges in expressing desire due to sensory sensitivities or difficulties with communication. The nuances of romantic relationships, including understanding social cues, reading emotional landscapes, or navigating intimate encounters, can be particularly overwhelming. These barriers may result in a significant disconnect between their internal feelings and how they can express those feelings externally, leading to frustration and isolation.

Men from working-class backgrounds often contend with societal expectations that prioritise stoicism, self-sacrifice, and duty over emotional needs. Such pressures can lead them to suppress their desires, creating an internal struggle as they grapple with the need to express emotions while adhering to cultural norms that dictate they should remain firm and unyielding. This conflict can create an emotional bottleneck, preventing them from seeking validation or support.

Ultimately, there is no singular "male experience" of desire; what remains universal is the fact that all men possess desire, yet many struggle to articulate it effectively. Understanding these diverse experiences can cultivate greater empathy and compassion in relationships, paving the way for more profound and meaningful connections.

What men truly desire often lies beneath the surface of their everyday actions and behaviours, obscured by societal expectations and personal struggles. For instance, a man's withdrawal from emotional interaction may not signify disinterest; instead, it could reflect a profound quest for safety and acceptance, unmarred by the shame that societal norms sometimes impose on vulnerability.

Likewise, sexual pursuits are frequently misinterpreted; they may disguise a deeper yearning for love, intimacy, and a desire to feel valued and cherished. Overworking, which can outwardly appear as ambition or a relentless commitment to career success, often masks an underlying longing for intrinsic value. Many men chase accomplishments in an attempt to prove their worth, revealing a desperate need for affirmation.

When a man seeks control within a relationship, it is rarely about asserting dominance; instead, it often signifies a desire for stability and reassurance amid emotional uncertainty. Emotional shutdown, frequently mistaken for apathy, can actually be a plea for the space to rest and recuperate without the pressure to constantly articulate feelings or justify actions. Furthermore, outbursts of anger, which are commonly viewed as mere aggression, may, in truth, be cries for relief from pervasive internal pain and turmoil.

As one insightful therapist has aptly noted, "Most men don't lack desire; they lack environments where their desire feels safe enough to be explored." Recognising and creating those safe spaces can help men articulate their feelings, leading to deeper connections and healthier emotional expression.

Clinical Research & Statistics

Research highlights the complexities surrounding men's emotional expression in profound ways:

- A significant 64% of men report feeling the need to suppress their emotional needs due to a pervasive fear of judgment from peers and society. This statistic underscores the substantial barriers that hinder open and honest expression of emotions, revealing deep-rooted cultural norms about masculinity that discourage vulnerability (Journal of Men's Health).
- Neuroscience research indicates that oxytocin levels, which are often linked to feelings of bonding and intimacy, are notably lower in men after intimate encounters when they do not feel emotionally safe. This suggests a crucial relationship between emotional connection and physical intimacy, emphasising that true closeness requires a foundation of trust and security (Neuroscience & Bio-behavioural Reviews).
- While one in three men still equate vulnerability with weakness, a perception that can prevent them from forming meaningful connections, an overwhelming 72% express a strong desire for deeper emotional connections. This reveals a dissonance in men's experiences, where cultural scripts of strength conflict with innate human needs for connection and intimacy (APA, 2022).
- Moreover, research shows that men who have experienced Adverse Childhood Experiences (ACEs) are 2.5 times more likely to express their emotional desires through maladaptive behaviours such as aggression, addiction, or avoidance. This highlights the

long-lasting impact of early life adversity on emotional health and coping strategies, underscoring the need for greater awareness and interventions to support emotional well-being (CDC Study, 2020).

This refined exploration provides a clearer understanding of the challenges men face in expressing their emotions and the critical need for fostering environments that prioritise emotional safety and connectivity.

A Partner's Perspective – What Gets Misread

Partners can often misinterpret male expressions of desire and emotional needs, as these may not align with traditional emotional indicators. For example, when a man spends long hours at work, it might be easy for a partner to perceive this as withdrawal or a signal of diminished interest in the relationship. However, this behaviour could stem from feelings of inadequacy or a sense that he does not deserve emotional closeness, leading him to seek comfort in work rather than connection. Additionally, when men pursue sexual intimacy, it is worth considering that this may not stem from a sense of entitlement or a purely physical desire. For many men, physical intimacy may serve as a vital means of establishing a deeper emotional connection and seeking validation. Thus, it's essential to recognise that their pursuit of sex might reflect a genuine yearning for intimacy rather than a superficial craving.

When a man responds with a terse "I'm fine," it often masks a more complicated emotional landscape. This simple phrase can conceal feelings of unease, vulnerability, or a profound fear of rejection. Silence in a conversation should not be interpreted as emotional withdrawal; rather, it could be a well-practised defence mechanism that he has developed to shield himself from pain or disappointment.

Partner Tip: Instead of framing your concerns with a question like "What's wrong with you?", consider approaching the conversation with gentler curiosity. Phrasing it as "What are you

278

needing right now?" can invite your partner to open up in a safe environment, fostering a deeper understanding and connection between you.

Life Coaching Insight – Desire as Data

In the field of life coaching, desire is not seen as a mere dramatic expression of inner turmoil; instead, it is recognised as insightful data that reveals deeper truths about an individual's aspirations. By freeing themselves from feelings of shame and judgment, individuals can embark on a journey of self-discovery that illuminates what they genuinely want from life. This process also serves to uncover their core values, which are essential for meaningful decision-making and personal growth.

For many men, the pursuit of significance can often feel daunting, leading them to opt for performance as a safer, less emotionally charged alternative. This focus on achieving measurable success, whether in their careers, relationships, or personal achievements, can obscure a more profound quest for fulfilment. A proficient life coach plays a critical role in this journey by helping clients navigate beyond superficial markers of success. Their true purpose lies in guiding men toward a deeper understanding of what brings meaning and joy to their lives, facilitating a path that aligns with their authentic selves and deepest desires. Through this transformative coaching relationship, individuals can redefine success in a way that resonates with their intrinsic values and ultimately leads to a more satisfying and fulfilling life.

Three Core Male Desires:

1. **To Be Seen:** This concept encompasses the profound desire to be acknowledged and appreciated for one's authentic self, rather than merely for the societal roles or facades one may adopt. It involves recognition that transcends superficial judgments, allowing individuals to express their true identities without fear of dismissal or

misunderstanding. Being seen means having one's unique qualities, experiences, and emotions valued by others, fostering a sense of belonging and acceptance.

2 **To Be Safe:** Feeling safe is fundamental to the human experience and encompasses emotional, physical, and relational security. This means creating environments where individuals can express themselves freely, explore their thoughts and feelings, and engage with others without fear of harm or retribution. It is about cultivating trust and stability in relationships, ensuring that one can navigate life's challenges without the constant worry of emotional distress or physical danger.

3 **To Be Significant:** This notion extends beyond mere accomplishments and accolades, emphasising the intrinsic value of individuals. Everyone deserves to feel that their existence holds meaning and that they have a place in the world beyond their achievements. Significance is rooted in the understanding that every person has unique gifts and perspectives, and that their worth is inherent to their identity. This recognition fosters a sense of purpose and connection, enhancing one's overall sense of fulfilment and belonging.

Therapeutic Reframe – You're Not Broken, You're Starving

Recognising the sense of emptiness that can follow the accomplishment of long-desired goals is an essential step in understanding our emotional landscape. This feeling should not be interpreted as a sign of being broken or inadequate; rather, it serves as a reflection of a more profound yearning for genuine connection, inner peace, and heartfelt closeness with others.

At the core of our existence lies the truth that what we truly desire, whether it's intimacy, freedom, or a deeper understanding of ourselves and those around us, does not diminish our worth as human beings. These desires are simply manifestations of our

280

fundamental needs and aspirations, pointing us toward what we believe can fulfil us.

The journey through this realisation is not about suppressing or fixing these desires; it's about learning to trust them again. By embracing what we yearn for, we can uncover the most authentic parts of ourselves, those aspects that resonate with our true nature. This exploration encourages us to cultivate a sense of worth that is rooted not in external achievements, but in the rich tapestry of our desires and the connections we seek to nurture. In doing so, we open the door to a more profound understanding of who we are and what it means to lead a fulfilling life.

Reflection Workbook – Decode Your Desire

1. Emotional Inventory

- Exploring Hidden Longings: What dreams, aspirations, or desires have I quietly nurtured but felt too ashamed to voice? Are there specific dreams I've dismissed due to societal expectations or fears of judgment?
- Identifying Triggers: Which events or experiences consistently elicit a strong emotional response in me? What underlying beliefs or past experiences make these triggers resonate so deeply within my emotional landscape?
- Creating Emotional Safety: When do I find myself feeling most emotionally secure? What specific factors, be it the presence of certain individuals, environments, or activities, contribute to my sense of safety during these moments?

2. Body Awareness

- Locating Unmet Longing: In which parts of my body do I feel the unfulfilled ache of longing? How do these sensations manifest physically, and what do they communicate about my unmet needs?

- Understanding Suppressed Desires: What physical sensations do I experience when I stifle my true feelings and desires? How does this suppression affect my overall well-being, both mentally and physically?

3. Desire Detox

- Evaluating Satisfying Pursuits: What activities or pursuits do I frequently engage in that ultimately leave me feeling unfulfilled? How do these pursuits distract me from uncovering and pursuing my true passions?
- Differentiating Social Conditioning from Authentic Desires: What desires have I adopted due to societal pressure, familial expectations, or cultural norms, rather than stemming from my own genuine interests? How can I reconnect with my authentic self to uncover what I truly want?

4. IFS-Based Prompts

- Exploring Protective Aspects: What protective mechanisms or parts of myself emerge when I confront my deeper desires? How do these parts shield me from potential pain or disappointment?
- Nurturing the Inner Child: What affection or connection does my inner child still seek? How can I reconnect with this vulnerable part of myself to provide the nurturing and validation it craves?
- Addressing Fears of Wanting: Which aspects of my personality harbour fears about desiring too much or yearning for more than I feel I deserve? How can I engage with these fears compassionately and work to dissolve them?

5. Relational Insight

- Assessing Emotional Vulnerability: How secure do I feel when it comes to being emotionally vulnerable with

others in my life? What barriers or fears prevent me from opening up fully in relationships?
- Communicating Desires: In what ways do I express my desires to those I care about? Am I straightforward and open, or do I find myself becoming defensive, guarded, or ambiguous in my communication?

6. Create a New Script

- Drafting a Desire Declaration: I affirm that I am allowed to want freedom, touch, rest, and success not because I've justified it with accomplishments or proven my worth, but simply because I am human. This declaration serves as a reminder that my desires are valid and inherent to my existence.

"Desire isn't the problem. Silence is. And when a man finds the courage to speak what he truly wants, without shame, he begins to reclaim his life."

Chapter 20

The Man You Were Meant to Be

There exists a man behind the man, a profound figure not shaped by the scars of trauma or restrained by the rigid expectations of society. This figure embodies instinct, intuition, and a deep ancestral wisdom, a connection to generations past that informs his understanding of self and the world. He transcends the limitations imposed by stereotypes and commercialisation; he represents the archetype, the essential self that pulses with vitality beneath the layers of performance and facade demanded by modern life.

In today's fast-paced and often superficial world, most men have lost sight of this profound identity that once thrived within the collective male psyche. This deeper self has historically manifested through the timeless roles of King, Warrior, Magician, and Lover. Each archetype serves as a vital component of a balanced and harmonious man. Yet, these essential identities have become fractured, repressed, misunderstood, or, in some cases, dangerously mutated in our contemporary landscape.

The King serves as a wise ruler, embodying authority and responsibility; the Warrior embodies courage and strength, acting as a protector; the Magician channels creativity and transformation; and the Lover connects deeply with passion and empathy. When these archetypes are in equilibrium, they create a holistic portrayal of masculinity that is nurturing and grounded. However, in the modern age, societal pressures and cultural shifts have often led to confusion and discord among these roles.

This exploration is not merely a quest to reinvent oneself or adopt modern identities; rather, it is a profound call to remember and reconnect with this ancient essence that lies dormant within. It challenges men to delve into their psyche, to unearth the forgotten wisdom of their forebears, and to reclaim the balanced, authentic selves that have been overshadowed by the chaos of contemporary existence.

The Four Cornerstones of Mature Masculinity

In 1990, authors Robert Moore and Douglas Gillette reignited the conversation surrounding masculine identity by presenting four essential archetypes that draw from Jungian psychology and mythological narratives. Each archetype symbolises a core energetic pattern inherent in every man, collectively contributing to a well-rounded and balanced identity. These archetypes are:

- The King: This archetype embodies qualities such as order, blessing, purpose, and generative leadership. As a stabilising force, the King cultivates an environment where potential can flourish, guiding others toward their best selves. He represents not only authority but also the responsibility to nurture and empower those around him, establishing a legacy of integrity and vision.

- The Warrior: The Warrior is marked by attributes such as courage, discipline, boundaries, and decisive action. He is a protector of values and integrity, fighting for what is just and honourable. In a world often rife with conflict, the Warrior embodies the strength to confront challenges head-on, demonstrating resilience and commitment to safeguarding those he cares about and the ideals he cherishes.

- The Magician: Serving as a figure of insight, intuition, knowledge, and transformation, the Magician brings wisdom and innovation into the mix. With a deep understanding of the world and a knack for fostering growth, the Magician encourages exploration and creativity. He acts as a bridge between the seen and the unseen, guiding individuals toward greater awareness and enlightenment as they navigate life's complexities.

- The Lover: Representing connection, emotion, sensuality, and vitality, the Lover engages with the world on a profound level. He is attuned to the richness of human experience, fostering relationships that deepen understanding and enhance life's beauty. Through empathy and passion, the Lover nurtures emotional bonds that enrich both personal and communal existence.

- While every man carries these four archetypes within him, contemporary society often overlooks the importance of nurturing them in balance. It is not uncommon for men to become excessively developed in one archetype while neglecting others, or to experience distorted expressions of all four. This imbalance can lead to personal dissatisfaction and a fragmented sense of identity.

These archetypes transcend cultural boundaries and have been manifested throughout history in diverse traditions. For example, they can be seen in the Samurai of Japan, who exemplified the Warrior's discipline and honour; the fierce Zulu warriors of Africa, who embodied protection and community; the Norse god-king Odin, representing wisdom and leadership as the King; and the wise indigenous tribal elder or the Native American shaman, who symbolises the transformative aspects of the Magician. Each of these figures illustrates pathways to responsibility, emotional regulation, spiritual depth, and embodied masculinity.

However, in our modern, often disconnected, digital landscape, many of these essential rites of passage have been lost or diminished. This disconnection strips away the intimate connections that are crucial in forming and understanding a man's true identity, leaving a void that many seek to fill without the guidance of these archetypal frameworks. In nurturing these aspects, men can work towards a more integrated and whole identity, ultimately leading to healthier relationships and a fuller engagement with life.

Let's rediscover these archetypes together.

The King: From Tyrant to Sovereign

The King archetype embodies more than mere dominance; it represents a profound sense of order, stability, and benevolence within his realm. A true King creates a nurturing environment where respect is both given and received, fostering a sense of purpose and belonging not just within himself but also among those he leads. He bestows blessings upon his domain, infusing it with core values and recognising the inherent potential in others, guiding them toward personal and collective growth.

However, the absence of positive role models can lead to the King devolving into a tyrannical, oppressive, insecure, and defensive person against differences that threaten his fragile sense of control. This transformation may manifest in destructive behaviours, and in extreme cases, the King may regress entirely, resulting in a man who feels passive, uncertain, or obsessively reliant on external validation to affirm his worth.

The essence of a healthy King lies not in ruling through fear, but in governing with alignment, wisdom, and compassion. This involves striking a balance between strength and gentleness, enabling the King to inspire loyalty and commitment rather than fear.
For many boys growing up in fatherless or unstable environments, the opportunity to receive the King's essential blessing is tragically diminished. These boys may transition into men who yearn desperately for validation yet harbour a profound distrust of authority figures, including their own inner guidance. When a man lacks the anchoring presence of a father figure, the internal throne of the King remains empty. This void leads to a lifelong quest for external affirmation, leaving an unfulfilled desire for recognition that has never been meaningfully addressed.

Awakening the King within entails a conscious choice to embrace structure over chaos, responsibility rather than reactivity, and a visionary outlook over the pursuit of fleeting validation. This journey invites men to reclaim their rightful place within the lineage of masculine wisdom, tapping into the power and purpose that can effectively guide not only themselves but also the younger generations who look up to them.

The Warrior: From Destroyer to Defender

The archetype of the Warrior embodies action, determination, and an unwavering movement toward noble goals. A true

Warrior possesses the strength to advance, protect, and stand firm in the face of adversity, prepared to defend those who cannot protect themselves. Yet, in a society where expressions of male power have often devolved into abuse and toxicity, many men find themselves suppressing their Warrior energy. This internal conflict typically leads to one of two detrimental outcomes:

1. The Destroyer: In this manifestation, the Warrior's innate strength becomes distorted, emerging as unchecked anger, reactivity, violence, and emotional immaturity. Rather than serving as protectors, such individuals may inadvertently engage in self-sabotage or become a source of harm to others.

2. The Passive Shell: Conversely, some men may become overly agreeable, anxious, and boundaryless, living in a state of shame about their identities and needs. This passive existence leaves them vulnerable, unable to assert themselves or stand firm in their beliefs.

An authentic Warrior is not aggressive but is instead assertive, embodying strength paired with respect. He stands firmly in his values and upholds them without inflicting harm on others. True strength resides in his ability to set clear boundaries, effectively communicating, "I will not forsake myself to ensure your comfort."

The absence of strong yet nurturing male role models has significantly contributed to distorted expressions of the Warrior archetype. In various cultures, traditional warrior rites often included mentorship from elder males, imparting not only the practical skills necessary for combat but also invaluable lessons in ethics, discipline, and emotional regulation. This guidance nurtured a balanced understanding of strength, helping young boys learn to harness their power responsibly. In the absence of such mentorship, boys may misinterpret the concept of strength as mere domination, or they may abandon the notion of warrior energy entirely, leading to a cycle of confusion regarding their identity and role in society.

In the journey toward reclaiming the Warrior, individuals are encouraged to explore their inner strength, allowing them to evolve from mere destructiveness into courageous defenders of truth, justice, and compassion.

The Magician: From Trickster to Alchemist

The Magician archetype embodies qualities of thoughtfulness, healing, and transformation. This figure possesses the extraordinary ability to perceive reality beyond mere superficial appearances. He is adept at interpreting symbols, understanding intricate systems, and navigating the complex landscape of human emotions, which allows him to unlock profound insights and revelations that can lead to personal and collective growth.

In modern interpretations of masculinity, however, the Magician is often undervalued or misinterpreted. His shadow manifests in two distinct ways that can distort his true essence:

1. The Detached Observer: This version of the Magician presents as highly intellectual and analytical. While he may excel in critical thinking, he often exudes a sense of cynicism and emotional detachment. This detachment can create barriers to genuine connection, leading to loneliness and frustration, as he may prioritise rationality over empathy.

2. The Trickster: This manifestation moves further away from the Magician's true nature, characterised by manipulation, self-serving behaviours, and evasiveness. The Trickster undermines trust and connection with others, often using wit and cleverness to deceive instead of embracing vulnerability and authenticity.

The true Magician achieves a balance by integrating intellect with emotional awareness. Rather than hiding behind purely cerebral pursuits, he recognises that insights should serve as tools for fostering wholeness both within himself and in the communities he engages with. This archetype flourishes in roles such as counsellors, strategists, artists, and coaches, who are instrumental in facilitating growth, understanding, and healing.

However, without emotional literacy, the Magician's valuable gifts can become twisted. Men, in particular, may find themselves stuck in cycles of overthinking, prioritising intellectual pursuits at the expense of meaningful, embodied experiences that foster genuine connection and understanding.

Reclaiming the essence of the Magician involves a commitment to honouring introspection while simultaneously avoiding the trap of isolation. It is about merging knowledge with empathy, and blending the mystery of deep thought with the mindfulness of lived experience. By doing so, the Magician can transform not only himself but also positively impact those around him, ultimately guiding them toward a more profound understanding of their own journeys.

The Lover: From Addict to Sacred Connection

The Lover archetype is intricately woven into the fabric of emotions and sensory experiences, representing a profound connection to beauty, intimacy, and deep relationships. As the most vulnerable of the four archetypes, the Lover often faces the risk of suppression, particularly in a society that frequently encourages men to distance themselves from their softer instincts.

In contemporary culture, there is a prevalent message that equates vulnerability with weakness and that encourages a disconnection from touch, often reducing it to mere sexuality. This misunderstanding can lead to an internal conflict for those embodying the Lover archetype. The shadow side of the Lover can surface in two prominent forms:

1. The Addict: This manifestation is characterised by a tumultuous emotional landscape, marked by chaotic behaviour, compulsive rituals of seeking pleasure, and a debilitating inability to manage intense feelings. The Addict may become ensnared in a cycle of seeking fulfilment through superficial or destructive means, often leading to emotional instability and turmoil.

2. The Avoidant: This archetype embodies emotional detachment, exhibiting numbness and an impenetrable barrier to intimacy. The Avoidant often struggles to process emotions, leading to missed opportunities for genuine connections and a sense of isolation from the richness of human experience.

A well-balanced Lover, however, navigates the delicate interplay between emotion and reason with grace. He neither allows his life to be dictated solely by feelings nor shuns them entirely. Instead, he embraces a spectrum of human experiences, joy, sensuality, presence, and even grief, acknowledging them as essential components of life. The Lover archetype acts as a crucial conduit between the heart and body, facilitating authentic connections with others and fostering a deeper understanding of oneself. By honouring the Lover within, individuals can cultivate a more profound sense of empathy, connection, and emotional resilience in their lives.

Identity Collapse: When the Archetypes Go Missing

When a man cannot access and integrate these four vital energies, he experiences identity fragmentation that can inhibit his growth and fulfilment. The symptoms often present as:

- Lost Direction (King): Lacking a clear sense of purpose or leadership.
- Poor Boundaries (Warrior): Unable to assert oneself or protect one's values.

- Overthinking Without Insight (Magician): Getting caught in a web of analysis without actionable understanding.
- Emotional Numbness or Chaos (Lover): Struggling to connect with feelings or experiencing emotional turbulence.

These manifestations are not mere personality flaws; they stem from developmental wounds that are frequently inherited and reinforced by societal factors. The modern man often grapples with digital distractions, the absence of father figures, and cultural shaming, which leave him devoid of these essential internal guides. Consequently, he can perform masculinity without ever truly experiencing it, leading to:

- Loud but Disconnected: Expressing outwardly but lacking depth in personal connections.
- Loyal but Resentful: Being reliable on the surface while harbouring inner conflicts.
- Strong but Hollow: Displaying strength outwardly while feeling emptiness within.

What is needed is not a heightened expression of masculinity but rather a quest for deeper masculinity that aligns with authenticity and self-awareness. When these archetypes remain unacknowledged, the narratives surrounding manhood are written by external influences, often labelling him as toxic, cold, or controlling. In reality, he may simply be a man struggling to stay attuned with his internal guide, leading to silence, intensity, or distance that society misinterprets as a threat. More often than not, this behaviour emanates from unprocessed grief, a deep longing for connection and understanding.

Rebalancing the Inner Council: A Journey of Self-Discovery

In the field of personal development, the exploration and integration of archetypes is essential for cultivating a well-rounded character. Each archetype represents a fundamental aspect of a man's psyche, forming an inner council that contributes to the multidimensionality of his personality. Rather than competing for dominance, these archetypes work in harmony, with a mature man adeptly invoking each one following the demands of various situations.

- The King: This archetype symbolises authority, vision, and purpose. He is the guiding force that provides clarity and direction in life, ensuring that decisions align with core values and long-term goals. The King nurtures a sense of stability and integrity, creating a foundation upon which other archetypes can thrive.

- The Warrior: Embodying strength, courage, and decisiveness, the Warrior stands as the protector of the King's vision. This archetype is characterised by his readiness to take action and defend what is essential, demonstrating resilience in the face of challenges. A balanced Warrior harnesses discipline and focus, channelling energy effectively to overcome obstacles.

- The Magician: Within the council, the Magician serves as the nurturer of creativity and wisdom. He brings insight, innovation, and transformative thinking to the table, allowing the King's vision to evolve and adapt. The Magician's ability to connect seemingly disparate ideas fosters a dynamic approach to problem-solving, encouraging growth and continuous learning.

- The Lover: As the emotional heart of the council, the Lover emphasises connection, empathy, and the importance of relationships. This archetype ensures that the other aspects of a man's character remain grounded in humanity and compassion. The Lover fosters self-acceptance and emotional resonance, enabling a deeper understanding of oneself and one's interactions with others.

When one archetype becomes overly dominant, it can lead to a disbalance that affects all areas of life. For instance, an overpowering King might suppress the emotions of the Lover, resulting in a lack of connection in personal relationships. Conversely, if a man neglects certain archetypes altogether, he can experience a profound sense of incompleteness, leading to internal struggles and a sense of fragmentation.

To restore equilibrium among the archetypes, engaging in introspective inquiries is crucial. Thoughtful reflection on questions such as the following can facilitate personal growth and understanding:

- Where am I over-identified with a specific archetype? This inquiry encourages examination of areas where one may be excessively attached to a singular facet of their identity, potentially at the expense of others.

- What parts of my being have I felt unsafe to express openly? This question invites exploration into suppressed emotions or characteristics that may be crucial for holistic self-expression and personal fulfilment.

- Which archetype feels foreign to me, and what might be the roots of this disconnection? Delving into feelings of estrangement from certain archetypes can uncover valuable insights about past experiences, societal influences, or fears that hinder authentic self-realisation.

Through this process of reflection, a man can cultivate a richer understanding of his inner council, achieving a harmonious interplay among the archetypes that ultimately leads to a more balanced and fulfilling life.

Bio-psychological Insight: Understanding Archetypes and Brain Patterns

From a bio-psychological perspective, each archetype corresponds to specific brain functions and emotional responses, highlighting the intricate relationship between our mental frameworks and neurological processes:

-   The King activates the brain's executive functions through the prefrontal cortex, which is responsible for higher-order thinking, decision-making, and emotional regulation. This archetype embodies leadership and vision-setting, allowing individuals to plan strategically and navigate complex situations with a sense of authority and calm.

-   The Warrior stimulates sympathetic arousal and leads to the release of dopamine, enhancing physical readiness and motivation. This archetype is characterised by focused action and resilience, empowering individuals to confront challenges with courage and determination. The Warrior's energy is essential in cultivating a drive that propels one toward their goals, especially in times of adversity.

-   The Magician resonates deeply with the brain's default mode network and the limbic system, facilitating insight and creative problem-solving. This archetype supports emotional tracking and reflective thought, enabling individuals to connect their intuitive knowledge with the broader context of their experiences. The Magician embodies transformation and mastery over one's circumstances, prompting personal growth and innovation.

-   The Lover triggers the release of oxytocin, known as the bonding hormone, and engages the brain's right hemisphere, which is associated with creativity and emotional intelligence. This archetype fosters connection, sensory integration, and a profound sense of empathy, allowing individuals to form deeper relationships and experience the richness of human connection.

It is essential to recognise that traumatic experiences can severely disrupt the natural communication pathways between the brain and body, leading to weakened connections to these archetypes. This disruption can manifest as difficulties in emotional regulation, motivation, and relational dynamics. Therapeutic interventions, including talk therapy, somatic practices, and mindfulness techniques, can aid in rewiring these pathways, fostering resilience and integration. However, it's crucial to emphasise the vital role that safe, supportive masculine spaces play in this healing journey.

Historically, mentorship has been a cornerstone in the rite of passage to manhood. In many ancient cultures, men were not left to navigate the complexities of adult life alone; they were guided by the wisdom of their elders through mentorship and initiation rituals. These practices provided not only guidance but also a sense of belonging and identity. In contemporary society, while therapy addresses deep-seated psychological wounds, mentorship remains pivotal in shaping a holistic understanding of manhood. Peer-led groups and wise elder figures serve as essential mirrors, reflecting back the multifaceted aspects of the male psyche that seek validation and embrace. These relationships foster a supportive community where individuals can explore their identities and grow into the fullness of their potential.

Coaching Interventions: Awakening the Man Within

To facilitate this journey of self-discovery and balance, several comprehensive coaching interventions can be employed:

Archetypal Inventory

- Connection Assessment: Begin by evaluating your relationship with each archetype on a scale from 1 to 10. Note how strongly you identify with each one and identify any archetypes that feel either exaggerated or suppressed in your life. Consider journaling your reflections to gain deeper insights into how these archetypes manifest in your daily experiences and relationships.

Daily Embodiment Practice

- King: At the start of each day, take a moment to set one clear and meaningful intention. This could be related to your professional life, personal growth, or relationships. Throughout the day, check in with yourself to ensure that your actions align with this intention, reinforcing your sense of responsibility and leadership.
- Warrior: Embrace the courage to assert your boundaries by practising saying "no" in situations where you have previously remained silent. This could involve declining a request for help or stating your needs in a group setting. Notice how it feels to stand firm in your decisions, and reflect on the empowerment that comes from valuing your own time and energy.
- Magician: Dedicate at least ten minutes each day to a period of reflective thought. Create a quiet space where you can explore your inner insights or brainstorm creative ideas. Consider using prompts to guide your reflection, such as "What is a challenge I am facing, and how can I approach it differently?" Allow your thoughts to flow freely, nurturing your imagination and innovation.
- Lover: Schedule a sensory experience where you can fully immerse yourself in beauty and connection, whether in nature, art, or music. Dedicate this time to be entirely distraction-free, no phones or other interruptions. As you engage with your chosen medium, focus on the sensations it evokes within you, allowing yourself to experience joy, peace, or any emotions that arise.

Father Story Reclamation

- Father Figure Reflection: Take time to reflect on your experiences with father figures in your life. This could include biological fathers, stepfathers, mentors, or other significant male figures. Consider the lessons you learned from them regarding the archetypes of the King, Warrior, Magician, and Lover. What positive teachings did they impart? Were there any lessons or emotional wisdom you feel were missing or unaddressed?

- Exploration of Absence: Reflect on how the absence of a father figure or emotional distance may have influenced your development in the King and Warrior archetypes. How has this absence shaped your ability to take charge, assert yourself, or lead in various aspects of your life? Journaling these reflections can provide clarity and help you reclaim your inner strengths.

Archetypal Goal Alignment

- Significant Life Decisions: Choose a significant life decision you are facing, whether it relates to career, relationships, or personal growth. For each archetype, King, Warrior, Magician, and Lover invite their unique perspective on the situation.
- King: What would a wise leader advise you to do?
- Warrior: What actions should you take to assert yourself bravely?
- Magician: What creative solutions can emerge from this situation?
- Lover: How can you ensure that your choices align with your heart's desires and connections with others?

By engaging deeply with these interventions, you can foster a greater sense of balance and understanding of the archetypal energies that shape your life.

Gentle Prompts for Self-Reflection

Engage with these reflective prompts to connect more deeply with your inner self and foster personal growth:

- In what moments do I feel most like a leader? Consider the specific situations where you naturally take charge or inspire others. Reflect on the qualities you exhibit during these times and how they align with your values and aspirations.

- Which battles am I fighting that are not truly mine? Take a moment to identify conflicts or challenges you may be facing that stem from external pressures or expectations. Ask yourself whether these struggles serve your true purpose or if they divert your energy away from your own path.

- How has my intellect become a defensive shield? Reflect on the ways you may rely on your intellect to protect yourself from vulnerability or emotional exposure. Explore how this defence mechanism influences your relationships and whether it fosters genuine connection or isolates you further.

- What beauty have I denied myself the chance to experience? Think about the opportunities for joy, art, or connection that you have overlooked due to self-doubt or fear. Consider how embracing beauty in its various forms could enrich your life and enhance your well-being.

- Which parts of me require affirmation to exist fully? Identify aspects of your identity or personality that feel neglected or undervalued. Contemplate how seeking affirmation from yourself and others could empower these parts to flourish and contribute fully to your life.

- Who in my life could help guide me back to the aspects of myself that I have long disowned? Reflect on the individuals who inspire, nurture, or challenge you in meaningful ways. Think about how their support can help you reconnect with lost parts of yourself and reignite your sense of purpose and direction.

Final Reframe: Embracing Wholeness

Ultimately, hold onto this profound truth: you are not broken; instead, you are a tapestry of various fragments yearning to be unified. You are not deficient or incomplete; instead, you are engaged in a beautiful process of remembrance, rediscovering the pieces of yourself that have been overshadowed by life's complexities.

The mature man is not merely an assembly of traits or accomplishments; he is revealed through the delicate art of rebalancing the multifaceted aspects of his nature that have been buried over time, each layer holding lessons and wisdom.

Consider the archetypes that dwell within us: The King, The Warrior, The Magician, and The Lover. These are not just ancient myths or symbolic stories; rather, they serve as vital mirrors, reflecting the rich and intricate depths of your humanity. Each archetype embodies essential qualities and virtues that, when harmonised, allow for a more integrated and authentic existence.

This journey is sacred work, not just for the surface-level performance of masculinity, but for embodying it with intention, balance, and integrity. The true essence of masculinity is not a collection of rigid norms, but rather a dynamic flow of strength and compassion. It invites you to embrace vulnerability and to nurture a spirit that blesses rather than bruises, fostering connection and understanding with others. This is the path toward a fuller, more meaningful expression of who you are meant to be.

Reclaim your archetypes. Reclaim your true self.

Chapter 21

The Voice He Never Learned to Use

Words wield significant power; they can inflict profound pain or serve as a balm for healing, and in the nuanced space between these two extremes, they play a crucial role in revealing hidden truths. For many men, the real challenge does not stem from silence itself, but from the struggle to articulate their emotions effectively. This difficulty manifests in various ways: some may share too much, leading to overwhelming conversations, while others speak too little, leaving their thoughts shrouded in ambiguity. Miscommunication frequently arises, causing frustration and confusion. As a result, some men might retreat from expressing themselves meaningfully, while others cling to safe, rehearsed phrases that have become their emotional armour, perpetuating the all-too-familiar mantra: "I'm fine."

Yet, the underlying reality is far more intricate. Most men do not lack emotional intelligence; instead, they navigate a complex landscape of feelings that often seems inaccessible or daunting. They have not lost their capacity for genuine expression; instead, they frequently find themselves without the words to articulate the depth of their inner experiences. This struggle can feel akin to being locked out of a crucial room within their emotional architecture, where vital thoughts and feelings reside, waiting to be acknowledged and understood. The challenge lies in bridging the gap between their rich internal world and the language needed to communicate it, fostering deeper connections and a more profound understanding of themselves and others.

The Lock Without a Key

Imagine a man sitting in a therapist's office, his arms tightly crossed, conveying a defensive posture that hides the emotional tempest roiling within him. His eyes flicker nervously, not as a sign of resistance or lack of engagement, but as a manifestation of deep internal conflict. He is grappling with an emotional burden that feels insurmountable, yet the words to articulate his feelings remain frustratingly out of reach. This experience can be described as the Linguistic Lock, a paralysing moment when powerful emotions surge, but the vocabulary to express them eludes him entirely. This phenomenon is not indicative of a failure of intellect or mere stubbornness; rather, it reflects a lifetime of cultural conditioning geared toward emotional suppression.

From an early age, boys are often inundated with messages that reinforce emotional restraint, such as:

- "Don't cry; it's a sign of weakness."
- "Don't complain; it burdens others."
- "Don't talk about your feelings; it makes you vulnerable."

These societal scripts shape their understanding of masculinity and emotional expression, creating an unspoken code that stifles openness. When they do find the courage to express their emotions, the societal expectation is often to cloak those feelings in layers of humour or practicality, steering clear of direct emotional discourse. It's as if they are gifted a grand piano but stripped of the black keys, thereby limiting their ability to create a truly harmonious piece; they can still produce music, but it lacks depth and variety.

What is sacrificed within this emotional confinement? The nuances of their experiences are dulled, stripping away essential elements like vulnerability, connection, and the opportunity for authentic self-repair. As a result, crucial moments of personal growth are overshadowed by the inability to engage with their own emotions honestly. The cost of such suppression is high, leading to deeper issues in relationships and a flawed understanding of oneself. In a world where emotional articulation is often seen as a weakness, the pursuit of true emotional expression becomes not only a personal challenge but a necessary path toward healing.

Cultural Conditioning: When Men Speak in Code

Men have historically cultivated a rich, metaphorical vocabulary to express their emotions, often using vivid imagery as a means of communication. When asked how they feel, a man might respond with phrases like:

305

- "I'm feeling like a pressure cooker ready to burst," illustrating pent-up frustration or anxiety.
- "My life feels like a broken engine; nothing's running smoothly," which conveys a sense of dysfunction and lack of control.
- "It seems like my game plan is unravelling," reflecting feelings of confusion or defeat in the face of challenges.

Instead of directly saying, "I'm scared" or "I feel abandoned," men might choose to assert, "I'm off my game" or "Something's just not right." Such expressions are not merely acts of avoidance; they serve as a nuanced translation of deep-seated emotions into a language that feels safer and more manageable to share in a world that often discourages vulnerability.

Culturally, men have leaned on a coded language historically communicating their innermost feelings through stories of valour, camaraderie in pubs, evocative lyrics in music, and even through expressions of physical intimacy. The long-standing societal expectation has been that actions speak louder than words, reinforcing the notion that to survive, men must do more while saying less. This unspoken code places a premium on stoicism and strength, often leaving emotional nuances unaddressed.

However, this approach can become a liability, especially within therapeutic settings or close personal relationships where healing demands the accurate identification and articulation of emotional wounds. When a man struggles to express the pain he feels, he risks embodying the very fears and stereotypes that society places upon him. The inability to voice these struggles can lead to internal conflict, isolation, and a perpetuation of the emotional barriers that hinder genuine connection and understanding. Acknowledging and articulating these feelings is essential for breaking the cycle and fostering a healthier emotional landscape.

Cultural Contrast: The Double Standard

When a woman becomes emotionally withdrawn, society often interprets her behaviour as a self-protective measure. This view emphasises her need to reclaim her inner peace and establish vital boundaries. In contrast, when men exhibit similar emotional withdrawal, they are frequently labelled as emotionally unavailable, indifferent, or even manipulative. This stark double standard complicates the emotional landscape for men, who are already navigating a cultural environment that discourages open expression of their feelings.

Understanding these dynamics is crucial for fostering deeper connections between genders. When we acknowledge the pressures men face, we can create a supportive atmosphere that encourages them to articulate their emotions. By breaking through the societal "linguistic locks" that restrict their ability to communicate, men can begin to share their feelings more freely, in a world that has traditionally rewarded silence and stoicism.

Furthermore, when men withdraw emotionally, they often confront a barrage of negative labels that suggest a lack of empathy or a failure to invest in relationships. This judgment can lead to internalised shame, creating a cycle of emotional hiding. In contrast, women who experience emotional shutdowns typically receive understanding and compassion, which highlights the inherent bias in how we perceive and respond to emotional distress across genders.

This glaring discrepancy can trap men in a no-win scenario. They feel the pressure to suppress their feelings to avoid judgment, yet this silence does not shield them from blame when relationships suffer. Consequently, seeking genuine emotional connection becomes a precarious endeavour, heavily laden with the fear of misunderstanding and rejection. By actively working to dismantle this double standard, we can pave the way for a more empathetic dialogue that honours the emotional experiences of all individuals, regardless of gender.

Psychology of Miscommunication

In Cognitive Behavioural Therapy (CBT), one of the essential tools employed by therapists is the "thought record." This technique encourages individuals to meticulously identify their feelings, label the corresponding thoughts, and critically challenge any cognitive distortions that may be present. However, a significant obstacle often arises: if a person struggles to articulate their feelings, they are consequently unable to access the underlying thoughts that accompany those emotions. This disconnect between feelings and thoughts can lead to impulsive actions and behaviours that are frequently misinterpreted by others.

The miscommunication that arises from this emotional disconnect can manifest in various ways, complicating interpersonal relationships. For instance:

- Anger: An outward display of anger may be perceived as an aggressive outburst, but it can be deeply rooted in feelings of frustration, helplessness, or a sense of being overwhelmed. Rather than being simply rebellious or hostile, the individual may be struggling with an inability to process or express their discomfort adequately.

- Detachment: This emotional state is often interpreted as indifference or coldness. In reality, it may stem from an internal conflict with vulnerability; the person might be grappling with the fear of being hurt or rejected. Their apparent emotional distance can be a protective mechanism, shielding them from the pain of deep feelings that feel unsafe to express.

- Cold Logic: When an individual defaults to rational thinking in emotionally charged situations, others may perceive this as a lack of empathy. However, this behaviour may indicate their struggle to navigate overwhelming emotions. By resorting to detached reasoning, they attempt to create a sense of order amidst emotional chaos, trying to regain control over situations that feel unmanageable.

In these contexts, behaviours that seem negative or troubling often stem from a deeper issue: a failure to effectively translate complex emotional experiences into articulate words. Many men are acutely aware that something feels off or amiss; however, the precise language to describe their inner landscape eludes them. This can lead to a profound sense of isolation, as they feel trapped in their emotional turmoil without the means to convey it to those around them. Understanding this dynamic is crucial for fostering empathy and improving communication in relationships.

Enter the Linguistic Lock pick

To effectively address the emotional challenges that many men face, it is beneficial to explore clinical frameworks derived from Neuro-Linguistic Programming (NLP) alongside somatic language patterns. NLP emphasises that the language we use deeply reflects our internal maps of reality; it has a profound influence on our beliefs, feelings, and subsequent actions. For men who often feel emotionally constrained or unable to express their true feelings, NLP offers a range of tools designed to unlock and process previously suppressed emotional experiences.

Consider the impact of reframing negative self-statements. For instance, the thought "I'm always failing" can be shifted to a more constructive perspective: "I haven't discovered what works for me yet." This subtle adjustment not only alleviates feelings of shame associated with failure but also encourages a growth mindset, opening the door to exploration and self-discovery. Similarly, the statement "I'm too much" may be transformed into "I've never been given the space to feel like I'm enough." This reframing acknowledges the external circumstances that may have limited self-acceptance, fostering a sense of validation and self-worth.

These nuanced yet powerful shifts in language can liberate men from the heavy burdens of shame and insecurity. By fostering greater emotional awareness and self-compassion, they create new pathways for authentic self-expression, enabling a richer, more fulfilling engagement with their own emotions and relationships. This transformation not only allows men to navigate their feelings more freely but also encourages a deeper connection with themselves and others, ultimately cultivating healthier emotional lives.

Expressing the Inexpressible: The Body as Translator

Somatic therapy emphasises the importance of body-based expression, recognising that when verbal communication falls short, our physical sensations can reveal deeper emotional truths. This therapeutic approach invites us to explore the intricate connections between our physical experiences and emotional states. For instance:

- A tight chest often signals profound fear, hinting at anxiety or unresolved trauma that restricts breath and movement. This physical tension serves as a reminder of feelings that might be too overwhelming to articulate.

- Clenching fists can be an embodiment of unexpressed anger, manifesting as a defensive posture against perceived threats or feelings of helplessness. This tight grip on our hands may indicate a struggle to channel anger constructively.

- Jaw pain frequently symbolises words that have been suppressed, suggesting that there are thoughts or feelings which one feels unable to voice. This tension in the jaw can reflect frustrations or disagreements that remain unspoken, trapping our emotions inside.

- Fidgeting hands might illustrate the internal conflict between a desire to express oneself and a simultaneous fear of vulnerability. This physical restlessness can be a powerful indicator of the difficulty in navigating one's own emotional landscape.

By guiding individuals to identify and connect these physical sensations with their underlying emotional experiences, somatic therapy offers a valuable pathway to expression. In this interactive process, the body emerges as a vital translator, articulating feelings that have long been silenced. This innovative approach not only enriches personal insight but also fosters a deeper connection to oneself, paving the way for healing and self-discovery.

Clinical Sidebar: Misunderstood Male Trauma

In psychiatric settings, the trauma experienced by men is often misinterpreted as conduct disorder or narcissistic behaviour. This mislabelling occurs for several interconnected reasons:

- Cultural Norms and Emotional Expression: Society frequently links emotional expression with weakness, particularly within male-coded social roles that emphasise stoicism and emotional restraint. This cultural stigma discourages men from openly discussing their feelings, leading to a façade of toughness that can obscure underlying emotional distress.

- Misinterpretation of Emotional Shutdown: When men exhibit emotional withdrawal or shutdown, it is often mistakenly viewed as a display of power or control. In reality, such behaviour may stem from a panic response due to overwhelming feelings of vulnerability or fear. This misinterpretation can prevent effective communication and support, further isolating the individual in their struggles.

- Perception of Anger and Rage: Anger is commonly interpreted as a threat, which can overshadow its true nature as an emotional response rooted in deep-seated trauma or as a symptom of a flashback. This perspective not only diminishes the understanding of a man's emotional experience but can also stigmatise their reactions, reinforcing feelings of alienation.

The consequences of these misunderstandings are significant. They can lead to misdiagnosis, where individuals are labelled with inappropriate psychiatric conditions that do not accurately represent their experiences. This can result in mistreatment, as therapists may focus on behaviours deemed problematic rather than addressing underlying trauma. Ultimately, this cycle creates an environment of internalised shame among men, hindering their ability to seek help and perpetuating their struggles with mental health. By recognising and addressing these misconceptions, we can foster a more compassionate and accurate understanding of male trauma, paving the way for better support and healing.

Rebuilding Vocabulary from the Ground Up

The journey toward emotional literacy is not an innate trait for many men; instead, it is a skill developed through deliberate practice, cultivated word by word and association by association. For some men, this transformative pathway may begin with journaling, a process that allows them to articulate their thoughts and feelings in a safe space. Others may discover clarity and insight through the pages of fiction, where they can explore complex emotional landscapes vicariously, or by engaging in conversations with others, listening to fellow men share their vulnerabilities and truths.

This essential work of developing emotional literacy involves several key shifts in communication:

- Instead of resorting to the blanket statement "I'm angry," men can strive for a more nuanced expression such as "I feel ignored and overlooked," which paints a clearer picture of the underlying feelings and context.

- When faced with fatigue, replacing "I'm tired" with "I feel emotionally depleted and overwhelmed" allows for a deeper understanding of the emotional toll that circumstances may exert on them, rather than merely focusing on physical exhaustion.

- Transitioning from the standard "I'm fine" to a more honest admission like "I don't feel safe enough to be seen right now" fosters a greater sense of vulnerability and authenticity, allowing for real connection and support.

By expanding their emotional vocabulary and engaging in these practices, men can reclaim their voices, enabling them to express their authentic experiences and foster deeper, more meaningful connections with themselves and those around them. In doing so, they not only enhance their own emotional well-being but also contribute to creating an environment where open dialogue about feelings and emotions is welcomed and normalised.

Cultural Illiteracy: The Silence We Inherited

In our societal structure, the emotional education of boys is, unfortunately, tragically neglected. From an early age, instead of nurturing their ability to articulate feelings and process emotions, we often prioritise punishment, pressure, and performance. This environmental condition them to view words merely as tools for manipulation or, even worse, as weapons intended for self-defence or offence. Consequently, this pervasive paradigm leaves many men ill-equipped to form genuine connections with others, overlooking the fundamental importance of communication as a pathway to understanding, empathy, and emotional intimacy.

As a result, men frequently grow up without acquiring essential emotional skills that are vital for healthy relationships and self-awareness. For instance, they may struggle with:

- Apologising without collapsing under the weight of shame or guilt: Many boys are socialised to view apologies not as a courageous act of humility and reconciliation but as a sign of weakness that undermines their masculinity. This can lead to prolonged conflicts and unresolved issues in their personal relationships.

- Expressing their needs without feeling embarrassed or vulnerable: This aversion creates a significant barrier, preventing them from voicing critical personal desires or discomforts. As a consequence, authentic relationships become stifled, and partnerships may falter due to misunderstandings or unexpressed needs.

- Asking for emotional closeness without it being automatically associated with sexual advances: This misunderstanding often creates rifts in their interpersonal relationships. Affection, which should be an expression of platonic care and connection, is frequently misinterpreted, leaving both parties confused and emotionally distant.

The cultural narratives available to them tend to reinforce these limitations, perpetuating harmful stereotypes. Boys and men are often portrayed through clichéd archetypes such as:

- The Strong, Silent Type: Lauded for their stoicism, yet this façade ultimately isolates them from meaningful connections, as shutting down emotionally becomes synonymous with strength.

- The Lone Wolf: Celebrated for their fierce independence, men who embody this archetype often miss out on the profound benefits of collaboration and community support, leading to feelings of loneliness and disconnection.

- The Fixer, Not the Feeler: They are encouraged to be problem-solvers rather than to engage with their emotions. This focus on fixing rather than feeling can leave their emotional landscape barren and devoid of deeper understanding.

When these men encounter difficulties in romantic relationships, society is quick to label them as "toxic," hastily characterising their struggles as flaws in character rather than symptoms of an emotional crisis. In therapeutic settings, their reluctance to engage or confront their feelings is often dismissed as "resistance," further alienating them from the help they may need. When they grapple with their pain or react defensively, they're branded as abusers, neglecting the systemic emotional illiteracy that has been cultivated throughout their upbringing. This lack of comprehension about emotions not only hampers their personal growth but also perpetuates cycles of misunderstanding and conflict in relationships, highlighting a profound need for change in how we approach the emotional development of boys and men.

Ethical Framing: Damned If You Do, Damned If You Don't

There exists a troubling paradox surrounding men's emotional expression, one that often leaves them feeling trapped. On one hand, when men choose to remain silent about their feelings, they are frequently perceived as distant, detached, or uncaring. This societal expectation pressures them to seem stoic, reinforcing the stereotype that emotional vulnerability is a sign of weakness. On the other hand, when they muster the courage to articulate their emotions, particularly in high-stakes situations like contentious arguments or custody disputes, their words risk being weaponised against them.

In legal settings, for instance, genuine emotional expression can be misinterpreted as volatility or instability. Instead of presenting a man as someone capable of vulnerability and empathy, these outbursts may be reframed as signs of emotional turmoil, casting doubt on his reliability and fitness as a partner or parent. Similarly, in the context of relationship breakdowns, moments of candour, where honesty and vulnerability should foster understanding, can be twisted into accusations of manipulation or aggression. This skewing of intent creates an environment where emotional honesty is fraught with peril.

315

Many men, therefore, opt for silence not because they lack care or concern, but because they live in a pervasive fear of the potential fallout from their emotional honesty. They fear that their attempts to communicate effectively will instead be turned into tools for blame or character assassination.

Reflecting on this profound struggle, a former client shared a poignant insight: "I wasn't trying to hurt her. I just didn't know how to be in a fight and stay." This statement encapsulates the desperate need for men to find guidance, support, and practical tools to navigate these complex emotional landscapes. It underscores the importance of fostering environments where emotional expression is met with understanding rather than judgment, allowing men to engage authentically without the fear of retribution. Only then can we hope to dismantle this paradox and promote genuine emotional communication for men in all aspects of their lives.

Cross-Cultural Voices

This emotional restraint is not simply an individual challenge; it represents a deeply ingrained cultural phenomenon, particularly prevalent in many African, Asian, and Middle Eastern communities. In these cultures, silence surrounding emotional expression is often passed down through generations, creating a strong societal expectation of emotional control. As Imran, a 41-year-old man reflecting on his upbringing, states, "I was taught not to cry, not to speak unless spoken to." This upbringing instilled in him a belief that vulnerability is a sign of weakness. When he relocated to the UK, he was taken aback by the open discussions surrounding emotional health and expression. However, he found that, despite the emphasis on emotional openness, practical guidance on navigating these discussions without experiencing shame or fear was often lacking.

Cultural norms and expectations further complicate men's attempts to articulate their emotions, particularly in mixed or Westernised contexts. The differing interpretations of emotional openness can result in confusion and miscommunication, leaving many individuals feeling isolated in their struggles.

Therapeutic Techniques: Unlocking Emotional Expression with Precision:

In therapeutic environments, it is essential to implement targeted techniques that empower men to express their emotions effectively. By focusing on how to unlock their voices with precision, we can facilitate healthier forms of communication, allowing for vulnerability without the burden of judgment. This approach fosters genuine connections and deeper emotional understanding among individuals.

Therapists and coaches trained in trauma-informed care employ a range of tools to encourage understanding, communication, and healing. One effective method is known as Parts Language, which draws on Internal Family Systems (IFS) therapy. This technique invites individuals to delve into their internal conflicts by exploring questions like, "What part of you shuts down when you feel criticised?" This inquiry assists individuals in identifying and acknowledging the various aspects of themselves, which ultimately enhances their emotional awareness and facilitates a journey toward self-acceptance.

Another valuable strategy is the use of Sentence Stems. These serve as prompts for self-reflection and expression, encouraging individuals to articulate their thoughts and fears. For example, a prompt like "I'm afraid if I say_____, then _____ will happen" allows men to confront their anxieties about vulnerability and its potential repercussions. Similarly, "What I really wanted to say was _____" invites clarification of feelings that might otherwise remain unexpressed, thus enhancing relational communication.

Metaphor Exploration acts as a powerful tool, enabling individuals to convey complex emotions in more relatable terms. Questions such as, "If your anger were an animal, what would it be?" or "What's the weather like inside you today?" provide avenues for individuals to visualise feelings that might seem overwhelming or complicated to articulate, thereby creating a pathway to deeper understanding.

Backwards Journaling is an introspective technique that begins with a specific behaviour and traces back to the emotions driving that behaviour. For instance, starting with a statement like, "I shouted," one might explore underlying emotions by asking, "What was I terrified of?" leading to realisations such as, "I was afraid I'd lose her," which may further uncover feelings of abandonment. This backwards exploration unearths fears and emotional triggers that can influence present behaviour, fostering self-awareness and emotional intelligence.

To cultivate a nurturing environment conducive to open communication, partners need to embrace the Role of Hearing Without Fixing. When individuals, particularly men, muster the courage to share their feelings, they often crave the space to express themselves without the pressure of correction or interrogation. They need the invaluable gift of being truly heard, rather than being immediately coached or fixed.

For partners wishing to support their loved ones, it's essential to:

-   Refrain from rushing to solve the problem at hand, allowing space for exploration instead.
-   Avoid using someone's vulnerability against them in future disagreements, fostering a safe emotional environment.
-   Engage in active listening by reflecting back what is heard, instead of projecting fears or assumptions onto the conversation.

Examples of practical reflections might include:

-   "So when you shut down, it's not that you don't care; it's that you're feeling overwhelmed?"

318

- "It sounds like this situation isn't just about the present moment; it's connected to something deeper, perhaps rooted in the past?"

This style of communication nurtures emotional literacy, allowing both partners to share and comprehend their feelings more openly and authentically.

Additionally, Gentle Prompts can function as linguistic keys that help uncover hidden emotions. Examples might include:

- "What word do I frequently use when I am unsure about my feelings?"
- "What emotion do I often judge myself for expressing?"
- "What physical signs indicate that I am shutting down emotionally?"
- "What's one sentence I wish I could say but find impossible to express?"
- "What underlying fear contributes to my silence?"

These techniques and prompts not only facilitate emotional expression but also strengthen the bonds of understanding and empathy between partners, ultimately promoting healthier and more fulfilling relationships.

The final reframe is essential for understanding your experience: You are not broken solely because you struggle to express your thoughts and feelings. Instead, it may simply be a reflection of being unpractised in articulating your emotions, perhaps because no one ever taught you the skills necessary for effective communication. It's essential to recognise that your moments of silence should never be perceived as signs of guilt or inadequacy. Instead, they reveal a more profound truth: the ability to express yourself has likely been constrained by various factors, such as past experiences or a lack of encouragement.

The encouraging news is that you have the power to reclaim your voice, one word at a time, one breath at a time, and one truth at a time. This process of rediscovery is not only possible, but it is also within your grasp right now. By embracing your journey and allowing yourself the space to practice and grow, you can learn to articulate your thoughts and feelings with clarity and confidence. Each step you take forward is a testament to your strength and resilience, guiding you toward a more expressive and fulfilling life.

Chapter 22

Truth Over Performance

There comes a pivotal moment in a man's life when mere survival no longer satisfies his spirit. Amid the mundane routine of daily existence, he begins to sense an unsettling void, a disconnection that gnaws at him from within. As he navigates the landscape of his life, his career marked by accomplishment, relationships that once sparked joy, and milestones celebrated, an undercurrent of discontent persists, manifesting as a nameless ache deep in his core.

This ache isn't rooted in a mere failure to achieve societal expectations or personal ambitions; instead, it emerges from a profound misalignment between his actions and his authentic self. He realises that, despite outward success, he has been caught in a cycle of performing tasks devoid of meaningful connection, engaged in interactions that feel superficial at best. This realisation catalyses a quest for something deeper, a yearning to rediscover purpose and fulfilment.

This profound introspection serves as the genesis of the Ethical Roadmap, a guide designed not as a set of rigid rules or moral checklists, but as a navigational tool that encourages him to explore the depths of his values, passions, and truths. The Ethical Roadmap aims to facilitate a transformative journey back to self-awareness, enabling him to evaluate his choices against the backdrop of his true essence. By reconnecting with what genuinely matters to him, he embarks on a path towards authenticity, empowering him to live with intention and meaning. In this journey, he finds not only a restoration of spirit but also the courage to embrace a life that resonates with his true self.

When Values Go Missing

Most men do not begin their journeys through life with the conscious intention of betraying their true identities. Instead, they slip into the roles society expects of them, provider, protector, performer, adapting to the demands of their circumstances. Initially, these roles might seem like badges of honour, symbols of their commitment to family and community. However, as time unfolds, these roles often devolve into monotonous routines that become suffocating, transforming into restrictive cages that confine their true selves.

In this transition, a critical shift occurs within him. He stops asking himself, "Is this right for me?" a question that invites introspection and alignment with his personal values. Instead, he begins to centre his thoughts around, "Does this keep the peace?" This subtle but profound change signifies a disconnection from his own moral compass, leading to a gradual erosion of his authentic voice. In this silence, he often feels an unsettling absence that he cannot quite name; it is not born from a lack of integrity or moral failing but emerges from a profound disconnection with his inner truth and core values.

As he navigates through life, unwittingly surrendering his beliefs for the sake of external expectations, he may find himself feeling increasingly unfulfilled and estranged from his own essence. The societal pressures that once seemed innocuous now weigh heavily upon him, creating a growing chasm between who he is and who he has become. It is this internal conflict, this quiet struggle for authenticity, that may ultimately drive him to seek rediscovery and reconnection with the values that once guided him.

The Ethics of Self-Abandonment

In therapeutic settings, we often find ourselves addressing boundary violations imposed by others' actions that infringe upon a person's autonomy and sense of self. However, a far more insidious betrayal frequently goes unnoticed: the violations a man inflicts upon himself. In a quest for external validation, he may compromise his own boundaries, choosing to seek approval over authenticity, avoiding conflict at all costs, or shying away from being labelled as "difficult."

These self-betrayals may seem negligible in individual instances, yet they accumulate quietly over time, creating a profound impact on his mental and emotional well-being. He may nod in agreement during discussions where he profoundly disagrees, suppress his voice when facing unjust treatment, or take on blame simply to quell tensions and restore peace. Each choice might appear minor in isolation, but collectively, they erode his self-esteem and authenticity.

Eventually, he finds himself not only losing his voice but also drifting away from his true self and personal aspirations. This personal erosion can lead to feelings of frustration, disconnection, and confusion about one's identity and desires.

This is precisely where the Ethical Roadmap becomes not just beneficial, but absolutely essential. It serves as a guiding framework, helping individuals navigate their internal and external landscapes, reinforcing the importance of self-respect, and empowering them to reclaim their voice and personal agency. By addressing these self-imposed boundaries, individuals can begin to rebuild a sense of direction and clarity in their lives, ultimately fostering healthier relationships with themselves and others.

Psychology: Moral Injury and Inner Conflict

Moral injury refers to the psychological harm that arises when an individual betrays their own deeply held values and principles. While it is frequently discussed in the context of military service, where soldiers may act in ways that contradict their moral beliefs, it extends far beyond that realm, affecting personal relationships, family dynamics, and workplace environments.

Consider the example of a man who places great importance on loyalty. He finds himself stuck in a corporate job where he is consistently exploited, working long hours without recognition or fair compensation. Every day, he grapples with the conflict between his dedication to the company and the disloyalty he feels towards himself for tolerating such treatment. This inner turmoil creates a palpable sense of moral discord, leading to feelings of guilt and resentment.

Alternatively, think of another individual who values honesty above all else. He is faced with a situation where telling the truth could cause undue pain to a loved one. In a moment of weakness, he chooses to fabricate a white lie, believing it to be a protective measure. However, each instance of dishonesty accumulates, eroding his self-esteem and contributing to a growing sense of shame for not living up to his own standards.

Then, consider a person who fundamentally cherishes peace and harmony in his life. Yet, despite his best intentions, he finds himself reacting with anger and frustration in everyday situations, such as traffic jams, work stress, or conflicts at home. Each angry outburst contradicts his core value of peacefulness, creating an internal conflict that manifests as anxiety and discontent.

In all of these instances, a profound inner rot begins to take shape. The mind attempts to rationalise these betrayals, spinning stories to soothe the conscience, yet the soul remains acutely aware of these inconsistencies. It silently keeps score, diligently recording the emotional and psychological toll of living out of alignment with one's true self. Over time, the cumulative effects of moral injury can lead to profound distress, disconnection, and a pervasive sense of dissatisfaction with life.

Biopsychology: The Body Remembers

When a man acts in contradiction to his fundamental values, his body registers this internal conflict as a source of significant stress. The emotional turmoil that ensues leads to elevated cortisol levels, a hormone closely linked to the stress response. This rise in cortisol can result in various physical manifestations that reflect his struggle. For instance, tension headaches may emerge as a consequence of suppressed feelings, where the frustration of unspoken words and unexpressed emotions creates a pressure that the body cannot ignore. Similarly, digestive issues often arise, stemming from the turmoil of thoughts left unvoiced, indicating that what we hold back can indeed affect our gut health. Chronic fatigue, too, becomes a common experience, representing the heavy burden of unresolved guilt and internal contradictions that he carries.

The nervous system operates independently from societal expectations and external validations; its focus is solely on the individual's inner sense of alignment. When this intrinsic alignment is missing, the body instinctively sends out distress signals. Symptoms may manifest in various ways, such as an unsettled stomach, tightly knotted muscles, and a feeling of constriction in the chest, all of which serve as stark reminders of his inner turmoil. Over time, his body transforms into a vivid billboard, vividly displaying the profound toll that a life lived in authentically takes. Each physical symptom becomes a testament to the ethical and moral conflicts he grapples with, illuminating the pain he can no longer endure in silence.

Coaching Insight: The Integrity Gap

From a coaching perspective, many men find themselves grappling with feelings of frustration, stagnation, or even burnout in various aspects of their lives. These experiences often leave them feeling disconnected and overwhelmed, prompting a deeper exploration into their personal journeys. It is in these moments of introspection that I encounter a significant concept I refer to as the Integrity Gap. This gap symbolisessymbolises the dissonance between a man's life and his authentic beliefs and values, creating a sense of inner conflict and dissatisfaction.

When addressing this Integrity Gap, it's essential to recognise that the solution does not lie in simply increasing motivation or imposing external pressures. Instead, what is truly necessary is the creation of a comprehensive roadmap that acts as a guide, steering him back toward his core values and principles. This is the essence of what I call the Ethical Roadmap, anan intentional framework designed to facilitate a return to one's foundational truths and convictions.

To elaborate, the Ethical Roadmap is built upon three essential pillars:

1. Truth over Performance: This principle emphasises the importance of prioritising authenticity and honesty in one's life. Men are encouraged to shift their focus from chasing external success or accolades to embracing their true selves. By doing so, they can foster a deeper sense of fulfilment and connection to their own identity, rather than remaining trapped in a cycle of superficial achievements.

2. Courage over Comfort: This pillar advocates for the bravery to confront and engage with the uncomfortable realities of one's life. Many men may be inclined to choose the easy path silencing their inner struggles or avoiding difficult conversations. Instead, this principle urges them to embrace discomfort as a catalyst for growth, understanding that facing uncomfortable truths often leads to genuine transformation and resilience.

3. Alignment over Approval: Finally, this aspect focuses on the significance of living in harmony with one's personal values and beliefs, rather than seeking validation from others. By concentrating on what truly resonates with them, men can cultivate a life that reflects their authentic selves rather than one moulded by societal expectations or the desire for approval from peers and authority figures.

Together, these pillars create a robust framework that empowers men to bridge the Integrity Gap. By guiding them back to their core values, the Ethical Roadmap not only helps restore their sense of purpose but also fosters a more authentic and fulfilling life journey.

Cross-Cultural Reflections: Different Worlds, Same Silence

Across diverse cultures, a pervasive stigma surrounds men who openly express their emotions, deeply rooted in traditional views of masculinity. In many societies, emoting is often perceived as a sign of weakness, suggesting vulnerability that contradicts the ideal of a stoic male figure. In other contexts, such expressions could be interpreted as a marker of instability or lack of control, further entrenching emotional suppression. Moreover, intersecting factors such as race, community dynamics, and religious beliefs shape distinct expectations of masculinity, significantly influencing whether men feel empowered or constrained in their pursuit of an ethical and emotionally fulfilling life.

For instance, one Indian man in therapy revealed, "If I cry, I'm disrespecting my father," which poignantly illustrates the intense pressure to maintain familial dignity, often at the cost of one's own emotional health. This sentiment resonates within many cultures where filial piety and respect for family legacy trump the necessity for personal expression. A Black client shared his experience, stating, "Where I grew up, strength meant silence. Emotions got you jumped," highlighting the harsh realities that can accompany emotional vulnerability in specific communities. Similarly, a Middle Eastern man articulated a gripping internal conflict, asserting, "My integrity is family honour, not personal happiness," indicating how cultural expectations of honour can overshadow individual pursuits of joy and self-identity.

This complex clash between cultural integrity and individual authenticity complicates the pursuit of personal fulfilment for many men. They often find themselves torn between the duty to uphold their heritage and the yearning for personal liberation and self-acceptance. The essential task lies in acknowledging and reconciling both dimensions: respecting ancestral legacies while embracing one's personal authenticity. This integration creates a bridge that allows them to navigate their identities, fostering a new understanding of masculinity that values emotional expression as a strength rather than a weakness, ultimately leading to a more fulfilling and balanced life.

Cultural Pressure: The Shame of Right Action

Men often encounter societal pressure and shame, not only for actions they take that may be perceived as wrong but also for choosing to act in ways that challenge traditional social norms. For instance, when a man decides to voice concerns about injustices, he may be met with dismissive comments like, "You're overreacting," which diminishes the validity of his feelings and the issues he's addressing. Conversely, suppose he opts to distance himself from a toxic environment, be it a harmful relationship or a detrimental workplace. In that case, he might find himself labelled as someone who "gave up" or lacks resilience, undermining his decision to prioritise his mental well-being.

Setting personal boundaries, essential for maintaining one's integrity, could elicit backlash that frames him as "selfish" or inconsiderate. This societal response can be especially harsh for men who have been socialised to seek approval and avoid conflict, often leading them to prioritise others' perceptions over their own ethical convictions.

There exists a profound cultural cost associated with pursuing ethical clarity, particularly for men who strive to remain true to themselves. Those who refuse to compromise their values may find themselves facing disapproval, isolation, or ridicule from peers, family, and society at large. For many, raised to be people-pleasers, this disapproval can manifest as a significant emotional burden, creating feelings of overwhelming failure and inadequacy when they choose to uphold their principles.

However, it's essential to recognise a fundamental truth: your ethics are not a matter for consensus or majority rule. You do not need the validation of others to affirm your choices. What you ultimately require is the ability to rest easily at night, confident that you have honoured your principles and remained faithful to your values. Embracing this truth can empower you to navigate societal pressures with resilience, knowing that true integrity comes from within.

NHS & Therapeutic Gaps: Overlooked Ethics

Within the framework of the National Health Service (NHS), a notable gap persists in addressing ethical alignment in the treatment of male mental health. While men are frequently encouraged to articulate their symptoms, discussions about their inner lives, such as their core beliefs, values, and moral dilemmas, are seldom part of the therapeutic dialogue. While they may receive interventions for mental health conditions like depression, the critical question of whether their current way of living truly reflects their innermost values and principles often goes unasked.

This oversight is significant, as ethical considerations are not merely philosophical musings but are intricately connected to our overall physiological and psychological well-being. When men diverge from their fundamental principles, they can unwittingly open themselves to a multitude of health challenges not just in mental health, but also affecting their physical health, interpersonal relationships, and spiritual wellness.

In integrative counselling, we strive to bridge this considerable divide by encouraging men to confront pointed, introspective questions that provoke deeper thoughts and self-reflection. For example:

- What did you value most before the weight of life's pressures became overwhelming or exhausting?
- What deeply-held beliefs are you prepared to advocate for, even in the face of societal or relational scrutiny?
- Who did you feel compelled to become to maintain the comfort of those around you, and what cost did that take on your true self?

These questions are far from abstract inquiries; they serve as a robust form of therapeutic medicine that can catalyse profound growth and healing. By exploring these dimensions, we can assist men in navigating their mental health more holistically, ultimately guiding them toward a life that is more congruent with their true selves.

Ethical Gas lighting: When Right Becomes Wrong

In a world where conformity often reigns supreme and the pressures to fit in can feel overwhelming, there comes a pivotal moment in a man's life when he musters the courage to speak his truth. This act of honesty, however, does not always elicit the support or understanding one might hope for. Instead, he is often met with discomfort and resistance from those around him, which can be bewildering. It is essential to recognise that this backlash does not arise from any perceived wrongdoing on his part; instead, it highlights his newfound refusal to be controlled by the expectations of others.

The phrases that surface in these situations, "You've changed," "You're selfish now," or "What happened to the old you?" are not merely expressions of concern; they are markers of an insidious practice known as ethical gaslighting. In this toxic dynamic, standing firm in one's integrity is unfairly rebranded as an act of betrayal, the betrayal of not only interpersonal relationships but also societal norms. In this context, simple acts of self-care, such as setting boundaries, can be misconstrued as abandonment, while prioritising self-respect is often twisted into an accusation of cruelty.

Many men who seek therapy recount experiences that resonate deeply with this phenomenon, expressing a profound sense of disillusionment. Common sentiments include, "I thought doing the right thing would bring me peace, but instead, I faced intense pushback from those I care about." This pushback, though painful, should not be viewed as a sign of failure; rather, it serves as a powerful testament to personal growth and evolution. It indicates that the individual is no longer willing to conform to oppressive systems that demand his silence and complicity in favour of harmony.

Embracing one's truth in a society that often rewards compliance can feel profoundly isolating, yet it signifies the beginning of a transformative journey toward authenticity. This journey may alienate him from some familiar circles but ultimately paves the way for deeper connections based on mutual respect and understanding. As he navigates this path, he learns that while the road may be fraught with challenges, the pursuit of genuine self-expression is an invaluable aspect of his quest for wholeness and fulfilment.

Fatherhood and the Ethics of Modelling

The role of a father extends far beyond the traditional responsibilities of provision and caretaking; it encompasses a profound and multifaceted responsibility of ethical modelling that shapes the moral compass of the next generation. Children, particularly sons, are particularly adept at absorbing lessons on ethics not through overt lectures or textbook teachings, but rather through careful observation of their father's actions, decisions, and interpersonal interactions.

For example, consider the father who routinely agrees to requests or obligations when deep down he truly means to decline. What message does this inconsistency communicate to a child? It signals a complex lesson about compliance and societal expectations over personal truth. Similarly, when a father apologises for behaviours in which he feels no genuine remorse, he inadvertently teaches his children about inauthenticity and the pitfalls of insincerity. These moments, however small they may seem, leave a lasting imprint on a child's understanding of honesty and emotional expression.

In contrast, a father who stands firm in his beliefs, especially during challenging times, instils in his children invaluable lessons about integrity and courage. By demonstrating emotional honesty, he shows them that vulnerability and strength can coexist and that expressing one's beliefs is an essential part of being true to oneself. This proactive and consistent modelling does not merely influence day-to-day interactions; it becomes a lasting legacy, inviting the next generation to break free from harmful cycles of behaviour, embrace a sense of self-acceptance, and embody the essence of authentic manhood. A father's

331

actions, therefore, create a roadmap for navigating the complexities of life with honesty and resilience, equipping children with the tools they need to forge their paths with confidence and integrity.

Therapeutic Tools: Mapping the Ethical Road

To navigate the complex terrain of ethical living, various therapeutic tools can serve as a comprehensive guiding framework. Here's an expanded exploration of these methods:

1. Value Excavation: Start with a deep, reflective exercise where you articulate ten core beliefs that resonate with your sense of self. These should be principles you've internalised throughout your life, even if they haven't come from formal teaching or societal norms. After compiling this list, take the time to analyse which of these values you've recently compromised in your actions or decisions. This reflection will help illuminate areas in your life that need growth and realignment, allowing you to prioritise living authentically in harmony with your beliefs.

2. The Ethical Audit: This exercise encourages introspection about a specific situation that left you feeling uncomfortable or conflicted. Consider this scenario carefully, examining it through the lens of your identified values. Reflect on whether you upheld your truth in that moment, or if you prioritised maintaining harmony or peace at the expense of your authenticity. This analysis can deepen your understanding of your decision-making processes and highlight areas where you may wish to assert your values more boldly in the future.

3. Guilt vs. Shame Sorting: It's essential to discern between guilt and shame, as both can significantly impact your emotional health. Guilt serves as a constructive acknowledgement, conveying the message, "I did something wrong," which can lead to reparative actions.

In contrast, shame is a more detrimental emotion that internalises blame, suggesting, "I am wrong." By identifying instances where you conflate these feelings, you can cultivate greater self-awareness, allowing you to address guilt as an opportunity for growth rather than succumbing to shame's damaging narrative.

4. Role Conflict Reflection: Create a comprehensive list of the various roles you occupy, be it father, partner, employee, friend, etc. Afterwards, analyse where the obligations tied to these roles may clash with your core values. This exercise can reveal conflicts that require your attention and resolution, ensuring that you strive for balance and alignment between your roles and values, rather than living in discord.

5. Ethical Witness Work: Visualise a version of yourself who stands apart and observes your life choices from a distance, acting as an impartial witness. Ask yourself probing questions: Would this observer feel pride in the actions you've taken? Would he sense feelings of abandonment or regret in how you're living? Engaging with this inner witness can provide crucial insights into your decisions and the person you aspire to be, guiding you toward more value-aligned choices.

6. Cross-Cultural Truth Inventory: Take the time to scrutinise the values you hold dear, distinguishing between those that stem from cultural conditioning and those that are intrinsic to your genuine self. Understanding where these influences align can foster authentic living, while recognising divergences will empower you to question societal expectations that do not serve your true self.

7. Somatic Check-Ins for Integrity: When faced with pivotal decisions, pause for a moment to conduct a somatic check-in. Tune in to your body's physiological responses. Do you notice an expansion in your chest,

signalling openness and readiness, or a tightening that signifies discomfort or resistance? Allowing your body's authentic reactions to guide your decision-making process can lead to more congruent and integrity-based choices, fostering a sense of alignment between your body, mind, and values.

By employing these therapeutic tools, you can navigate the complexities of ethical living with greater clarity, self-awareness, and authenticity.

Gentle Prompts – The Ethical Roadmap

To enhance your journey of introspection, consider reflecting on the following thought-provoking prompts:

- When was the last moment I felt a deep sense of pride in how I expressed my true self? What were the circumstances that led to this feeling, and how did my expression resonate with those around me?

- Which core values have I chosen to mute or overlook in the name of maintaining harmony in my relationships or environments? What might I be sacrificing in the process, and how does this affect my sense of self?

- In what ways does my decision to compromise my integrity benefit others? Who gains from my silence or conformity, and at what cost to my own principles?

- What beliefs and convictions do I hold close to my heart that I have stopped advocating for, either out of fear or complacency? Why have these beliefs become quieter in my life, and what would it take to revive them?

- As I reflect on the man I am becoming, do my actions and choices align with the vision I have for myself? Are there any discrepancies that I need to address to live authentically?

- From whom did I inherit the values that no longer resonate with me? What experiences have led me to realise that these values no longer serve my growth and individuality?

- What does a harmonious state of alignment feel like within my body? Can I identify the sensations, emotions, and mental clarity that accompany this state, and how can I cultivate it further in my daily life?

Final Reframe

You do not need to be plunged into a crisis to spark meaningful change in your life. All it takes is a steadfast moral compass. While society may provide you with maps that promise pathways to success, power, status, and control, your soul inherently holds a more profound navigation system, a blueprint for truth, which I like to call your Ethical Roadmap.

Following this roadmap may not always win you popularity or accolades; in fact, it can often be a challenging and lonely pursuit. Yet, the journey toward living following your principles ultimately leads to a profound state of freedom unlike any other experience.

A man who commits to living authentically, aligning his actions with his values, boldly speaking his truth, and advocating for justice does not merely exist in this world. Instead, he becomes a catalyst for transformation. His unwavering integrity and genuine character inspire change in others, encouraging them to embrace their own authentic selves. In this way, he not only affects his surroundings but also ignites a ripple effect, prompting a collective awakening to the importance of integrity and truth in our lives. Each step he takes on his Ethical Roadmap contributes to a larger tapestry of positive change, reminding us all that true power lies not in dominance, but in the courage to live transparently and justly.

Chapter 23

The Power You Didn't Know You Had

He presents a façade of calm, a polished exterior that skilfully conveys an impression of ease and control. Yet, beneath that thin veneer lies a cacophony of silence, reverberating with a profound and unsettling sound: the slow, rhythmic tick of a heartbeat stifled behind an impenetrable fortress of emotional barriers. These defences, meticulously constructed over the years, are fortified by past experiences and a relentless desire to protect himself from a world that often misinterprets vulnerability as weakness.

As he navigates through life, he shoulders an immense burden: unspoken guilt that gnaws at him during quiet moments, persistent grief that lingers like an ever-present shadow, and the paralysing fear that he may never live up to the towering expectations set by society, family, or even his own unyielding standards. For the outside world, he may appear stoic, his expressions carefully curated to reflect confidence and stability. However, within the confines of his mind, this façade is a vital act of survival. This delicate balancing act keeps him from crumbling under the weight of his unacknowledged emotions.

In moments of solitude, when the chaos of daily life fades away, the truth becomes harder to suppress. Memories of loss and missed opportunities swirl around him, taunting him with what could have been. Each heartbeat seems to echo the disappointments, amplifying the pressure to maintain the illusion of composure. He feels trapped in a paradox: the more he strives to meet others' expectations, the more distant he becomes from his own sense of self. Yet he clings to his self-control, even as it becomes a heavy chain that he's afraid to break, fearing what lies beneath the surface.

The Disappearing Man

Over the years, he has adeptly navigated life as a man who seldom acknowledges the profound cost of upholding such a carefully crafted façade. His education, a double-edged sword, has armed him with leadership skills that fuel a relentless drive for success; yet, it is also within the walls of his upbringing that he learned to don an emotional mask, presenting an illusion of unwavering strength to the world. This duality permeates his existence at home. He was taught that vulnerability is synonymous with weakness. At. At work, he absorbed the unwritten rule that silence is synonymous with dignity and respect, qualities that are revered in a competitive environment.

However, as night falls and the protective layers of his façade begin to crack under the weight of unacknowledged emotions, he is consumed by a profound tremor of anxiety. This surge of introspection reveals a disquieting reality that leaves him unsettled and vulnerable, exposing the fragility beneath his constructed exterior.

Within him resides a hollowness, an ever-present emptiness that no amount of providing, protecting, or pretending can fill. This existential void is not merely a sign of weakness or fragility; it is a manifestation of an overwhelming fatigue, a slow-motion crisis unravelling within the intricate confines of his psyche. Each day feels like a battle as he grapples with the dissonance between his carefully curated reality and the chaotic emotional landscape he navigates to survive.

In a culture that equates masculinity with control and emotional stoicism, he finds himself ensnared by the very silence he so expertly manages. His body aches in ways he cannot articulate, muscles tense and weary, as if carrying an invisible weight that drains his spirit. At times, he zones out during conversations, lost in a swirling vortex of thoughts and feelings that remain unspoken, leaving him feeling detached from those around him. He avoids mirrors, unable to confront the emotional stranger staring back, a person he hardly recognises anymore.

What once was a lifeline, a phone filled with messages from friends and family, has become a source of distress. Unread notifications blink at him like reminders of his growing isolation; loved ones reach out in genuine concern, yet he feels paralysed, incapable of responding, as if words would betray the turmoil swirling inside. He exists in the physical space of his life but feels as though he is gradually fading away, a mere ghost haunting the edges of his own reality.

The Unseen Crisis

The statistics surrounding male mental health are not just alarming; they are stark and chilling, effectively painting a harrowing portrait of a silent crisis. In Western countries, three out of every four suicides are committed by men, illuminating a troubling trend that demands urgent attention. According to the Office for National Statistics in the UK, suicide tragically remains the leading cause of death among men under the age of 50. This grim reality is echoed across the Atlantic, where men are nearly four times more likely than women to take their own lives. In many emerging economies, the situation is even more dire. Marginalised groups such as veterans, Indigenous men, and those fulfilling the roles of fathers and partners often find themselves living in the shadows of these alarming statistics, battling their struggles in silence, largely ignored by a society that increasingly prioritises superficial standards of masculinity over genuine emotional health.

Despite these shocking figures, male depression frequently falls under the radar when it comes to diagnosis and treatment. This oversight can be attributed to the fact that male depression often manifests in ways that differ from traditional markers. Instead of displaying obvious signs of sadness, such as tears or overt emotional distress, men may exhibit a range of symptoms, including anger, irritability, emotional numbness, social isolation, or engagement in risky behaviours. These outward expressions can mask the internal pain they endure, complicating the process of recognition and support. The deep-seated cultural misconceptions about masculinity and emotional expression further exacerbate this crisis, fostering an environment where vulnerability is stigmatised and emotional struggles remain unaddressed. The result is a pervasive silence surrounding male mental health, leaving countless individuals to confront their battles alone, trapped in a cycle where their pain is both invisible and unacknowledged.

Common Threads

He might be a man of considerable wealth, basking in the lavishness of luxury cars and opulent homes, enjoying the high life that success can bring. Yet, beneath that polished surface, he could also be wrestling with the fear of financial instability, his mind racing with worry over assets that could disappear or investments that might falter. Perhaps he is a military veteran, navigating the daunting transition back to civilian life, haunted by memories of service while trying to adapt to the ordinary rhythms of everyday existence. Alternatively, he could be an everyday labourer, whose hands are calloused from long hours of hard work, facing the relentless ebb and flow of the job market, grappling with both the challenges of physical demands and the small victories of completing a tough day's work.

As a devoted father, he strives to provide not just for the physical needs of his children but also to nurture their hopes and dreams, often sacrificing his own desires in the process. As an affectionate son, he finds himself caught in the intricate web of family loyalty, feeling the weight of expectations from parents and siblings alike. In the sleek, polished environment of corporate boardrooms, he may don a confident smile, exuding an air of competence and authority, skilfully navigating high-stakes discussions with poise. Yet, behind the closed doors of his office, the façade can crumble; he feels the invisible burdens of stress and anxiety press down on him like an insurmountable weight, leaving him engulfed in a profound loneliness that no one sees.

In public, he holds his child's hand with a steady grip, radiating an aura of comfort and safety, embodying the perfect father figure. However, internally, his heart aches with silent struggles, layered beneath the expectations of success and stoicism that society imposes. In a world that celebrates resilience, he grapples with an overwhelming sense of paralysis, burdened by the belief that he has no right to voice the turmoil that lies heavy on his heart. The thought echoes in the recesses of his mind: "I'm not okay."

Clinical Insight: Hypoarousal – The Quiet Collapse

When life becomes overwhelmingly demanding, the body can respond with a phenomenon known as hypoarousal, which manifests as a profound emotional and physical shutdown. This neurobiological reaction occurs when the brain is flooded with stress hormones, particularly cortisol, as a result of sustained pressure or trauma. In this state, the body instinctively detaches from reality, employing hypoarousal as a coping mechanism to survive the intense demands placed upon it.

Individuals experiencing hypoarousal often exhibit a range of signs such as numbed emotions, which may make it difficult to connect with feelings or express joy, leading to a pervasive sense of mental fog that clouds their ability to think clearly or make decisions. This condition can also engender an overwhelming lethargy, where daily activities feel insurmountable, and social withdrawal becomes common as individuals retreat from interactions that seem taxing or overwhelming.

It is vital to recognise that men who find themselves in this state are not simply being lazy, broken, or weak; instead, they are relying on the only coping strategies their bodies have learned in response to extreme stress. Hypoarousal is not merely a sign of dysfunction or weakness; it should be understood as an adaptive response to overwhelming stressors that may have accumulated over time.

However, when hypoarousal is left unchecked, it can take on more serious implications, such as masquerading as clinical depression or contributing to the development of chronic health issues. The long-term effects of this state can further complicate one's emotional health and interpersonal relationships, ultimately creating rifts between men and the very support systems that are vital for their recovery and healing. Understanding this response is crucial in fostering empathy and offering the necessary support to those grappling with its effects.

Archetype: The Provider Who Fades

He embodies the archetype of the Provider, a role defined by an unwavering commitment to create a sense of safety and stability for those around him. He meticulously constructs the foundations of support upon which family and friends depend, consistently prioritising their needs over his own, often at significant personal cost. This selflessness, while admirable, frequently leaves him feeling drained and unrecognised, as he sacrifices his own well-being for the comfort of others.

Yet, beneath this façade of strength lies a profound struggle. He grapples with a disconcerting reality he feels lost and adrift, navigating through life without a compass or a clear roadmap leading him back to his own heart. The mask he wears is not a badge of honour; it is a heavy burden, reflecting the weight of ancestral expectations and outdated beliefs that equate vulnerability and emotional softness with weakness.

In a world that frequently demands unwavering resilience and stoicism, he often finds solace in silence, retreating into himself to avoid the pressures and judgments of society. Deep down, he yearns for a sanctuary, an environment where he can shed his armour and openly express his genuine emotions without fear of judgment. He longs to be seen for who he really is: a complex man, imperfect yet deserving of understanding, empathy, and compassion. In his quiet moments of reflection, he dreams of embracing his authenticity, shedding the shackles of expectation, and finding peace in the acceptance of his true self.

Poetic Break – Remember This

He is much more than just the roles he assumes or the tasks he performs daily. Beneath the surface of his actions lies a profound essence that transcends mere outputs or measurable accomplishments. Within him exists a quiet promise and a sacred commitment to his true self, a commitment that, over time, he may have inadvertently overlooked in the hustle and bustle of life.

This inner essence is the hallmark of actual power: it does not stem from the successful completion of duties but from the authentic, unwavering presence he brings to each moment. This deep presence has been part of him since the very beginning, its significance evident even in times when he might have failed to acknowledge it. When he fully embraces this aspect of himself, he not only transforms his own life but also radiates a transformative energy to those around him, reminding them of the importance of genuine connection and self-awareness. In this realisation, he finds a renewed sense of purpose and clarity, reaffirming the belief that true worth emerges not from external validation but from an inner alignment with one's essence.

Mini Coaching Sidebar: Post-Traumatic Growth

Therapist Insight: After enduring a prolonged period of living in survival mode, the nervous system enters a crucial yet hopeful phase of reorientation. This critical transition signifies the moment when authentic healing begins to unfold, providing an opportunity for an individual to evolve from merely surviving their pain to actively reshaping the narrative of their life. It's essential to recognise that one does not need to achieve complete healing before embarking on this transformative journey; all that is required is a moment of unfiltered honesty and the courage to confront and embrace the truth of one's current emotional and mental state.

Post-Traumatic Growth (PTG) represents this transformative process, wherein individuals emerge from adversity not just intact but enriched with deeper insights, a more profound sense of meaning, and strengthened emotional resilience. This journey is not simply about bouncing back to a previous state; it is about cultivating a more robust foundation for the future, one built on the lessons learned from hardship and a renewed perspective on life's possibilities. Through this process, individuals may discover new strengths, forge more meaningful connections, and develop a renewed sense of purpose, ultimately transforming their experiences of pain into catalysts for personal growth and fulfilment.

Gentle Prompts:

- **Responsibility vs. Reclamation:** Take a deep and honest look at your identity as a man. What are the fundamental responsibilities that shape who you are, and how do they reflect your values and aspirations?

  Consider the moments when the weight of these responsibilities transforms from a healthy sense of duty into a burden that feels like self-erasure, leading you to suppress essential facets of your authentic self. What does it feel like to prioritise expectations over your true desires?

- **Emotional Disconnection:** Reflect on your past experiences: when did you first feel compelled to project an image of strength instead of allowing yourself to genuinely feel and express your emotions?

  Think back to a moment that stands out vividly for you. As you delve into this reflection, which emotion do you find particularly challenging to acknowledge or articulate? What fears are tied to expressing that emotion, and how has this perspective shaped your interactions with others?

- **Who He Used to Be:** Imagine if your inner child could speak about their perspective on the journey of growing up. What secrets would this child divulge regarding the joys and pains that shaped you? Contemplate the dreams, hopes, and parts of your spirit that still crave validation, recognition, and nurturing in your current life. How can you reconnect with these aspects to enrich your present experience?

- **Redefining Strength:** Pause and consider what strength truly means to you today. Is it solely about the physical weight you can bear, or does it encompass a deeper understanding of vulnerability and emotional resilience? Explore the idea that true strength might include recognising moments when it is necessary to set those burdens down and seek support. How can redefining strength change the way you approach challenges?

- **Body Check:** Pay attention to how stress manifests itself in your body. Where do you physically hold tension or discomfort, be it in your shoulders, stomach, or elsewhere? How does your body signal when emotions remain unvoiced or unprocessed? Reflect on what safety feels like within your nervous system. Is that sense of safety a comforting presence, or does it seem always just out of reach?

Bookmark This Truth:

Often, a man finds himself on shaky ground, constructed from the words and expectations he has gathered from family, friends, and society. He may feel trapped until he learns the crucial art of looking inward. The first courageous step is to reclaim a clear understanding of himself, his values, beliefs, and passions. Even as he begins to rediscover his inner strength, self-doubt may still rear its head. Sometimes, the hardest voice to quiet is his own, filled with insecurities, fears, and remnants of past criticisms.

The key is not to continue fading into the shadows. Instead, the journey involves re-emerging to reconnect with oneself, not as a version moulded by external pressures, but as the man who has continuously resided beneath the layers of silence and expectation. In this journey of reclamation, the goal is to embrace and celebrate your whole self.

"Sometimes, the bravest act a man can take is to show up fully for his own life."

Act Three: Reclaiming Connection
(Love Brotherhood, Legacy)

Chapter 24

The Addictive Loop: Why Men Escape What They Can't Name

He tells himself it's just a drink, just a puff of smoke, just one more scroll through his endless social media feed, one more bet placed in desperation, one more late-night binge-watching session that remains hidden from the world. Yet deep down, he understands that this isn't truly about the substance itself; it's about the fleeting silence it provides, a temporary escape from the chaotic noise of his own mind, a brief reprieve from the turmoil he feels inside.

For millions of men, the spiral into addiction often doesn't begin with the quest for pleasure. Instead, it unfolds quietly in the shadowy corners of unacknowledged wounds, the unspoken pain, the heartache, and the deep-seated fears that they were never taught to confront, articulate, or understand. As the years pass, many come to believe that numbness is not only safer than vulnerability but a necessary armour against the tumult of emotions that threaten to overwhelm them. They convince themselves that shielding their hearts from feeling is a form of strength, not a weakness.

This chapter delves into this destructive loop: the slow, gravitational pull that exists between deep-seated pain and the craving for an escape. It highlights a cycle marked by emotional shutdown, pervasive shame hidden from friends and family, and a fleeting sense of relief that is frequently mistaken for resilience. Men aren't just addicted to substances; they are profoundly addicted to the silence and numbness those substances promise. This silence, however, is deceptive. It whispers lies of safety while leaving emotional scars that run deeper than any drug can touch, trapping them in a cycle of despair that is hard to escape.

The Addictive Loop: Pain → Numb → Shame → Repeat

Addiction is rarely a conscious choice; instead, it often emerges as a coping mechanism born from necessity. When emotional pain persists as a chronic condition, and societal norms render the expression of feelings unacceptable, many men instinctively turn inward. They tend to bottle up their emotions, distract themselves through a myriad of activities, or seek to override their anguish with substances such as stimulants and sedatives. In this context, numbing their feelings becomes a survival strategy, with the belief that experiencing no pain is preferable to confronting the often overwhelming weight of emotional suffering.

Counselling Insight:

Within therapeutic circles, this phenomenon is commonly referred to as affect dysregulation, which denotes the struggle to manage intense or fluctuating emotional states effectively. Men grappling with unprocessed trauma or unresolved childhood neglect frequently resort to external regulators, including alcohol, pornography, or illicit drugs. Their reliance on these substances is not born from a mere desire to indulge; rather, it is a desperate attempt to cope with the internal chaos fuelled by their emotional turmoil.

Biopsychology Note:

The biological response to emotional threat significantly shapes behaviour. Under such stress, the male brain activates the amygdala, responsible for processing fear, while at the same time, it inhibits the prefrontal cortex, which governs decision-making. This biological interplay elevates cortisol levels, the body's primary stress hormone, further intensifying the state of distress. In their quest for relief, men often unconsciously gravitate toward dopamine-driven behaviours, which can include substance use, casual sexual encounters, compulsive scrolling through social media, or participating in high-risk activities.

However, the relief provided by these behaviours is invariably short-lived. As the initial euphoria fades, feelings of shame and inadequacy frequently emerge: questions like "What's wrong with me?" "Why can't I stop doing this?" and "I must be weak" begin to surface. This shame transforms into another layer of emotional pain, which propels the individual back into the cycle of addiction, creating a vicious feedback loop that is hard to escape.

It is critical to understand that addiction is not a mere failure of willpower; it is a complex survival adaptation that develops in response to significant emotional distress. Much like any tool forged from trauma, these coping mechanisms often backfire, exacerbating the individual's suffering rather than alleviating it. Recognising this complexity is a vital step in addressing the root causes of addiction and fostering pathways toward healing and recovery.

Common Male Addictions: Beyond the Obvious

Most people often link the term "addiction" with overtly harmful substances like heroin, crack, or other narcotics. However, the spectrum of addiction extends far beyond these substances and can be much subtler, frequently escaping the notice of those surrounding the individuals affected.

Top Male Addictions:

- Alcohol: Commonly woven into social settings and associated with camaraderie, drinking can often disguise deeper emotional struggles, such as depression or anxiety. The societal acceptance of alcohol can make it difficult to recognise its potential to mask unhappiness or serve as a coping mechanism.

- Cannabis: While many use cannabis to alleviate anxiety or find relaxation, prolonged usage can lead to emotional numbness and a sense of disconnection from reality. Instead of providing relief, it can create a cycle of dependency that complicates emotional health.

- Cocaine: This powerful stimulant can offer a temporary surge of confidence and euphoria, appealing to those who feel powerless or inadequate in their everyday lives. However, the crash that follows often plunges users deeper into feelings of despair, which can lead them back to the drug in a vicious cycle.

- Porn and Sex: Frequently viewed as a means of escapism from the complexities of genuine intimacy, the use of pornography and casual sexual encounters can create challenges. They often generate feelings of shame and performance anxiety, leading to a distorted understanding of relationships and intimacy.

- Gambling: This habit can provide a thrilling escape, offering the illusion of control in situations that feel chaotic or uncertain. The rush of placing a bet can temporarily distract from underlying stressors, yet it often leads to financial ruin and emotional turmoil as the stakes escalate.

- Steroids: Employed to enhance physical appearance and build muscle, steroid use is frequently a reaction to feelings of inadequacy and emotional vulnerability. While they may provide a temporary confidence boost, the long-term effects on mental and physical health can be detrimental.

- Workaholism: Often praised in today's fast-paced society, workaholism is the last socially acceptable form of addiction. By burying emotions under constant work, individuals may gain recognition and success outwardly, while inwardly they struggle with loneliness and emotional deprivation.

- Gaming and Social Media: In a world where face-to-face interaction can feel daunting, gaming and social media platforms offer easy access to instant gratification and dopamine hits. However, this can lead to increased isolation, as superficial connections take the place of meaningful relationships.

While these behaviours may present uniquely, the common thread among them is an emotional coping mechanism aimed at distracting, detaching, and avoiding the confrontation of more profound, painful truths. Ultimately, these addictions tend not to stem from a pursuit of pleasure but from a fundamental desire to escape and avoid emotional pain.

What These Substances Do to the Male Brain

Understanding the complexities of addiction extends far beyond simply identifying behavioural patterns; it necessitates a deep comprehension of the brain's desperate struggle to regain equilibrium in the face of emotional upheaval.

- Alcohol: This substance inundates the brain with dopamine, offering a temporary escape from fear and anxiety. However, this euphoria is fleeting, leading to a downward spiral into more profound depressive states. Chronic alcohol use can result in notable shrinkage of the hippocampus, the brain region crucial for memory formation, consequently impairing cognitive functions and exacerbating challenges in emotional regulation.

- Cannabis: By activating cannabinoid receptors integral to mood regulation, appetite control, and memory functioning, cannabis can create a sense of relaxation and euphoria. Yet, with prolonged use, users often experience a significant decline in motivation, impaired emotional processing, and an increased susceptibility to anxiety. Long-term consumers may find that their ability to experience pleasure diminishes, complicating their emotional well-being.

- Cocaine: This powerful stimulant causes dramatic spikes in dopamine, eliciting feelings of invincibility and heightened energy. However, as the brain adapts to these surges, it reduces its natural dopamine production, leading to a detrimental cycle where users may find themselves trapped in escalating feelings of paranoia, depression, and emotional instability, as they chase the elusive high.

- Pornography: Frequent consumption disrupts the brain's reward system, training it to seek ever-greater novelty and intensity. This desensitisation process not only diminishes the pleasure derived from everyday experiences but also fosters a growing disconnect in real-life relationships, as genuine intimacy becomes overshadowed by unrealistic expectations.

- Gambling: This form of addiction activates the same neural circuits as cocaine, where sporadic wins trigger erratic surges of dopamine. These temporary highs can compel individuals to gamble persistently, even in the face of severe financial distress and mounting personal losses, leading to a dangerous cycle of risk-taking and desperation.

- Steroids: These substances artificially elevate testosterone levels and can enhance physical strength and aggressive behaviours in men. However, long-term use disrupts the body's natural hormone production, leading to diminished empathy and extreme mood swings. Users may also grapple with the psychological fallout of these shifts, finding it challenging to maintain healthy relationships or emotional stability.

- Workaholism: This addiction is often overlooked but engages the brain's dopamine and cortisol pathways, creating a rush that superficially masks feelings of emptiness or inadequacy. Over time, relentless overworking can lead to severe burnout, resulting in disconnection from interpersonal relationships, diminished mental health, and an overall sense of dissatisfaction with life.

In summary, addiction in its various forms reveals not only the intricate interplay between substance use and brain chemistry but also the profound personal and relational consequences that often ensue.

Trauma & Substance Use: What Was Never Healed Gets Replayed

A man's journey into addiction often has its roots embedded deeply in his childhood, extending far back to experiences that precede his first drink or drug use. These early years play a critical role in shaping his future coping mechanisms and emotional responses.

Adverse Childhood Experiences (ACEs): Extensive research indicates that individuals who endure multiple adverse experiences during their formative years, such as violence, neglect, abuse, or parental separation, are at a significantly greater risk of developing substance misuse issues later in life. Each negative encounter alters the brain's wiring, conditioning it to prioritise survival instincts over the formation of genuine emotional bonds. The result is a landscape of internal chaos where emotional connection becomes challenging, potentially leaving an individual feeling isolated and desperate for relief.

The Power of Neglect:

 Emotional neglect can prove just as harmful, if not more so, than physical abuse. This experience encompasses not just the absence of overt violence, but also the deprivation of nurturing interactions and emotional attunement. A lack of comforting touch and attentive listening can breed a profound sense of invisibility and unworthiness. Children who are not openly acknowledged or whose feelings go unacknowledged may internalise the belief that their emotional needs are excessive or that their suffering is insignificant. This pervasive emotional erasure teaches boys, in particular, to suppress their feelings, creating a chasm of unaddressed pain and confusion.

Thus begins a vicious cycle: the accumulation of unresolved emotions can lead an individual to seek solace in substances, attempting to silence the chaos within. This quest for numbness becomes a desperate attempt to escape from the overwhelming weight of feelings that have been buried and ignored for far too long. In this way, the journey into addiction is often not just about the substances themselves, but rather about an ingrained struggle for understanding, connection, and ultimately, healing.

The Biology of Numbing: Understanding the Compulsion to Escape

When men experience chronic stress, whether stemming from traumatic childhood events or the relentless demands of daily life, their neurochemical systems undergo significant transformations that profoundly influence their overall well-being and behaviour.

One key player in this process is dopamine, a crucial neurotransmitter linked to feelings of pleasure, reward, and motivation. Dopamine levels typically surge during rewarding activities, such as engaging in sexual encounters, playing video games, or participating in high-risk adventures. Initially, these behaviours provide a sense of joy and satisfaction, offering a temporary distraction from stress. However, as stress becomes a recurring theme in their lives, men may find themselves increasingly reliant on these activities to elicit positive emotions. This dependency can create a cycle where the brain demands more stimulation to achieve the same level of pleasure, often leading to riskier behaviours or compulsive habits as the initial rewards diminish.

Cortisol, frequently dubbed the stress hormone, plays a critical role in this dynamic. During prolonged periods of stress, cortisol levels can remain elevated, triggering a cascade of adverse effects on physical and mental health. This prolonged elevation disrupts the body's natural equilibrium, resulting in heightened feelings of anxiety, irritability, and even depression. Physically, men may experience symptoms such as chronic fatigue, increased susceptibility to illness, and various cardiovascular issues. These disruptions can also severely affect daily functioning, leading to irregular and fragmented sleep patterns that further exacerbate mental health issues, creating a vicious cycle of poor sleep and increased stress.

Additionally, GABA (Gamma-Aminobutyric Acid), a neurotransmitter essential for promoting calmness and relaxation, is often found to be deficient in individuals with chronic stress or a history of trauma. This deficiency can significantly contribute to heightened feelings of restlessness, agitation, and an overwhelming inability to manage stress effectively. Without adequate GABA, the brain becomes less capable of regulating anxiety and moderating stress responses, intensifying the overall experience of stress and making it increasingly challenging to find relief. This cycle can perpetuate itself, leading to a worsening of both emotional and physical health over time.

Understanding these neurochemical changes is crucial for addressing the effects of chronic stress and finding effective strategies for recovery and well-being.

Shame & Secrecy: The Impenetrable Barriers

Why do men often resist seeking help for their struggles? The answer frequently lies in a complex interplay between addiction, deep-seated shame, and the weight of societal expectations. Addiction is not just a personal battle; it casts a long and dark shadow of shame that can feel insurmountable to those affected.

Society often paints an image of the "real man" as someone who exhibits absolute self-control and dominance over his circumstances. This cultural archetype cultivates an environment where vulnerability is seen as a weakness. For many men grappling with addiction, the loss of control that comes with substance use can lead to profound feelings of inadequacy and shame. They may internalise the belief that they are somehow less than their peers, reinforcing an identity rooted in unworthiness.

Counselling Note:

Shame is perhaps the most potent and paralysing emotion that men resist confronting. While guilt communicates the message, "I did something wrong," shame conveys a far more damaging narrative: "I am something wrong." This distinction is critical, as it often leads men to conceal their struggles, resulting in a façade of strength. They may tell loved ones that they will overcome their addiction, only to continue spiralling into its depths in silence. This deceptive cycle of reassurance to others and self-deceit can spiral into an unbearable intensity, fostering deep isolation and loneliness.

Moreover, addiction transcends the mere issue of substance use; it morphs into an internal conflict that challenges one's self-image. For many men, the struggle is not only with the addiction itself but also with the ongoing battle to embrace self-acceptance amid the scrutiny of societal norms. The journey toward recovery often involves dismantling these entrenched beliefs about masculinity and learning to confront and embrace feelings of vulnerability as a crucial step toward healing.

Masculine Culture: When Societal Norms Fuel Addiction

The pressure to conform to societal ideals of masculinity is an unyielding force that shapes a man's life, evolving rather than diminishing as he ages. Phrases such as "Just one more," "Don't be a pussy," and "All the lads do it" encapsulate the subtle yet pervasive peer pressure that men encounter at various stages of their lives. These expressions serve as constant reminders that societal expectations surrounding masculinity are deeply ingrained, impacting behaviour and self-identity well into adulthood.

A prominent arena where this peer pressure is particularly pronounced is within gym culture. In this environment, many men feel an acute obligation to push beyond their physical limits, propelled by a mix of personal ambition and an implicit need for validation from their peers. The overwhelming desire to meet or exceed these expectations often leads individuals to adopt extreme measures, including the use of performance-enhancing substances like steroids. These choices frequently reflect not genuine pursuits of health or fitness, but rather a compelling need to shield oneself from feelings of inadequacy and vulnerability. Consequently, the journey toward achieving an ideal physique is transformed from a straightforward health goal into a defensive mechanism where physical prowess becomes synonymous with validated masculinity, especially within competitive settings.

Similarly, the societal glorification of workaholism places men in a precarious position where their self-worth is often equated with their professional achievements. This narrative promotes the idea that sacrificing personal happiness and family time is not only admirable but also expected. The relentless pursuit of productivity might create an illusion of success; however, it frequently serves as a distraction from deeper emotional issues and personal dissatisfaction. Men may find themselves chasing after an ever-elusive notion of achievement, often at the expense of meaningful relationships and their own mental well-being. In navigating these pressures, the cycle of striving for approval in both physical and professional realms can leave men feeling isolated, disconnected, and grappling with their own sense of identity.

Recovery Isn't Weakness: Pathways to Healing

The healing journey is not simply a quest to transform into someone new; rather, it is about the profound process of rediscovering and reconnecting with one's authentic self. This journey involves understanding who you truly are, beyond the labels and limitations that life's experiences may have imposed upon you.

Effective Recovery Paths for Men:

- 12-Step Programs: These well-established frameworks provide a structured approach to recovery, emphasising accountability and community support. While they have helped countless individuals achieve sobriety, their spiritual components may not resonate with everyone. Participants engage in a series of steps designed to foster personal reflection, connection to a higher power, and community fellowship.

- SMART Recovery: This program stands out by utilising a science-based approach and integrating techniques from Cognitive Behavioural Therapy (CBT). It equips individuals with practical tools to manage their recovery on a day-to-day basis, focusing on self-empowerment and rational thinking. This structure appeals particularly to those who prefer a more secular path to recovery.

- Trauma-Informed Therapy: Approaches such as Eye Movement Desensitisation and Reprocessing (EMDR), Internal Family Systems, and various somatic therapies delve deep into the underlying trauma that often fuels addiction. By addressing these root issues, individuals can begin to heal from past pains, fostering a deeper understanding of themselves and their behaviours.

- Peer Support Groups: Communities such as Andy's Man Club, MenSpeak, Soberistas, and numerous forums on platforms like Reddit provide essential safe spaces for men to share their experiences and struggles candidly. These groups cultivate an environment free of judgment, where members can offer support, share tips, and celebrate victories, creating a sense of community and belonging.

- Psychoeducation: Gaining knowledge about how trauma influences behaviours can be an empowering tool in recovery. Understanding these dynamics helps individuals identify negative patterns and develop healthier coping mechanisms. This education fosters a greater sense of control over one's life and decisions.

Ultimately, recovery is not just about relinquishing harmful substances or habits; it is a holistic process aimed at reclaiming what may have been lost throughout your journey: self-confidence, meaningful connections with others, and a renewed sense of joy in everyday life. This multifaceted approach to recovery emphasises the importance of healing the whole person rather than just the symptoms of addiction.

Intersectionality: Navigating Class, Race, and Sexuality in Addiction

It is essential to recognise that addiction does not affect all men in the same way; its impact varies significantly among different demographics due to cultural, social, and economic factors.

- Working-Class Men: These individuals often grow up in environments that uphold rigid gender norms and provide limited access to mental health resources. This upbringing fosters a culture of silence regarding emotional struggles and vulnerability, where expressing feelings is often viewed as a sign of weakness. As a result, many working-class men feel compelled to suppress their mental health challenges, leading to a cycle of unresolved issues and increased susceptibility to addiction, which can be passed down through generations.

- Black Men: Statistically, Black men are less likely to seek support services for addiction, a trend influenced by a combination of societal stigma, discrimination, and a historical context of criminalisation related to substance use. This community often faces significant barriers, including institutional mistrust, negative stereotypes, and a lack of culturally competent resources, which complicates their path to recovery. The stigma surrounding addiction within their communities can also lead to feelings of shame and isolation, making it even more challenging to seek help.

- Gay and Bisexual Men: Many from this demographic grapple with a unique set of challenges, including compounded feelings of shame, particularly concerning issues related to sex or pornography addiction. The pressure to conform to hyper-masculine ideals often found in recovery spaces can render these environments unwelcoming, alienating many gay and bisexual men. This lack of safe, affirming spaces can hinder their recovery efforts, creating a need for more inclusive and understanding approaches that address their specific experiences.

In conclusion, while addiction is undoubtedly a deeply personal struggle, it is inextricably linked to broader societal contexts that shape individual experiences and challenges. Understanding the intersections of race, class, and sexual orientation is crucial for developing effective support systems and interventions that promote recovery across diverse populations. Addressing these nuanced experiences can lead to more equitable and practical solutions in the fight against addiction.

The Protector Within: IFS and Archetypes

According to Internal Family Systems (IFS) therapy, addiction is not merely a sign of weakness or a failure of willpower. Instead, it serves a vital role as an internal protector. Within the framework of IFS, the "Addict" part represents a coping mechanism that emerges in response to deep emotional pain, often tied to an exiled inner child. This part of ourselves engages in behaviours aimed at numbing emotional distress, providing distraction, and creating a semblance of safety from the intense feelings of grief, shame, or trauma that may be too overwhelming to confront directly.

The journey toward healing from addiction does not involve the outright rejection or banishment of this protective part. Instead, it requires a compassionate approach that reassures this inner protector that it no longer has to bear the burden alone. By working to integrate and understand this part of ourselves, we can cultivate a deeper sense of safety, acceptance, and connection not only with ourselves but also with others.

From a Jungian psychological perspective, men in recovery often embody powerful archetypes that mirror their path toward wholeness. These archetypes include:

- The Wounded Healer: This archetype represents individuals who have endured significant pain and struggle themselves. The Wounded Healer chooses to use their personal experiences as a source of strength, guiding and assisting others on their healing journeys. Their intimate understanding of suffering allows them to offer profound empathy and support to those grappling with similar challenges, fostering a sense of community and shared resilience.

- The Lost Boy: This character represents the part of ourselves that yearns for nurturing, guidance, and connection. In the process of recovery, learning to re-parent oneself becomes essential. This involves recognising and addressing the unmet emotional needs of our inner child, providing the compassion, affirmation, and love that may have been lacking during our formative years. By nurturing this aspect of ourselves, we can heal old wounds and develop healthier relationships.

- The Initiated King: This archetype embodies a man who bravely confronts his shadow, those repressed parts of his psyche that harbour fear, guilt, and unresolved issues. The Initiated King exemplifies integrity and responsibility, utilising his strength not to dominate or control but to lead with wisdom and compassion. By integrating the lessons learned from grappling with his shadows, he emerges as a figure who can guide himself and others toward a more fulfilled and authentic existence.

Through the exploration and integration of these archetypes, men in recovery can embark on a transformative journey, fostering a deeper understanding of themselves and ultimately paving the way for healing, connection, and wholeness.

Recovery Toolkit: Reflective Prompts

Journal Prompts:

- What feeling is hardest for me to sit with, and when did I first learn to run from it?
  Reflect on your childhood experiences and identify the origins of your discomfort. Consider the emotions you struggled with as a child: were they sadness, anger, or fear? Explore how these experiences led you to develop coping mechanisms, such as avoidance or denial, and think about how these patterns may still affect you today.

- What am I afraid will happen if I stop numbing?
  Delve deeply into your fears surrounding vulnerability and acceptance. What do you envision when you think of facing your feelings without distraction? Explore the potential risks you fear, such as rejection, overwhelming pain, or feeling inadequate, and contemplate how these fears have influenced your choices and behaviours.

- Who would I be if I didn't need to escape?
  Take a moment to envision your life free from the need to escape through substances or certain behaviours. Consider the traits and qualities that would emerge in a more authentic version of yourself. What passions might

363

you explore? Who would you connect with authentically? Reflect on the potential for personal growth and the fulfilment that could come from embracing your true self.

- What am I truly seeking when I reach for that substance or behaviour?
  Identify the deeper desires or unmet needs driving your actions. Are you seeking comfort, validation, connection, or relief from pain? Reflect on whether these needs can be met in healthier, more constructive ways, and how understanding this can shift your relationship with these cravings.

Grounding Tips for Cravings:

- 5-4-3-2-1 Sensory Grounding:
Engage your senses to anchor yourself firmly in the present moment. Look around and identify 5 things you can see; notice their colours and shapes. Then, find 4 things you can touch and allow yourself to feel the textures. Next, listen for 3 distinct sounds around you, whether it's the hum of silence or the rustle of leaves. Then, identify 2 scents; perhaps it's fresh coffee or a favourite candle. Finally, choose 1 thing to taste; it might be a sip of water or a piece of fruit. This practice can help redirect your mind and calm your body.

- Ice in the Palm Technique:
  Holding a small piece of ice can serve as a powerful sensory experience to distract from cravings. Focus on the sensation of the cold as it melts against your skin. This physical anchor not only interrupts the craving cycle but also brings your attention back to your body and the here and now.

- Box Breathing:
  This structured breathing technique helps to soothe the nervous system. Inhale deeply for four seconds, hold your breath for another four seconds, exhale slowly over

four seconds, and then pause for another four seconds. Repeat this cycle a few times; it can significantly reduce feelings of anxiety and help regain emotional balance during moments of overwhelm.

- Calling a Trusted Friend Instead of Using:
Reach out to someone who understands your journey and can provide emotional support. This connection offers an alternative to engaging in harmful behaviours, fostering a sense of companionship and shared experience that can lighten your load.

Before You Quit:

- Don't go it alone:
Find a trauma-informed space where you can share your experiences openly. Support from those who understand the complexities of addiction can make a significant difference in your healing journey. Connect with support groups, therapists, or trusted friends who can offer guidance and empathy.

- Replace, not remove:
Instead of merely trying to eliminate addictive behaviours from your life, focus on identifying healthy self-soothing alternatives that can nurture your needs. Whether it's through creative expression, physical activity, or mindfulness practices, find what fulfils you and helps you cope without relying on substances.

- Track your wins: wins: (Continue with specific strategies or affirmations that align with your goals for quitting.)

This comprehensive approach encourages deeper reflection and equips you with tangible strategies to navigate your journey.

Final Reframe: You Are Not Your Addiction

You are not weak; you are not broken; you are not beyond help. You are a resilient man who has navigated through unimaginably difficult circumstances and experiences that many may not even dare to speak of. Yet here you are, at a pivotal point in your life, ready to embark on a profound journey that goes beyond mere survival.

The road ahead is not easy, but the bravest thing you can do is to confront the emotions and thoughts you were taught to suppress. It takes immense courage to face what you've hidden away, to acknowledge the pain and struggles that have shaped you. By embracing the full spectrum of your feelings, both the joyful and the sorrowful, you create a pathway to true healing.

This journey is not just about surviving; it's about rediscovering yourself and reclaiming your life. Each step you take toward allowing yourself to feel deeply is a step toward transformation. You will learn to be present with yourself, to honour your experiences, and to cultivate a richer, more meaningful existence. This is where genuine healing begins and where you can redefine what it means to truly live.

Chapter 25

The Bond Forger: The Man Who Holds Everyone Together (But Falls Apart Alone)

Some men are born to lead, while others possess the ability to build and innovate. Yet, there exists a rare and enigmatic third type, a man who lingers in the background, often unnoticed but profoundly impactful. This is the man who has mastered the fundamental art of connection.

He doesn't crave the spotlight or thrive in the clamour of public acclaim. Instead, he serves as a silent anchor, the steadfast presence that brings warmth and security. People are drawn to him, not by grand gestures or soaring speeches, but by the invisible thread of his empathy and understanding, which binds them together.

This is the Bond Forger.

This man embodies qualities that go far beyond superficial niceties. He is the one who checks in on a friend during tough times when others are preoccupied. He senses the subtle nuances of emotion, attuned to the flicker of resignation or anxiety behind someone's eyes, even when they wear a mask of composure. He remembers the small yet significant moments: a birthday that deserves celebration, a disagreement that lingers in the air, or a brief mention of a loved one facing health struggles that weighs heavily on another's heart long after the conversation has ended.

When he embraces someone in a hug, it transcends a mere reflexive action; it's a heartfelt gesture that communicates a depth of compassion and authenticity. The warmth of his support envelops others, offering solace in a world that often feels isolating.

Yet, here's the poignant truth:

The world frequently overlooks him. In a society that often values overt achievements and visible triumphs, the Bond Forger stands as a quiet testament to the power of connection, revealing that sometimes the most profound contributions are made not in the spotlight, but in the tender spaces of understanding and care.

The Emotional Architect

Bond Forgers are the emotional architects of human connection, wielding a remarkable ability to nurture relationships not through flamboyant gestures or overt displays of affection, but rather through unwavering consistency and quiet assurance. Their approach is rooted in an instinctive capacity to ask the right questions, delving beneath the surface of conversations to grasp the underlying emotions and intentions of those they engage with. This genuine curiosity allows them to forge deeper connections by truly understanding others, as they listen with intensity and purpose, not merely biding their time until it's their turn to speak.

These individuals excel in creating bonds where many only see fractures and gaps. They possess a rare gift for sitting comfortably in silence, recognising the intricacies of human feelings and honouring the complexity of unspoken thoughts without the compulsion to fill the air with words. Their presence becomes a safe haven for others, a space where vulnerability is met with empathy and understanding.

Yet, despite their profound emotional insight and resilience, Bond Forgers often find themselves misunderstood in a world that frequently values toughness and self-sufficiency. Misguided labels such as "soft," "sensitive," "over-attached," or even "weak" are often cast upon them, obscuring the true essence of their character. In reality, they embody a different kind of warrior

368

spirit, one that is not defined by physical prowess or aggression but by an unwavering emotional presence that encourages others to connect and share.

The journey of the Bond Forger is not one marked by grand theatrics or dramatic gestures, but rather by a quiet yet steadfast devotion to nurturing the relationships that enrich their lives and the lives of those around them. Through their faithful commitment and deep emotional intelligence, they illuminate the transformative power of genuine connection in an often fragmented world.

The Loneliness of the Connector

The role of a Bond Forger carries significant emotional weight. While it may seem noble, it often entails a quiet, isolating pain that emerges from their profound sensitivity to both their own struggles and those of others. This unique capacity to empathise allows Bond Forgers to feel the burdens of the people around them, even as they carry their own emotional burdens in silence. Their steadfast commitment to nurturing relationships often goes unnoticed, yet this very dedication forms the backbone of genuine human connection. As they honour their own feelings alongside the feelings of others, they navigate a complicated emotional landscape, sometimes feeling like solitary guardians in a world that can misinterpret the essence of forging profound connections.

While they perceive the world around them with acute awareness, there is an underlying irony: few truly see them. Bond Forgers continuously create space for others, offering a listening ear or a comforting shoulder, but, in return, they often find that others seldom reciprocate this generosity. They take on multiple roles, such as the friend to lean on, the unwavering anchor in turbulent times, and the safe haven that those in distress so desperately seek. Yet, over time, this self-denying behaviour begins to wear them thin.

They grapple with haunting questions that linger in their minds:

- Does anyone ever check in on me, just to see how I'm holding up?
- If I were to cease my efforts to reach out, who among my friends would genuinely notice my absence?
- If I begin to struggle or unravel, who would choose to stand beside me, steadfast in their support?

Despite these doubts, the intrinsic nature of the Bond Forger compels them to show up for others. Deep down, they identify with this term, which embodies those who prioritise meaningful connections, often placing the emotional needs of others before their own.

From a psychological standpoint, Bond Forgers frequently operate from a secure or earned-secure attachment style. They may have been fortunate enough to flourish in a stable environment that nurtured emotional health, or they have taken significant strides to establish a secure foundation in the aftermath of trauma. These individuals comprehend the necessity of boundaries; they articulate their needs with clarity and honesty while embracing the nuances of intimacy. They possess the wisdom to grant space when appropriate, navigating the complexities of closeness with deftness.

In the realm of relational therapy, this quality is referred to as relational integrity, the capacity to maintain meaningful connections while safeguarding one's own identity and sense of self. For many men, embodying this concept represents a radical departure from societal norms that often equate emotional dependence with weakness. The Bond Forger upends this narrative, recognising that connection is not only desirable but essential for emotional well-being.

However, this journey comes with its own set of challenges, most notably reflected in the phenomenon known as the Burnout of the Unseen. Unlike typical burnout arising from overexertion, the fatigue experienced by Bond Forgers often springs from a lack of reciprocity in their relationships. They unwittingly bear the emotional weights of others without consent, adeptly absorbing the prevailing moods of their surroundings in a quest to create a harmonious atmosphere. Their ability to anticipate and address the needs of those around them often before those needs are explicitly articulated can ultimately lead to their own emotional depletion.

As this relentless giving continues, Bond Forgers may begin to retreat into silence rather than express their fatigue through anger or frustration. Their withdrawal is subtle, marked not by dramatic exits but by a gentle fading into the background. It is within this silence that the risk of losing a Bond Forger looms significant, not due to grand gestures or conflicts, but rather through their unacknowledged absence.

As one voice poignantly articulated, "In my family, the men worked. That was the expectation. Emotions? Those weren't the topics of conversation. You didn't ask if someone was okay; you just carried on. I was the first to challenge that norm, and doing so made me feel like a stranger in my own skin." Diego, 45. This reflection underscores a broader societal issue: The Gendered Blind Spot. When women express empathy, they are often lauded for their emotional intelligence. In stark contrast, men's emotional expressions can be misconstrued as signs of pathology, leading to labels such as clingy, co-dependent, or overly intense. The very behaviours for which women receive praise can result in men being dismissed or ridiculed, perpetuating a damaging double standard that not only frustrates but also erases men's emotional experiences.

Men like Diego frequently withdraw not from a lack of desire for connection, but because their sincere attempts to provide emotional support are met with criticism or misunderstanding. In the intricate dynamics of relationships, within the confines of courtrooms, and even in therapeutic settings, their heartfelt contributions can be misconstrued as attempts at control. Often, their genuine presence is perceived as mere performance, rather than authentic engagement, which only deepens the chasm of connection.

The Social and Psychiatric Mismatch

Within NHS pathways, a significant number of individuals classified as "Bond Forgers" often go unnoticed, trapped in a cycle of misunderstanding and inadequate support. Unlike typical portrayals of distress, which might include outward displays of rage or reckless behaviour, these individuals primarily experience a profound sense of fatigue, relational burnout, and quiet despair.

They present themselves as compliant and polite, skills developed to navigate a world that often overlooks their struggles. However, beneath this exterior lies a deep well of exhaustion; they are quietly battling their challenges in isolation, frequently navigating complex emotional landscapes without the systemic support they desperately need.

Rather than failing to engage with the resources available to them, Bond Forgers are overextending themselves emotionally. They pour their energy into maintaining relationships and fulfilling responsibilities, often at the expense of their own well-being. This dynamic not only contributes to their sense of despair but also highlights the critical need for recognition and tailored support systems that genuinely address their unique experiences and challenges.

NLP and Somatic Markers: Reading the Hidden Strain

Bond Forgers often display intricate micro-expressions that frequently go unnoticed by those around them. For example, a clenched jaw may emerge during group discussions, signalling underlying stress or tension. Similarly, rapid blinking can occur when their personal well-being is questioned, suggesting discomfort or vulnerability. Even seemingly innocuous gestures, such as fidgeting hands when instructed to simply "relax," serve as indicators of significant inner turmoil that may be bubbling beneath the surface.

In the field of Neuro-Linguistic Programming (NLP), this dissonance between verbal communication and non-verbal signals is described as incongruence. For Bond Forgers, there can be a profound disconnect: their bodies might convey a clear message of overwhelm or distress, while their words insist, "I'm fine." This inconsistency creates a complex layer of communication that is often met with scepticism or disbelief by society, which tends to accept verbal reassurances at face value and overlook the deeper emotional struggles these individuals face.

Somatic therapists are especially attuned to recognising these subtle cues. Signs such as shallow breathing, perpetually tense shoulders, and an elevated heart rate, particularly when discussing sensitive childhood experiences, are not merely quirks in behaviour. Instead, they are significant indicators of emotional pain that the individual may be trying to mask with a facade of stoicism. This deep-seated emotional distress calls for a compassionate approach, as it reflects the individual's journey of grappling with their feelings while striving to navigate a world that often demands resilience and composure.

Therapeutic Tools for the Bond Forger

Reciprocity Mapping

Start by mapping out your emotional ecosystem to gain insight into your interpersonal relationships. Identify the individuals you support unconditionally, those whom you are always there for, no matter the circumstances. This could include close friends, family members, or partners. On the flip side, take note of those who offer you support, those who uplift you, listen to you, and provide comfort in times of need.

As you reflect on these connections, pay attention to any imbalance in your emotional investments. Are there relationships where you feel you are giving more than you are receiving? Acknowledge areas where your support may be disproportionately one-sided, which can lead to feelings of burnout or emotional exhaustion.

Needs Inventory

Take a moment for self-reflection to clarify your personal needs. Write down what you truly require from your relationships and life in general. Consider aspects such as emotional support, reassurance, understanding, and quality time. Be as specific as possible, avoiding vague statements, which will empower you to articulate your needs more effectively. Once you have your needs outlined, practice expressing them clearly and confidently, remembering that it's okay to voice what you want without feeling guilty or making excuses.

Boundary Rehearsals

Engage in role-playing exercises where you practice saying "no" in various scenarios. This could involve setting limits with a friend who often demands your time or declining additional responsibilities at work that could overwhelm you. Pay attention to the feelings that emerge during these exercises, especially any guilt or discomfort when you refrain from overextending yourself. Acknowledging and exploring these feelings is crucial for understanding how they impact your behaviour and self-worth. This practice will help you establish and maintain healthier boundaries, allowing you to invest in relationships that are reciprocal and fulfilling.

Core Wound Work

Reflect on the early experiences that taught you the belief that love must be earned through acts of service or personal sacrifice. Consider the moments when you felt that affection was conditional and linked to your ability to meet the needs or expectations of others. What core assumptions drive this belief? Explore how these experiences might compel you to prioritise performing for others rather than allowing yourself to receive love and validation, potentially leading to a cycle of overexertion and emotional depletion.

Ethical Framing

Take time to reflect on specific instances in your life where expressing your genuine emotions led to negative consequences, such as punishment or ridicule. Were there moments when showing vulnerability resulted in feelings of shame? Examine the internal conflict that arises from this. Ask yourself: "Have I been shamed for openly sharing my feelings, only to face shame again when I opted for silence instead?" This cycle may influence your willingness to communicate your needs and desires in relationships, creating barriers to authentic connections.

Cross-Cultural Check-In

Consider the messages you absorbed regarding male emotions during your upbringing. Reflect on the societal and cultural norms that shaped your understanding of acceptable emotional expression for men. What were the explicit or implicit rules about vulnerability and emotional availability? Did your cultural background endorse the stereotype that men should be stoic or emotionally reserved? Contemplate how these influences have formed your current perspectives on emotions and intimacy, possibly limiting your expression or connection with others.

Gentle Prompts – The Bond Forger

Who are the individuals in my life for whom I unfailingly show up, driven solely by love and unwavering loyalty, without a moment's hesitation? I often think about the sacrifices I make and the time I dedicate to supporting these people. In contrast, how many of these same individuals demonstrate the same level of commitment to me? Are there those who arrive by my side when I find myself in need, without requiring me to voice my struggles or ask explicitly for their help?

I also wonder about the deeper aspects of my inner self. What fears reside within me at the thought of relinquishing my role as a giver, the caretaker, the one who always seems strong? When did I first realise that the love I freely offer often carries hidden strings, entangled with expectations, service, and sacrifice? Reflecting on past experiences, I can trace moments where I felt my worth was tied to how much I give rather than simply being.

If I were to allow someone to take on my burdens, even if just for a brief moment, how might that reshape my existence? Would accepting help challenge my long-held sense of independence and self-reliance, or could it instead usher in a refreshing wave of relief and connection, allowing me to experience the beauty of vulnerability?

In times when I feel neglected or undervalued, how do I navigate that emotional turmoil while maintaining a facade of cheerfulness to the outside world? I often wonder what it would be like to fully immerse myself in love, freed from the constraints of guilt and obligation, embracing affection with open arms and a willing heart. Could this shift in perspective allow me to truly connect with others, and in turn, foster deeper, more genuine relationships?

Final Reframe

You are not excessive or overly emotional; instead, your feelings reflect a deep human experience that underscores your desire for connection. This yearning does not signify weakness; instead, it reveals the profound strength of a Bond Forger. You possess a remarkable ability to create connections and build bridges in a world that often insists on erecting barriers and divisions.

Yet, within this incredible capacity to foster relationships, it's vital to remember an equally important truth: you also deserve the opportunity to cross those bridges you construct. You deserve to be embraced in moments of vulnerability and to feel the warmth of another's presence. You deserve to be seen for who you truly are, your thoughts, your emotions, and your unique essence.

Even in this very moment, recognise that you are worthy of love, understanding, and connection. Your journey is just as important as those you bring together.

Chapter 26

The Intimacy Deficit – Why Men Struggle to Let Love In

The Heart He Forgot He Had

He longs for the warmth of touch, craving the kind of connection that can only come from genuine intimacy. Yet, when that moment arrives, his instinct is to instinctively recoil, as if the warmth itself has turned to fire. He yearns for meaningful relationships, but as those connections deepen, he often feels suffocated, like a bird trapped in a cage it once believed was safe. He insists that he is perfectly content with his solitude. Still, the truth is revealed in the quiet hours of the night when he lies awake, wrestling with a profound sense of being misunderstood and hopelessly isolated in a crowd of faces.

For many men, the realm of intimacy is not a comforting refuge but rather a tumultuous battlefield, fraught with emotional landmines laid by past experiences and societal expectations. Each step forward can trigger a haunting echo of previous wounds, making every intimate moment feel perilously risky.

To him, love can often be equated with exposure to vulnerability, a state that transforms into a trap from which he feels there is no escape. Even when he encounters the right person, someone who embodies safety and offers emotional support, his instinctive reaction may be to withdraw, to push that person away, or even to disappear entirely from the situation. This dynamic creates a painful dichotomy; he craves closeness yet fears it like a shadowy adversary.

His struggle transcends mere romantic relationships; it delves deeply into the very wiring of his brain, shaped by an intricate web of past traumas and the conditioning he has received about what love truly demands of him. Each experience adds another layer, complicating his ability to embrace love without hesitation and, in turn, reinforcing the walls he has built to protect himself from further pain. The conflict within him is palpable, a visceral tug-of-war between the desire for intimacy and the instinct to shield his heart from potential harm.

Hormones of Closeness: The Neurobiology of Love and Fear

Men are not inherently broken or flawed; instead, their brains have evolved with a specific focus on survival, shaped by both biological imperatives and societal expectations. When the emotional closeness inherent in a relationship triggers the release of cortisol, the primary stress hormone, it does not signify a lack of affection or desire. Instead, it highlights how a man's nervous system often interprets vulnerability as a significant threat. This physiological response can create a conflict between the desire for intimacy and the instinct to protect oneself.

The bonding hormone oxytocin, essential for cultivating deep emotional connections, is released in men at a slower rate compared to women. Meanwhile, the presence of testosterone, predominant in male biology, can further complicate emotional expression by inhibiting the openness necessary for fostering close relationships. This hormonal landscape creates a unique challenge for men when navigating their feelings.

In the male brain, the perception of emotional threats activates the same areas responsible for processing physical pain. Therefore, feelings of being misunderstood, dismissed, or emotionally criticised can resonate with men in a manner as acute and damaging as experiencing a physical injury. Faced with such distress, rather than seeking comfort and connection from others, the instinctive response may be to shut down, withdraw, or resort to avoidance tactics.

It is vital to understand that this behaviour should not be mistakenly categorised as mere detachment. Instead, it can be more accurately described as dysregulation, a multifaceted response to emotional stressors that often stems from early formative experiences and lessons. Many men grow up learning that emotional expression is unpredictable and can lead to vulnerability, a state they may have been taught to view with caution or even fear. Consequently, when confronted with love, especially a love that fully acknowledges and embraces all facets of their identity, it can feel akin to handing over a detailed blueprint of their vulnerabilities to another person, an act that may trigger defence mechanisms rather than open-hearted engagement.

Polyvagal Theory: The Safety Switch in Love

Polyvagal Theory suggests that the autonomic nervous system operates in three distinct states: fight/flight, shutdown, and social connection. These states influence not only our physical responses to perceived threats but also our emotional experiences in relationships. When men experience love that triggers feelings of threat or anxiety, they may unconsciously enter a dorsal vagal shutdown state. This state can manifest as emotional numbness, withdrawal, and a sense of disconnection from both their own emotions and from their partners. As a result, they may struggle to engage deeply in their relationships, fearing vulnerability or intimacy.

On the other hand, the ventral vagal state is characterised by feelings of safety, social engagement, and the genuine capacity for love and connection. Unfortunately, for some men, particularly those who have experienced childhood trauma or neglect, the concept of emotional safety may be foreign. When intimacy is perceived as potentially dangerous, these individuals may instinctively recoil from close relationships, interpreting trust and emotional closeness as threats rather than sources of comfort and joy.

Therefore, love transcends a simple emotional experience; it is intricately intertwined with our neurological wiring and the pathways our nervous systems navigate. Understanding this can shed light on why some may find it challenging to fully engage in loving relationships and illustrate the importance of fostering emotional safety for deeper connections to flourish.

The Window of Tolerance

Dr. Dan Siegel introduces the concept of the "Window of Tolerance," which describes the optimal range of emotional arousal within which individuals can think clearly, feel appropriately, and engage meaningfully with others. This window is crucial for healthy emotional regulation and interpersonal relationships. However, men who have experienced trauma often find themselves operating outside of this window, leading to extreme emotional states that severely hinder their ability to connect with others.

In the realm of love and relationships, these men may swing between two opposing states. Hyperarousal is marked by intense anger, heightened reactivity, and impulsivity; in these moments, they may lash out or feel overwhelmed by emotions. Conversely, hypoarousal reflects a state of emotional numbing, characterised by a sense of disconnection and withdrawal from both their own feelings and from those around them. This oscillation is not simply a failure of will or character; rather, it is a deeply ingrained response shaped by a history of emotional turmoil and instability.

Understanding this dynamic is key to recognising that the struggle for emotional connection stems from learned responses to trauma, rather than a lack of desire or ability to love. Until these individuals embark on a journey of healing that expands their "Window of Tolerance," they are likely to perceive feelings of safety as threats, leaving them trapped in a cycle where meaningful emotional connections remain elusive. Healing involves not only recognising these patterns but also developing tools and practices that promote emotional resilience, allowing them to reclaim their capacity for connection and intimacy.

When Masculinity Isn't Universal

Not every man enters the realm of love with the same narrative or understanding, shaped as they are by unique societal influences. For many Black men, the experience of love often arrives tangled up with a profound double-bind. From an early age, they are socialised to embody hypermasculine traits, not merely as a choice but as a means of navigating a world that consistently marginalises and devalues their existence. Ironically, this narrative of strength and stoicism, which society lauds, can become a source of internal conflict and shame when they yearn to express affection, vulnerability, or tenderness. The very qualities that could foster deeper connections can feel like betraying the ideals they've been taught to uphold.

In contrast, queer men traverse the landscape of love under the weight of intricate societal pressures and complications. They often face the haunting spectres of rejection, self-denial, and internalised shame, wrestling daily with the messages that communicate they are either too much, too flamboyant, too emotional, too expressive or not enough, burdened by the stigmatising question of their legitimacy as "real" men. This battleground of expectations can create significant emotional barriers, rendering intimacy a daunting prospect fraught with fear of judgment or inadequacy.

Working-class men confront their own reality when it comes to love, often finding the pursuit of affection overshadowed by foundational concerns such as financial stability and the imperative of providing for themselves and their families. In these circumstances, the act of expressing emotional depth and vulnerability may feel trivial, even self-indulgent, compared to the pressing demands of economic survival. This can lead to a disconnect where emotional needs are relegated to the background, overshadowed by the urgency of societal obligations that insist on practicality over emotional exploration.

As a consequence, love can transform from what should be a natural expression of human connection into a performance fraught with risk and hesitation. When intimacy is shaped by cultural backgrounds, historical trauma, and socioeconomic class realities, the journey toward healing and forming meaningful relationships becomes all the more complex. It requires a thoughtful and intentional approach that acknowledges these myriad influences. As the influential writer and cultural critic bell hooks wisely asserted, "Love is an action, never simply a feeling." This statement serves as a potent reminder that love requires conscious effort and engagement, inviting individuals to redefine their expressions of affection in healthier, more authentic ways.

Brotherhood Before Romance

The discourse surrounding male friendships often lacks the nuance it deserves. Many men tend to lean heavily on romantic relationships to satisfy their emotional needs. However, this reliance can leave them without the critical foundation of emotionally secure brotherhoods, which serve as invaluable rehearsal spaces for exploring vulnerability. Authentic friendships provide essential lessons in navigating complex emotions; they teach men how to embrace moments of silence without feeling the urgent need to "fix" a situation, how to listen with genuine empathy rather than passing judgment, and how to express physical affection like hugs simply for the sake of connection, without waiting for a special occasion.

When a man cultivates deep emotional intimacy with a close friend, he enhances his capacity to receive and express love within romantic contexts as well. This profound bond fosters an understanding that being truly seen and acknowledged by someone does not equate to exposure, shame, or judgment. Unfortunately, emotional fluency, the ability to articulate and manage one's feelings, rarely comes from conventional education or societal teachings. Instead, it is often honed through lived experiences and exemplary role models in friendships. These relationships not only enrich a man's emotional toolkit but also empower him to navigate the complexities of intimacy and connection in all areas of life.

The Trauma Template: Attachment, Abandonment, and Avoidance

Many men enter relationships bearing emotional wounds that originate from their past experiences, particularly those linked to childhood. These wounds, often rooted in attachment trauma arising from neglect, control, or emotional shaming, contribute to two predominant patterns of emotional behaviour: one group may cling tightly to their partners, while the other may withdraw altogether.

For some, this manifests as over-giving, an incessant drive to prove their worth through acts of service, whether by sacrificing their own needs or constantly seeking approval from others. They believe that by being indispensable, they can secure love and acceptance. On the other hand, some become "ghosts," retreating from intimacy when it feels vulnerable or overwhelming. This avoidance often stems from a deep-seated fear of emotional connection and the potential for rejection, leading them to shut down or disengage from those who want to draw closer.

In both cases, the essence of love becomes a performance, where the true self is masked behind a façade, driven by the belief that unveiling one's authentic self could result in emotional pain or abandonment. This leads to a cycle where genuine connection is sacrificed for the illusion of safety.

The journey toward authentic intimacy begins when individuals confront their fears and set aside their pretences, allowing themselves to be truly seen and understood by their partners. As Gabor Maté insightfully points out, "Trauma is not what happens to you. Trauma is what happens inside you." Thus, embracing vulnerability and fostering open communication can pave the way for deeper emotional connections, healing past wounds, and nurturing healthier relationships.

The Ego's Defence: Narcissistic Shields and Shame Collapse

Certain men often construct emotional barriers to intimacy, employing narcissistic shields as a defence mechanism. They mistakenly equate external admiration, such as praise and recognition, with genuine love, failing to recognise that true emotional connection involves vulnerability and authenticity. For these individuals, control becomes a misguided substitute for meaningful relationships, as they seek to manage interactions rather than engage in them fully.

On the other hand, some may experience a profound shame collapse. This occurs when an individual feels inherently unworthy and, as a result, retreats into silence and isolation. Their self-esteem, shaped by past experiences, prevents them from reaching out to others and accepting the love and support that could foster healing. These ego defences are linked to trauma and are not flaws of character; instead, they are survival mechanisms developed in environments that lacked healthy emotional modelling, where feelings were either dismissed or invalidated.

The journey toward healing requires a pivotal shift in perspective. True intimacy does not demand perfection or the absence of flaws; instead, it thrives in authentic engagement. It calls for individuals to show up as their true selves, allowing both themselves and others to experience their feelings fully. This journey fosters connections rooted in mutual understanding, acceptance, and the recognition that vulnerability is an essential aspect of meaningful relationships. By embracing authenticity and cultivating emotional safety, individuals can dismantle these barriers and forge deeper, more enriching connections with others.

The Relationship Mirror: Conflict as Communication

Couples therapy unveils a fundamental truth that many men have not been taught: conflict is not simply indicative of failure in a relationship; instead, it is often a manifestation of the desire for a deeper emotional connection. In therapeutic practices, primarily through approaches such as Imago Therapy, men begin to grasp that their romantic partner serves as a mirror, reflecting their own emotional landscape rather than standing as an adversary. The triggers that surface during intimate moments frequently resonate with unresolved issues from their past, allowing for a clearer understanding of how childhood experiences shape adult emotional responses.

Emotionally Focused Therapy (EFT) introduces the vital concept of co-regulation, which emphasises that men can soothe their partner's distress while still maintaining their own self-awareness and emotional presence. This co-regulatory process highlights the importance of emotional safety, an aspect of relationships that should not be perceived as a weakness or an obstacle to be avoided. Instead, emotional safety is depicted as a profound source of wisdom and strength that can lead to transformative growth within relationships. By fostering this safe environment, couples can navigate their emotional landscapes more effectively, gaining insight and ultimately building a more resilient bond grounded in understanding and connection.

Mis-attunement and Emotional Labour

In many heterosexual relationships, the burden of emotional labour predominantly falls on women. This dynamic is evident as women often take the lead in initiating repair efforts after conflicts, articulating the emotional climate of the partnership, and shouldering the emotional needs and vulnerabilities of both themselves and their partners. This imbalance of responsibility is not an inherent or natural disposition but rather a societal construct that has been passed down through generations, shaped by cultural norms and expectations.

Men, too, can learn and take on emotional responsibilities, which allows them to share the psychological load in the relationship. By doing so, they can foster deeper mutual love and intimacy. When both partners are actively engaged in emotional exchanges, the relationship transforms into a genuinely reciprocal partnership, where both individuals feel valued and understood.

Being present in a relationship goes beyond simply being physically close to one another; it embodies an active and transformative force that is essential for nurturing a healthy bond. This presence requires a heightened level of awareness, an ability to discern not only one's own feelings but also to empathise with the partner's emotional state. It demands the courage to embrace vulnerability, allowing both partners to share their innermost thoughts and fears without fear of judgment. Cultivating this depth of connection significantly strengthens the foundation of the partnership, creating a safe space for both individuals to thrive emotionally and spiritually together.

Jungian Archetypes and Love

Carl Jung introduced the concept of the Anima, which embodies a man's inner feminine essence. This psychological archetype is crucial for personal development and emotional health, as it encompasses qualities traditionally associated with femininity, such as intuition, empathy, and nurturing. When a man suppresses the Anima, he risks becoming emotionally rigid and disconnected, which can severely limit his ability to foster not only himself but also his relationships with others. The denial of this aspect can lead to difficulties in expressing vulnerability, forming deep emotional bonds, and receiving love, ultimately resulting in a superficial existence.

Conversely, embracing and integrating the Anima can significantly enrich a man's life. By acknowledging this inner feminine, he unlocks a wellspring of empathy, sensuality, and nurturing qualities, allowing for more intimate and fulfilling connections with partners, friends, and even family. This integration fosters emotional intelligence, enabling him to navigate relationships with greater understanding and compassion.

In addition to the Anima, Jung also highlighted the concept of the Shadow, which contains the repressed or denied parts of one's psyche. This aspect often emerges in times of conflict or stress, revealing the traits in ourselves that we find most irritating in others. These projections can serve as mirrors, reflecting qualities we have yet to confront or accept within ourselves. By recognising these facets, we can embark on a transformative journey of self-discovery and healing.

As Jung profoundly stated, "Only the wounded physician heals," underscoring the idea that our personal struggles and healing journeys are integral to our capacity to help others. This perspective invites individuals to consider their own healing as a vital component in fostering healthier relationships and supporting the emotional growth of those around them. Emphasising self-awareness and the integration of both the Anima and Shadow ultimately leads to richer, more authentic lives and connections.

Digital Disconnection: Faux Intimacy and Numbing Loops

In today's digital age, the widespread availability of pornography, dating apps, and various forms of virtual escapism constructs a landscape filled with superficial intimacy. These modern tools provide an enticing promise of excitement that is fueled by dopamine, yet they fall short in fostering the depth and richness that come with genuine human connection. This often results in superficial validation, which, while temporarily satisfying, is devoid of the essential element of vulnerability that meaningful relationships require.

Many men find themselves ensnared in this cycle, not necessarily due to a lack of desire for authentic love and companionship, but rather because the profound sense of vulnerability that genuine relationships demand can be daunting. The fear of rejection, the risk of emotional exposure, and the uncertainty of true intimacy can feel overwhelming, leading many to seek solace in easier, yet ultimately hollow, alternatives.

To mend these fractured ties and move toward authentic connections, these individuals must be willing to relinquish the fleeting highs associated with performance-driven interactions. Instead, they need to embrace the lasting satisfaction that comes from being fully present with another person. This shift away from transient pleasures paves the way for men to cultivate deeper, more meaningful relationships, allowing them to experience the joy and fulfilment that genuine intimacy offers. By prioritising authenticity and vulnerability, they can transform their interactions into rich experiences that nourish the heart and soul.

Bio-psychological Expansion

The nervous system plays a fundamental role in shaping the dynamics of intimacy in relationships. When we experience a sense of emotional safety, our parasympathetic nervous system is activated. This activation leads to a physiological state characterised by relaxation, where the heart opens and the body calms down. In this nurturing environment, we are more inclined to express vulnerability, fostering deeper emotional connections and trust between partners.

On the other hand, when we perceive emotional threats, be they from past traumas, misunderstandings, or external stressors, our sympathetic nervous system kicks in, initiating a fight or flight response. This shift triggers a state of heightened alertness, making us more defensive and potentially reactive. Such dysregulation can manifest as avoidance behaviours, withdrawal, or even aggression, severely straining intimate relationships.

Recognising these patterns is essential for fostering healing and growth. It requires self-awareness and a willingness to delve into our emotional triggers. Engaging in practices like mindfulness can help us stay present, allowing us to better manage our reactions. Breath-work serves as a powerful tool to calm the nervous system, guiding us back to a state of balance. Furthermore, co-regulation with partners where we support each other in creating an emotionally safe environment can significantly aid in rewiring these ingrained, often automatic responses. By nurturing this emotional safety together, we pave the way for healthier, more fulfilling connections in our intimate relationships.

Practice Letting Love In: A Healing Toolkit

- Mirror Affirmation: Stand confidently in front of a mirror, making direct eye contact with your reflection. Take a moment to breathe deeply, then affirm with sincerity, "I am safe to be loved in the places I once hid." This practice not only fosters self-acceptance but also cultivates emotional openness by allowing you to face and embrace your vulnerabilities. Repeat this affirmation daily, particularly during challenging moments, to reinforce your commitment to self-love.

- Somatic Awareness: Begin by tuning into your body during moments of praise or comfort. Close your eyes and focus on where you feel a lightness or warmth, perhaps in your chest, shoulders, or a sense of release in your stomach. By identifying these specific areas of relaxation, you can learn to anchor feelings of safety and joy within yourself. This awareness can act as a powerful tool, helping you to reconnect with your body and emotions in times of stress or anxiety.

- Journaling Prompt: Reflect deeply on the question, "When did I first learn that love might cost me myself?" Consider pivotal moments from your past, such as relationships, family dynamics, or societal expectations that may have shaped your understanding of love. Exploring this question can help you uncover limiting beliefs that may still influence your current relationships, leading you to a path of liberation from past emotional wounds and a healthier, more authentic way of loving.

- Breathing Tool: Develop a structured breathing technique: inhale slowly for a count of 4, hold that breath gently for another count of 4, and exhale deeply for a count of 6. This simple yet effective method can be beneficial during moments of argument or discomfort in intimate situations. By focusing on your breath, you can restore a sense of calm, allowing for more transparent communication and emotional connection with your partner.

- Legacy Ledger: Take time to contemplate, "What kind of intimacy do I want to model for the next generation?" Write down your ideals and aspirations regarding love and connection. This exercise encourages intentionality in how you demonstrate affection, respect, and vulnerability to those who come after you, ensuring that you foster healthy relationship patterns and an environment where future generations can thrive.

These small yet intentional practices, when applied consistently, can cumulatively build your capacity for profound intimacy and authentic connection, enriching your relationships and enhancing your emotional resilience.

When Performance Isn't Presence

Many men mistakenly believe that being physically present for someone is synonymous with being emotionally present. In their effort to support loved ones, they often prioritise tangible actions such as earning income, solving problems, and providing protection. While these efforts are commendable, they can overshadow a crucial aspect of relationships: the power of actual presence. Authentic connection does not require men to be perfect; instead, it calls for them to be genuine and vulnerable.

Children crave engaged, real fathers who are deeply involved in their lives, not just as providers but as active participants who show interest and share experiences. Partners, too, yearn for the emotional depth that comes from men willing to express their thoughts and feelings. It's within those raw, unpolished moments of honesty and vulnerability that the most meaningful connections are forged. When men allow themselves to be open about their struggles and fears, they invite others to do the same, creating a space for deeper understanding and intimacy. Ultimately, it is through this authenticity that relationships can flourish and individuals can truly support one another.

The Unconscious Imitation: How the Father Wound Sabotages Love

For many men, becoming like their fathers isn't a conscious choice, but rather a reflexive imitation shaped by the complexities of their upbringing. This involuntary replication of emotional patterns often occurs without awareness; many men unconsciously mirror the behaviours they observed during their formative years. If a father is emotionally distant, consistently unavailable, or prone to reactive outbursts, these behaviours typically become the default modes of interaction for his sons. Breaking this cycle demands a proactive, conscious awareness of these ingrained patterns. By recognising the thought, "This reaction isn't genuinely me; it's who I learned to be," men can begin to identify the scripts that govern their responses. This process of self-discovery encourages them to choose different emotional reactions, enabling them to redefine their approach to intimacy in a more authentic and fulfilling manner.

From Shame to Sacred: The Spiritual Rebirth of Intimacy

Intimacy encompasses a profoundly spiritual dimension that is rarely discussed among men, yet it has the power to transform relationships and personal identities. Engaging deeply with another person allows individuals to tap into the sacred essence of our humanity, an experience that transcends mere physical attraction or polished interactions. True intimacy involves being fully seen, felt, and embraced in one's authentic truth, creating a space where vulnerability is honoured and reciprocal. In this sacred realm, love becomes a transformative force, not because it fills a void in one's life, but because it reveals the inner self that has always existed, allowing individuals to step into their fullest potential.

Legacy of Connection: The Silent Lessons of Love

A man who learns to let love into his life not only embarks on a profound personal healing journey but also becomes an influential teacher for the next generation. Through his actions, he can demonstrate tenderness to his son, providing a living example of what affection and emotional safety look like. This nurturing behaviour fosters a secure environment where his son can appreciate the value of vulnerability as a strength rather than a weakness. Similarly, to his daughter, he embodies the essence of security, illustrating that she can thrive in a world where openness and gentleness coexist with strength.

Furthermore, he manifests to his partner that masculinity can be expressed gracefully through gentleness, thereby retaining its inherent power and depth. In this way, he not only rewrites his own narrative but also enriches the understanding of love and connection for his lineage. Ultimately, intimacy is not the antithesis of masculinity; it is, in fact, its highest and most profound expression, highlighting the significant role emotional intelligence plays in defining manhood.

Final Reframe: You Are Lovable Even in the Places You Were Taught to Hide

You do not have to disappear or diminish yourself to find love. You are not required to solve every flaw or insecurity to be entirely accepted and cherished. Remember, you are not too much to handle; you are not beyond healing, and certainly not beyond hope. Your worthiness of love is intrinsic and profound. It's a love that sees you for who you truly are, recognising and nurturing the boy within, celebrating the man he evolves into, and perceiving the depth of the soul that lies beneath both layers of identity.

This kind of love is compassionate and patient; it understands that everyone carries their own scars and stories. Ultimately, the journey toward receiving such love begins with your readiness to embrace it. Opening yourself up requires vulnerability and trust, but it is in this willingness that you find the transformative power of love. This love invites you to be authentic, encouraging you to grow, heal, and thrive just as you are.

Chapter 27

Brotherhood – Why Men Heal in Circles

He sat with his arms crossed, not out of coldness, but as a learned posture of self-preservation amid chaos. This stance had evolved into a protective shell, a way to navigate the turbulent waters of a world that often felt unbearable. Encircling him were six other men, each settled in their own mismatched chairs, forming a loose yet cohesive circle. Some cradled steaming cups of coffee that released tendrils of warmth into the air, while others stared blankly at the worn wooden floor, lost in their thoughts. One man fixated on a scuffed patch of wall, his gaze lingering there as if seeking answers in the imperfections. The atmosphere crackled with a palpable silence, a heavy cloak woven from threads of unspoken understanding. It wasn't an uncomfortable hush; instead, it served as a comforting armour, shielding their vulnerabilities like a fortress against the outside world.

He hadn't arrived intending to unfold his own story; instead, he found himself here because the weight of his thoughts had become too heavy to carry alone. Something inside him had splintered, a fracture he struggled to name or even comprehend. He came in response to a simple nudge from a friend, a gentle encouragement wrapped in the casual phrase, "Just try it once, mate." That small invitation had propelled him into this unfamiliar territory, a step that felt both daunting and necessary.

This space was far removed from any conventional therapy room. There were no framed diplomas that decorated the walls like gold medals of expertise, nor sterile couches looming ominously in the corners. Instead, the setting embraced a stark minimalism: a circle formed by mismatched chairs, a humble side table bearing an open packet of biscuits, whispering promises of comfort. The kind-eyed facilitator, with a face slightly weathered by life's own hardships, bore the unmistakable marks of someone who had traversed similar valleys of grief and confusion.

In this quiet yet uncomfortable sanctuary, healing was poised to begin, not through well-meaning advice or empty platitudes, but through the genuine presence of men who comprehended the unarticulated struggles of one another. They were no longer isolated in their pain; together, they embarked on a shared journey toward understanding and, perhaps, redemption.

Why Men Don't Talk to Their Friends

The modern man navigates a landscape filled with companions: he enjoys the camaraderie of drinking buddies over laughter-fueled nights, engages in the lively banter of WhatsApp groups that buzz with memes and jokes, and shares quick jests with colleagues under the unforgiving glow of fluorescent office lights. Yet, when posed with the question of who he could lean on during his darkest moments of despair, an unsettling silence envelops the space, revealing a more profound, hidden truth.

Cultural conditioning, passed down through generations, has ingrained in men the notion that emotions are burdensome and that tears are an emblem of weakness. Society has perpetuated the insidious belief that silence equates to strength, pushing men to bottle up their feelings instead of reaching out for support. This conditioning breeds a façade of resilience while masking an undercurrent of vulnerability.

As a result, men become adept at discussing a plethora of topics: sports scores, work projects, romantic escapades, and workout routines. Yet, when it comes to addressing their own pain and struggles, they often stumble. They carry the weight of their emotional burdens, believing they must do so with a sense of pride, until, inevitably, the pressure becomes too much to bear, leading to a breaking point that can manifest in various ways, from anger to depression.

In many male friendships, the subject of emotional depth hovers like an unacknowledged elephant in the room. Conversations skim the surface, rarely venturing into the complexities of grief, shame, fear, or failure. It's not that these men lack the capacity for depth; instead, they were never equipped with the tools to explore and express it. The societal expectation to maintain a stoic demeanour leaves many feeling disconnected and misunderstood.

This creates a quiet crisis: millions of men find themselves surrounded by acquaintances yet feel emotionally starved and isolated. Despite the illusion of companionship, an underlying loneliness persists, as they navigate their inner turmoil in silence, yearning for authentic connection but unsure of how to forge it. The need for conversation that transcends superficiality has never been more pressing; it is time for a cultural shift that encourages men to embrace their emotional lives fully, fostering bonds that provide solace and understanding.

Brotherhood: The Unspoken Language of Healing

What unfolds in men's circles goes far beyond the boundaries of traditional therapy; it delves into something more ancient and primal. In these gatherings, men sit across from one another, engaging in deep, meaningful conversations that transcend superficial interactions. Here, the act of listening becomes a profound exchange; each man recognises his own journey reflected in the struggles and triumphs shared by others. This environment often represents a pivotal moment in a man's life, the first time he encounters a space where he isn't being "fixed" or judged. When he quietly admits, "Sometimes I think about ending it," he is met with unwavering compassion rather than discomfort.

Unlike casual conversations in a pub, where laughter serves as a veil over unresolved issues, these circles provide a safe haven for vulnerability. The genuine eye contact and heartfelt engagement create an electrifying connection that fosters trust. It is in this sacred space that a man lays bare his innermost thoughts, those he has never dared to vocalise and discovers that the room holds space for his honesty without any hint of judgment.

The efficacy of this approach lies in a deceptively simple yet profoundly impactful concept: witnessing. When a man feels truly seen in all his complexity, his fears, struggles, and truths, unfiltered by judgment, correction, or minimisation, it establishes a profound sense of safety. This emotional sanctuary can be challenging to replicate, even in conventional therapeutic settings.

Within this sacred masculine space, the process of healing does not come from outside interventions; rather, it is something that is subtly permitted and gently encouraged. Men learn to rediscover their innate resilience and strength together, forming bonds that honour their individual stories while also celebrating their shared humanity. In these moments, healing becomes a collective journey, allowing men to navigate their experiences in a way that fosters growth and understanding.

The Neuroscience of Shared Pain

Group spaces serve a crucial psychological function by dismantling the pervasive loop of shame that many individuals grapple with. According to bio-psychological research, shame activates specific neural regions associated with physical pain, most notably the anterior cingulate cortex and the insula. This neural activation not only triggers an emotional response but also initiates a parasympathetic collapse, characterised by a slowed heart rate and increased cortisol levels. As a result, individuals often withdraw inward, feeling isolated and vulnerable for extended periods.

In contrast, when shame is openly verbalised and met with genuine empathy from others, it effectively disarms the brain's natural threat detection systems. This empathetic engagement creates a supportive environment, prompting an increase in oxytocin levels often referred to as the "bonding hormone." This hormonal shift fosters a sense of connection among participants, enhancing emotional safety.

Moreover, the engagement of mirror neurons plays a pivotal role in this process, allowing individuals to resonate with and reflect the emotions of those around them. As the limbic system, the part of the brain responsible for emotional processing, signals a state of safety and belonging, participants may internally affirm, "We're safe now." This collective reassurance paves the way for healing and deeper emotional expression.

In summary, group circles facilitate the regulation of the nervous system through authentic connections among participants. They underscore the notion that, in their emotional journeys, men often need connection, not correction, to navigate their experiences effectively. By fostering these supportive relationships, group spaces become vital arenas for transformation and growth.

Intersectionality: When Brotherhood Isn't Always Safe

The Complexity of Brotherhood and Emotional Expression

It is crucial to recognise that the sense of brotherhood does not resonate equally with all men. For many working-class men, the societal pressure to uphold traditional masculine ideals often leads to the ridicule of emotional expression. In their environments, vulnerability is frequently perceived as a weakness or a betrayal of these ideals, which may prevent them from seeking or participating in supportive spaces. For these men, the concept of a sharing circle might initially appear unappealing or threatening. However, when they finally engage in this experience, they may discover a profound sense of strength and connection that arises from shared vulnerability. This transformative realisation can begin to reshape their understanding of masculinity and brotherhood.

For Black and ethnic minority men, the interplay of cultural expectations and deep-rooted systemic mistrust adds layers of complexity to their relationship with mental health resources. Historical marginalisation and stigmatisation mean that even the idea of "opening up" to mental health services can seem alien or intimidating. Research highlights that these men are significantly less likely to seek help, motivated by both a valid fear of further discrimination and a cultural narrative that often neglects or politicises their mental health needs. Thus, any initiative aimed at fostering brotherhood and emotional openness must actively work to dismantle these barriers, providing culturally competent support that understands and respects their unique experiences and histories.

Similarly, gay and bisexual men, many of whom have endured shame or exclusion from conventional male spaces, confront a complex relationship with the ideal of brotherhood. For them, it is often intertwined with feelings of trauma and alienation. The quest for a safe and accepting brotherhood requires a concerted effort to cultivate inclusivity, transcending mere performative gestures. True brotherhood calls for the establishment of secure spaces where all men can authentically express their thoughts and emotions, regardless of whether they conform to traditional definitions of masculinity.

Rites of Passage: Reconstructing Meaningful Transitions

Through the ages, nearly every ancient culture defined rites of passage that were instrumental in guiding boys into manhood through rigorous trials and challenges. These rites often tested their physical strength, mental discipline, and spiritual resilience. Young men might confront formidable wild animals, endure periods of isolation, undergo fasting, or embark on vision quests that are intended to foster personal growth and self-discovery. The sacredness of these transitions was primarily rooted in the mentorship and wisdom imparted by elders, individuals who provided guidance and support during these pivotal moments.

In stark contrast, modern society often lacks structured frameworks for such rites of passage. Many young men now navigate a nebulous landscape between adolescence and adulthood, frequently feeling lost, overwhelmed, and uncertain of their identities. Contemporary rites of passage have become ad-hoc rituals, such as cold plunges, nights of truth-telling, or communal experiences of vulnerability. These modern practices emphasise the importance of emotional growth and community over traditional notions of toughness. In sharing circles, men can reclaim this essential rite, assuming roles both as mentors and initiates, ultimately fostering a holistic sense of self and belonging.

Digital Brotherhood: Navigating Connection in a Virtual World

In an increasingly digital age, where physical gatherings may not always be feasible, men are increasingly turning to online platforms to forge connections. Communities such as Andy's Man Club, Men's Group, and 7 Cups provide anonymous, guided opportunities for men to engage in meaningful conversations and support one another. Social networks on platforms like Discord and Reddit have thrived by promoting emotional literacy, enabling men to connect and share their experiences across geographic boundaries.

The advantages of these digital spaces are numerous; they offer enhanced anonymity, flexible participation, and accessibility for those who may find it challenging to engage in person. However, significant challenges accompany these environments, such as the absence of physical presence, diminished accountability, and the risk of harmful venting without constructive dialogue. Despite these obstacles, the fundamental reality remains that men are rediscovering opportunities to connect with one another, fostering a digital brotherhood that transcends screens and distances. In doing so, they embark on a journey towards reimagining what brotherhood can mean in the modern world, creating supportive networks that can lead to lasting change in how they relate to themselves and each other.

What to Look for in a Circle (And What to Avoid)

It's essential to recognise that not every circle cultivates authentic connection and healing. Finding the proper environment is crucial for personal growth and emotional support. Here are some essential characteristics to consider:

Green Flags:

- Trained Facilitators: Seek out leaders who are not only experienced but also trauma-informed. These facilitators should have undergone specific training in emotional support, allowing them to navigate sensitive topics with care and empathy. Their expertise can help create a safe and nurturing space for participants.

- Clear Ground Rules: A well-structured circle should establish clear ground rules that emphasise the importance of safety, confidentiality, and mutual respect. These foundational principles help create an atmosphere where every participant feels valued and secure, enabling open and honest communication.

- Allow Silence: An effective environment should embrace silence as a natural part of the sharing process. Participants may need time to process their thoughts and feelings, and it's crucial that no one feels pressured to speak before they are ready. Allowing moments of silence can deepen reflection and create a more thoughtful dialogue.

- Voluntary Participation: While participation in discussions should be encouraged, it should never be forced. Individuals should feel comfortable simply being present, whether they choose to share or not. This respect for personal autonomy fosters a sense of belonging without the stress of obligation.

Red Flags:

- Performative Leaders: Be cautious of domineering leaders who venture into performative behaviour rather than creating an egalitarian space for all voices. "Alpha" leaders may prioritise their authority over group dynamics, which can stifle individual expression and honest participation.

- Shame-Based Tactics: Avoid environments that resort to shame-based challenges or coerce vulnerability through pressure. Such approaches can lead to mistrust and emotional harm, instead of fostering a supportive atmosphere conducive to healing.

- Hierarchical Dynamics: Genuine brotherhood flourishes in spaces that promote equality. Be wary of any signs of hierarchical dynamics, where some individuals may feel superior to others. A proper healing environment should support each person's right to be heard and valued equally.

A meaningful brotherhood goes beyond merely following healing protocols; it actively cultivates the conditions necessary for organic healing to take place. By being mindful of these green flags and red flags, you can better navigate circles that genuinely support your emotional well-being and personal journey.

The Psychology Behind It

From a counselling perspective, the insights of Carl Rogers underscore the vital importance of unconditional positive regard, the fundamental belief that healing truly begins when an individual is embraced for their authentic self, free from judgment. This principle finds profound resonance in men's circles, where acceptance and support foster an environment conducive to personal growth and emotional healing.

Within these group settings, Jungian archetypes naturally emerge, enriching the collective experience. Figures such as the Wounded Healer, who embodies the transformative power of personal suffering, the Wise Elder, who offers seasoned wisdom and guidance, the Warrior, representing strength and courage, and the Shadow, which reveals the often-unacknowledged aspects of oneself, all invite men to delve deeper into their inner worlds. These archetypes, when reflected back through the experiences and insights of peers, provide invaluable opportunities for men to confront and integrate parts of themselves that have long been suppressed or ignored.

The Internal Family Systems (IFS) model further enriches this exploration by illustrating how men frequently cultivate stoic "manager" roles to protect their most vulnerable aspects from the harsh realities of life. In the safe space of sharing circles, these protective roles can be gently disentangled. Through open dialogue and mutual support, men are encouraged to reconnect with their inner child, the source of their creativity, spontaneity, and genuine emotional expression, free from the fear of judgment or ridicule. This courageous engagement not only fosters individual healing but also strengthens the bonds of brotherhood and understanding among participants, paving the way for deeper connection and collective resilience.

Banter vs. Bonding

Many men often find it easier to engage in humour and light-hearted banter as a mechanism for communication, rather than diving into the depths of authentic honesty and emotional vulnerability. This inclination towards humour serves a vital role as a protective barrier, allowing them to maintain a sense of emotional distance that feels safer. During these interactions, banter becomes a shared language, a tool that facilitates connection without the discomfort of exposing one's true feelings and fears. While this approach can create a semblance of camaraderie, it risks fostering only surface-level relationships. Genuine bonding, however, necessitates a willingness to take emotional risks and confront vulnerabilities head-on.

For many men, the landscape of connection has often been significantly influenced by shared suffering or hardship, rather than a foundation built on safety, openness, and trust. This reality can cultivate what is known as trauma bonding, where intense, challenging experiences are mistakenly equated with deep intimacy and connection. In these contexts, shared struggles create a narrow understanding of friendship. The weight of these hardships can obscure the path to authentic relationships, leading individuals to form connections based on pain rather than mutual support.

In contrast, true brotherhood emerges not from collective experiences of brokenness but from a shared commitment to healing and personal growth. It is in the expansive space of mutual support, understanding, and sincerity that deeper, more meaningful connections are formed. When men can transcend the comfort of banter and embrace their vulnerabilities, they craft a richer tapestry of relationships, one that honours both the light-heartedness found in shared humour and the profound strength discovered in authentic emotional exchanges. Ultimately, such connections not only enhance their bonds but also promote personal growth and emotional well-being, demonstrating the transformative power of vulnerability in building lasting friendships.

Gentle Prompts for Reflection

- How would it feel to occupy a space where no one is trying to "fix" you or change who you are? Imagine a setting where acceptance prevails, allowing you to simply be yourself without the pressure of societal expectations.

- When was the last time you experienced a genuine sense of being seen and understood by another man? Reflect on those moments of connection where your thoughts, feelings, and experiences were fully acknowledged.

- What aspects of your true self do you find difficult to share with others? Consider the vulnerabilities you hold back, whether it's fears, ambitions, or insecurities, and why these parts feel so daunting to reveal.

- In your friendships, have you ever conflated loyalty with remaining silent during challenging times? Explore how this belief might affect your relationships and whether it hinders open, honest communication.

- Which elements of your identity feel most secure and affirmed when you are surrounded by other men? Think about the qualities or experiences that help you feel at ease and connected, fostering a sense of belonging within the group.

Final Reframe:

Remember, achieving clarity can be a profound experience; it allows you to perceive yourself not as a burden or a problem, but as a valuable individual deserving of life, love, and joy. This shift in perspective is transformative, enabling you to embrace your unique essence and potential.

The journey of self-discovery is far from a sign of weakness. It is not merely an indulgence or a fleeting moment of introspection; rather, it serves as a powerful initiation into a deeper understanding of who you are. This process requires courage, vulnerability, and an openness to explore the complexities of your thoughts and emotions.

In the end, one of the bravest actions a person can take is to gather with others in a safe space, where they can courageously voice what they have kept hidden for far too long. By uttering the words "Me too," you not only share your own struggles but also create an avenue for connection and understanding. This simple yet profound statement can foster an atmosphere of empathy and compassion, reminding both you and those around you that, in our shared experiences, we find solace. You are not alone in your journey; through openness, we cultivate healing and the strength that comes from collective support.

Chapter 28

Loving Him Through the Silence — When the Man You Love Is Struggling

When your partner is wrestling with inner turmoil yet struggles to articulate his pain, that unspoken tension can linger heavily in the spaces between you. It hangs there like a storm cloud, suffusing your shared moments with an unshakeable weight. You sense it in the frequent, weary sighs escaping his lips, the heaviness subtly concealed behind the smile that no longer reaches his eyes, and the emotional distance that has shifted from being a comfortable space to an aching absence. This void leaves you feeling eerily alone. Your love for him runs deep; still, you find yourself at a loss, grappling with uncertainty about how to truly reach him during this difficult time.

This chapter is dedicated to the women who recognise these subtle yet profound cracks forming in their relationship, yet feel adrift without a clear guide to navigate the complex landscape of emotional distress. It speaks to those who cautiously tiptoe around their partner's feelings, constantly questioning not only whether he still loves them but also grappling with the burden of their own role in his pain. How can one assist a man who firmly holds back his requests for help, shrouding his struggles in silence?

The harsh reality is this: most men don't reach out for support, often choosing silence over vulnerability. This reluctance doesn't stem from a deficit of trust or love. Instead, it is deeply rooted in societal conditioning, which teaches them that vulnerability is a sign of weakness, a loss of their masculinity. Phrases echoing from childhood, "Man up," "Don't be soft," "Boys don't cry", impose a rigid, rugged exterior, leading many to internalise their suffering rather than express it. For countless men, the act of seeking help is often misconstrued as an admission of defeat, while the notion of breaking down aligns with the fear of being fundamentally broken.

Yet, you see him. You see beyond the silence, recognising the turmoil churning just beneath the surface. You're grappling with an essential question: how can you extend your support to him without neglecting your own emotional well-being? It is a delicate balance, one that requires compassion for both him and yourself. Understanding and patience are essential, as is the realisation that while you can be there for him, you must also remain anchored in your own feelings. This journey may be challenging, but your willingness to engage in it speaks volumes about your love and commitment.

Understanding the Male Mind in Crisis

Understanding His Withdrawal

When men encounter mental or emotional struggles, their reactions often diverge sharply from societal expectations. Rather than openly expressing sorrow through tears or seeking solace through conversation, many choose to withdraw into themselves. This retreat can easily be misconstrued as personal rejection, yet it is often a deeply ingrained coping mechanism. In these moments, he seeks refuge in solitude, a space where he can feel a semblance of control amid inner turmoil.

Signs of Withdrawal

Understanding the signs of withdrawal can help in navigating this complex emotional landscape. Key indicators include:

- Diminished Expression: A noticeable quietness prevails; his laughter and voice become less frequent, leaving an echoing silence.
- Decreased Affection: A sudden withdrawal from physical affection may occur, which can naturally lead you to question his feelings and commitment.

- Avoidance of Intimacy: He may shy away from eye contact and avoid deep conversations, opting instead for superficial interactions that don't demand emotional investment.
- Excessive Busyness: He might immerse himself in work or hobbies as a distraction, using busyness to avoid confronting his thoughts and emotions.
- Mood Instability: An observable increase in irritability or frustration may manifest, with mood swings that seem abrupt and uncharacteristic.
- Altered Sleep Patterns: His sleep habits may shift drastically, whether he's oversleeping in an attempt to escape reality or struggling through sleepless nights filled with anxious thoughts.

His withdrawal is not an indication that he is shutting you out; instead, it reflects his attempt to create a barrier against a world that feels overwhelmingly heavy and chaotic.

The Challenge of Communication

The struggle for many men when it comes to emotional expression is often rooted in the cultural narratives they internalise from a young age. Growing up, they frequently encounter societal messages that equate emotional vulnerability with weakness. This deeply embedded belief system teaches them to suppress their feelings, leaving many at a loss for words when faced with emotional turmoil.

Even if there exists a genuine desire to open up, they may find themselves lacking the necessary vocabulary to articulate their pain and struggles. Additionally, the fear of being misunderstood or judged can be paralysing, leading him to opt for silence rather than risk vulnerability. This conundrum leaves both partners in a difficult position, craving connection and understanding yet often unable to bridge the emotional gap.

Recognising these patterns can foster greater compassion and patience in the relationship, encouraging a supportive environment where he may eventually feel safe enough to share the emotional battles he faces.

He Still Loves You, even if He Can't Show It

Understanding the dynamics of emotional distance in relationships is crucial. It's essential to recognise that when he pulls away, it doesn't necessarily mean he loves you any less. For many men, this isolation stems from a misguided belief that separating themselves can shield those they care about from their internal struggles. They often feel that by withdrawing, they are preventing you from bearing the weight of their challenges. Still, this tactic can inadvertently create a deep sense of disconnection in the relationship.

To navigate this situation effectively, it's essential to look beyond his behaviour and try to comprehend the emotional turmoil he may be experiencing beneath the surface. This requires patience and empathy, as well as a willingness to engage in open communication when he's ready. Acknowledging what he might be going through can provide you with a clearer perspective and help you find meaningful ways to offer support.

At the same time, it's equally important to prioritise your own emotional health during this process. Balancing your well-being with his needs is vital; it allows you to remain grounded and present, ensuring that you're able to support him without compromising your own mental and emotional stability. Remember, self-care isn't selfish—it equips you to navigate the complexities of the relationship more effectively and compassionately. By taking care of yourself, you create a healthier dynamic where both individuals can grow and thrive together.

What Not to Do

1. Don't Take It Personally

It's crucial to grasp that your partner's struggles with mental health are not a reflection of your own worth or the overall value of your relationship. When he experiences feelings of inadequacy or emotional withdrawal, these issues often originate from within himself rather than being caused by anything you've done or said. Taking his silence or distance as a direct affront may intensify his feelings of guilt and shame, which can lead to even greater isolation. Instead, remind yourself that his mental health challenges are a complex battle he's facing internally and, importantly, not a judgment of your love or commitment.

2. Don't Try to "Fix" Him

In your role as a partner, it's essential to understand that you are there to support, not to play the role of a therapist or healer. Attempting to "fix" your partner can inadvertently convey that he is somehow broken or inadequate, reinforcing the notion that he is a project needing repair rather than an individual worthy of love and acceptance as he is. Healing from trauma is a deeply personal journey; it requires professional intervention and personal work. Instead of trying to solve his problems, focus on being a consistent, caring presence in his life. Listen empathetically, validate his feelings, and encourage him to seek the help he needs, all while showing him that he is valued and loved just as he is.

3. Don't Shame or Compare

When your partner opens up about his feelings, it's vital to approach the conversation with sensitivity and empathy. Avoid using comparisons or minimising his experiences by saying things like, "Other people have it worse" or "Why can't you just talk to me?" Such statements can inadvertently deepen his sense of shame, making him feel misunderstood and further alienated. Remember that each person's emotional landscape is unique; what may seem insignificant to one may be monumental to another. Acknowledging and validating his feelings is key to fostering a supportive environment. Show him that his emotions matter and that you're there to walk alongside him on his journey.

What You Can Do

1. Hold Space, Not Pressure

Creating a safe emotional environment is essential for fostering open communication and trust. Let him know through your presence that you are there for him, without imposing the expectation of immediate explanations or responses. Simple affirmations can offer reassurance that your support is unwavering. Phrases like, "You don't have to talk right now, but I'm here whenever you feel ready," or "You're not alone; I see you even in your silence," can bring comfort during difficult times. This act of being present, without pressure, can provide a profound sense of healing and solidarity, allowing him to feel safe in his vulnerability.

2. Understand the Language of Withdrawal

Withdrawal can manifest in various ways, often appearing as mundane activities like walking the dog, scrolling through social media, or simply sitting in silence. These actions may serve as his methods of communication or coping mechanisms rather than outright disengagement. By recognising that these moments of quiet or distraction can be forms of connection, you will be better equipped to bridge the emotional distance that sometimes arises. It's valuable to interpret these behaviours as opportunities for understanding and connection rather than signs of disconnect.

3. Encourage Help Without Shaming

If the topic of therapy or seeking professional help arises, approach it with care and compassion, consciously avoiding accusatory or judgmental language. Instead of saying, "You need help," express your love and concern by phrasing it as, "I care about you deeply and want to help you through this. Do you think talking to someone could be beneficial for both of us?" Sharing articles or insights about mental health that resonate with your experiences can also gently open the door for these essential conversations, normalising the idea of seeking support without applying undue pressure or stigma.

4. Learn His Triggers

Understanding what specific stressors lead to his withdrawal is crucial for fostering a supportive environment. These can range from work deadlines and family tensions to personal insecurities. By becoming aware of these triggers, you can respond with empathy and foresight, anticipating moments when he might be feeling overwhelmed. Recognising patterns in his emotional reactions not only helps you understand him better but also allows you to create a nurturing atmosphere that pre-empts potential negative spirals before they begin.

5. Mirror Calm

Your emotional state can have a significant impact on his. When he feels overwhelmed or anxious, your calm and composed presence can serve as a reassuring beacon. This doesn't mean you should suppress or ignore your own feelings; instead, grounding yourself enables you to be a stabilising influence in his turbulent moments. Your ability to maintain composure can act as an anchor, helping him navigate his emotions and providing a sense of stability amid chaos.

6. Offer Choices, Not Commands

Rather than issuing directives such as "You need to do this," consider reframing your approach by presenting options. Utilise phrases like, "What do you need right now?" or "Would it help to take some time for ourselves, or would you prefer to spend time together?" This empowers him to express his needs and desires, fostering a collaborative rather than confrontational dynamic. By offering choices, you create a sense of agency and mutual respect, allowing him to feel more in control of the situation while strengthening your connection.

When You're Burning Out Too

Supporting someone you love through their pain can be an emotionally demanding journey, often leading to compassion fatigue. It's essential to recognise that while you can care deeply for someone, it is equally vital to carve out time and space for your own emotional well-being.

Signs You're Burning Out:

- Resentment and Frustration: You may find yourself feeling increasingly resentful or frustrated, not only at the situation but potentially at the person you are trying to support. This can create an emotional distance in your relationship.

- Constant Anxiety or Exhaustion: If you notice a persistent feeling of anxiety, fatigue, or being overwhelmed, it's a clear indication that your emotional reserves are running low.

- Neglecting Personal Needs and Interests: When you become so immersed in caring for someone else, you might lose sight of your own needs, interests, and passions. This neglect can lead to a sense of identity loss and unhappiness.

Many supportive partners inadvertently fall into the "rescuer trap," assuming full responsibility for their partner's emotional well-being. However, it's vital to remember that you can't pour from an empty cup; when your own emotional resources are depleted, neither you nor your loved one can thrive.

What You Can Do:

- Seek Support for Yourself: Engaging in therapy, counselling, or support groups can provide you with a safe space to process your feelings. Sharing your experiences with others who understand can offer new insights and alleviate some of the pressure you may feel.

- Set Emotional Boundaries Without Guilt: Establishing limits on how much emotional support you can provide is not a sign of weakness; it's an act of self-care. By setting boundaries, you promote a healthier dynamic where both partners can share responsibility for emotional wellness.

- Prioritise Solo Time for Recharging: Make it a priority to spend quality time alone, engaging in activities that rejuvenate your spirit. This could include hobbies you enjoy, physical exercise, meditation, or simply taking a walk in nature. These moments of solitude can help you gain clarity and restore your emotional strength.

Remember, being strong for someone else does not mean sacrificing your own emotional health. Prioritising your well-being is essential, as nurturing yourself enables you to offer genuine support to those you love. Only when you are in a stable emotional state can you truly be there for others in a meaningful way.

If He Refuses Help

Sometimes, despite your gentle and well-meaning offers of support, he may resist seeking the assistance he needs. Navigating this complex situation can be particularly challenging; here's a thoughtful approach to handling it with both care and understanding.

1. Know Your Limits

It's crucial to recognise that you cannot desire his healing more than he does. While your intention is to provide unwavering support, you must acknowledge the boundary that exists between offering help and taking on the full weight of his struggles. Understand that you can provide a listening ear, empathy, and emotional space, but you cannot shoulder the burden of his pain alone. By clearly defining your limits, you protect not only his well-being but also your own mental health. This understanding enables you to be there for him without losing yourself in the process.

2. Focus on Safety

If there are indications of emotional, verbal, or physical abuse within the relationship, maintaining your safety and well-being must be your top priority. Love should never come at the expense of your personal health and security. Establishing a safety plan, seeking external support, or confiding in trusted friends or professionals can be vital steps to ensure your protection. Remember that you deserve to be treated with respect and care in any relationship. It's essential to acknowledge that prioritising your safety is a fundamental act of self-love and self-respect.

3. Hold the Door Open

Even if he isn't ready to accept help right now, your consistent compassion can serve as a catalyst for change in the future. Healing often begins in hindsight, when the burden of pain becomes too overwhelming to carry alone. By maintaining an open, non-judgmental presence, you create a safe environment that encourages him to seek support when he feels ready. Your willingness to be there, without pressure, can be incredibly powerful. It signals to him that change is possible and that he is not alone in his struggles.

4. It's Okay to Walk Away

Choosing to step away from a relationship that undermines your well-being is not a failure or betrayal; rather, it is an act of courage and self-preservation. Love, while profound, should not require you to endure discomfort, emotional instability, or neglect of your own needs. Walking away can be an empowering decision, allowing you to reclaim your peace and pursue healthier relationships that honour your worth. By prioritising your own emotional health, you create the opportunity for personal growth and fulfilment, paving the way for healthier connections in the future.

Closing: Love as Witness, Not Fixer

Loving a man who grapples with mental health struggles is a profoundly sacred act, akin to walking alongside him on a path filled with both shadows and light. It means choosing to be present with him during his most challenging moments, even when the silence between you is thick with unspoken pain, a reminder of the weight he carries. In these times, your steadfast support serves as a powerful affirmation that vulnerability does not diminish his value as a person; your affection is not contingent on his ability to meet societal standards of perfection.

As a partner, you hold the transformative power to act as a mirror, reflecting back not only his humanity but also the complexity of his strengths and struggles. By acknowledging both the light and the darkness within him, you help him see himself with greater clarity and compassion. Yet, this journey of reflection must be reciprocal. It's crucial that this mirror also reflects your own experiences and feelings, allowing you to engage in necessary self-reflection and self-care.

To truly support him in finding his way to the light, it's vital to ensure that you never dim your own spirit. Prioritise your well-being and personal growth; engaging in activities that nurture your own happiness and resilience will empower you to be a more supportive partner. Together, you can navigate the intricacies of love, understanding that while his journey may be fraught with challenges, your love can be a beacon of hope, not just for him, but for both of you as you forge a more profound connection amidst the complexities of life.

Gentle Prompts for Partners

- What emotional and practical burdens am I currently carrying that aren't truly mine to bear, and how can I begin to let go of those responsibilities for my own well-being?
- In what ways can we actively create an environment of open communication and mutual support within our relationship, ensuring that both of our needs are met and acknowledged?
- During which moments do I experience a profound sense of connection with him, and conversely, when do I sense a distance or disconnect between us? What specific situations or actions contribute to these feelings?
- What specific emotional and psychological needs do I have to feel safe, genuinely seen, and fully supported in this partnership? How can I express these needs clearly to foster understanding and intimacy?

Affirmation for Partners

"I am a witness, not a rescuer. In this role, I consciously choose to offer love that honours both his journey and my own well-being. His pain is a personal battle that I cannot take on as my own to heal, but I can stand by him with a heart full of compassion, clarity, and unwavering strength. While I extend my support, I also make it a priority to nurture my own light, ensuring that I maintain my own balance and resilience. This approach allows me to provide meaningful companionship, fostering a space where he feels understood and valued, yet reminded that his path is uniquely his to navigate."

Chapter 29

The Inner Reconciliation — Masculine and Feminine Integration

Where the War Ends: The Masculine-Feminine Reunion

He was never meant to choose between strength and softness, between fire and water, between the unwavering act of showing up and the profound depth of his feelings. Yet, that's precisely the dichotomy the world imposed upon him. Society's rigid expectations echoed relentlessly in his ears, proclaiming, "Be a man." However, no one took the time to teach him how to honour and nurture the fragile boy still residing within him, the one full of hopes, dreams, and vulnerabilities.

In the eyes of the world, he was celebrated for his unwavering control, stoicism, and toughness, hailed as a bastion of resilience that others turned to for strength amid adversity. Yet, there were harsh penalties for exhibiting empathy; moments of stillness, introspection, and the courage to surrender were met with disapproval, as if such traits were weaknesses in a world that prized relentless strength above all. To navigate this societal pressure, he crafted two distinct personas, each reflecting the conflicting expectations placed upon him.

One persona, forged in the crucible of relentless ambition, protective instincts, and a logical mindset, thrived in the spotlight, often pushing him to excel and succeed at any cost. This figure became a shield, fiercely guarding against the perceived vulnerability that came with showing emotion. In stark contrast, the other persona, characterised by intimacy, intuition, and tenderness, was relegated to the shadows, buried deeply under

419

the weight of performance, shackled by the chains of shame, and shrouded in silence.

This internal division epitomises the profound wound of modern masculinity, a complex struggle that many men face in a society that often fails to embrace the full spectrum of human experience. The journey toward healing commences not with choosing one side over the other, but with the courageous act of embracing both aspects fully. It is in this integration that true strength lies, allowing him to emerge as a whole person, capable of vulnerability and connection, while still harnessing the power that comes with resilience and determination. Only then can he begin to dismantle the rigid constructs that confine him, paving the way for a more authentic existence that honours both his strength and his softness.

The Psychological Divide: Attachment and Inner Polarity

The concepts of masculine and feminine energies extend far beyond the confines of biological gender; they represent archetypal forces that exist within the psyche of every individual, regardless of their gender identity. Psychologically speaking, many boys are raised in environments where emotional safety is intricately tied to their ability to conform to societal expectations of masculinity. When early attachment figures, such as parents or caregivers, exhibit emotional inconsistency or withdraw affection during moments of vulnerability, boys quickly learn that exhibiting their true feelings or seeking closeness can be fraught with danger.

As a result, to protect themselves from perceived emotional threats, these boys may adopt a defence mechanism that involves a hyper-identification with traditionally masculine traits. They start to prioritise actions such as doing, fixing, and performing, often at the expense of exploring or embracing their feminine qualities, traits that encompass being, feeling, and receiving. This internalised split leads to a frequently rigid and stoic persona, which becomes a shield against vulnerability.

Over time, this psychological division becomes deeply entrenched, causing the man not only to disown his own softness and vulnerability but also to project wariness upon those who exhibit these traits. As he has rejected these qualities within himself, he begins to distrust them in others, fostering a cycle of emotional disconnection. This dynamic can hinder meaningful relationships and prevent the development of a more balanced emotional landscape, where both masculine and feminine energies coexist harmoniously.

Carl Jung and the Inner Anima

Carl Jung articulated a profound concept in understanding the human psyche: every man possesses an Anima, which symbolises his inner feminine aspect. This Anima embodies qualities typically associated with femininity, such as emotionality, intuition, and nurturing and is integral to a man's overall psychological health. When men suppress this aspect of themselves, it can lead to emotional rigidity and a disconnect from their authentic selves. They may project unacknowledged emotions onto others, distorting their relationships and hindering personal growth. Jung poignantly observed, "Only the wounded physician heals," suggesting that embracing one's vulnerabilities is essential for proper healing and self-understanding.

By reconnecting with his Anima, a man embarks on a transformative journey toward wholeness. This journey doesn't diminish his masculinity; rather, it enriches it. He learns to experience his emotions without becoming overwhelmed, to lead with empathy rather than dominance, and to love genuinely without clinging or attempting to control. This more profound connection with the Anima allows a man to access a broader emotional range and fosters healthier, more fulfilling relationships.

Furthermore, Jung warned against the Shadow, which encompasses the unacknowledged, disowned, or denied facets of our psyche. Often, the very traits that men disdain in others, such as vulnerability, emotional sensitivity, and softness, are the characteristics they have been conditioned to fear or suppress within themselves. This fear can lead to a cycle of self-punishment and rejection. The process of integration involves a courageous journey of reclaiming and accepting these shadowed parts of the self. Rather than allowing these traits to manifest destructively, men can learn to embrace them as integral components of their identity.

This reclamation fosters profound personal growth and enhances their ability to connect meaningfully with others. By bridging the divide between the masculine and feminine aspects within themselves, men can cultivate a sense of balance that ultimately enriches their lives and relationships. Embracing both the Anima and the Shadow leads to a more complete, authentic existence. In this state, men are not only stronger in their masculinity but also more compassionate and understanding toward themselves and those around them.

Trauma and the Ego Split: Understanding the Fear of Vulnerability

"Trauma is not what happens to you. Trauma is what happens inside you." – Gabor Maté.
When love feels unsafe, the nervous system instinctively faces a critical dilemma: to protect or to perish. To shield themselves from emotional pain, many men unconsciously develop protective ego defences, such as:

Narcissistic Shields: This defence manifests as a tendency to conflate admiration with genuine love. It often arises from a deep-seated need to project an image of invulnerability and strength. For many, being perceived as strong becomes synonymous with feeling secure, leading to a self-reinforcing cycle where authentic emotional connection is overshadowed by the pursuit of external validation. As a result, relationships may lack depth, with partners feeling more like admirers than genuine companions.

Shame Collapse: This pattern is characterised by emotional withdrawal, where individuals become convinced that they are unworthy of love unless they adhere to a façade of perfection. This belief, often rooted in past experiences of rejection or ridicule, prompts a retreat into a protective shell, stifling genuine emotions and authentic connections. The layers of shame that accumulate create a barrier to vulnerability, making it difficult for them to engage in intimacy or seek support from others.

It is vital to understand that these defensive patterns are not simply character flaws; they are survival mechanisms developed in response to past traumas. These coping strategies, while initially protective, can hinder the opportunity for emotional growth and connection. Merely surviving does not equate to a rich and fulfilling life. Acknowledging and addressing these patterns is essential for fostering deeper, more meaningful relationships and embracing the full spectrum of human experience.

Biopsychology of Reconnection: The Role of Safety in Emotional Integration

The nervous system plays a crucial role in facilitating emotional integration and reconnection among individuals. According to Polyvagal Theory, true love can only be fully experienced when one is in the ventral vagal state, characterised by a profound sense of safety, connection, and the capacity for co-regulation with others. This state allows individuals to engage with their emotions and those of others in a way that fosters intimacy and authentic connection.

However, many men find themselves stuck in maladaptive responses known as the dorsal vagal shutdown or the sympathetic arousal state. The dorsal vagal shutdown is often experienced as emotional numbness or incapacitating withdrawal, wherein individuals feel disconnected from their emotions and from others. In contrast, the sympathetic arousal state manifests through heightened feelings of anger, anxiety, and agitation. This emotional dysregulation contributes to a common perception among men that love is inherently unsafe.

Paradoxically, this perception stems not from love itself being a threat, but rather from the way love can mirror the chaos of earlier life experiences that were traumatic or distressing.

Dr. Dan Siegel's concept of the Window of Tolerance further elucidates this issue by illustrating that emotional intimacy exists within a relatively narrow band of emotional states. When men experience triggering situations, such as conflict, vulnerability, or the fear of rejection, they often find themselves moving outside of this window. This may result in extreme responses: they might withdraw entirely, shutting down emotionally, or they may erupt in frustration or anger, reacting disproportionately to the situation at hand. The overarching goal of emotional integration is to expand this Window of Tolerance, allowing individuals to experience a broader range of emotions more healthily. By doing so, they can foster greater emotional resilience, improve interpersonal relationships, and cultivate an authentic capacity for love and connection.

Hormones of Wholeness: The Biological Factors at Play

Understanding the physiological foundations of emotional expression is essential for fostering deeper interpersonal connections. Research indicates that oxytocin, often referred to as the bonding hormone, increases gradually in men compared to women. This disparity can hinder men's ability to form profound emotional bonds and connections, as oxytocin plays a pivotal role in promoting feelings of trust and intimacy.

Moreover, the influence of testosterone can create barriers to emotional openness. Elevated testosterone levels are often associated with traditional masculine behaviours that prioritise stoicism over vulnerability, making it difficult for some men to express their emotions authentically. Compounding these challenges, cortisol, often called the stress hormone, can surge during periods of high stress. This reaction is particularly pronounced when vulnerability is perceived as a potential risk, leading to an instinctual withdrawal from emotional sharing.

To navigate and harmonise these complex biological systems, men are encouraged to actively practice co-regulation. Co-regulation involves engaging in mindful activities that facilitate emotional connection and well-being. Techniques such as controlled breathing can help mitigate stress responses and promote a sense of calm. Being fully present in the moment fosters mindfulness, allowing for genuine interactions. Gentle touch, whether through a comforting hug or a reassuring hand, can also signal safety and support. Furthermore, mutual emotional attunement with loved ones, being attuned to one another's emotions and needs, creates a foundation for deeper understanding and connection. By incorporating these practices, men can cultivate healthier emotional habits and strengthen their relationships.

Cultural Constructs: Navigating Societal Expectations

Cultural narratives play a significant role in shaping how men express their emotions, often placing them under intense societal pressures that can be detrimental to their emotional well-being. For instance, Black men frequently navigate the expectation to embody a façade of invincibility, which can lead to a reluctance to show vulnerability or seek help. This pressure to appear strong can prevent them from fully engaging in emotional connections, both with themselves and others.

Queer men often face a different yet equally challenging set of societal standards, where expressing softness or vulnerability can be met with stigma and shaming. In many cases, they are pressured to conform to hypermasculine ideals, making it challenging to embrace and communicate their emotions openly. This creates a conflicting narrative where being true to oneself is at odds with the fear of societal judgment.

Additionally, working-class men are conditioned to prioritise survival and economic stability, often viewing emotional expression as a luxury they cannot afford. This perspective is rooted in a historical context where emotional stoicism is valued as a means of confronting hardship. The overarching message in these narratives emphasises the need to produce, protect, and prove oneself, ultimately establishing barriers that inhibit authentic emotional connection.

In light of these complex dynamics, it is crucial to recognise that the pursuit of love that is contingent upon performance or specific behaviours is inherently flawed. Authentic love is not a reward to be earned through achievements or strength; rather, it is a natural experience that benefits from vulnerability and mutual sharing. As bell hooks insightfully articulated, "Love is an action, never simply a feeling." This perspective invites us to redefine love not as a transaction but as an active process grounded in acceptance, compassion, and emotional availability.

The Coaching Lens: Practical Questions for Rebuilding Emotional Frameworks

Life coaching offers a profoundly supportive environment where men can begin to unravel the complexities of their identities and societal expectations. It serves as a transformative space for introspection and growth by encouraging individuals to explore vital questions that challenge traditional notions of masculinity. Some thought-provoking inquiries include:

- Where am I over-performing masculinity at the expense of living my authentic truth? This question invites reflection on the ways societal standards might compel men to adopt behaviours that mask their true selves, pushing them to prioritise performance over authenticity.

- What instances in my past have taught me that softness is punishable? This prompts a deep dive into personal history, exploring moments that may have communicated the message that vulnerability and emotional expression are weak, thus shaping one's self-perception.

- How does the integrated version of myself feel, not just in terms of appearance, but in emotional depth? This encourages exploration beyond the surface, asking individuals to consider what it truly means to be whole, and how emotional richness and self-acceptance enhance overall well-being.

- What emotional legacy do I aspire to leave for the next generation of men in my life? Here, men are prompted to think about the values and emotional intelligence they wish to impart, shaping a future where vulnerability and authenticity are celebrated rather than shunned.

Through coaching, individuals can reframe their understanding of masculinity, moving beyond the traditional roles of protector and provider. It encourages the development of an authentic presence that creates a sense of safety and trust, both internally within oneself and externally in relationships and communities. This journey not only enhances personal relationships but also contributes to a healthier, more compassionate understanding of what it means to be a man in today's world.

Rehearsing Wholeness: Integrative Practices for Emotional Integration

To support the journey towards wholeness and a more integrated understanding of identity, several transformative practices can be employed:

- Mirror Work: Stand in front of a mirror and, with intention, recite affirmations such as, "It is safe for me to hold both strength and softness." This practice allows for the internalisation of the duality of masculinity, encouraging self-acceptance and fostering a compassionate dialogue between different aspects of oneself. By affirming these qualities aloud, one begins to break down barriers and embrace a broader definition of what it means to be masculine.

- Somatic Journaling: Dedicate time to reflect on physical sensations associated with tenderness and vulnerability. As you write, pay attention to how these feelings manifest in your body—whether it's a warmth in your chest or a lightness in your limbs. This exercise not only enhances body awareness but also deepens the connection between emotional experiences and physical states, allowing for a richer understanding of one's emotional landscape.

- Internal Family Systems (IFS) Visualisation: Engage in a dialogue between the 'masculine part' and the 'feminine part' within yourself. Begin by finding a quiet space and visualising each aspect as a character. What does the masculine part look like? How does it express itself? What are its strengths and fears? Conversely, explore the feminine part and its unique qualities. Invite both aspects to communicate their needs and desires to one another, fostering a deeper understanding and collaboration between these sometimes opposing forces.

- Shadow Dialogue: Identify a part of yourself that you have long rejected or ignored. Write a letter from this shadow aspect, articulating its truths and emotions. What fears, desires, or messages does this part wish to communicate? This exercise can lead to valuable insights, as it encourages recognition and acceptance of the parts of oneself that are often considered unworthy or shameful.

- Embodiment Rituals: Experiment with alternating between power poses, such as standing tall with hands on hips, and surrendered postures, like sitting with your head bowed or lying down with arms open. Take note of how these physical expressions impact your emotional state and self-perception. This practice encourages exploration of how strength and vulnerability coexist within the same body, promoting a sense of balance and wholeness.

By engaging in these practices, men can cultivate a nuanced understanding of self, integrating both strength and vulnerability as essential components of their identity. This approach not only enhances personal growth but also fosters healthier relationships with others, as it encourages authenticity and emotional openness.

Narrative Therapy: Rewriting the Masculine Myth

You are not solely defined by your past experiences or the expectations imposed by society; you hold the power to be the author of your own narrative, shaped by your choices and intentions. Embrace this unique opportunity to rewrite your story with unwavering conviction and genuine authenticity. Allow this new chapter to resonate intensely, reflecting both your strength and your vulnerability:

"He was not a diminished man for shedding tears; rather, he emerged as a whole man, courageously exploring the depths of his emotions. Each tear shed was a testament to his resilience, a clearing of the soul that revealed not weakness, but a profound connection to his true self."

"He didn't lose his identity when he embraced love; instead, he embarked on a journey of rediscovery, unearthing the parts of himself that had long been overshadowed by fear and self-doubt. In allowing love to flourish, he found the courage to confront his insecurities, transforming them into stepping stones towards self-acceptance."

"He no longer felt the need to choose between the warrior's fierce strength and the healer's compassionate heart; instead, he learned to embody both elements, harmonising their powerful qualities. With the warrior's determination complemented by the healer's empathy, he forged a new path, a balanced identity that radiated confidence and compassion, reflecting the multifaceted nature of his being."

Legacy of Balance: What He Teaches Without Speaking

A man who harmonises both the masculine and feminine energies within himself evolves into a powerful force for good, embodying a rich tapestry of qualities that enhance his relationships and contribute to his community:

- As a partner, he listens deeply, offering undivided attention and profound empathy. He leads with unwavering integrity, navigating challenges with a steady hand while creating a supportive space where both partners feel valued and heard. His ability to engage in open, honest communication fosters trust and intimacy, enriching the bond he shares with his loved one.

- As a father, he stands as a steadfast protector, exemplifying strength and resilience. Yet, he also embraces his nurturing side, knowing how to soothe and provide gentle affection. By creating a safe emotional haven, he encourages his children to express themselves freely, allowing them to explore their identities and emotions without fear of judgment.

- As a son, he sheds the need for external validation through performance or achievements. Instead, he embarks on a journey of self-discovery, living his truth authentically. Through this authenticity, he reflects unconditional love to those around him, fostering deeper connections with family and loved ones and encouraging them to embrace their own truths.

- This evolution is a natural progression from the narratives explored in "The Father Wound" and "The Villain Construct," poignant chapters where men confront their internal conflicts and embark on a transformative journey toward healing. This man's life serves not only as a testament to personal growth but also as a beacon of hope, granting permission for other men to embrace their vulnerabilities, explore their emotions, and embark on their paths of integration. His journey exemplifies that true strength lies in balance and authenticity, inspiring others to break free from societal constraints and redefine what it means to be a man.

Final Reframe: Integration Is Not Weakness. It Is Mastery.

You are not required to forsake or diminish your masculine traits to embrace your feminine side; these elements of your identity can coexist in a rich and fulfilling way. Similarly, connecting with your deeper emotions does not mean you have to abandon rational thought; in fact, these facets of yourself can beautifully complement one another. You don't have to choose between exhibiting strength and embodying nurturing qualities; instead, you can harmoniously integrate both, creating a more complete and resilient self.

Real men understand the importance of rejecting societal pressures that promote internal division. They bravely reclaim all aspects of their being, including those that have been conditioned or suppressed due to fear or societal expectations. In doing so, they embark on a journey of self-healing and growth, ultimately becoming the holistic figures that the world genuinely longs for.

This journey manifests in three essential ways:

- Wholeness: They embrace every dimension of their identity, acknowledging both their masculine and feminine traits, and doing so without shame. This acceptance fosters inner peace and confidence.
- Presence: They commit to living fully in the moment, engaging with their surroundings and the people in their lives. This presence allows for deeper connections and a richer understanding of their experiences.

- Authenticity: They strive to show up as their genuine selves, unguarded and unapologetic. By being authentic, they inspire others to do the same, leading to collective healing and growth within their communities.
- By embodying these qualities, men not only enrich their own lives but also contribute to a more compassionate and understanding society.

Chapter 30

The Masculine Rebirth — A New Path, A New Legacy

Where the Ashes Turn to Soil

Every ending opens a doorway to new beginnings, and this moment signifies not the death of masculinity but its profound rebirth into a form that resonates with authenticity and depth. This transformation is not about perpetuating the aggressive archetype that society often celebrates, nor is it a mere echo of what remains after shame and fragility. Instead, it emerges as something sacred, grounded in reality, unshakable in conviction, and expansively open to the full spectrum of human experience.

This new manifestation of masculinity breaks free from the chains of performative expectations, power struggles, and inherited pain, instead taking root in a purposeful existence infused with meaning. It invites men to embrace vulnerability as strength and to redefine success beyond societal metrics.

The journey of masculine rebirth begins when a man consciously shifts his focus from the crippling question of "Am I enough?", a question that often breeds insecurity and comparison to a more empowering inquiry: "What legacy do I wish to leave for future generations?" This profound shift not only transforms individual lives, fostering personal growth and fulfilment, but it ultimately has the power to alter the very fabric of society, leading to more compassionate and equitable interpersonal dynamics.

As men begin to explore what it means to embody this new masculinity, they discover the strength in collaboration over competition, the courage to express their emotions freely, and the wisdom in fostering connections that uplift rather than diminish. In doing so, they pave the way for younger generations to inherit a world where masculinity is defined by respect, responsibility, and resilience, where, indeed, the ashes of the past turn into fertile soil for a brighter, more inclusive future.

From Survival to Sovereignty

In the journey of trauma recovery, the final stage transcends mere healing; it is an awakening into the realm of creation and self-actualisation. After enduring the profound silence of inner turmoil, the suffocating numbness, the explosive and unchecked rage, and the tumultuous reckoning with deep-seated emotions, there emerges a powerful clarity of vision. This vision does not reflect the man he has been conditioned to be by external pressures and past experiences; rather, it embodies the man he has consciously chosen to become through introspection and personal growth.

This transformative process marks a pivotal shift from merely surviving to embracing a state of sovereign manhood, where he begins to construct his life not as a reaction to past traumas, but as a deliberate expression of his innermost desires and aspirations. In this phase, he realises that true sovereignty entails liberating himself from the shackles of living solely as a response to past pain. Instead, he claims authorship over his narrative, crafting a life that resonates deeply with his core values and beliefs.

No longer driven by the need for validation from others, he discovers the liberation of living authentically. His choices reflect not just who he is on the surface but resonate with the essence of his being. Here, authenticity is not merely an ideal; it becomes a guiding principle, allowing him to navigate the complexities of life with confidence and purpose. In this empowered state, every step forward is a testament to his strength and resilience, as he actively shapes a future that honours both his journey and his truth.

What the New Masculinity Looks Like

The reborn man transcends the limitations of a commercialised persona or a meticulously crafted image; instead, he embodies coherence and authenticity in all aspects of his life. He possesses a profound understanding of his emotions, demonstrating an exceptional level of emotional intelligence that allows him to fully acknowledge and embrace his feelings without judgment or fear. This wisdom enables him to hold space for not only his own emotions but also for those of others, offering a nurturing and supportive environment.

His personal power is not rooted in a desire for domination or control; instead, it flows from an inherent strength that uplifts and inspires everyone around him. He safeguards the well-being of those he loves by establishing healthy boundaries, allowing him to offer his love and support unconditionally while respecting their autonomy.

This man creates not out of a need for external validation or recognition, but from a deep, intrinsic motivation that fuels his passion and purpose. He willingly embraces vulnerability, understanding that true strength lies in being open and honest. He expresses love freely and without hesitation, discarding the emotional armour that many wear to shield themselves. Rather than seeking to impress others, he focuses on making a meaningful and lasting impact in the lives of those he touches. Through his actions and relationships, he embodies the essence of authenticity, compassion, and strength.

Intersectional Insight: Many Paths, One Rebirth

Rebirth does not wear a single face; it is a rich tapestry woven from diverse experiences, histories, and identities. For some men, the concept of legacy may manifest as the profound act of nurturing a child, fostering an environment where they can grow up free from doubt and imbued with an unwavering sense of their own worth and potential. This nurturing goes beyond mere protection; it involves the intentional cultivation of emotional

435

intelligence, empathy, and resilience, ensuring that the next generation is equipped to navigate life's challenges.

For others, rebirth signifies a courageous journey of breaking cycles of generational violence and trauma. It can mean confronting the harsh realities of an upbringing steeped in pain and adversity, where healing becomes both a personal and collective endeavour. This journey often involves deep self-reflection, community support, and perhaps even therapeutic practices, a testament to the strength required to confront deep-seated racial traumas or the scars left by marginalisation.

For a Black man raised in survival mode, rebirth may reveal itself through the invaluable lesson of learning to rest and prioritise self-care for the first time. It involves acknowledging that vulnerability is not a weakness but a strength, enabling him to recharge and grow beyond merely surviving to truly thriving.

In the case of a gay man, this personal renaissance may require reclaiming the beauty of softness, sensitivity, and love, all qualities that have been scorned and ridiculed in a societal framework that often prizes stoicism and aggression. This process of reclamation can serve as a powerful assertion of identity, encouraging an embrace of one's authentic self in the face of societal rejection.

For a man who has navigated the harsh realities of poverty, the pursuit of creating stability within his bloodline may feel like uncharted territory. This quest encapsulates the desire to build a foundation of security and hope for future generations, perhaps through education, entrepreneurship, or community engagement. It's a commitment to transforming the narrative of his family's legacy from one of struggle to possibility, paving the way for a brighter future.

Ultimately, this transformative process transcends the personal; it is deeply ancestral, cultural, and resonates on a global scale. It invites all men, regardless of their beginnings, to envision and embody their own unique paths of rebirth, encouraging them to honour their past while forging a new narrative that encompasses strength, healing, and hope. Each journey is a testament to resilience, illustrating a collective movement towards a more inclusive and understanding world.

Bio-psychology of Becoming: Hormones of Vision and Legacy

In this transformative journey of rebirth, biology is reimagined as a potent catalyst for personal growth rather than a restrictive constraint. Testosterone, traditionally viewed as a hormone synonymous with dominance and aggression, is reframed to serve as a vital source of motivational energy. This energy fuels a renewed sense of direction and purpose, steering one toward constructive ambitions rather than destructive impulses. Meanwhile, oxytocin, once regarded with trepidation as a marker of vulnerability, emerges as the essential connective tissue that nurtures deep, meaningful relationships with others, fostering a sense of belonging and trust.

Cortisol, often labelled the hormone of stress and urgency, no longer wields authoritative control over daily life. Instead, the individual learns to implement effective down-regulation techniques, allowing for the mitigation of stressful responses. This mastery elevates dopamine levels, encouraging a joyful engagement with passions and pursuits, all while maintaining balance within one's own Window of Tolerance, a framework that delineates optimal emotional functioning.

As personal development unfolds, he evolves into a thermostat rather than merely a thermometer; he takes an active role in regulating his emotional state while simultaneously influencing the emotional climate around him. Through continuous emotional engagement, the brain undergoes significant reshaping, giving rise to new neural pathways that challenge and ultimately replace the entrenched fight-or-flight responses that once dictated his behaviour. The prefrontal cortex, responsible for higher-order decision-making and impulse control, begins to regain its dominance as the limbic system, the emotional epicentre of the brain, finds its equilibrium.

This journey is a testament to neuroplasticity, the brain's remarkable capacity to reorganise itself based on experiences and practices. It transforms the aspiration for change into a tangible reality through consistent effort, intentional repetition, meaningful rituals, and the courage to embrace emotional vulnerability. Each moment of aligned action contributes to this process of neural reprogramming, reshaping his identity at profound levels.

This is not merely a theoretical exercise; it signifies a profound, embodied biochemical transformation that fundamentally redefines who he is and who he can become. The integration of these biological insights into everyday life catalyses a holistic metamorphosis, empowering him to navigate the complexities of existence with resilience and authenticity.

The Final Shadow: Outgrowing the Wounded Identity

Yet, there exists an unspoken cost to this healing journey, one that often remains hidden from view. To truly attain wholeness, he must confront and ultimately release the survival mechanisms he adopted during both turbulent and challenging times. This transformation involves shedding identities that have served as armor in the face of adversity, such as the tough guy who persistently hides vulnerability, the pleaser who tirelessly seeks validation from others, the numb achiever who disconnects from emotions in relentless pursuit of success, the emotionally distant father who struggled to connect, and the overlooked son who faded into the background of family dynamics.

Healing is not simply about moving forward; it requires an arduous process of outgrowing these versions of himself, the very constructs that once helped him navigate the darkest and most chaotic chapters of his life. Grieving the loss of these identities is an essential step in the healing process. Each one, while flawed, played a crucial role as a protector and saviour during his most challenging times. Acknowledging that these personas served their purpose, albeit imperfectly, is vital as he walks this path.

438

However, it is crucial to understand that the paths to healing and growth cannot be traversed while holding on to the past.

Inevitably, there will be moments when the temptation to revert to old habits looms large. The numbing tactics that once provided him with a façade of control may feel familiar and enticing, offering a deceptive sense of safety. The psychological armour he once wore to shield himself from emotional pain now lingers as a comforting relic, creating a conflict between the safety of the known and the courage required to embrace the unknown. Embracing his rebirth means enduring the discomfort of being fully seen and vulnerable, despite the uncertainty regarding who will choose to stay in his life as he undergoes this transformative journey.

In the depths of this struggle, a shadow whispers insidiously: "It's safer to disappear." Yet, he begins to realise that the concepts of safety and true aliveness are not synonymous. Proper safety lies not in hiding but in authenticity, in allowing himself to feel and experience the depths of his humanity, no matter how daunting it may seem. Embracing vulnerability may lead to new connections and a richer existence, illuminating the path of resilience and personal growth.

Counselling Integration: Post-Traumatic Growth in Male Clients

Research on post-traumatic growth (PTG) uncovers a profound reality: men who skilfully transform adversity into a sense of purpose often undergo significant and multifaceted changes in their lives. These transformations can manifest in several key areas:

- Greater Emotional Authenticity: Through their experiences, these individuals learn to express their true feelings without the lingering fear of judgment. This courageous openness enables the establishment of genuine and deep connections with others, fostering an environment of trust and empathy.

- Re-evaluation of Priorities: Distress can serve as a catalyst for introspection. As a result, what once appeared to be essential, such as material success or societal approval, may shift dramatically. This newfound perspective often leads to heightened self-awareness and a commitment to pursuing more meaningful and fulfilling goals that align with their authentic selves.

- Deeper Spiritual Awareness: Many individuals report a renewed connection to their spiritual or philosophical beliefs following adversity. This may involve a resurgence of faith, the exploration of new spiritual practices, or a profound contemplation of life's meaning. Such spiritual frameworks can offer vital support in understanding and navigating life's challenges, helping them find solace and purpose.

- Stronger Relationships with Peers: As these men open up about their experiences, they often forge deeper and more authentic bonds with family, friends, and peers. This vulnerability not only strengthens their support systems but also encourages others to engage more profoundly, creating a network of mutual understanding and resilience.

- Renewed Commitment to Legacy: Adversity can inspire a powerful desire to make a positive impact on future generations. Many feel compelled to shape a legacy that emphasises connection, authenticity, and compassion, often leading them to engage in mentorship, community service, or other forms of contribution that uplift others.

This transformation is not merely a return to a previous state but signifies a profound evolution, a realisation of their true essence and potential. In this pivotal journey, the role of therapists, coaches, and healers becomes indispensable. Rather than imposing their visions of healing, these professionals create a nurturing space that fosters support and acceptance, allowing the individual to navigate their own path of rebirth. They hold space for the realisation that the individual is no longer broken; instead, they are engaging in a transformative process of becoming, embracing their complexities and emerging with renewed strength and clarity.

Archetypal Integration: Warrior, Lover, Magician, King

In the sacred expanse of the throne room, a reborn man stands as a living embodiment of a profound integration of his past selves, the Warrior, the Lover, and the Magician, all converging to form the essence of the King he is destined to become.

The Warrior, fierce and unyielding, ignites within him a relentless courage that empowers him to face adversities head-on. He draws on a reservoir of inner strength, confronting life's numerous challenges with a heart full of valour and an unshakeable resolve. This archetype not only instils a sense of discipline and determination but also cultivates resilience, enabling him to rise after each fall and to protect what is just.

In contrast, the Lover beckons him to embrace vulnerability, teaching him that true strength is deeply rooted in connection and emotional authenticity. This aspect of his being encourages him to open his heart to celebrate love, nurture relationships, and foster empathy. It is in the warmth of these connections that he finds the foundation of his humanity and the wisdom to balance passion with compassion.

Guiding the way is the Magician, whose deep insights and boundless wisdom enable him to discern the complexities of the world around him. Through a lens of curiosity and understanding, the Magician unveils hidden truths and possibilities, prompting him to question the status quo and explore new realms of thought. This archetype sparks creativity and innovation, allowing him to weave a tapestry of knowledge that enriches his decisions and actions.

Only through the harmonious blend of these archetypes, the Warrior's courage, the Lover's compassion, and the Magician's wisdom, can he fully embrace his rightful role as a King. In this sacred union, he is capable of leading with clarity, compassion, and unwavering integrity, crafting a legacy that reflects not just power, but the profound depth of his journey and the love he shares with his kingdom.

The Legacy Blueprint: What He Leaves Behind

The reborn man envisions a legacy that transcends the confines of his individual existence; he aspires to be a beacon of hope and guidance for future generations, illuminating their paths with wisdom and compassion. Rather than seeking validation through fame or chasing the number of followers he accumulates, he values the profound, lasting impacts of his actions, echoes of his presence that resonate long after he has departed from this world.

He nurtures a son who learns to embrace the full spectrum of his emotions, understanding that tears are not a sign of weakness but rather an essential aspect of humanity. This son grows up to be emotionally intelligent, capable of expressing vulnerability without shame and cultivating empathy towards others.

His daughter emerges as a strong, independent individual, grounded in the knowledge of her inherent worth and capabilities. She is unyielding in her belief that her dreams deserve pursuit, and she embraces challenges with a resilience that empowers her to break barriers and defy societal expectations.

In his partnership, he fosters an environment of unconditional support and trust, where his partner feels a profound sense of safety. She knows she can express her true self without the fear of being silenced or dismissed, allowing for an open dialogue that nurtures both personal growth and mutual understanding.

Ultimately, he strives to create a world that reflects his unwavering values and teachings, even in his absence. His approach to life is marked by a commitment to active listening, ensuring that he creates space for others to share their thoughts and feelings without interruption. He remains present, especially during discomfort, facing difficult conversations head-on with courage and sincerity.

In moments of misstep, he practices humility by offering heartfelt apologies, shedding defensiveness and owning his imperfections. He is dedicated to feeling deeply, showing up consistently for those he loves, and cultivating connections that inspire both strength and resilience. Through his legacy, he aims to foster a sense of belonging and empowerment, encouraging future generations to live authentically and to embrace the beauty of human connection.

Life Coaching Frame: Stepping into Legacy Living

In the context of coaching, a transformative moment often arises, known as the identity shift. This pivotal juncture signifies a significant evolution in personal goals, which begin to metamorphose into guiding principles that shape a profoundly meaningful life. At this critical point, the individual makes a conscious decision to abandon the facade he has constructed, one that previously veiled his pain and grief. Instead, he embarks on the journey of building his life with a foundation of integrity, rooted in truth and authenticity.

This process compels him to engage in deep self-reflection through a series of powerful inquiries that challenge and inspire personal growth. For instance:

-   Who am I without my wounds? This inquiry invites him to explore the essence of his true self, stripped of the narratives of trauma that have long defined his existence. It encourages a courageous confrontation of his vulnerabilities, allowing for the emergence of a more resilient identity that transcends past experiences.

-   What future am I designing with every choice I make today? Here, he begins to appreciate the significant weight of his daily decisions. Each option, whether conscious or unconscious, plays a crucial role in shaping the legacy he aspires to cultivate. By acknowledging this, he shifts from a passive existence to one where he actively participates in creating a future that aligns with his values and desires.

- Who benefits from my becoming whole? This question opens a pathway for him to recognise the broader implications of his healing journey. By understanding that his growth and transformation can foster positive change in the lives of those around him, he begins to view his healing not just as a personal endeavour, but as a catalyst for uplifting others. This perspective cultivates a sense of responsibility and interconnectedness, inspiring him to invest in his own well-being for the sake of his loved ones and community.

Through this profound process, he learns that stepping into his true legacy requires immense courage, a willingness to embrace vulnerability, and a steadfast commitment to emotional honesty. By weaving these qualities into the fabric of his life, he shapes a narrative that not only inspires his journey but also uplifts others, creating a ripple effect of positivity and resilience in the lives he touches.

Practices for Masculine Rebirth

Legacy Letter: Set aside an hour in a peaceful and inspiring environment to compose a deeply heartfelt letter from your future self, envisioning yourself at the age of 85. In this reflective exercise, draw upon the rich tapestry of your life experiences and the insights you've garnered over the years. Contemplate the moments you hold dear, the pivotal lessons you want to share with your present self, and any regrets you wish to acknowledge with compassion. What are the core values and beliefs that you hope will define you and that you want to be remembered for by those you love? This letter will serve as a poignant testament to your journey of growth, aspirations, and the wisdom you wish to impart.

Symbolic Death Ceremony: Select a meaningful object that encapsulates your former self. This could be a piece of clothing that no longer resonates with who you are, a memento from a time in your life you view with regret, or a written memory that reminds you of past struggles. Find a location that feels significant, perhaps a serene natural setting or a quiet corner of your home. Holding the object, take a moment to articulate the emotions attached to it, expressing your gratitude for the lessons it has taught you. As you confront and acknowledge what you're ready to release, you can choose to burn it safely in a fire or bury it in the ground. This act symbolises a powerful severance from that part of your identity, marking a fresh start and a commitment to embrace the person you are becoming.

Affirmation Mirror: Stand before a mirror in a quiet space, and look directly into your own eyes, connecting with your inner self. Recite the affirmation: "I am not who hurt me. I am who I choose to become." Speak these words with conviction and belief, allowing yourself to feel their weight and significance. Repeat this affirmation daily, building a strong and positive self-image. This practice empowers you to shape your identity through intention and resilience, rather than being defined by the pain of your past.

Embodied Visioning: Take a moment to envision your future self with vivid clarity. Stand confidently in a posture that you associate with your ideal future self, a stance that embodies power, relaxation, and confidence. As you engage your physical presence, breathe deeply and practice speaking with the voice that reflects the wisdom and assurance of your envisioned self. Allow these qualities to permeate your demeanour, inspiring your daily actions and guiding your decisions toward the life you aspire to lead.

Daily Impact Check-In: At the close of each day, set aside a few moments to engage in thoughtful reflection. Ask yourself, "What did I stand for today?" Evaluate whether your actions and choices align with your core values and principles. Did you express the qualities you aspire to embody? This daily reflection cultivates a sense of accountability and helps sharpen your focus on living a life that is true to your values and aspirations.

Legacy in Action: Daily Habits of the Reborn Man:

- Emotional Naming: Each morning, take a moment to identify your feelings. Acknowledge their presence and the impact they have on your day. This practice fosters emotional intelligence and a deeper awareness of your emotional landscape.
- Radical Ownership: Commit to exercising radical ownership over at least one decision every day. This could be a choice within your personal life or a professional context. By taking responsibility, you empower yourself and cultivate a more profound sense of autonomy.
- Connection Calls: Dedicate time each week to make one phone call aimed at deepening a meaningful connection, whether it's reaching out to a friend, family member, or colleague. These connections enrich your life and contribute to a supportive network.
- Legacy Projects: Engage in a project that transcends your lifetime, such as planting a tree or initiating a community-focused initiative. By investing in something that will grow and flourish long after you are gone, you shift your focus from immediate rewards to creating a lasting legacy that benefits future generations.

The Final Reframe: The Return of the King

In the rich tapestry of mythology, the King represents the quintessential archetype of mature masculinity. He stands apart from the tyrant, whose reign is fueled by fear and the desire for control, as well as from the coward, who is rendered immobile by self-doubt and insecurity. The King learns from the trials and tribulations of life, integrating those lessons to govern with profound wisdom, genuine compassion, and a mindful presence that inspires those around him.

A true King recognises that his value lies not in conquest or dominance, but in his commitment to serving others and safeguarding the vulnerable. He cultivates an environment where kindness and strength coexist, offering support to loved ones and extending a helping hand to those in need. He embodies this regal energy not through the adornment of a crown, but through everyday actions, exercising integrity in moments of solitude, demonstrating loyalty and care in his relationships, and engaging with the world around him with purpose and authenticity.

With this profound understanding of life's significance, each day becomes an opportunity to live meaningfully. The question then arises: how will you choose to embrace this gift? How will you live each moment, aware that life is not a rehearsal but a precious journey? This consciousness invites us to act with intention, striving to honour the legacy we create through our choices and interactions, ultimately embodying the noble qualities of the King within ourselves.

The journey of masculine rebirth is not a singular event but rather a continuous rite of passage. It requires daily commitment to remembering that wholeness is not synonymous with perfection; it embodies authenticity and realness. You're not striving to be an idealized version of yourself because you are already enough.

Closing Prompt: Your Throne Room Moment

Close your eyes and visualise entering an expansive, tranquil throne room, where the atmosphere hums with reverence and calm. The walls, adorned with intricate craftsmanship, seem to embrace you in a comforting shelter, inviting you to step fully into your authenticity. You stand not merely as a visitor seeking validation but as a sovereign ready to claim your rightful space and identity in this sacred sanctuary. In this moment of reflection, delve deeply into the core of your being, contemplating your values, your passions, and what you

447

staunchly stand for. Allow yourself to feel the weight of your purpose and the essence of your journey as you prepare to declare your legacy.

Now, write your Declaration of Legacy, a single powerful paragraph that begins:

"I am the man who..."

For example: "I am the man who speaks with truth, even when it shakes."

Let this declaration capture your essence and aspirations, becoming a guiding principle for your future.

Authors Chapter

When the Pint Hits the Pain – Talking Man to Man (and Woman)

Let me share something candidly, without sugar-coating it or filtering my words. If you had sat with me in a bustling pub five years ago, you might have seen a confident smile lighting up my face, a pint in my hand, and heard the jokes flowing effortlessly from my lips, as if I were performing in an elaborate comedy routine. But beneath that cheerful facade? I was sinking into a quiet despair. It wasn't an obvious crisis, no dramatic breakdowns or public meltdowns, but rather an insidious, gnawing emptiness that seeped into every corner of my being.

That's the essence of this book. It's not going to delve into airy theories or rehash well-worn self-help clichés. It's about real men navigating the often suffocating silence that surrounds us, grappling with the heavy burdens we've carried for far too long, usually without a single resource to light our way. This chapter isn't tailored for a TED Talk audience; it's raw and unpolished, the kind of truth that emerges when the evening grows late, the joyful noise of the pub fades to a whisper, and bravado slips away like the last remnants of a drunken promise. It's in those quiet moments when it's just you and your closest friends, sharing a drink and finally allowing yourself to voice the truths that have been lodged in your throat, stifled for too long.

And to the women reading this, I urge you to stay close and listen. Approach us not as if unravelling a complex riddle, but with the intent to genuinely understand the weight that life has placed on our shoulders. The outdated stereotypes of masculinity aren't just relics; they are dangerously misleading and emotionally damaging. They continue to influence how we interact with our feelings and the world around us.

We Were Taught to Survive, Not to Feel

Let's face it: many of us were never armoured with emotional tools for navigating life. Instead, we were wrapped in a cloak of societal expectations that dictated our behaviours from a young age. Feeling angry? We were told to "calm down." If we shed a tear, we hear "man up." Longing for comfort earned us the label of "soft." These phrases became mantras that echoed throughout our upbringing, conditioning us to suppress our emotions.

Thus, we learned to lock our feelings away, donning masks of resilience in every situation. We performed flawlessly at work meetings, family events, and social gatherings that seemed functional on the surface but were slowly crumbling beneath. When people looked at us, puzzled by our emotional distance, we were left to wrestle with their confusion. It's not that we don't feel deeply; instead, we were never taught how to navigate our emotions. We were raised to lead, protect, and provide, yet no one showed us how to create a safe space for our own emotions or to foster that safety in others.

What does this upbringing create for a man? An internal pressure cooker, simmering with pent-up feelings and no avenue for release. When we finally reach our boiling point, the consequences can be devastating: we might implode, facing depression or suicidal thoughts, or we might explode outward in rage or emotional withdrawal.

If You've Ever Loved a Man Who Shut Down

This next section speaks directly to the women partners, mothers, sisters, and friends. Have you ever loved a man who seemed to go cold when connection mattered most? The one who retreated into silence at pivotal moments? Who snapped over minor issues or vanished emotionally just when you needed him?

Understand this: he wasn't being unkind. Instead, he was responding to years of conditioning, battling a storm of emotions that felt far too vast to articulate. Behind that stoic exterior lies a man wrestling with grief too profound to name, fear that wraps itself around him like chains, and anger he's unsure how to confront.

This reality isn't an excuse for harmful behaviour, but it does shed light on the silence, the withdrawal, the vacant expressions. It clarifies the moments when he flinches as you reach out or the times he requires a few drinks before he can finally find the courage to voice those deep-seated feelings. Most men aren't intentionally distant; they're just trying to avoid the collapse that feels imminent if they dare to be vulnerable.

The Male Mind: Not Simpler, Just Safer by Default

People often describe men as "simple," but that assertion is a dangerous oversimplification. We're not inherently simple; we're merely guarded. Viewed from a distance, we may appear straightforward, yet this is only due to the conditioning that teaches us to display one dominant colour: strength.

In reality, we resemble a kaleidoscope filled with vibrant hues, emotions spanning the whole spectrum. Yet, somewhere along the way, we were taught that the world only welcomes shades of blue and grey. So we bury our reds and golds deep within, stifling our true selves.

Men process emotions like a slow-cooked stew; they simmer over time, thickening with memories and experiences, ultimately emerging in unpredictable bursts when least expected. Yet, far too often, we resist this outpouring. We fear that sharing our innermost feelings will render us weak or, more importantly, that it will place an emotional burden on those we care about. Instead, we channel our emotions into silence, lost hours at work, the numbing escape of pornography, or the obsessive tracking of sports stats anywhere but into our spoken words.

What I've Learned from Writing This Book

I didn't write this book merely to preach or dispense wisdom; I wrote it out of a deep personal necessity that I believe many can relate to. Each chapter is crafted as a heartfelt conversation, an intimate dialogue I wish I could have shared with my closest friends during my most vulnerable moments. These reflections represent the thoughts and insights I desperately needed to hear while I was busy masking my struggles behind a façade of perfection and composure.

As I embarked on this transformative journey, I experienced a profound realisation. This narrative isn't solely about the pain we endure, but rather about the vast possibilities that lie ahead for each of us. It's about men healing, not by forcing themselves into a mould of someone entirely different, but by courageously embracing their own wholeness, flaws, and authentic selves.

What we truly require isn't a superficial fix or a quick solution to our emotional turmoil. We need to feel understood, to be seen in our entirety, our joys, our sorrows, our complexities. It is essential to cultivate spaces where we can openly discuss our anger without fear of being labelled as aggressive or dangerous. We need environments where shedding tears is not an act of weakness but a healthy expression of our humanity, free from the oppressive weight of shame. We must strive to create communities that offer the safety to voice our loneliness and struggles without the looming threat of ridicule or judgment.

Through these conversations, I hope to foster a sense of solidarity and connection, empowering us to explore not just our struggles, but also the rich tapestry of our shared human experience. Let's work together to build a culture that embraces vulnerability as a strength, inviting healing and authenticity into our lives.

To the Men Reading This

If you've taken the time to read these words, I want you to grasp something profoundly important: there is absolutely nothing wrong with you. Society has a powerful way of conditioning us to remain silent about our struggles, pushing us to project an image of unwavering strength despite our inner turmoil. We often find ourselves caught in a relentless cycle of overwork and self-neglect, mistakenly equating our value with constant productivity and the ability to function under pressure.

However, let me assure you, a different path is not only available but also within your reach. You do not have to stifle your feelings or hide your vulnerabilities to feel secure in this world. It's a common misconception that love must be earned through tireless effort, and that showing any sign of weakness will lead to rejection or judgment. In truth, embracing your emotions, whether they be joy, sadness, anger, or fear, can be an incredible source of strength.

The journey to self-acceptance involves acknowledging that it is entirely possible to be open about your feelings and still command respect from others. You can articulate your truth passionately and stand firm in your beliefs without compromising your integrity. Taking the time to rest and recover, prioritising self-care, and allowing yourself to be human does not diminish your worth; in fact, it enhances it.

Embracing the full spectrum of your emotions allows for a richer, more authentic experience of life. Remember, you are enough just as you are, and taking care of yourself is a vital part of your journey. You deserve to be heard, to feel, and to thrive without the weight of societal expectations holding you back.

To the Women Reading This

You are not imagining things. The distance you feel from your partner is not a reflection of a lack of love or commitment. Instead, it likely arises from his difficulty in forming deep emotional connections, a struggle rooted in his past experiences where he may have faced emotional pain but lacked the tools to navigate it effectively. This reality does not imply that you should shoulder the weight of the relationship single-handedly or take on the responsibility of "fixing" everything that feels broken.

However, consider the possibility of offering him space, not as a means of withdrawal, but as a chance to be fully present, to observe his emotions, and to witness his journey without the urge to intervene or pressure him into changes. In doing so, you might uncover something truly remarkable: the man you love is not stagnant but instead taking significant strides toward becoming the person he has always aspired to be. This process may require patience and understanding, as he learns to navigate his emotions and deepen his connections, allowing him to transform and grow in ways that could strengthen your bond in the long run.

Final Round Before We Go

This moment isn't just the conclusion of a discussion; it signifies the dawn of a meaningful dialogue among men who have grown disillusioned with the superficial roles they've been assigned. It's a call to those who have lost touch with their true selves and a lifeline for women seeking to comprehend the complexities and struggles that men face. It also extends to fathers aspiring to be better role models and sons who are still longing for the reassurance that they are seen, valued, and significant in a world that often overlooks them.

Masculinity isn't in crisis because men are inherently flawed; instead, it's in crisis because the prevailing narrative we've been fed fails to align with our lived experiences and true identities. This disconnection can leave many feeling isolated and misunderstood, as if they are forced to wear a mask that doesn't fit. Perhaps that dominant story never truly encapsulated our essence, and now, more than ever, it is crucial to forge a new narrative, one that celebrates authenticity, vulnerability, and the multifaceted nature of what it means to be a man in today's society.

So now close this book and let's embark on a mission to write a new story together.

About Author

I never set out to be a writer.

For most of my life, I've been the person others lean on during crises, the problem-solver, the housing officer, the probation worker, the individual who stands sentinel between chaos and calm. My career has unfolded in a myriad of challenging environments: prisons filled with desperate individuals, council offices addressing urgent community needs, high-stakes crisis meetings where every word can cut deep, and domestic abuse shelters brimming with heartache. I've witnessed human vulnerability at its lowest ebb and have been privileged to watch countless individuals claw their way back from depths that many wouldn't survive.

My journey into writing began not from a place of ambition, but from an urgency to express the profound truths and painful realities I encountered daily. It emerged from a desire to voice the stories that rarely make headlines, the silent mental health crises that often play out in men's lives, the heart-wrenching wounds inflicted by societal expectations of strength in a world that frequently fails to comprehend the true nature of that concept.

Every book I've penned is rooted in reality tales born from experiences lived and felt. I've sat across from men who struggle to utter the word "help," their hands trembling at the mere suggestion of vulnerability. I've witnessed the devastating silence that shrouds those who've never been given permission to cry. I've stood by the side of survivors battling the ghosts of abuse, addiction, trauma, homelessness, and the relentless cycles of reoffending and I've felt the weight of despair when systems meant to protect them falter and leave them to fend for themselves.

Yet amid the hurt, I've also glimpsed a different truth: the quiet strength found in vulnerability and the raw power of honesty. I've seen how a single line in a book can resonate deeply, cracking open the armour of someone who believed they were unreachable, a flicker of hope in a darkened room.

I don't aim to sugar-coat the reality of these experiences. I don't write to follow trends or to gain popularity. My pen is devoted to the man who lies awake at 2 a.m., grappling with an unshakeable sense of loneliness that he can't quite define. I write for the survivors of violence, the ones who have borne the weight of silence and self-doubt, those who have never had their stories told without the heavy shroud of shame.

I believe, wholeheartedly, that understanding can save lives. That honesty can be a profound form of healing. And that the concept of masculinity deserves a substantial redefinition, not merely as an abstract theory but as a heartfelt truth.

So, if you're engaging with my work, know this: you are not alone in the struggles you've faced. You are not weak for feeling broken. And you are not beyond the possibility of rebuilding your life.

I'm Josiah Cornell. I write stories that matter, grounded in the lived experiences of those who've wrestled with what so many only encounter in print and on screen.

This isn't just writing; it is survival transformed into a purposeful mission.

Bibliography

bell hooks, 2000. *All About Love: New Visions*. New York: William Morrow Paperbacks.

Bowlby, J., 1969–1980. *Attachment and Loss*. Vols. 1–3. New York: Basic Books.

Cooper, A., 2013. *The Insecurity of Freedom*. London: Routledge.

Dana, D., 2018. *The Polyvagal Theory in Therapy: Engaging the Rhythm of Regulation*. New York: W.W. Norton & Company.

Hendrix, H. and Hunt, H.L., 1988. *Getting the Love You Want: A Guide for Couples*. New York: St. Martin's Press.

Johnson, S., 2008. *Hold Me Tight: Seven Conversations for a Lifetime of Love*. New York: Little, Brown Spark.

Jung, C.G., 1981. *The Archetypes and the Collective Unconscious*. 2nd ed. Princeton, NJ: Princeton University Press.

Jung, C.G., 1989. *Memories, Dreams, Reflections*. London: Vintage Books.

Maté, G., 2008. *In the Realm of Hungry Ghosts: Close Encounters with Addiction*. Berkeley, CA: North Atlantic Books.

Maté, G., 2011. *When the Body Says No: Exploring the Stress-Disease Connection*. Toronto: Vintage Canada.

Neff, K., 2011. *Self-Compassion: The Proven Power of Being Kind to Yourself*. New York: William Morrow.

Porges, S.W., 2011. *The Polyvagal Theory: Neurophysiological Foundations of Emotions, Attachment, Communication, and Self-Regulation*. New York: W.W. Norton & Company.

Siegel, D.J., 2012. *The Developing Mind: How Relationships and the Brain Interact to Shape Who We Are*. 2nd ed. New York: Guilford Press.

Siegel, D.J., 2012. *The Pocket Guide to Interpersonal Neurobiology: An Integrative Handbook of the Mind*. New York: W.W. Norton & Company.

van der Kolk, B., 2014. *The Body Keeps the Score: Brain, Mind, and Body in the Healing of Trauma*. New York: Penguin Books.

Additional Resources Referenced in Text (non-book)

CALM (Campaign Against Living Miserably), n.d. [online] Available at: https://www.thecalmzone.net/

Andy's Man Club, n.d. [online] Available at: https://andysmanclub.co.uk/

NHS Talking Therapies, n.d. [online] Available at: https://www.nhs.uk/mental-health/talking-therapies-medicine-treatments/

Crenshaw, K., 1991. *Mapping the Margins: Intersectionality, Identity Politics, and Violence Against Women of Color*. *Stanford Law Review*, 43(6), pp.1241–1299.